NECESSARY NOISE

Necessary Noise

MUSIC, FILM, AND CHARITABLE IMPERIALISM
IN THE EAST OF CONGO

Chérie Rivers Ndaliko

OXFORD
UNIVERSITY PRESS

OXFORD
UNIVERSITY PRESS

Oxford University Press is a department of the University of Oxford. It furthers
the University's objective of excellence in research, scholarship, and education
by publishing worldwide. Oxford is a registered trade mark of Oxford University
Press in the UK and certain other countries.

Published in the United States of America by Oxford University Press
198 Madison Avenue, New York, NY 10016, United States of America.

Library of Congress Cataloging-in-Publication Data
Names: Ndaliko, Chérie Rivers, author.
Title: Necessary noise : music, film, and charitable imperialism in the east of Congo/Chérie
Rivers Ndaliko.
Description: New York City : Oxford University Press, 2016. |
Includes bibliographical references and index.
Identifiers: LCCN 2015049373 | ISBN 9780190499570 (cloth : alk. paper) |
ISBN 9780190499587 (pbk. : alk. paper) | ISBN 9780190499617 (oso)
Subjects: LCSH: Music—Congo (Democratic Republic)—History and criticism. |
Music—Social aspects—Congo (Democratic Republic)
Classification: LCC ML350.5 .N32 2016 | DDC 306.4/8420967517—dc23
LC record available at http://lccn.loc.gov/2015049373

9 8 7 6 5 4 3 2 1

Paperback printed by Webcom Inc., Canada
Hardback printed by Bridgeport National Bindery, Inc., United States of America

For mama Karen Rivers and mama Yukabed Kahindo Sikulimwenge, with my deepest gratitude for your constant wisdom and your unconditional love!

And for all the youth at Yole!Africa, with ferocious faith in your futures. . .

Contents

List of Illustrations

CHAPTER 4: JAZZ MAMAS

Acknowledgments

IN THE SPIRIT of the Swahili proverb *Kama mti umeanja kutoa majani mapia, mwenye sifa ni mzizi* (if the tree sprouts new leaves, give the credit to the roots), I want to express my deepest gratitude to the monumental "roots" that helped me sprout *Necessary Noise*. To the host of generous people in Congo who opened their lives to me, shared their stories with me, and inducted me into the beauty and the madness of Goma—*asante sana*! Special thanks to the Yole!Africa family in Goma: to Ganza Buroko, whose loyalty and conviction is unsurpassed and who is, quite simply, the rock on which so many of us stand in times of need; to Stella Ramazani for teaching me, with unwavering grace, the hardest-won lessons of Congolese womanhood; to Gaius Kowene for his contagiously buoyant optimism and his invaluable skills of translation; and to Batumike Chambu for sustaining and nourishing us all with his unparalleled cuisine, wisdom, and humor. Thank you to the all artists, young and old, whose talents, wit, and faith transform the Yole!Africa compound into a place of magic. Thank you to the global Yole!Africa team as well: to Samuel Yagasse, Excellence Juma Balikwisha, Ndungi Githuku, Atieno Odenyo, Yehudi van der Pol, Thomas "jumanne" Gesthuizen, Maurice Carney, Mathieu Roy, Olivier Lechien and Ebba Kalondo, Alain Cannone, Makena Kibiti, Guido Convents, Gilbert Bwete, Bruno Hegel, Lynn True and Nelson Walker. And to all the "s/heroes" whose fingerprints have made their way into this book—you know who you are! *Tuko pamoja!*

I want to offer exuberant thanks to the intellectual mentors and colleagues who have supported me through the numerous incarnations of this project. To Kay Kaufman Shelemay for her endless supplies of wisdom and tea, and for her unanticipated humor in the face of personal and professional revolutions—without her neither my life nor my work would be what it is; to Biodun Jeyifo, whose profound compassion, formidable intellect, and impeccable guidance are of monumental inspiration and whose humility affirms, beyond the shadow of a doubt, the real-world relevance of academic study; to Ingrid Monson for her adventurous scholarship and her willingness to encourage the same from me; to Evelyn Brooks Higginbotham for whose intellectual courage I have the most profound respect and who gave me the life-altering gift of encouragement to integrate my scholarship and my activism. For their mentorship and support during my years at Harvard I also want to thank Abiola Irele, Henry Louise Gates, Jr., John Mugane, Werner Sollors, Caroline Elkins, Jacob Olupona, and my many dear colleagues in the departments of African and African American Studies and Music.

I wrote *Necessary Noise* while teaching at the University of North Carolina at Chapel Hill, where I am surrounded by the rare gift of colleagues whose intellectual rigor and deep humanity inspire me daily. In the music department: Mark Katz has ushered me into deeply fulfilling professional experiences and has ceaselessly encouraged me to push boundaries; Louise Toppin is a stunning example to me of strength, elegance, and wisdom; Jocelyn Neal has been a selfless mentor and friend and has set a formidable example of what it means to be superwoman; Evan Bonds has far exceeded his role as mentor and has instead become a friend and an inspiration; Annegret Fauser, Tim Carter, and David Garcia have challenged and supported me deeply in my efforts to bring the principles of my scholarship into my teaching, which has measurably benefited both. I also want to thank Terry Rohdes, Emil Kang, Severine Neff, Phil Vandermeer, Stefan Litwin, and the many others in the Music Department who have encouraged and supported me in bringing the arts of Congo to UNC. Additionally, I am blessed with colleagues outside my primary department who are invaluable to me. Joseph Jordan has been my intellectual compass, guiding me with elegance as I transpose my habits of intellectual activism onto a new campus; Georges Nzongola-Ntalaja has opened many opportunities to me and has been selfless in his support of my work on art and culture in Congo; Alphonse Mutima has generously become my "uncle at the *barazza*"; Patricia Parker has built invaluable bridges for me with the Department of Communication; and Anne Johnston, my fellow Thorpe Faculty Engaged Scholar, has buoyed me with her collaboration and faith in the value of socially engaged scholarship. I am also grateful to the interdisciplinary community of scholars and artists who have encouraged and inspired me along the way, including Emily

Burrill, Carol Magee, Victoria Rovine, Jessica Tanner, Barbara Friedman, Genna Rae McNeil, Bill Ferris, and Pierce Freelon.

In this litany of thanks, I have to pause and say that *Necessary Noise* quite simply would not exist without the courageous and elegant influence of Suzanne Ryan and her team at Oxford University Press. As an editor, Suzanne has a mystical ability to transform both books and people for the better. In the case of *Necessary Noise,* she immediately identified the most unconventional aspects of the manuscript and, rather than corralling them into more traditional form, worked tirelessly to help me craft them into the crowning jewels of this book. I am deeply grateful to have an editor who supports those of us pushing the boundaries of scholarship and only hope that through this process I have been permanently infused with even a dose of her inimitable confidence.

I am also grateful to the many people who read drafts of this manuscript throughout its evolution. Thank you to my anonymous reviewers, whose rigorous engagement with my work enhanced it tremendously. Thank you to my cohort of Fellows at the Institute of Arts and Humanities for their valuable feedback: Anna Agbe-Davis, Stephen Anderson, Cemil Aydin, Michele Berger, Lucia Binotti, Anne MacNeil, Townsend Middleton, and Jennifer Smith. Thanks also to the scores of students who have read portions of this manuscript in my classes Media and Social Change in Africa; Hip Hop and Social Justice; Soundtracks of the Black Atlantic; and Music, Film, and Aid in Contemporary Africa. Special thanks to the members of my seminar, Culture and Activism in Congo: Ethics and Methods, who offered valuable feedback on the manuscript: Amanda Black, Barkley Heuser, Kori Hill, Alex Marsden, Meg Orita, Dawn Stevenson, and Sarah Tomlinson, with special mention to Carlee Forbes for lending her art history skills to selecting the images and creating the map for this book.

Numerous grants supported this project. I am grateful to the Harvard Committee on African Studies; the W.E.B. Du Bois Institute; Harvard's Department of African and African American Studies; and Harvard University for support in the forms of a Presidential Fellowship, a Presidential Dissertation Completion Grant, the Frederick Sheldon Traveling Fellowship, the Phillipe Wamba Traveling Fellowship, and a FLAS. I have also received generous financial support from the University of North Carolina at Chapel Hill. I am grateful to the Institute for Arts and Humanities for a faculty fellowship that allowed me to draft this book; to the Sonja Haynes Stone Center for Black Culture and History, where I was scholar in residence when I wrote this book; to the Carolina Center for Public Service for the Thorpe Faculty Engaged Scholars Fellowship; to the College of Arts and Sciences for the 2013 Interdisciplinary Initiatives Grant; to the Center for Global Studies; and to the University Research Council for a publication grant that supported this book. I am also deeply appreciative of the moral and financial support I received from the Skywords Family Foundation under the leadership of Michael Davis and Jyll Johnstone.

Then there are those people—friends and family—without whom I cannot imagine living. I have enjoyed the warmth, generosity, and excitement of each and every member of the Katondolo family, many of whom have been indispensable to me in writing this book. I am eternally indebted to Mama Yukabed Kahindo Sikulimwenge without whom none of this would exist—*asante sana mama mama*! I thank Isabelle Furaha and her beautiful family for literally and metaphorically saving my life repeatedly; Modogo Mutembwi for becoming my brother in the best sense of the word; Zibi Katondolo for pulling resources out of thin air; Justine Masika for being a true Super Star; Sarah Bihamba for the gift of sisterhood; Sekombi Katondolo for sharing his memory; Emma Katya and Jobu Madibo for taking the mic; and Linda Kahambu and Emily Katondolo for their magic with children. I am grateful to the entire Rivers Clan; to my cousins, my uncles, and specifically my aunts Daisy, Celeste, and Bang for believing in me against all odds and reminding me that being a Rivers means always raising the bar. Special thanks to those dear friends who have allowed Yole!Africa to enter their hearts so deeply: to Josselyne Schwartz for her tenacity and precision and to Allason Leitz for being the best cheerleader a person ever had. I have tremendous gratitude and awe for two of the strongest and most precious women in my life, who contributed immeasurably to this book: my generous and selfless colleague and friend Andrea Bohlman, whose intellectual, creative, and culinary brilliance is unsurpassable, and to Polly Cherner, who is an unparalled source of wisdom.

Finally, none of this would have been imaginable without the ongoing encouragement of my family, whose history of bold perseverance in the face of impossibility humbles and inspires me daily. To my mother, Karen Rivers, whose faith in the power of unconditional love makes miracles, I owe everything; to my father Isaac Rivers, whose heart and vision were larger than life and whose strength taught me to reach for the impossible; to my stepfather Michael Cohen, who touched my life with his uncanny ability to show up and changed it forever with his uncanny ability to stay, listen, and grow; to Amani and Malaika Katondolo for forcing me at times to stop writing and play; to Mokozi Rivers Ndaliko for reminding me just how beautiful the world can look through the eyes of a child and for entrusting me with the promise of his future. And, lastly, to Petna—for his unwavering dedication to making the world a better place and for sharing it daily with me!

List of Abbreviations

AFDL	Alliance of Democratic Forces for the Liberation of Congo
ALT2TV	Alternative to TV
FESPACO	Festival panafricain du cinéma et de la télévision de Ouagadougou (the Pan-African Film and Television Festival of Ouagadougou)
JMI	Jeunesses Musicales International
MONUC	United Nations Organization Mission in the Democratic Republic of the Congo
MONUSCO	United Nations Organization Stabilization Mission in the Democratic Republic of the Congo
NGO	Nongovernmental organization
RCD	Rally for Congolese Democracy
RTNC	Radio et télévision national du Congo (National Radio and Television)
SKIFF	Salaam Kivu International Film Festival
UJADEP	Union des jeunes artistes dessinateurs et peintres
UN	United Nations
UNHCR	United Nations High Commission for Refugees

FIGURE 0.1 Map of Congo. Courtesy of Carlee Forbes.

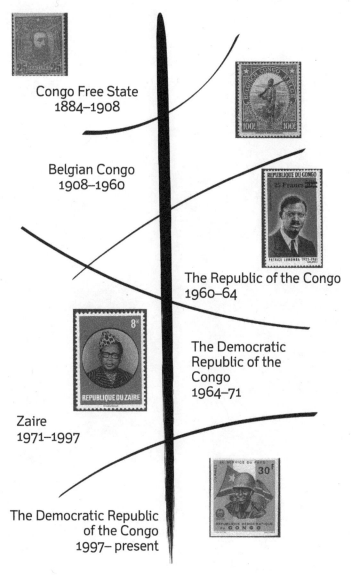

Congo Free State
1884–1908

Belgian Congo
1908–1960

The Republic of the Congo
1960–64

The Democratic
Republic of the
Congo
1964–71

Zaire
1971–1997

The Democratic Republic
of the Congo
1997– present

FIGURE 0.2 Historical Timeline of Congo. Courtesy of Dr. Andrea Bohlman. Stamps from author's own collection.

About the Companion Website

www.oup.com/us/necessarynoise

Username: Music3

Password: Book3234

Oxford University Press has created a password-protected website to accompany *Necessary Noise*. The site includes sound files, music videos, short films, and additional archival photographs that give readers the opportunity to engage directly with sights and sounds from the east of Congo. These audiovisual materials are linked to specific parts of the book and are indicated with the icon ▶. Readers are strongly encouraged to hear and see for themselves the songs and films in this book.

NECESSARY NOISE

*The song arises from what has gone before and it leads
to what follows.*
NGUGI WA THIONG'O, Decolonizing the Mind, p. 45[1]

INTRODUCTION

ONE DAY IN late October 2012, when my husband, Petna Ndaliko Katondolo, and I were living in Chapel Hill, North Carolina, we came home to a series of missed calls from our family in Goma, which is the capital city of the North Kivu Province in the east of the Democratic Republic of the Congo. It was when the M23 rebel army was advancing on the city, and we were worried that a family member had been injured or killed. For more than twelve hours we called repeatedly, our panic mounting as we failed to reach anyone. When, eventually, we got my mother-in-law on the phone, we skipped the usual formalities and demanded, with urgent concern, *"muko aje?! Batu bote biko bien?" Shida ni nini??!"* (are you OK?! Is everyone OK?! What happened?!). But she could not hear us because she was too busy asking us the exact same questions, *"muko aje?! Batu bote biko bien? Shida ni nini??!"* You see, according to the television news in Congo, America was "under water" in the aftermath of Superstorm Sandy. There were dire reports of flood, destruction, and death; buildings were shown collapsed and people stranded with no discernable mention of specifics (i.e., that the storm hit the northeastern rather than the *entire* United States). Even as we received reports of the city being invaded by the M23, she begged us to come home to Goma, where we would be safe.

Then again, in December of the same year, after the M23 had officially taken Goma despite the fortified UN forces, we came home to another series of missed calls. This time, when we finally got through, my mother-in-law was distraught, begging us, again, to come home where it was safe. She had seen the news about

Sandy Hook elementary school, where twenty children had been killed by a gunman. Even as we could hear bombs going off in the background, she was insisting, vehemently, that Goma might have its moments of unrest but at least children do not get slaughtered when they go to school, which, in her mind, is the epitome of savagery (though of course that word is seldom used to describe Americans).

Then there were missed calls during the riots in Ferguson, and then again when three Muslim students were slain down the road from us in Chapel Hill, and again with the death of nine African Americans in their church in Charleston, South Carolina. With every event, the urgency in her voice escalates.

The point of this story is perspective. In the mind of my mother-in-law, America was taking shape as a place of terror: natural disasters made worse by human barbarism, racial (parallel in her mind to "ethnic") tension, corruption, and lawlessness. What was, for local communities in the United States, a series of exceptions to the otherwise cohesive norm of their daily lives was being reduced, for her, to a defining inventory of failures. This is an obvious result of the stories and information to which she was exposed. What was absent from her vantage point was any account of the daily interactions and negotiations that define collective identity in a place as complex as the United States, the infinite details—from the transcendent to the ordinary—that make up the connecting tissue between newsworthy events. From afar, she could not see the intimacies of place and history that cumulatively make home.

Yet, were she so inclined, my mother-in-law could, with comparative ease, familiarize herself with the lives of her global peers in the American cities featured, temporarily, in her news outlets. She could access a wealth of materials—images, films, written texts, songs, social media platforms, etc.—that offer more nuanced insight into the multivalent layers of daily existence on the other side of the world. Even though such investigation would be far from comprehensive, it would yield poignant details: names and faces of ordinary people and places, popular song lyrics, favorite games, and a wealth of other concrete visual and sonic material with which to fill in the gaping craters left in her imagination by the horrific reports of violence and natural disaster.

The same is not as readily true in reverse. Like the United States, Congo too is a place of profound complexity. It has a legacy—both colonial and postcolonial—of unparalleled brutality, of exaggerated violence, and of spectacular failures. For more than a century, it has been branded in the global psyche as a heart of darkness; now, as a "postcolonial" nation, it is fraught with what anthropologist Ann Laura Stoler refers to as "imperial formations" of the most insidious sort. Indeed, Congo is a textbook example of "mutant, rather than simply hybrid, political

forms that endure beyond the formal exclusions that legislate against equal opportunity, commensurate dignities, and equal rights."[2] One can, with ease, cite
proofs of such mutant political forms as substantiating evidence for a diagnosis
of Congo that is a global exception. And yet, like every other nation, Congo also
has everything else: it has its own intimate nuances of place and history that
cumulatively make home, its own daily interactions and negotiations that define
collective identity for its communities. But insight into the multivalent layers of
daily existence in Congo is significantly harder to come by from a distance. There
is a comparative dearth both of representational materials such as images, films,
songs, etc. and of scholarly studies that offer perspective on the details that make
up the connecting tissue between newsworthy events.

Yet the magnitude of newsworthy events in Congo is catastrophic, which leads,
in turn, to equally catastrophic craters left in global imaginings of this place.
Necessary Noise aims to fill in one such crater. Through stories and analyses of
music and films in and about the east of Congo, this book introduces people,
places, sounds, and images that populate daily interactions and ordinary moments in one of the world's most volatile conflict regions. It is a work designed
to counteract the historic exclusivity of focus on fields—economics, development, governance, aid, etc.—traditionally designated to the study of war and to
foreground the critical necessity of rigorous studies of art and culture in regions
susceptible to foreign charitable interventions. It argues, quite simply, that understanding the production and consumption of art yields important insight into
the opinions and extant mechanisms of sociopolitical action—both those that
succeed and those that fail—within local communities.

As the (imagined) "international community" and an army of charitable and
nongovernmental organizations (NGOs) from the West continue to expand their
interventions into Congo's ongoing wars and crises, intimate understanding of
local communities is urgent. Analysis of economics and politics along with met-
rics of development are simply not sufficient to measure need or best practices in
communities caught in the historically complex conflicts in which the entire world
is implicated. And indeed, practices of international aid are subject to scathing
criticism not only for the ethical quagmires inherent to mandates that simultaneously protect basic human rights for all while also condemning those who commit
atrocities, but also for the many failures that result from ill-informed plans of
action. To my mind, many such ill-informed plans are the inevitable result of the
cultural ignorance that festers when studies of human catastrophe are divorced
from studies of human creativity.

To combat this trend, *Necessary Noise* introduces a study of art into the literature on the east of Congo. This book sets out to accomplish three primary tasks: it

is an ethnography (of sorts) of the Yole!Africa cultural center in Goma, a study of art (specifically music and film) and conflict in the east of Congo, and a reflection on global cultural activism. What follows is an introduction to each of these facets of the book; an introduction to Congo and to its current conflict, history, and geography; a reflection on my role in constructing this text in which I speak, interchangeably, as scholar, participant, administrator, and spouse; and finally, a definition of key terms.

Let me start by introducing Yole!Africa. The organization was originally founded by the acclaimed Congolese filmmaker Petna Ndaliko Katondolo and the Dutch anthropologist Ellen Lammers in 2000 in Kampala Uganda; then in 2002, Petna founded a second branch in Goma (about which this book is written). Yole!Africa was created in response to the dire fragmentation and hopelessness that accompanies prolonged violent conflict. The word *Yolé*, common in many East African languages, means "come together" and was originally used by shepherds, goat herders, and cattle drivers to call flocks together in times of danger. And the center is just that: a space for young people to come together, to learn, exchange, and create community as an alternative to being inculcated into perpetual cycles of violence. On a practical level, Yole!Africa provides trainings and workshops in digital arts, music, dance, journalism, computer literacy, and foreign languages as well as community galvanizing events such as public debates, film screenings, jam sessions, and festivals; on an ideological level, Yole!Africa is a space that promotes critical thinking and community autonomy. I often introduce Yole!Africa as an "unlikely cultural center" because, beyond the obvious questions of the viability of an art center in an active warzone, it has survived the eruption of the volcano Nyiragongo in Goma, systematic underfunding, theft and looting, and the threatening power dynamics that accompany the influx of international NGOs. Yet despite the challenges, to date more than 90 percent of the musicians, filmmakers, and dancers and roughly 40 percent of journalists from North Kivu who have achieved international acclaim have trained at the center. In terms of scope, approximately fourteen to seventeen thousand young people participate in Yole!Africa's activities in any given year (this includes active registered members who complete special workshops and trainings as well as people who participate in ongoing public events). The majority of participants are between eighteen and thirty-five years old, which is how I define *youth* throughout this text, but there are a growing number of younger children (ages six through eighteen) becoming actively involved in the center at the time of writing. Thus, in terms of prestige and magnitude, locally Yole!Africa has a reputation not only for being the longest-standing organization supporting cultural activism, but also as an institution of artistic excellence.

The portrait of Yole!Africa in *Necessary Noise* has many ingredients. I have woven together empirical examples drawn from the ethnographic research I have been conducting at Yole!Africa since 2008; insights that I have gained through the administrative position of co-director (later executive director) of the center, which I took on in late 2010; and scholarly analyses of Congo's history and present that are grounded in the academic disciplines of ethnomusicology, film/media studies, and African studies. This book also includes still images from films and recently recovered archival photographs of Yole!Africa and Goma that add visual markers and introduce people and places in the city. Further, there are transcribed (and translated) lyrics of songs and, in some cases, links to audio and visual examples of works produced in Congo as well as an accompanying website. This multigenre presentation is both the standard fare of ethnographies in the age of digital humanities and my part in the strategic effort by youth at Yole!Africa to curate an array of poignant details that collectively render the east of Congo more vivid in the global imagination.

The backdrop against which the young people at Yole!Africa (and I) work to render such details vivid is both the physical reality and the global narration of historic and ongoing violence. Whether or not one accepts that Congo's exceptionally brutal colonial history continues to shape the nation, there is no doubt that the current war in the east of Congo, which has taken more than six million lives in the past two decades, shapes the daily experience of the nation's residents. In the face of this degree and duration of violence, creating art is, by definition, a political and a radical act. It is a means of self-expression, a source of community cohesion, and a strategy to break the cycle of reductionist representations through visual and sonic assertions of normalcy. Arguing for an ethnomusicological approach to understanding conflict through music, ethnomusicologist John M. O'Connell suggests that "music offers the possibility of an imaginary ideal, a shared goal that promotes cooperation between groups while respectful of individual cultural identities," qualities that, to a large extent, also apply to interactive filmmaking processes.[3] In short, art and creativity are domains in which citizens, young ones in particular, can assert agency in a powerful but non-violent fashion. Indeed, in many cases witnessing the impact of their creativity, whether within the local community or as rising international stars, confirms to young people that art has the potential to catalyze sociopolitical transformation.

But endorsing the power of art as a catalyst of social change is a double-edged sword, particularly in conflict regions. In the east of Congo, a growing number of artists are turning to creative expression as a vehicle of resistance to the conflict and to the corruption and inequity that characterize the response of the local government and the international community. These artists have identified globally celebrated mediums—particularly music and film—as being potent in galvanizing communities to action. These artists align themselves with historic movements of artistic resistance (such as the anti-apartheid movement in South Africa) and actively position themselves within contemporary global underground networks. At the same time, many charitable and humanitarian organizations have also identified art (particularly music and film) as a potent means of conveying information to local populations and communicating to potential donors in emotionally powerful forms. Such organizations often appeal to audiences sympathetic to the impulse of artistic resistance, which, on the surface, seems to align with the motivations of local artists. But when NGOs, most of which are qualified to offer disaster relief, medical relief, and structural aid, begin to commission and promote art, then issues of ownership, censorship, money, and international corporate politics enter into the equation in a radically different form.

There is a perception among local artists from Yole!Africa that many NGOs use music and film in ways that undermine artists' efforts toward professionalism and autonomy. Grossly oversimplified, the pattern is for NGOs to approach local artists, specifically those associated with resistance or "speaking truth," and commission, and then censor (or in more politically correct language "modify" or "edit") a song or film to fit organizational criteria. From the organizational point of view, this is fair practice; they commission artists like any other skilled workers and they have the right to get what they want and pay for. From another point of view, this practice is a total corruption of the most potent channels of resistance because it generates diluted songs, films, paintings, etc., that are marketed as "the voice of the people."

The problem is that in Congo, as in other global disaster regions, having access to "local voices" is now a global craving. Many of the scathing criticisms humanitarian and charity projects have received center on organizations' refusal to listen to locals. To combat this impression, a flood of NGOs have started producing artistic and cultural pieces that create the illusion of a "utopian fantasy of a global village of moral concern," an illusion that encourages donors and volunteer to equate *hearing* the words and voices of locals with *listening* to local needs.[4] But listening to local needs is not possible through the songs and films that are "edited" or "modified" by the organizations that script and pay artists to record their messages. At the same time, there are also songs, films, and other artistic works that remain uncensored and that *do* reflect local perspectives unapologetically. The trick is that it is hard now to tell the difference. Indeed, artists in Goma complain that NGOs are in the process of absorbing, distorting, and reusing aesthetics of resistance with systematic precision, to the extent that, to the naked eye—or ear—many people cannot tell the difference between actual resistance and its commercial equivalent. This works, in large part, because of the centrality of audio and visual rhetorics of suffering, which introduce emotion, often guilt and compassion, as a distracting façade behind which the industry of aid is free to erode the potency of cultural resistance. But regardless of whether the global craving for local voices is fulfilled by propaganda or by genuine expression of community perspectives, the words and voices of locals are being cited as supporting evidence for strategies developed abroad to meet the needs of Congolese at home.

This is the urgency in this book: for many people living in the east of Congo, their lives and livelihoods hang in the balance of global strategies of aid. To the degree that art contributes to soliciting donor support that is based on the feel-good factor or the illusion that a given organization is collaborating with rather than imposing itself on locals, it makes a material difference in people's lives. It made a difference, for example, to the highly respected local musician Tonton Lusambo, who, after performing at the 2014 Amani Festival in Goma, was evicted from his home with his wife and four children when he failed to pay a sudden increase in rent; his children were also expelled from school when he failed to pay their overdue fees. The reason the landlord and the school administrators were merciless with Lusambo's family was that they had seen the live broadcast of his performance on television and they (quite logically) assumed, from the publicized $274,000 budget of the festival, that Lusambo had been handsomely compensated for his performance. When he insisted that in reality he, like all the local performers, was not paid anything (not even money for transportation), they accused him of lying and left him and his family on the street. Indeed, it was incomprehensible to the landlord or the school that an "NGO festival" aiming to bring peace to the region would treat local musicians with anything less than the deep respect and generous compensation they afforded foreign stars.

These are the circumstances in which art is being produced in the east of Congo. As a study of art and conflict, *Necessary Noise* works to parse the nuances of artistic production, to position the resultant songs, films, albums, and festivals within context, and to analyze their aesthetics and their sociopolitical impact with relevant theories. Because so much of the context and theory relevant to artistic production in Goma is related to NGOs, this book is also about the dynamics and trends of global activism. Against the backdrop of the Congo conflict, which is commonly referred to as the deadliest humanitarian conflict since World War II, the topography of Western humanitarian and charitable (in)action comes into sharp relief. Variations on global activism are evident in many artistic collaborations taking place in Congo, some of which reveal profoundly inspiring innovations that support artistic autonomy and others expose profoundly disturbing dynamics of censorship and authorial power struggles. Indeed, there is a wealth of information about aesthetics and ethics buried in the artistic works coming out of the east of Congo, all of which are being produced both by radical artists and by humanitarian NGOs. Collectively the histories and analyses of these cultural products offer insight into the politics of production that go into making and marketing art in a war zone, and into how resistance movements fighting to meet the needs of local communities clash with the international industry of doing good.

To articulate the complexities of cultural activism in the east of Congo, I have developed specific language drawn from my research experience. Whether or not I knew it at the time, this project began in a crowded restaurant in Kinshasa where Mweze Ngangura, the celebrated pioneer of Congolese cinema, and Petna Ndaliko Katondolo were having a reunion of sorts over lunch. I was there as a graduate student, conducting field research for my doctoral dissertation on music, film, and youth-led movements of social change in Africa. I had met Ngangura years prior at the FESPACO film festival in Burkina Faso, where I had conducted a short interview with him about film as a tool of social change. With his characteristic generosity, Ngangura took time out of their passionate luncheon discussion of Congolese politics to ask me about my research. When I told him that my research in Congo was still related to my project about *cinema éngagé* (the French term for films associated with projects of social or political change), he looked, slowly, from me to Petna and then slammed his fist down on the table with enough force that our dishes rattled loudly and everyone in the restaurant turned to stare. Looking directly into my eyes with an intensity that made me tremble, and rhythmically jabbing his finger in Petna's direction he said, "There is something you have to understand. There is a difference between *éngagé, activist,* and *militant.*" Not confident that I had fully grasped his point, he continued, "If you are studying brother Petna here, you are not studying *cinema éngagé,* you are studying the most militant cinema Congo has."

Between my struggle to parse the nuance of his sophisticated French (in which I was only moderately fluent at the time) and my lack of deep familiarity with Petna's work (this encounter took place within the first week of my research in Congo), I did not immediately recognize the magnitude of Ngangura's statement. But years into my study of and engagement with Congo and Yole!Africa, his words came back to me as I struggled to articulate the dynamics I witnessed. Indeed, after the proverbial dust of my enthusiasm to be involved with Congo settled, I came to understand that behind the rhetoric of solidarity, even unity, expressed by the countless social actors advocating for or against this or that in or about Congo, there are significant rifts between numerous factions. The more I reflected on the tensions between groups and individuals who all articulate similar objectives, the more frequently I began to return to the map Ngangura had given me when he delineated engagement, from activism, from militantism.

What I discovered when analyzing the situation from this perspective is that the range of activities that are generally summed up in the term *activism* is in fact a broad enough spectrum of ideologies and practices to require the distinct terminology Ngangura suggested. The connecting tissue is certainly the desire to make positive change in a given region or on a given issue, but the strategies, the tactics, and most importantly the *stakes* differ considerably among groups. As applied to film production, engagement refers more to the practice of filmmakers making films about a social or political issue. Such films are generally commissioned by an NGO or other entity, and generally define or prescribe solutions to a specific problem such as illiteracy, hygiene, or voting rights. Activism is generally positioned as more radical than engagement because it is linked with progressive ideology rather than being directly associated with monetary compensation. Many activists undertake campaigns, whether cinematic, musical, political, etc., without any promise of payment simply because they are concerned about an issue and feel compelled to catalyze change. When successful, such projects or campaigns often become targets of collaboration on the part of NGOs, which are positioned to introduce money and power into movements that started at the grassroots level; equally common are activist initiatives that directly seek the sponsorship of a powerful entity, through which they have a larger platform to make a given point, but which sometimes requires certain compromises to qualify for funding. I have come to understand that militantism is more radical still because it is the stance that refuses ideological compromise at all costs. There are associations of violence with the term *militant*, but let me be clear, that is not how I am using it in this text. Like the artists who self-designate as militant, I use the term to distinguish from the sea of activists a growing coalition of nonviolent social actors (in this text primarily artists) whose commitment to the populations they serve and the issues they tackle is not negotiable in the face of financial support or in the face of power.

These categories are porous. I do not cite them to create the illusion of fixed identities but rather to tease out how similar rhetoric can serve such radically divergent agendas as it does in the east of Congo, where organizations and individuals regularly undertake categorically oppositional projects all in the name of peace or women's rights (for example). Indeed, critical anslysis of the strate of Congo advocacy efforts reveals a thick web of social actors, organizations, personalities, issues, and histories at work. The common denominator is the desire to do good. What is not common is any shared definition of the good that needs doing. Everyone agrees on the overarching needs: Congo needs peace, stability, and a strong state. But what people mean by "peace," "stability," or a "strong state," and how they go about advocating for those goals, is contradictory to the point of brutal antagonism.

I am not the first to make this point. Since the explosion of NGOs in Africa in the 1980s, there has been a growing literature from scholars, journalists, and activists (in the meta sense of the term) who are pointing out the tensions and contradictions among the complex network of international NGOs, humanitarian and charitable organizations, governments, grassroots organizations, and individuals working in various global conflict regions toward sociopolitical change. Many of these critiques center on power, politics, and ethics[5] and the surreptitious, often destructive, relationships between "local voluntary organizations" and "transnational-level entities."[6] In Congo, like other humanitarian zones, studying these entities reveals the common pattern of transnational organizations that are aligned with power in their Western countries of origin yet seek to operate (or at the very least appear) as grassroots organizations on the ground.

In fields from law, political science, and African studies to sociology, anthropology, and economics, rigorous studies question the efficacy and ethics of NGO presence in Africa.[7] The urgent concerns extend to issues of human rights more broadly in which, thanks to the proliferation of NGOs, "the production of an international agenda for human rights is increasingly marked by a dominant concern to make the 'civil society' a co-equal partner [with] ... corporations and other economic entities."[8] The result, as legal scholar Upendra Baxi sees it, is that "the paradigm of the Universal Declaration of Human Rights is being steadily, but surely, *supplanted* by that of a trade-related, market-friendly human rights."[9] In a closely related vein, scholars and critical journalists raise potent questions about "the horror of the cost of a good deed."[10] Collectively this literature makes frequent reference to the association of humanitarian action with good deeds, drawing attention to how, beneath the utopic idealism of charity as a selfless act of service, doing good is in fact an industry. And one in dire need of scrutiny.

In addition to the scholarly literature, there is also a host of popular articles on the subject of humanitarianism, human rights, and the effects of international NGOs. Indeed, halfway through writing this book I woke up to start my writing session early one morning and found an email from a colleague and friend alerting me to an article by Arundhati Roy. The article, "The NGO-ization of Resistance," is a pointed critique of the global pattern of international NGOs strategically undermining meaningful social movements by coopting and corporatizing the rhetoric of resistance. In reading it, I was at once elated and distressed—elated because someone (whose work I admire) was making the same argument as I was, distressed because she made it first and it only took her one page.

Collectively these, and other, texts have opened many people's eyes to the notion that the ratio of good to harm done by many international NGOs is suspect. But that has done little to ebb the tide of students flocking to tell me that the NGO *they* support is different, that *their* work in Africa is *actually* helping people, despite the linguistic, historical, geographical, and political odds. True, there is now the requisite preamble criticizing other foreign interventions, the conspiratorial denunciation of the failings of humanitarianism and charity that is designed to suggest awareness of the problems and to confirm that, finally, brilliant new strategies have been identified from hard-learned lessons. But in such conspiratorial exchanges, what is clearest to me is that the critiques of charity and aid are perpetually perceived as applying to someone else.

My better self recognizes in this the genuine desire on the part of idealistic young (and not so young) people to make the world a better place. Indeed, that is a desire I share deeply. However, as an African American woman with family across the African continent, my concern is that, historically speaking, the Western version of making the world a better place has had catastrophic consequences for the browner people of that world. It is not politically correct to say these things anymore. But they are still true. And if we trace them back even one or two degrees, they lead us directly to the complex of Western saviorism that, in its own encounter with political correctness, has subjected the historic language of moral superiority to the global appeal of resistance (or solidarity with resistance). The result is a new paradigm of action defined by the urgent desire and fervent belief in the ability to "get it right" this time; but as investigative journalist Michael Maren points out, "the belief that we [Westerners] can help is an affirmation of our own worth in the grand scheme of things."[11] Indeed, history is in the process of proving that the vast majority of efforts are still not working, that beneath the veneer of solidarity with resistance movements or "collaborations" with local communities the nearly compulsive Western—specifically American—dedication to playing the hero and the equally compulsive—specifically European—stance of paternalism marches on uninterrupted.

Thus, despite the fact that many of the ideas I offer in this text are not new, I decided to soldier on, to continue the painstaking task of writing a case study that not only sheds light on the overarching (and established) fact that charitable intervention is often more charitable for the intervener than for the intervened upon, but also illuminates how this dynamic works in an age when people believe they know better. This is not a book that aims to condemn international NGOs or the people who work for or donate to them. This is a book that aims to expose the underbelly of good intentions through specific examples drawn from my own experiences in the east of Congo. In this book I argue that revolution is in the details, but I believe the same of revelation. Through exposure to the details of mundane as well as life-changing experiences the small choices that create big problems become clear.

As much as I agree with the host of scholars, journalists, and activists who shout the urgent message from the world's proverbial rooftops that aid does not work, as a teacher I am convinced that there will be no ebb in the tide of well-intentioned but ill-informed people setting out to save the world until they begin to understand the little ways in which their NGOs *are* in fact like all the rest. And this is a harder lesson to learn with regard to art and culture than just about any other topic because creative expression (and in some cases beauty) in the midst of suffering and depravity often becomes a kind of moral oasis that shifts focus away from critical scrutiny of the conditions of its production to sentimental celebration of its very existence. As such I consider myself a custodian of detail as much as anything else. Many of the details I offer might not be comfortable to read, but they are part of the larger project of aligning paradigms of cultural activism with their utopic potential. Let me state clearly that I believe there *is* a place for cross-cultural collaboration in Congo advocacy, even if, to date, that place needs greater critical consideration. My motivation for writing this book is based on the receptiveness I have witnessed from NGO workers, volunteers, students, and even funders, the genuine interest they express when given the opportunity to see—and hear—things from a different perspective.

The examples and stories in this book are recent, but I approach the practice of ethnography and the analysis of aesthetics and cultural activism as both a historic and a contemporary project. In Congo, as in many postcolonial nations, the specific influences of space and time are formative and require rigorous narration of details to counteract the popular (and nebulous) generalities that reduce this vast territory to a handful of key words (such as war, gorillas, rape, and rainforest). The particulars of Congo are many, and in various chapters I dedicate significant time to its history. In introducing this book it is important, for context, to make a few general observations and offer a brief historic timeline.

Any study of Congo is, by default, set against a backdrop of extremes. For perspective, Congo is the twelfth largest country in the world by area, it is 4.25 times bigger than France (3.37 times bigger than Texas), it has between 250 and 487 ethnic groups depending on how one defines things, and regardless of how one defines things it has tremendous diversity. Congo is at once among the wealthiest nations on earth in terms of natural resources and yet it is ranked second-to-last (sometimes last) on the Human Development Index and has a greater disparity between wealthy and poor than almost any nation on this planet. Since its encounter with the Western world in 1483, Congo's vast wealth has lured a revolving cast of explorers, monarchs, missionaries, and investors whose collective interactions with Congo are the stuff of legend. When, in 1885, the territory was formally colonized, it was as the private personal property of the Belgian King Léopold II, who plundered what he (rather ironically) called the Congo Free State with no restrictions. The fortune he amassed through slave labor enriched Belgium (and Léopold) exponentially and cost Congo the lives of more than ten million people, leaving a legacy of terror and social fragmentation that still lingers today.

Then, in 1909, thanks to the celebrated persistence of Edmond D. Morel and the Congo Reform Association, Belgium was forced to buy the Congo from Léopold and assume formal colonial authority over what was renamed the Belgian Congo. In this configuration, Congo's wealth continued to serve Belgium until 1960, when Congo won its independence and elected Patrice Lumumba as its first Congolese prime minister. Visionary in his understanding of global politics and economics, Lumumba was adamant that Congo's successful development was directly tied to the nation's ability to control its own resources and to sever neocolonial ties with Belgium. But in the Cold War atmosphere of the 1960s, Lumumba's position was not popular with Western powers, particularly as Congo had supplied the uranium for the atom bombs dropped on Hiroshima and Nagasaki. Afraid Lumumba's proposed autonomy might allow alliances to develop between resource-rich Congo and the Soviet Union, the United States, British, and Belgian governments ordered Lumumba's assassination, which was carried out by his former disciple, Joseph Mobutu, in January 1961.

With the loss of its visionary leader, Congo plummeted into chaos until, in 1965, Mobutu was installed as president with the support of Belgium, the United States, and England. Mobutu proved to be a good ally for the West, exchanging control over Congo's resources for support in maintaining his dictatorship over the country, which he renamed Zaire. As the Cold War came to an end and other urgent geopolitical factors—including the 1994 genocide in neighboring Rwanda—took priority for Western nations and influenced their position toward Zaire, Mobutu lost much of his support from the West. Thus weakened, Mobutu's colorful dictatorship came to an end in 1997 when the rebel leader Laurent Kabila overthrew him and set out to return the nation, which he renamed the Democratic Republic of the Congo, to a democratic state. But by then Congo was embroiled in a series of large-scale wars that erupted as hundreds of thousands of people fled Rwanda and entered Congo's eastern provinces, where, incidentally, a new set of coveted resources had been discovered.[12]

The cumulative effect of long-term oppression, lack of infrastructure, corruption, and extreme wealth positioned (and still positions) Congo as nearly impossible to govern. In January 2001 Laurent Kabila was assassinated and his son Joseph installed as interim president. In 2006 Joseph Kabila was voted president in Congo's first democratic elections since the 1960 election of Lumumba. Although the fact of his election and reelection in 2011 signaled progress (of a sort), the reality is that wars continue to rage in the east of Congo, corruption is still rampant, infrastructure is still dysfunctional, and the ethos of terror and fragmentation introduced by Léopold II continues to reverberate. Indeed, as I write this Introduction, there is tremendous political unrest triggering deadly riots in Congo against President Kabila's attempt to change the constitution to allow himself another term in power. In response to the unrest in the streets, the military police are actively asserting their authoritative presence, which includes periodically cutting off Internet and cell phone services to the entire nation, which generates a flurry of hypotheses and fantastical accounts of what may or may not be happening. In short, the cycle of crises—economic, political, cultural, psychological, and representational—continues.

Historic vacillations of this magnitude cannot but affect—even define—people in deeply personal ways. In interviews with members of an older generation, I have been told, "I was born in the Belgian Congo, went to school in the Republic of the Congo, worked in Zaire, and retired in the Democratic Republic of the Congo, all without leaving my village." This results in comical stories of identity crises brought on by the ostensibly simple task of claiming nationality on a customs form as people are torn between identifying as Congolese, Zairian, or Belgian, or as they reflect whether to claim their Christian names or those imposed under Mobutu's regime of *authenticité* depending on the circumstances. Yet not so comically, these continued transpositions have resulted in a kind of cultural schizophrenia that sees young people dissociated from their own history and the identity (potentially) embedded within it.

My motivation in writing this book was to explore the growing popular claim that art can remedy such social ills. Had Lumumba's vision for Congo come to fruition, I would not have written it. Indeed, Congo would have a thriving economy and would be a significant geopolitical power, and the questions of culture and its production would be radically different. But Lumumba's vision did not come to fruition. Instead he was assassinated and every effort was made to extinguish his legacy and frame his ideology as a specifically Congolese failure. Yet that failure was—and still is—the result of both local and global political realities. In most accounts of the current conflict, echoes of this failure are present; they reverberate through the debates, reports, and scholarly texts addressing issues of economics, politics, structural and development aid, and crisis management. But Lumumba's vision for Congo and the global enthusiasm it catalyzed for widespread liberation from oppression also introduced the promise of a new utopia, a promise that, though it failed in Congo's independence era, still infuses global engagement with the nation.

The dire circumstances of conflict in Congo prevent people from mobilizing around notions of utopia in nearly all domains of life. Except art. Indeed, it is in cultural activism and in the enthusiasm to produce art as a remedy for the social ills of war that the utopic rather than the failed vision of Lumumba lives on. This impulse is at once deeply rooted in compassion and at the same time highly problematic in how it substitutes the euphoria of utopia for objective critical scrutiny. "Art" has become a way for Westerners from Europe and America to engage, positively, with Congo. But art has also become the vehicle through which to inflict new kinds of domination. Both are equally true: art is, in many senses, a kind of last utopia in the east of Congo, but in just as many ways it is a battlefield on which much more insidious issues are playing out. As the examples in this book show, the universalist humanist appeal of art and creativity allows otherwise rational organizations and individuals to endorse, in conflict regions, projects whose equivalents would be ludicrous if proposed in the fields of economics, governance, or medicine. But because it is about creativity rather than more quantifiable matters, the whistleblowers join the cheerleaders in celebrating "art" as a set of inherently positive practices and products without distinguishing between imperial formations or a genuine impulse to realize a Lumumbist utopia.

In *Necessary Noise* I apply critical analysis to art production with the intention of casting the same level of rigor to studying cultural activities as is routinely applied to issues of economics, government, development, and structural aid. Collectively the chapters of this book form a reflection on the meanings and values we ascribe to art making in postcolonial spaces. This analytical approach yields a series of principles about aesthetics and about activism that emerge in each chapter. I have structured the narrative in an arc that starts with an introduction of the local development of music and film production in Goma, then considers the relationship between art and history, and concludes with a series of empirical examples that expose the underbelly of creative production in the current conditions of conflict, with an eye to its implications for the future of the region. In sum, this book mirrors the trajectory articulated by Ngugi wa Thiong'o in the epigraph of this introduction: it follows the songs (and films) as they arise from what has gone before and as they lead to what follows.

The first chapter, "Art on the Frontline," describes the founding of Yole!Africa through a contrapuntal reading of politics and culture in North Kivu in the years from 1995 through 2010. This was a particularly tumultuous period in the east of Congo, which experienced the aftermath of the Rwanda genocide, the overthrow of a thirty-two-year dictatorial regime, two significant wars, assassination of the nation's revolutionary-turned-president, Laurent Kabila, and the ongoing political power struggles characterized by ever-more-violent rebel groups and an increasingly fragmented state. At the same time, there were significant artistic advances that are the foundation of the current artistic resistance movement. Indeed, this same period saw the birth of Congolese hip hop culture, production of the first Congolese music videos, the beginning of Yole!Africa's project Alternative to TV, and the international success of a number of the musicians and filmmakers who trained at the center. Chapter One documents this specifically local history with particular attention to the development of hip hop music, the emergence of the first cinema of proximity in Goma, the evolution of digital technologies, and the volatile political climate of the Great Lakes Region. The principle that emerges through the stories and analyses in this chapter is that, in a conflict region, control of one's own image and voice is a matter of utmost urgency.

Chapter Two, "Re-Membering Congo," is a study of popular history; it explores the relationship between historical knowledge and self-perception in a complex postcolonial state. In 2010, against the backdrop of a nation celebrating fifty years of independence from Belgium, Yole!Africa launched its curriculum of popular history as part of the center's larger objective of reviving the many stories of local heroism that were excised from Congo's official history as institutionalized by its colonizers. Yole!Africa's curriculum of popular history includes a series of films that document well-known (and less-known) historical moments from alternative perspectives. Following screenings of these films, the center facilitates interactive community discussions, which are often quite passionate as young people begin to question information that had previously been presented as absolute Truth. In Chapter Two I analyze five important films in Yole!Africa's curriculum of popular history that explore Congo's colonial, independence-era, dictatorial, and postdictatorial pasts. The analyses are culled from my experiences participating as a researcher and later as an administrator in screenings and debates with students at Yole!Africa. This chapter draws on the theoretical work of writer and literary scholar Thiong'o, who sees literature (and storytelling writ large) as a way of re-membering dismembered histories, and on the work of film scholar Teshome Gabriel, who ties the power of historical storytelling to the positive psychological effects on communities of guarding popular memory. The principle that emerges in this chapter is that understanding Congolese versions of history is a matter of urgency both for local communities seeking to recalibrate their collective identity and for foreign activists and organizations seeking to intervene effectively in the current crisis.

Chapter Three, "Peacemongers," flashes forward to the present. It is about the tensions that are currently arising in Goma as campaigns designed to capitalize on art as a vehicle of sociopolitical change are more torn than ever between the local demands of resistance and the global demands of capitalism. This chapter offers a series of case studies that expose the politics of production behind humanitarian music and film projects, the commodification of suffering, and the now popular practice of marketing peace through art. These analyses draw on the ideas economist Manfred Max-Neef put forward in his study of Human-scale Development, in which he defines nine fundamental human needs that are nonhierarchical and consistent across cultures and throughout time, and then differentiates these needs from their culturally and historically specific satisfiers. The aim of this chapter is to provide detailed examples of the human stakes of modes of activism that are based on economies of people versus those that are based on economies of things. The principle at work is that there is a difference between, on the one hand, the rhetoric and practices of international NGOs that *use* art for change and on the other hand militant artists who insist that if sociopolitical change is going to happen *through* art, it must be art created with intellectual and creative autonomy. The extension of this principle is, of course, that there are consequences to both models.

Having established the historic and contemporary dynamics of Congo's cultural and political landscape, in the final chapter, "Jazz Mamas," I present a collection of stories about rape and sexual violence that never make the news. This chapter takes as its title the historic appellation bestowed on Congo's powerful women as a heuristic move to reconnect stories of empowerment from the past with contemporary examples. It challenges dominant narratives of Congo as a place of extravagant savagery and pitiful victims, by introducing instances of extraordinary agency and daily choices that call into serious question campaigns that take the powerlessness of Congolese women as the launching point of their calls for action. Specifically, this chapter details two of Yole!Africa's projects, Twaomba Amani and Jazz Mama, that have had significant impacts on legal, economic, and educational issues in North Kivu, particularly for women. In recognizing the local initiatives that are effectively addressing the challenges local communities face, the analyses in this chapter indirectly explore the motivations and consequences of maintaining a single story of sexual violence. This chapter parses some of the ways in which exposing urgent truths vacillates between being a noble practice and a calculated publicity strategy. The principles at work in Chapter Four are many. As author Chimamanda Adichie insists there are indeed many dangers to a single story, dehistoricizing a conflict inflicts real violence on recipients of "aid," and for all its overstated glory, revolution is ultimately in the details.

Necessary Noise is a book that sits at many intersections. It is about Congo, creativity, war, and humanitarianism, but it is also an effort to put the east of the nation on the cultural map. There are numerous things that set the east of Congo apart from other parts of the country. For one thing, Kiswahili is the most prominent indigenous language, which linguistically connects the east of Congo more to the Great Lakes Region than to the capital city, Kinshasa, in the west of Congo. This linguistic division also mirrors historic and ongoing political divisions between disparate parts of the nation. In certain times the country has been so divided that travel between the east and west was prohibited for citizens, and different currencies were introduced on the two sides. The result is that travel is still much less costly and much easier between the east of Congo and other Great Lakes countries such as Rwanda, Burundi, Uganda, and Kenya than it is between the east and the west of Congo. This has led, in turn, to many cultural influences from the Great Lakes Region that are not as audible or visible in the art coming out of Kinshasa as that coming out of Goma, Bukavu, Lubumbashi, or Kisangani. Yet to date, with the exception of Guido Convents's French text on the history of Congolese cinema, which includes a section on the east, there are few studies of contemporary art and culture specific to the east of Congo. As this is the site of the ongoing war, an important premise of this book is that regionally specific study of culture is directly relevant to sustainable sociopolitical initiatives.

Much of my thinking about culture in the east of Congo grows out of my own interaction with the scholarly disciplines of ethnomusicology, film studies, and African studies. To each of these it aims, in turn, to make a contribution. Its intended contribution to ethnomusicology is to the growing body of literature on music and conflict and music and conflict resolution. To date little of that literature if any has addressed the conflict in the east of Congo, despite its magnitude. This text thus aims to introduce into urgent ethnomusicological consideration of the very real issues surrounding conflict, a case study of the east of Congo, a region full of vibrant musical traditions that are generally overlooked in favor of Kinshasa and other regions of the country. To the extent that this book contributes to film studies, it is as an applied ethnography of Third Cinema in theory and practice, again in a region that has not been addressed by scholars of African cinema. It is a text that complements the growing body of literature addressing the works of Mweze Dieudonné Ngangura, Balufu Bakupa-Kanyinda, Zeka Laplaine, Jean-Michel Kibushi Njate Wooto, Monique Phoba, Djo Tunda Wa Munga, and others whose films from the west of Congo have put the nation's cinema tradition on the global radar. Finally, this book's contribution to

African studies is simply the addition of a text addressing culture production in one of the most vibrant and most fraught regions of the continent, a region in which cultural questions have taken a back seat to questions of war, politics, and development.

Equally central to my conception of this book as are disciplinary considerations are the questions that emerge at the intersection of social engagement with intellectual study. I am fortunate to be coming of age as a scholar at a time when academic study is reconverging with activism, however tentatively. I have the privilege of having as my intellectual models brilliant scholars who have instilled in me an appreciation of rigorous academic study as well as the value of placing intellectual endeavors in the service of society. As a result of grappling with what (potentially) distinguishes socially engaged scholarship from many of the initiatives I criticize in the following pages, I came to recognize that, like any discipline, practices of social engagement require their own reflexive treatment. To me, social engagement is not simply the act of coupling a service project with an intellectual one; the scholarship that results from social engagement is, for me, not simply the articles or books we write *about* our projects, but the intellectual scrutiny we bring to bear on this particular brand of activism. In the case of *Necessary Noise*, this scrutiny is present in my overt critique of the practices of activism that are interwoven with my ethnography of Yole!Africa and its various projects.

These are some of the intersections I bring to the book. But I have also tried to write it in such a way that it will be of interest and of use to diverse readers. For those with a general interest in Congo, this is one in a cluster of texts that collectively describe one of Africa's richest nations. I hope that in exploring some of the ways artistic production in the east of Congo is simultaneously bound by national and regional histories, readers will begin to see the unique cultural qualities of this conflicted region. For those with interest in getting involved in advocating around Congo's ongoing conflict, I would like this book to provide the opportunity to learn from the experiences of others. For such readers, this book is better read as a list of ingredients than as a prescription or a recipe. For those readers who come to it as part of a quest for better ways to contribute (time or money) to existing organizations, my goal has been to tease out some of the distinctions between a number of paradigms of action and to preserve some of the more uncomfortable conversations and negotiations that take place behind the scenes of the polished press releases and websites competing for support. There are many references throughout the text to local organizations and their international counterparts. This is not intended to create the illusion that either category is unified; nor is it to appeal to the knee-jerk reaction of many to support the underdog on principle. Among the most sacred core objectives of Yole!Africa is to foster in youth the desire to ask questions; that has been my model in writing this book. My aim is that through the stories, analyses, and historical information in *Necessary Noise*, readers will identify questions that they, in turn, might use as barometers against which to measure their own choices.

The research that led to this book was driven by questions of my own: Why in the age of global media is the Western world largely unaware that a conflict of such magnitude is happening right now? What role, if any, can art or culture play in raising awareness? Does changing the stories we tell change how people respond to a crisis? How is art a vehicle for socio-political change on the ground in Congo, if at all? Why are international NGOs trained in medical aid and disaster relief commissioning songs and films in conflict regions? What are the ethics and politics of such productions? What impact do they have on local artists and global audiences? Although these are a handful of the most basic questions that spurred my early research, the text of this book is not driven by answers but by stories. The one truth that remains incontestable in my findings in the east of Congo is that there is no single story. Not of the conflict, not of resistance, not of humanitarianism or charity, not even of local versus foreign interventions. As political scientist and Africanist Mahmood Mamdani argues, endorsing any single or even merely bifurcated analytical frame that either "champions rights" or "stands in defense of culture" is indeed a "paralysis of perspective" that obscures the underlying issues hindering African advancement.[13] For every ingredient of this complex situation there is a web of stories, each with its own adherents and advocates. I have selected a handful of those stories that best illuminate the dynamics I witness in the east of Congo as a cast of local and foreign actors navigate perceptions and issues of social justice through art and culture.

I have already referenced, in general terms, the benefit of coming of age as a scholar at a time when academic study is reconverging with activism. Concretely, for me, those benefits have been many. Working both as a scholar and an (increasingly militant) activist has forced me to confront and remedy weaknesses in my thinking as well as in my ways of engaging in the world. In the early years of my field research and my more recent years as executive director of Yole!Africa, I have been privy to many dynamics that slip under the radar of international and even local media coverage. As a scholar-activist I engage these dynamics in theory and in practice alike, which has fortified my intellectual activity and clarified my activist priorities. It has also made plain to me that they are not separate practices, but deeply interconnected.

This means I am implicated in much of the story I tell about Yole!Africa. A colleague of mine once offhandedly referred to Yole!Africa as my "laboratory," and then quickly retracted the comment for fear of offending me with implications of mad science, or, more worryingly, ethically questionable human experimentation. I do not experiment on people, but I like this metaphor for two reasons. First, Yole!Africa *is* a place of experimentation, even if the experiments in question are artistic rather than chemical or biological. And second, Yole!Africa is, for me, the space in which I watch at the front row as dynamics reveal themselves, the place where I participate actively in probing intellectual questions in search of underlying truths. Indeed Yole!Africa has metaphorically been for me what a laboratory is for my colleagues in the world of science. That my own participation in some of the projects I analyze in this book informs my perspective is inevitable; such is the cost and the benefit of a front row seat in a cultural battle for identity in a conflict region. If anything, this is the greatest strength of my perspective: it is from the ground, informed by a brutally honest group of peers in Congo who, over the years, have not held back from pointing out my own errors of logic or behavior. This is not to say I speak for Congo or for Yole!Africa in this book. I don't. I speak for myself and share, through my own experiences, the dynamics I have witnessed and the insights I have gained.

But, of course, my own experiences and insights are inextricably linked to Congo, to Yole!Africa, and to its founder, Petna Ndaliko Katondolo, with whom I share the values that brought us both to this work and the life we have built together as co-directors of the center, as intellectual and creative collaborators, and as husband and wife. Our partnership has many facets. Young people at the center frequently comment on the positive changes they perceive as resulting from gender-balanced leadership; beyond issues of gender, our partnership certainly brings a distinct mix of artistic, academic, and activist perspectives into often tense negotiations between powerful entities in the world of Congo advocacy. But the deeper strength our marriage brings to our respective and collective work is rooted in the principle of our partnership. After our wedding, we opted to follow the Nande tradition of hosting a kitchen opening ceremony. This ritual involves newlyweds gathering the community and then publicly preparing a meal and serving each and every person. The highpoint of the ceremony is the couple's attempt to make *ugali* together. The dish is a staple in the east of Congo made from dried cassava root pounded into flour and then mixed with boiling water, which must be rigorously kneaded into a doughy consistency with a large wooden paddle. This requires significant physical effort; one partner has to hold the pot of boiling water firmly to the ground while the other vigorously works the mixture. Making ugali as a couple is a metaphor for (and test of) the teamwork required in marriage; feeding the community the food prepared in partnership symbolizes a couple's commitment that their union is in service of the community rather than just for personal benefit. As two individuals who, in the same generation, have immediate family ties to Africa (east, west, north, south, and central), Europe, and the United States, we conceive of our community as global in a very literal sense. Thus the translation of the kitchen opening ceremony into practice has required us to figure out how our partnership fortifies our abilities to serve a global community. This book is part of that project.

At the same time, this is a scholarly text, so let me clarify five additional points to establish my own subject position. First, despite his significant artistic career, in *Necessary Noise* I confine my discussion of Petna Ndaliko Katondolo to quotes from interviews with him about his films and to those aspects of his biography and artistic work that are directly relevant to the formation of Yole!Africa. This means I have left out much about his role in the Great Lakes Region as an influential presence and formative mentor to many filmmakers, dancers, painters, actors, actresses, and musicians; I have also left out analysis of his films except where they are pivotal to Yole!Africa's curricular developments, as is the case with *Lamokowang* (discussed in Chapter Two) and *Jazz Mama* (discussed in Chapter Four). I am confident a comprehensive study of his life and work will one day be published, but for now I leave that to another scholar.

Second, although it is unconventional to refer to artists or subject of analysis by their first or given names, in this text I will refer to Petna primarily by first name from here forward, to avoid illusion or artificial distancing and to avoid confusion since we share a family name.

Third, by marrying Petna I married into a particularly vibrant family that is engaged with many social and political issues in North Kivu. Indeed, this family's commitment to the local community traces back at least to Petna's maternal grandfather, André Kataliko, who inherited his family's knowledge of traditional healing and was later selected by American Protestant missionaries to be among the first Congolese in the region trained in Western medicine. His legacy as a healer established a precedent in the family that continues to manifest. His daughter (Petna's mother), Yukabed Sikulimwenge Kahindo, is the founder and matriarch of Tulizeni, a local widow's association that supports hundreds of women and children after the death of their husbands and fathers. Her efforts, in turn, have influenced her children, many of whom are central figures in Goma's civil society and whose work is thus relevant to this text. I write, for example, about Petna's elder sister, Justine Masika, a renowned women's rights activist who was nominated for the Nobel Prize in 2005 and won the Human Rights Tulip in 2008; I write about Modogo Mutembwi, an elder brother of Petna's who trained at Yole!Africa and has become a pivotal figure in Goma's nascent fiction film scene; I write about Emma Katya, Petna's younger brother who trained at Yole!Africa and has gone on to win international music prizes; I also write about Sekombi Katondolo, another younger brother whose training at and later contributions to Yole!Africa prepared him for his eventual work establishing the Mutaani independent radio station and music label in North Kivu. With the exception of Sekombi, whose familial relationship is relevant to Yole!Africa's history, in the text I write about family members as activists and artists (not as siblings) because that is how they function in Goma. I mention their familial relationships here simply for the sake of full disclosure.

Fourth, let me lay out, clearly, the history and specific responsibilities I carry at Yole!Africa. As indicated earlier, I conducted traditional field research at Yole!Africa starting in 2008. During this period I engaged as a participant observer in musical projects, film screenings, and debates and also collected interviews. Starting in late 2009, I began helping with translation projects at the center as well as occasional small-grant writing. In 2010 I participated in an organizational review (discussed in Chapter Two) and was later asked to step in as temporary co-director of the center with Petna. After a second organizational review, in 2011 my position as co-director was retitled "executive director" (differentiated from Petna's reconfigured position as "artistic director") and extended for a five-year term, which I am serving at the time of writing. My responsibilities as executive director include grant writing; educational outreach between Yole!Africa and global partner organizations; project development and implementation, which I do in collaboration with the centers' artistic director, Petna and coordinator, Ganza Buroko; and attending to administrative details. At the time of writing I continue to act as executive director of the center, which affords me greater insight into the inner workings of the organization and has given me access to much of the information presented in this book.

In addition to my research and administrative roles at Yole!Africa in Goma, in 2012 I oversaw a project with students at the University of North Carolina at Chapel Hill who formed a nonprofit 501(c)(3) sister organization to the center in Congo called Yole!US, This is an educational organization that brings greater awareness to the conflict in the east of Congo through cultural exchange. In practice, Yole!US facilitates opportunities for American college students to engage directly with the artistic pieces being produced in Congo and to work collaboratively with the artists making them. For example, students have written collaborative songs and produced collaborative music videos by sending digital files back and forth and communicating through online platforms such as Skype, Facebook, and WhatsApp. Yole!US has also created an arts curriculum that introduces elementary, middle, and high school students at public and charter schools in the United States to art projects and their accompanying critical issues in

Congo and other African countries. My responsibilities at Yole!US include over-seeing curricular and administrative tasks relevant to implementing projects and directing the board. In my work with Yole!US, I have been privy to a new set of dynamics that come into play when young people in the United States set out to get involved in Congo advocacy work. These experiences, too, inform my writing.

The final point relevant to my subject position in this book is the simple fact that I am an actor in this story. Beyond my role as author of this book, and beyond the many ways Yole!Africa has shaped me as a scholar and an activist, my finger-prints are also visible on elements of the center's evolution during the years of my involvement with it. The formative influences I have had on Yole!Africa are two. I am the first African American participant in the organization, so my presence, the values I hold, and the history I represent have introduced important new con-versations and channels of exchange to the youth at Yole!Africa. Prior to my ar-rival, there was a general if abstract respect for icons of African American popu-lar culture, but little or no understanding of the intricate history and cultural contributions of African Americans writ large. Through informal conversations, *barazza* discussions, and formal curricular changes, I have expanded the dialogue about the African American and African diasporic past and present, which has allowed many young people at Yole!Africa to deepen their understanding of the global Black experience. This is a pivotal shift that has materially disrupted the previous monoscopic focus on colonizing nations and instead provided opportu-nities for Congolese youth to see their African American counterparts as peers in the Global South.

The second arena in which I recognize my own influence on Yole!Africa is the intellectual and scholarly material I have introduced into the center's various curricula. Yole!Africa has always been a radical organization that looked to fig-ures like Frantz Fanon, Kwame Nkrumah, Patrice Lumumba, and Paulo Freire as intellectual role models. My presence as a scholar at the center has expanded this intellectual lineage to include a wider range of historic and contemporary thinkers dedicated to liberation ideology. I see this as the establishment of a dia-logic relationship between theory and practice; in this regard my colleagues at Yole!Africa summarize my presence as a force that has inspired the organiza-tion to zoom out, think, rethink, and theorize as well as take concrete action in real time.

Thus through my own participation, my marriage, and my professional engage-ment, over the years of my work at Yole!Africa my position has shifted from out-sider researcher to insider community member, wife, and mother. I value this shift, above all, for the trust it reflects. Indeed, I measure the evolution of my relationship to the community in Goma by the evolution of names I have been given, which started with the formality of being called by my family name and then moved to tentative—and creative—substitutes for my given name that grew out of shared experiences. Finally, at the surprise party organized for me in June 2012 at Yole!Africa to celebrate the completion of my doctorate, with great solemnity the students announced that they would, thence forth, refer to me as "*mama*," which is the highest sign of respect conveyed to women (the male equivalent is *mzee*). Calling a woman *mama* indicates appreciation for her wisdom, and for the role she plays as a matriarch in the community; it also communicates, in no uncertain terms, an increased level of responsibility and expectation toward the community. I speak from all of these places in this text: as a scholar with objective insights and analyses, as an adopted community member with deference to cultural mores, as a researcher-turned-wife with personal stakes in the community in question, as an African American woman with deep African roots and my own personal commitment to liberation ideology based on my family's experiences in the United States and in West Africa, and finally, as an activist convinced that, globally speaking, we all have a stake in and responsibility to Congo.

What remains in this Introduction is for me to define certain terms. One is *mental colonization*. I trace my use of this notion back to Fanon's writing on the psychological condition that resulted from colonial regimes, which strategically undervalued African practices and overvalued their European counterparts. On mental colonization, Ngugi wa Thiong'o writes

> Colonialism imposed its control of the social production of wealth through military conquest and subsequent political dictatorship. But its most important area of domination was the mental universe of the colonized, the control, through culture, of how people perceived themselves and their relationship to the world. Economic and political control can never be complete or effective without mental control. To control a people's culture is to control their tools of self-definition in relationship to others.[14]

Evidence of mental colonization is visible in many facets of life. Two examples are the internalization of whiteness as the absolute standard of beauty that leads African women the continent over to mold their bodies to White norms, chemically straightening their hair and bleaching their skin with toxic lotions despite serious health risks; and the reflex by many Africans to accord Westerners respect based on nationality rather than character or achievement and to pursue relationships (commercial or personal) on the basis of the belief that proximity to whiteness is a symbol of status. I agree with anthropologist James Ferguson's point that African "yearnings for cultural convergence with an imagined global standard . . . can mark not simply mental colonization or capitulation to cultural imperialism, but an aspiration to overcome categorical subordination."[15] Not all interactions between Africans and Westerners boil down to mental coloniza- tion. But in Congo, where colonization gave way to dictatorship, which in turn gave way to a humanitarian/charity complex imbued with the power to influence states, mental colonization is a real condition that cannot be overlooked in any strategy that aims to intervene meaningfully in the current crisis.

Another term that requires explanation is *NGO*; indeed it is one of the sticki- est and most frequently evoked terms in this book. *Nongovernmental organization* means many things to many people in many places. Technically, Yole!Africa is an NGO, for that is the only legal category available to nonprofit organizations in Congo. At the same time (for example), World Vision, Save the Children, Oxfam, and the American Red Cross, organizations with annual budgets ranging from US$5.3 billion on down to $863 million, are also NGOs. Clearly, an organization with an annual budget greater than those of entire countries has wildly different reach, power, and access to resources than does a private cultural center. This is, in part, what Ferguson refers to when he calls attention to the problems of con- flating politically powerful transnational entities with local grassroots organiza- tions. There are also a host of NGOs that occupy a kind of middle ground between the two poles. Solidarité Internationale and Search for Common Ground are two examples. These are both international NGOs with significantly higher profiles and larger donor bases than the Yole!Africas of the world, but they are not as powerful as organizations like Oxfam. Without intending to conflate their orga- nizational priorities or approaches, I have reserved the term *international NGO* for all foreign humanitarian and charitable organizations working in Congo.

Related to the designation of international organizations as NGOs is the ques- tion of what to call their local equivalents. There are a number of Congolese NGOs that operate in surprisingly similar fashion to their international peers. By and large I do not address such organizations in this text (were I to, I would refer to them as Congolese NGOs). Instead I focus on *local organizations*, which is what I call Yole!Africa throughout the text. I chose this term not because it has any legal significance, but because it allows me to foreground defining characteris- tics of grassroots initiatives and to delineate how local grassroots organizations cannot be conflated with even the most benevolent and considerate international organizations.

It is also necessary to define *charitable imperialism*. Although the term is origi- nal, the idea is not. Scholars and writers from a host of disciplines have pointed out that the impulse toward imperial domination takes many shapes, includ- ing cultural imperialism and humanitarian imperialism. These ideas have long intellectual histories that trace back at least to the 1960s, when poststructuralist and postcolonialist theorists were actively drawing attention to various mediums through which powerful nations exercise control over foreign territories. Charitable imperialism is much the same thing. It is the dynamic that political analyst David Rieff refers to when he calls humanitarianism an adjunct to imperial domination. I have chosen to focus on the noun form of this dynamic, and on charity rather than humanitarianism, to foreground the subject position assumed by those interested in doing good. For all the recent criticism it has received, the notion of charity remains fundamentally associated with good-personness. Ultimately what *Necessary Noise* asks is that we (re)consider, carefully, our definitions and expectations of doing good not as part of an identity rooted in illusions of heroic grandeur or paternalism but as part of an effort to define globally responsible citizenship.

Let me conclude by defining *necessary noise*, to which I have already referred, repeatedly if indirectly. What I am calling necessary noise is both the frenzy of stories generated by foreign activists and organizations (trapped as they are between the perils of speaking out and the deadly consequences of remaining silent) and the increasingly vocal opinions of local artists and activists for whom immediate and personal questions of life or death hang in the mix of global policies. All of this is justified by its makers as *necessary*—whether to raise awareness or to enact resistance. In referring to these efforts as "noise," I am simultaneously doing many things. First, "noise" refers to the figurative volume produced by the frenzy of global actors intervening in Congo; second, it references (indeed shows my own allegiance with) the historically powerful force of embodied protest in music, dance, film, and other expressive mediums that have been reappropriated by Black bodies in many parts of the Global South as a direct critique of the colonial mislabeling of African-origin expressive styles and a reclaiming of their cultural power.

But beyond defining the double entendre of the term, this book questions the validity of the dynamic the term endorses. Here is the contradiction at the heart of this issue: the songs and films produced by charitable and humanitarian organizations are framed as part of the efforts—or noise—deemed necessary to rouse the world from complacency about the atrocities taking place in Congo. This is the noble side of the equation. The problem is that, despite the universal appeal of art and the feel-good reflex it triggers, such songs and films also have consequences, not the least of which are the insidious ways in which they coopt and corporatize the noise of resistance, which local activists also deem necessary. I do not take issue with the necessity of raising awareness or of resisting—in the face of the conflict in Congo I agree that, globally, we need to take action—but I want to question how citing necessity selectively validates certain noise and then influences global consumption of the noise it validates. This is where the stakes lie for artists and communities: the noise the world listens to determines how the world responds, and in the case of the Congo, the world's response is mediated through international NGOs. So necessary noise, in this text, is about sounds (or noise) but also about their makers and the contexts and politics that surround their making. Currently there is cacophony; what *Necessary Noise* sets out to do is to parse how much of that noise is in fact necessary, for whom, and why.

NOTES

1. Ngugi wa Thiong'o, *Decolonizing the Mind: The Politics of Language in African Literature* (New Hampshire: Heinemann, 1986), 45.

2. Ann Laura Stoler, ed., *Imperial Debris: On Ruins and Ruination* (Durham and London: Duke University Press, 2013), 8.

3. John M. O'Connell and Salwa El-Shawan Castelo-Branco, eds., *Music and Conflict* (Urbana: University of Illinois Press, 2010), 5.

4. David Rieff, *A Bed for the Night: Humanitarianism in Crisis* (New York: Simon and Schuster, 2002), 37.

5. Michael Barnett and Thomas Weiss, eds., *Humanitarianism in Question: Power, Politics, Ethics* (Ithaca, NY: Cornell University Press, 2008), 36.

6. James Ferguson, *Global Shadows: Africa in the Neoliberal World Order* (Durham, NC: Duke University Press, 2006), 101.

7. See, for example, Issa G. Shivji, *Silences in NGO Discourse: The Role and Future of NGOs in Africa* (Oxford: Fahamu, 2007); Robert Pinkney, *NGOs, Africa and the Global Order* (Basingstoke: Palgrave Macmillan, 2009); Sarah Michael, *Undermining Development: The Absence of Power Among Local NGOs in Africa* (Oxford: James Currey, 2004); Makau Mutua, ed., *Human Rights NGOs in East Africa: Political and Normative Tensions* (Philadelphia: University of Pennsylvania Press, 2009); Firoze Manji, and Carl O'Coill, "The Missionary Position: NGOs and Development in Africa," *International Affairs* 78, no. 3 (2002), 567–83; Kingston Kajese, "An Agenda of Future Tasks for International and Indigenous NGOs: Views from the South," *World Development* 15, no. 1 (1987), 79–85; Hans Holmén, *Snakes in Paradise: NGOs and the Aid Industry in Africa* (Sterling, VA: Kumarian Press, 2010); Mahmood Mamdani, *Citizen and Subject: Contemporary African and the Legacy of Late Colonialism* (Princeton: Princeton University Press, 1996); Mahmood Mamdani, *Saviors and Survivors: Darfur, Politics, and the War on Terror* (New York: Pantheon Books, 2009); James Dawes, *That the World May Know: Bearing Witness to Atrocity* (Cambridge: Harvard University Press, 2007), 189.

8. Upendra Baxi, *The Future of Human Rights* (New Delhi: Oxford University Press, 2006), 122.

9. Ibid., 132.

10. Rieff, *Bed for the Night*, 56.

11. Michael Maren, *The Road to Hell: The Ravaging Effects of Foreign Aid and International Charity* (New York: Free Press, 1997), 2–3.

12. These resources include coltan, a composite of tantalite and cassiterite, which conducts electricity without heating up and is consequently used in portable electronic devices (cell phones, computers, digital cameras, etc.), the transportation industry (automobiles and airplanes), and medical devices (such as pacemakers); illegal export of coltan from the east of Congo is a major factor in the current conflict.

13. Mamdani, *Citizen and Subject*, 3.

14. Thiong'o, *Decolonizing the Mind*, 153.

15. Ferguson, *Global Shadows*, 20.

1

ART ON THE FRONTLINE

SOMETIMES STORYTELLING IS a matter of survival. When one's story is one's only possession of value, telling it becomes a matter of life or death, becomes the only means of inscribing, in the impenetrable course of war, a trace of humanity. Yet, when the momentum of war has calibrated a community's expectations— even self-perceptions—for more than a century, the impulse to preserve human dignity through stories is easily extinguished. In such conditions storytelling becomes a radical, often dangerous act. In the east of Congo, as in other African conflict regions, reviving subversive storytelling traditions does indeed usher one into the battle over Africa (as the epigraph above suggests) in the most literal sense. Arguably, at its best, storytelling, more than taking arms, restores agency to those who have historically been the subject, indeed the collateral damage, in this battle. The optimists among us might even go so far as to suggest (or at least hope) that in the battle over Africa the pen is mightier than the sword, that ideas outlast and ultimately triumph over force. But it is hard to gain access to the proverbial pen in a postcolonial war zone. Both weapons have, of course, been updated—machine guns have replaced swords, and cameras (and other digital recording technologies) have been substituted for pens—but, if anything, this has increased the disparity of access. Indeed, in Congo obtaining a gun is a matter of ease while accessing—to say nothing of using—a camera is a nearly insurmountable feat.

For perspective: the first time I turned on my camera in Congo I was nearly arrested by five heavily armed agents of the secret police. I was in the back of a car driving down the Boulevard de 30 Juin on a beautiful Sunday morning when, with the approval of veteran filmmaker Petna Ndaliko Katondolo and his seasoned production manager Stella Ramazani, I decided to shoot some footage of Congo's distinct urban beauty with my small handheld video camera. Within moments of removing the lens cap, our vehicle was surrounded by highly polished black SUVs with impenetrable tinted windows. We were forced to a halt in the middle of the four-lane boulevard, and before I knew it, a man with a large gun had wrenched open my door and was lunging across my lap, aggressively grabbing for the camera, while four other armed men positioned themselves on all sides of the car. After over an hour of heated arguing, during which I produced certified copies of the $250 filming permit that it had taken me nearly a month to obtain as well as copies of my embassy-issued travel visa and proof of academic affiliation, we were eventually released, with the ironic and nonapologetic explanation by the chief officer that it is their duty to ensure that no one gets negative images of Congo.

That was in 2009, when the war had officially ended. And I had an American passport. Imagine what it was like in 1997, when the country was reeling from the overthrow of a thirty-two-year dictatorship and careening full throttle from kleptocracy to guerrilla state. Then take away the protection of the American passport, and you can start to picture what it was like for Congolese attempting to document, articulate, or critique the conditions of their nation. Obstacles were particularly severe for citizens in the east of Congo, which is far removed from the capital and thus has fewer of the resources or protections surrounding the seat of power. Furthermore, the rebel leader, Laurent Kabila, who had overthrown the dictator Mobutu Sese Seko and assumed the presidency, had gathered much of his army in the east, branding the eastern provinces as rebellious and dangerous in national and global analyses. Thus, restrictions preventing artists and intellectuals in these provinces from telling their own stories were nearly absolute.

These are (some of) the preconditions that led to the founding of Yole!Africa in Goma—the increasing urgency for youth caught between the dire need to express themselves and the near impossibility of inscribing in the impenetrable course of war a record of local resistance. By the mid-1990s, Yole!Africa's founder, Petna (who was born in 1974), was emerging as an influential youth leader in North Kivu in part for his increasingly militant ideas about cultural activism and in part because of his pioneering role in Congolese cinema in the east of the nation. At the time, Petna was among a small handful of Congolese in the east to have obtained both the training and the technology to film; contrary to his fellow cameramen, who either worked for the national television or filmed social or religious events, he was the only one to put these skills and technologies to use in an artistic or storytelling capacity (to date, Petna is still the only internationally acclaimed Congolese filmmaker to be born and to work in the east of the nation). His experiences illustrate the challenges of the time; indeed, beyond the nearly insurmountable issues of getting access to cameras was the precarious project of not getting killed by suspicious, often corrupt, agents of law enforcement. *Debrouillardaize,* the culture of harassment and impunity established by Mobutu, was still the order of the day, and when Petna was not being hassled, detained, or arrested by state officials, he was subjected to costly manipulations of official documentation procedures as, with each production, he had to fight anew for state-issued accreditation to film.

Provided he managed to get a functional camera, train a competent and courageous crew, and secure and pay for a permit, there was still the problem of retaining his footage. He tells countless stories of fighting from the break of dawn to film events, only to have a soldier or policeman (who was drunk as often as not) confiscate his footage at the end of the day and destroy it out of paranoia of what might appear on one of the tapes. Foreign journalists were a customary sight, but a local with equivalent technology was terrifying to the state. There is the now-infamous example of Petna being asked to film Goma's participation in World Ecology Day in 1997: after he spent the day filming people happily planting trees, law enforcement officers arrested him and detained him by force in their headquarters for hours while they puzzled over how to confirm that his images were not somehow compromising. In this particular case, intervention on Petna's behalf by a high-ranking colonel eventually led to his release and salvation of the footage, but despite this "successful" negotiation of law enforcement, for members of the ecological movement the lingering sentiment was that documenting what was to be a celebration of a growing environmental consciousness in Goma ended up as an antagonistic confrontation with the state.

During this same period, musicians, who had long been central to preserving and expressing popular opinion in Congo through stories and songs, were also severely restricted by the political climate. Mobutu's dictatorial cultural policy, which legislated music (and other performance forms) as a vehicle of state control, had nearly eradicated any inclination toward musical dissent among artists. Even instances of criticism buried in allegory resulted in songs and albums being banned; for example, Koffi Olomide and Quartier Latin's veiled critiques of Mobutu resulted in the banning of their 1994 album *Magie.* In the east of Congo, the tension around musical content was further complicated by the complete lack of infrastructure to support musical production; there were no recording studios, and performance venues were limited to small nightclubs, churches, and schools.

Collectively, this created a peculiar dynamic in Goma: longing for musicians to speak out against the oppression and confusion of the times, audiences of popular music began to hunt for hidden meanings buried in song lyrics, particularly in songs from Kinshasa; at the same time, for local musicians in the east, political criticism through music was unfathomable with the regional volatility triggered by the genocide in Rwanda. To navigate opposing pressures, popular musicians in Goma wrote and performed—but did not record—songs that decried war and violence in general terms and that, in equally vague terms, implored people, presumably including politicians, to "make peace."

The majority of the music and the handful of films produced during this time were popular but politically innocuous. They skirted the boundaries of storytelling without fulfilling the community's growing need to revive subversive narrative traditions. Yet, in later interviews, artists of this era identify it as an incubation period for the movement that is currently (re)vitalizing the tradition of cultural dissent in the east of Congo. Indeed, many of the socially and politically active musicians and filmmakers trace the roots of their current artistic radicalism—and in some cases even militancy—to a number of events, starting in 1995, that seemed disparate at the time but that collectively shifted the trajectory of artistic production in Goma.

Many of these events were not artistic, but political. The 1990s were a time of radical upheaval in the east of Congo; the 1994 genocide in Rwanda led to a mass migration of hundreds of thousands of people into North Kivu, which strongly inflected the urbanization of cities like Goma, and at the same time there was tremendous political instability throughout Congo (then Zaire) as American support for Mobutu's dictatorship diminished, allowing vying factions to assert alternative modes of governance until Kabila overthrew Mobutu's government in 1997 and attempted to introduce democracy. In all of this there was a renewal of long-simmering ethnic and economic disparities that had been introduced under Belgian colonial rule and were further exacerbated by the post-independence decline (if not outright dysfunction) of infrastructure and the continued unregulated exploitation of natural and human resources.

These powerful political factors forced people in the east of Congo to navigate an evolving state of emergency. But, as sociologist AbdouMaliq Simone points out, in addition to introducing conditions of crisis, "emergency [also] describes a process of things in the making, of the emergence of new thinking and practice still unstable, still tentative in terms of the use to which such thinking and practice will be put."[1] In Goma, the artistic productivity between 1995 and 2010 reflects precisely such a process of emergence/emergency. Indeed, the particular combination of political upheaval, rapid urbanization, and charismatic individuals catalyzed radically new thinking and new practice in the domains of music and film production that have expanded, concentrically, to influence social and political choices in the region. This period marked the advent of hip hop in the east of Congo, the beginning of the region's first cinema of proximity, and the founding of Yole!Africa, Goma's first independent cultural center. These developments parallel the evolution of increasingly accessible and inexpensive digital technologies, all of which, collectively, supported aspiring young artists in reclaiming expressive mediums as vehicles through which to tell their own stories.

Viewed retrospectively, the coinciding artistic, political, and personal influences of the time cohere into a specifically local history of bourgeoning cultural activism, or to revisit my earlier metaphor, an effort to reclaim the proverbial pen. But if the result is a (somewhat) cohesive vision of the power of artistic expression in the east of Congo, the process by which local artists arrived at this vision was all but cohesive. Instead it was the result of an intricate web of influences and interactions that require a "contrapuntal reading."[2] Counterpoint, in music, describes a relationship between independent but interconnected voices; it is defined as a texture in which "voices are brought into relief against each other functionally and by virtue of their relative importance."[3] This is both literally and figuratively a particularly apt analytical frame through which to understand the evolution of artistic radicalism in the east of Congo; it is an ongoing process in which individual and collective voices are brought into often sharp relief against each other and against the larger machinations of global politics in ways that shed light on their relative importance. To extend the analogy further, the language of tension and resolution that describes the movement of interlocking musical melodies parallels the convergences and divergences of intersecting artistic and political forces in Congo, as they are all beholden to an internal structural integrity that dictates the variations and manipulations of their respective themes.

In this light, I read the development of cultural activism in Goma as a kind of counterpoint between politics and culture writ large, between specific mediums of expression (in this case music and film), and between individual actors whose biographies shaped (and continue to shape) artistic practices in the region. Accordingly, this chapter explores the period from 1995 to 2010 in Goma, during which many of the voices and themes that dominate the current artistic landscape were evolving; it charts interactions that brought these voices into relief and theorizes what that meant for their relative importance in a cultural economy that is considerably influenced by external (particularly charitable) actors. The chapter is divided into three sections—"On Sound and the Founding of Yole!Africa," "On Image and the Emergence of Radical Aesthetics," and "Intersections"—that move roughly chronologically through this period, interweaving historic and aesthetic developments that cohere at some points thematically, and that diverge dramatically at other points, revealing the ebb and flow of artistic emergence in conditions of crisis. (The most obvious deviation from chronological organization is the withholding of certain political history until the second section of the chapter, which I have done to foreground the differing political factors affecting music versus film production in the east of Congo.)

The object of this, as in any contrapuntal analysis, is to create a map of interrelationality in which the momentary foregrounding of a given voice or theme exposes the development of them all. This is not intended as a comprehensive artistic history of the city; for that I have made too many omissions, particularly with regard to the vibrant artistic projects affiliated with many Protestant and Catholic churches. Instead what follows is a transcription of the specific cultural movement in Goma that positions artistic expression in general and storytelling in particular as a human necessity in a global economy animated by narrations of war.

ON SOUND AND THE FOUNDING OF YOLE!AFRICA

To the extent that any historical account has a beginning, this story starts with music. By the early 1990s, hip hop was a genre of growing interest on the African continent, with rising emcees and expanding audiences in many countries, but in Goma, like most of Congo, there were not yet any well-established Congolese rap groups. Mobutu's dictatorial cultural policies were largely to blame as he categorically rejected Western influence in favor of "authentic" and "traditional" Congolese music and liberally ordered severe physical, economic, and psychological punishments for anyone who disobeyed his regime of *authenticité*. It is no wonder, then, that hip hop did not take root in Congo as early as it did elsewhere on the continent; yet, as an increasingly popular genre associated with global belonging, dissent, and liberation ideology, its eventual popularity in Congo's environment of oppression was inevitable. Indeed, by the mid-1990s, there were traces of an emerging "youthscape" in Congo—that is, "a site that [was] not just geographic or temporal, but social and political as well"—that was deeply rooted in hip hop culture and in imagined participation in an aesthetic renewal of global pan-African belonging.[4]

In Goma this process began in 1995, when a group of three high school students formed South Cross, the first rap group in the region. At the time, Black American culture was extremely popular in North Kivu; for years Michael Jackson had been a beloved superstar of Congo, and in fact local Congolese pronunciation of his famous lyrics "just beat it" eventually yielded the term "*djanspilé*," a word (both adjective and noun) used across Congo that designates everything inspirational and popular that comes from America. Popular American music was called djanspilé as a genre designation, people who performed this music were called *mdjansa* (*m* being the prefix that designates humans in Bantu languages) and all music, dance, clothing, etc., that appealed to people as related to American popular musicians was described as djanspilé.

Eddie Murphy was another local superhero as he opened the eyes of young people to the potential that a Black man could "kick white ass" (to quote the youth). Hip hop icons MC Hammer, Bobby Brown, and Naughty By Nature were also extremely popular, and even though the majority of *Gomatriciens* (as people of Goma refer to themselves) did not understand the English lyrics, they expressed their solidarity by meticulously fashioning their clothing, hairstyles, and gestures on their American idols. They also learned all of the dances. By 1995 there were already local hip hop dance groups, but it was not until Francophone artists MC Solaar and Benny B became popular that youth in Goma began to understand the potency of rap lyrics. The sense for them was that for the first time they had access to Black role models, and in watching and listening to "positive" Black people they had finally discovered how they too could, indeed should, be. Naturally, they tried to emulate this model of Blackness in every possible way, including in the case of South Cross their music.

Notably, instead of recognizing overtures toward a global tradition of dissent or street culture in South Cross's early lyrics, parents and school officials viewed their raps as poetry that demonstrated linguistic prowess in French and thus encouraged the young people enthusiastically. Despite the youths' conception of their works as songs, older generations did not readily associate this "noise" with music, which, for them, had certain prescribed aesthetic characteristics that were inaudible in the relentless drive of hip hop beats. Yet none of this deterred the group from classifying their songs as both musical and political. In retrospect, Dyna Icy, a founding member of South Cross, recognizes that the politicality of the early songs was minimal, in large part because overt critiques were not tolerated under Mobutu's regime and the group was simply not old or experienced enough to launch a large-scale campaign of dissent.[5] Yet, despite the absence of an underground hip hop scene in the east of Congo, burgeoning roots of politicism are evident in the group's very insistence that, unlike other popular genres of Congolese music at the time, such as Rumba, R&B, and djanspilé, hip hop was not a genre for love songs, but a genre reserved for critiquing social and political ills. The popular topics of complaint in the era were unemployment, poor education, and the general grievances of living under dictatorship. Yet, even though these pressing social issues were the inspiration for the songs, the lyrics themselves were far from scathing. For example, here are the opening verse and refrain of South Cross's first song, "Expression":

Debout les révolutionnaires de l'an 2000	stand up revolutionaries of 2000
personne ne peux nous faire taire	no one can silence us.
a cause de nos révolution	Through our revolution
pour qu'en on ai des évolution	we will bring evolution
de nos institution	to our institutions
a fin que la jeunesse retrouve	for the youth to find
sa place dans cette société	our rightful place in society
rangé des inégalité	full of inequality
et d'injustice	and injustice
une société dans la quelle les toubibes sont de venu	a society where doctors have become
des metteures de feux	orchestrators of destruction (lit. fire)
les enfants traité comme des bidonnerons,	the children treated as useless,
drogue et alcool sont devenu	drugs and alcohol have become
le passetemps favori au détriment de l'école . . .	the favorite pastime instead of school...

Refrain:

par cet rap nous voulons exprimer	with this rap we want to express
nous voulons exprimer	we want to express
toute nos penses . . .	all our thoughts . . .
(repeat three times)	(repeat three times)

The remainder of the song does in fact express many (if not quite all) of their thoughts, but it does so in a language caught between the opposing forces of revolutionary spirit, dictatorial restriction, and the urgency of adolescence.

Of this triumvirate of forces, revolutionary spirit eventually gained the upper hand, due, in part, to the sheer determination of the young people to forge a hip hop culture in Goma and due, in equal part, to the political circumstances of the time. When South Cross decided to record "Expression," which incidentally was the first hip hop song recorded in North Kivu or South Kivu, they came face to face with the war in the region. The year was 1996, and the aftermath of the 1994 genocide in Rwanda was still playing out in the east of Congo in the form of political instability caused by insurgent rebel groups aiming to overthrow Mobutu, and by hundreds of thousands of migrants and internally displaced persons making their way from Rwanda into Congo. It was in the home of a Rwandan refugee, known locally as "Jean-Jacques," that South Cross discovered the technology they needed to record their song. That the flight from genocide was the circumstance through which recording technology entered North Kivu and became available to aspiring hip hop artists is a pointed fact in the evolution of the genre in the region that irrevocably connects hip hop to the recent history of war by the material conditions of production. Indeed, in this instance the studio itself emerged as a microcosm of those "postmodern geographies" that effectively "re-entwine the making of history with the social production of space."[6] Inhabiting the studio, however temporarily, was thus an embodied act that made visible to young people their own agency in both the production of history and the inscription of new meaning on the recording studio and on the soundscapes of future listeners, however few, as viable social spaces.

Inspired by the experience of recording their first track, South Cross decided to make a music video to accompany the song and amplify its meaning. For this they approached Petna, in part because he was known in North Kivu as one of the few Congolese to have modern video camera equipment (television stations at the time did not yet have equivalent equipment), and in part because of his status as a rising powerful leader of youth opinion. By commissioning Petna to direct and produce their video, South Cross aimed both to elevate the profile of the video and to lend it, by affiliation, greater social capital.

The music video for "Expression" was the first one made in Goma, and its production represents the first convergence of music and film in the city's nascent hip hop scene. The video itself was buried under the lava of the 2002 eruption of the Nyiragongo volcano, but discussions with participants in this project suggest that the circumstances of production say as much as the final product about the revolutionary spirit of Goma's hip hop pioneers. Indeed, like the recording of the song, the filming of the video was framed by issues of power and material scarcity that result from political instability. For example, in Goma in 1996, "modern" video camera equipment was still extremely cumbersome and editing technologies were not available outside of national television channels, which were fiercely controlled by Mobutu.

For readers from the digital age for whom even the comparatively recent mini DV technology is already an ancient ancestor of the agile HD or 4K cameras with automatic audio sync and a full spectrum of digital aftereffects, it is worth describing the production of "Expression" in some detail. Since there was no way of accurately syncing audio to video, the sound had to be embedded directly into the VHS tape, which prompted the production team to

FIGURE 1.1 1996 Music Video Shoot. Photo courtesy of Yole!Africa.

surreptitiously "borrow" Petna's elder brother's giant boom box (when he was out of town), then scrounge together enough money to buy the twelve double D batteries the machine required to operate for a few hours. The boom box was then attached via long cables to the Panasonic 300M camera, which itself was plugged into a (somewhat) portable power source like a car battery. In this configuration, which is visible in Figure 1.1, filming a single image required a team of assistants to run behind the camera and keep cables and power supplies portable, untangled, and out of the shot all in perfect silence. On top of this was the added complication that, in the absence of editing facilities, Petna had developed a tactic of editing on camera, which meant that musicians and assistants had to be perfectly choreographed to time the cuts and transitions (from one location to the next) that would appear, untouched, in the final film. In short, it was a guerrilla production in the tradition of revolutionary cinema, which requires filmmakers to exercise extraordinary ingenuity and construct a culturally relevant local aesthetic out of whatever materials are at their disposal. By all accounts, the final music video for "Expression" was just that: a unique perspective on the east of Congo that showed young people engaged in positive social activities and scrupulously avoided cliché images of war-torn Africa.[7]

Yet, for all the personally transformative micropolitics of latent revolutionary production, the musical and visual critiques put forth in "Expression" were still quite mild. But when Laurent Kabila overthrew Mobutu and the cultural regime of authenticité began to be dismantled, hip hop in Goma emerged as a vehicle for more overt dissent. By 1997 a handful of other hip hop groups had formed, including White Beret, and Damaniz, followed later by SW Rough, TNG, Z1 Crew, and C Tribe, all of which expressed allegiance to the revolutionary rather than commercial aspects of the genre. Songs like "L'oeuil anxious" by White Beret replaced the comparatively docile texts of earlier songs like South Cross's 1995 "Expression."

"L'oeuil anxious" includes this verse sung by Damas Masudi, one of the group's lead rappers:

Moi Damas avant j'étais encore gosse	I, Damas, before I was still a boy
maintenant j'ai grandi dans le rap,	now I've grown up immersed in rap
oh Afrique notre continent	Oh Africa, our continent
où est tu parti le Congo démocratique	where has democratic Congo gone?
dans le ciel, Dieu réuni ce qui s'aime en vérité	in heaven God reunites true loves
et comme je suis un garçon libre	and since I am a free man
je parle la vérité	I speak the truth
pour satisfaire nos grands parents	to avenge our grandparents
c'est pas vrais leurs mensonges	to expose their lies
nous entoure comme «chinangambaya»	surrounding us like evil spirits
écoute mes frères	listen my brothers
ces dirigeantes en foirés nous trompent	these despicable leaders deceive us
avec leurs démocratie à chié	with their bullshit democracy
autour de nous, toutes en vérité	the truth surrounds us
les massacres nous tuent comme des animaux,	we die in massacres like animals
de quoi tu parles mon frère ?	what are you talking about, brother?
mon frère je parle de la guerre	I'm talking about war
tribale du Rwanda	about ethnic war in Rwanda
de l'Afrique déjà déchiré par la guerre tribale raciale.	about Africa already torn by ethnic war.
oh Afrique de Mandela,	Oh Africa of Mandela,
de Kwame Nkrumah,	of Kwame Nkrumah
Afrique de Lumumba	Africa of Lumumba
où elle est parti?	where has she gone ?
Je parle à la guerre comme Charles	I speak of war like Charles
qui parle à Adèle, la belle	who speaks to Adèle, the beautiful[8]
je souffre comme dans le future	I suffer when I think of the future
allure de vivre	I long to live
je sais que tout cela c'est toujours l'injure	I know that this is the eternal insult
de toute ces massacres africaine,	these African massacres
j'accuse toute ces peuples	I accuse those people
qui acceptent de se battre,	who agree to fight
j'accuse tous ces dirigeants	I accuse all the leaders
qui escroquent l'économie du pays	who defraud the nation's economy

pour se faire enrichir	to enrich themselves
car j'étais appelé à barré la route	I was called to block the path
de ceux qui s'attaquent aux frères ...	of those who attack their people ...

The overt denunciation of local, national, and international political and military leaders in "L'oeuil anxious" marks a significant departure from earlier hip hop songs in Goma, which alluded to corruption in subtler ways. The language of these lyrics, in which Masudi accuses various powers of orchestrating social ills and positions himself as gatekeeper of social values, suggests a profoundly enhanced conception of musical and artistic agency, which, coupled with references to Mandela, Nkrumah, and Lumumba as visionary leaders, asserts allegiance to a growing sentiment of Pan-African solidarity among youth in the east of Congo. Despite its limited circulation, for local audiences in Goma, this song can be read as an example of—even a contribution to—global Black musical traditions as they function as a symbolic "archive of pan-African feeling, practice, and imagination."[9]

But even though analysis of the lyric content of "L'oeuil anxious" reveals mounting courage among young people to critique politicians, the actual risk of voicing political criticism was minimal, as hip hop still did not have a large audience in Goma. The primary connoisseurs of hip hop were still the age mates and classmates of the artists themselves and, although this group of youth eventually became a distinguished generation of university graduates, at the time they were simply high school students with an affinity for American music and as such were not taken very seriously by officials.

Then, in 1998, the imagined solidarity with pan-African networks became a reality when the popular American hip hop group Arrested Development performed live in Goma. This marked a significant step forward in Goma's hip hop scene. South Cross had the opportunity to open for Arrested Development, which was the local group's first public performance outside of school-affiliated events. When, in the aftermath of the successful concert, South Cross and other emerging groups realized hip hop had an audience in Goma, it opened the doors for a series of local concerts. No individual group at the time could fill an entire venue (or program for that matter), but South Cross and others formed a coalition, called "Empire Z,"[10] with four or five bands of different genres, mostly R&B and hip hop, and collectively set out to establish a new popular concert tradition in Goma. Empire Z began organizing shows in outdoor nightclubs with the support of progressive proprietors and, eventually, amassed a following of approximately one thousand dedicated fans.

The growing popularity of rap music led to a corresponding demand for music videos. Following the logic of South Cross's early effort to lend their songs greater politicality and social value, rap groups frequently approached Petna to direct and produce their videos. The convergence of music with video marked a moment when the evolution of artistic radicalism in the east of Congo became inextricably linked to the biography of Petna. Thus my contrapuntal narrative must momentarily foreground those aspects of his personal story that were formative for subsequent artistic developments.

By 1997 Petna was gaining more and more traction as a youth leader. He had his own radio show, *Tamtam Chrome*,[11] at the North Kivu branch of the National Television and Radio Broadcast Association (RTNC), where he discussed the latest music and cultural politics with a growing loyal following. He was also known as a public figure for his work with Maïdeni, which he founded in 1992 as a youth organization dedicated to raising awareness about sociopolitical and environmental issues through art and culture. Simultaneously, his reputation as the most prominent socially engaged filmmaker in the province won him both esteem in the eyes of young people and suspicion in the eyes of the revolving cast of military leaders. Initially, navigating the political and military personalities was a matter of striking a balance between humility and wit while maintaining a public profile, but then, in 1998, Petna wrote and released a series of plays, including *Victime de la guerre, La contre-offensive foudroyante,* and *Mon combat noir,* which were overt in their radical denunciation of the political and humanitarian climate of the time. As a result he and his closest colleague were targeted and eventually kidnapped; his colleague, who had less influence in the region, was killed and Petna narrowly escaped to Uganda in secrecy. During Petna's absence, any overtures toward revolutionary filmmaking in Goma ground to a halt, but not so hip hop music; even without the support of a youth leader, rappers in Goma continued to produce songs of greater or lesser dissent.

Petna's exile in Uganda resulted in a temporary divergence of film and music in Goma, but it also led to the formation of Yole!Africa. When he arrived in Kampala, Petna began working with throngs of East African refugees in his role as research assistant for a Dutch anthropology Ph.D. student, Ellen Lammers, who was conducting research with urban refugees with a focus on their experiences with the United Nations High Commission for Refugees (UNHCR).[12] As he gained deeper access and accordingly became more intimately aware of the contradictions and failings of the humanitarian system, Petna began to seek an alternative way to meet some of the needs of the masses of young people whose lives were disrupted by the various wars raging between their nations (at the time there were wars between Ethiopia and Eritrea; Rwanda, Burundi, and Congo; what is now North

Sudan and South Sudan; and in Somalia; notably the Ugandan army was active in most of these wars). Unable to alter either the political climate or the industry of humanitarianism, Petna turned to what he knew—art—and created, in his living room, a space where people could come together to express their frustrations and seek camaraderie. When participants discovered that, despite the linguistic and cultural differences that posed such serious problems when attempting to navigate the official system, they were able to communicate across barriers through art, these gatherings became extremely popular, and what began as an informal opportunity to paint, dance, and make music quickly snowballed into a thriving cultural hub.

In concert with the theoretical concepts that underscored Lammers's anthropological research, Petna began to develop his own analysis of crisis and displacement. His personal experiences of exile and migration confirmed for him that effective human rights advocacy must extend beyond meeting basic material needs of sustenance and shelter to also address the equally fundamental human needs for communication, interaction, and mutual understanding (to name a few). What he witnessed in the impromptu artistic gatherings in his living room was a local iteration of the celebrated (and highly theorized) capacity for creative expression to catalyze profound personal and interpersonal transformation. On this principle, he and Lammers formed Yole!Africa as a nonprofit cultural center. [(▶) files 1.1, 1.2, 1.3]

Yole!Africa quickly became an extremely popular space in Kampala's youth-scape. It started as a center for refugees, but as it grew, Ugandan youth petitioned to join as well and, out of deference to the center's founding principles of inclusivity and community, Petna and Lammers opened the space to everyone. Within months of its founding, the center was positively influencing enough young people that it caught the attention of major international organizations such as the United Nations; the French, Belgian, and Dutch embassies in Uganda; the Global Pan-African Movement; and the Unilever Omo brand, as well as such Ugandan institutions as the National Theatre and Makerere University. Thus, in addition to being a space for creativity and healing, Yole!Africa also became an influential structure that helped young people navigate larger institutions. As Yole!Africa continued to grow in Kampala, many Congolese youth from Goma migrated to Uganda and joined the center, where, in addition to learning English, they were exposed to new artistic practices and aesthetics including new aspects of hip hop culture.

It is important, at this point in the narrative, to underscore the significance of young people from Goma aligning themselves with hip hop culture in Uganda. Both geographically and geopolitically, Uganda is part of East Africa, whereas

Congo is classified as Central Africa, despite the fact that its eastern regions identify geographically and culturally with other East African nations. What this means for local populations in the east of Congo is that the political decisions made in the capital, Kinshasa, are not always congruent with the lived realities they experience in (or, in geopolitical terms, on the periphery of) the Great Lakes Region, which leaves with citizens the challenge of navigating often conflicting demands of allegiance. This political fragmentation also manifests artistically as evidenced by the tensions between musical and cinematic aesthetics from the east versus the west of Congo, which, on a smaller scale, are not entirely dissimilar from the tensions between East Coast and West Coast hip hop in the United States. To fully illustrate this dynamic, it is important to contextualize the evolution of cultural activism in the east with a detour that briefly outlines the concomitant development of hip hop in the west of Congo.

At the same time young people from Goma were aligning themselves with East African hip hop through their work with Yole!Africa in Kampala, hip hop in the west of Congo, specifically in Kinshasa, was also gaining momentum. Hip hop became popular in Kinshasa in the late 1980s and had some notable moments of political engagement (for example, in 1991 rappers protested "Black September," which was a public massacre of citizens by Mobutu's soldiers) but, by the late 1990s when hip hop exploded in the capital city, there was a strong divide between commercial and political rappers. Similar to Goma, many young people there were enamored of the aesthetics of what they considered the quintessential American genre, and like their peers in the east, they modeled their physical appearance and dance moves on American hip hop artists. But in Kinshasa, with its thriving popular music scene, many musicians who decided to pursue hip hop initially borrowed the rhythms and effects that gave them a sense of global belonging more than they took inspiration from the impulse of dissent. Similarly, in the absence of an active radical cinema tradition in the capital since the revolutionary filmmaker Balufu Bakupa-Kanyinda had been forced into exile in 1986, the hip hop music videos being produced in Kinshasa were an outright imitation of the aesthetics that were imported with commercial American hip hop: fast cuts, aggressive angles, and a general glamorization of bling. Thus it was primarily commercial hip hop that was rising in popularity in Kinshasa until, when Congo's National Censorship Commission attempted to ban hip hop, the genre took on a much more uniformly political role than it might otherwise have assumed.

Ironically, the attempted ban was about control of image, not control of lyrics. As digital technologies enabled Kinois (the local term for inhabitants of Kinshasa) hip hop groups to begin to produce music videos quickly and inexpensively, they began to saturate the television channels in the capital. At the time, hip hop was considered a youth genre and was not incorporated into the state-run system of artistic control, until rapper ODJI decided to take his video to the National Censorship Commission for official approval and the government realized that, prior to him, they had not been controlling hip hop songs or videos, as was their practice with all popular music productions. The structure of the commission is such that artists are required to submit their songs and/or videos and pay a fee to have them censored, after which they receive an official letter of authorization for the song or video. When, in compliance with this law, ODJI paid the commission to censor his song (which, incidentally was not remotely political), the National Censorship Commission called an internal meeting and, with the support of the state, solicited a prosecutor to draft a letter prohibiting dissemination of Congolese hip hop, which they distributed to all television and radio stations. According to Lexxus Legal, who is one of Congo's most influential and militant rappers, the issue was not about music or lyrics, but about money and control: "They thought that if they banned hip hop, we, the rappers, would be obliged to go to the Commission and pay, which mattered to them because more of our videos were being diffused than all the rumba musicians put together. The difference was that we produced our own videos, even the rumba musicians had to come to us to make their videos—they were already the minority, and we already had control."[13]

Regardless of the government's motives, its effort to control hip hop catalyzed a fierce—if short lived—unity among rappers in Kinshasa, who organized a campaign against the ban. These artists gained the support of local and international media outlets, which covered their protests in front of the censorship commission's building, and gave them television airtime during which they called, among other things, for the commission to justify their decision in light of the post-Mobutu constitution's inclusion of "freedom of expression." Particularly in Belgium and France, the international media attention proved embarrassing to the government, especially as rappers demanded the government detail exactly what in their music and videos warranted censoring. (A much-repeated sound bite at the time was of Lexxus Legal stating, "If, for example, they want to tell us that showing a topless woman is banned, then many national monuments will have to be removed"). Eventually the commission was obliged to retract their ban on hip hop, and with this victory, hip hop artists realized the power of the genre as a medium of political activism.

Although fighting the censorship commission temporarily united the rappers of Kinshasa, it did not lead to a uniform relationship between music and activism. Instead it was a moment of unity that dissolved into a broad spectrum of engagement in the capital. There were artists who preferred to develop commercial styles that, with the exception of language, are nearly indistinguishable from American or European hip hop. There were others for whom the politicality of hip hop was in the synthesis of traditional Congolese musical genres with driving beats and electronic effects, which, they argued, linked Congo's soundscape to the global present. There were also rappers who were (and still are) overtly political, the most prominent of whom is Lexxus Legal, whose lyrics in songs such as "L'art de la guerre" ("The Art of War") offer strong sociopolitical critiques and who, with many others, has done much to put the nation's hip hop tradition on the world stage.

The breadth of Kinshasa's spectrum of political engagement in hip hop is a reflection of a larger confluence of forces that had a radically different impact on the west than on the east of Congo. Unlike in Goma, the political situation in Kinshasa was, though volatile, less immediately menacing to young people in the form of incessant recruitment into rebel armies or throngs of refugees fleeing in desperation. The instability of the country was certainly palpable in Kinshasa, as it was everywhere, but the symptoms of war in the capital were rapid political turnover and corruption, whereas in the Kivus houses were being bombed and people killed in the streets. These divergent immediate experiences of war gave youth in the west different foci for their lyrics from their peers in the east. Furthermore, from 1998 to 2002, which were formative years of Congolese hip hop, Congo was essentially divided in half and communication and transport were cut off between the west and the east of the country. Thus, in addition to having different immediate experiences of the war(s), there was no way for artists on one side of the country to hear what their peers were doing. Even though popular music was among the only commodities disseminated across the nation, hip hop was not yet included in the officially sanctioned repertoire. Indeed, despite the popularity of Kinois hip hop in the west of Congo and in the European diaspora, this music and the artists making it were simply not known in Goma, while in Kinshasa there was equal ignorance of Goma's hip hop scene.

The disconnect between Kinshasa and Goma was reconfirmed with the eruption of the Nyiragongo volcano in 2002, the aftermath of which is partially depicted in Figure 1.2, which shows how severely devastated the city was by lava. The eruption had little impact if any on the cultural scene in Kinshasa, yet in Goma it was a pivotal moment that set the city on its current trajectory of cultural activism. Here again, the evolution of art in the east of Congo converges with the biography of Petna, who, for the first time since early 1998, returned to Goma after the eruption. Still in exile for his political stand, Petna's objective was to sneak across the border in order to quickly usher his family to safety in Kampala, where his career as a filmmaker was thriving. But what he found when

FIGURE 1.2 Goma Post-eruption, 2002. Photo courtesy of Alkebu Film Productions.

he arrived in Goma was a city that bore almost no resemblance to his place of birth, a city that had deteriorated socially, politically, and economically to the extent that the choices for young people were reduced to three: join a rebel militia, be killed by a rebel militia, or seek refugee status, with all the humiliations this entailed at the time. Indeed, all institutions and centers that provided what were deemed "nonessential" services (either by the Congolese government or by the governments of the citizens operating them) were shut down. This included cultural and religious centers as well as, in many cases, schools.

Haunted by memories of the bountiful opportunities that defined his rich childhood in Goma, Petna decided to start a second branch of Yole!Africa in Goma. At first Yole!Africa in Goma was somewhat of an experiment to determine whether creative expression as a means of individual transformation and community cohesion would be equally potent in the face of the specific sociopolitical and economic problems in North Kivu. The objective was to create a space, both literally and in the sense of a postmodern geography, that provided youth in North Kivu with an alternative to violence and allowed them to reimagine themselves as social agents. Logistically this was complicated, as Petna himself was still not at liberty to stay in Congo and the Congolese students at Yole!Africa in Kampala were not yet qualified to direct a second branch of the organization. Thus Petna established a team to direct the center in Goma under his advisement from Kampala. The original team included the journalist Tuver Wundi, who was the representative of Yole!Africa for its first years in Congo; and Batumike Chambu, a former commander of the Alliance of Democratic Forces for the Liberation of Congo (AFDL) and then Rally for Congolese Democracy (RCD) armies, who had returned to Goma after resigning in disillusionment and joined Yole!Africa to support his longtime colleague Petna in offering young people an alternative to his own experiences of war. In the early years of Yole!Africa in Goma, the organization's main focus was to send aspiring local musicians and dancers to Kampala and other east African cities to perform and train with their peers.

By 2004 Yole!Africa in Goma was thriving. Late that year, the center expanded its operation and began offering workshops in Goma, which were initially coordinated by Sekombi Katondolo, Petna's younger brother, who had been trained in dance and cultural administration at Yole!Africa in Kampala. Through these workshops, musicians in Goma had opportunities to exchange with their peers in other east African cities, which exposed them to the influences of east African hip hop and eventually led to a second wave of hip hop in Goma. Artists in this second wave built on the revolutionary spirit of their predecessors by incorporating specifically local critiques with stylistic elements and political analyses that connected their music more broadly to east Africa. Their confidence to advance social and political critiques through music was further enhanced by their growing awareness that there was a larger culture of and audience for conscious African hip hop.

Thus Yole!Africa emerged as the hub of hip hop in North Kivu. This meant that, in addition to fostering creative development of artists aesthetically, the center had to start supporting material production of artistic works. To that end Yole!Africa began importing recording equipment, computers, and software from Uganda and, eventually, training recording technicians. This dramatically improved the production value of the music and, in conjunction with frequent regional exchanges between Uganda and Congo, notably increased the audience base for hip hop music coming out of Goma.

As rap and other musical genres grew in popularity in Goma, Yole!Africa recognized the further need for the aspiring musicians to have performance opportunities, so the center started monthly musical gatherings called Jam Sessions. When Jam Sessions first started informally in 2005 then formally in 2006, they were the only venue for live music in Goma that was not controlled by a foreign NGO, a politician, or a church. In practice, Jam Sessions are outdoor performances similar to open mic sessions that allow both seasoned and inexperienced artists to perform up to three songs, either with the accompaniment of a live backup band or with their own prerecorded tracks. Audiences for Jam Sessions are made up of locals from a wide spectrum of socioeconomic classes, religions, ages, and ethnic groups as well as expats. Through these Jam Sessions, individual musicians began to make names for themselves locally, which, in many cases, led to nationally and internationally successful careers. It is worth citing a few examples of artists whose careers started at Yole!Africa to illustrate the magnitude of this trend: rapper Emma Katya has won international awards for his songs and performed in Europe and a number of African countries; rapper S3 performed in Brazil after winning the 2012 Fair Play competition; singer Prince Agakahn is becoming a prominent music manager; singer-songwriter/producer DJ Fonkodji is currently traveling the world performing his original music; singer Innocent Balume (now known as Innoss'B) has recorded with Akon and performs live concerts to audiences of thousands all over the world; singer and guitarist Robert King is locally revered as the region's *griot*; reggae musician Makaveli has opened a professional recording studio and started a record label in Goma; and singer Wanny S King is known throughout the Great Lakes Region as an important popular musician.

This (only partial) list of musical accomplishments confirms that by the mid-2000s hip hop and other popular music genres had taken root in Goma. It is important to note that not all of the popular music being made in the east of Congo at this time was conceived by its makers as advocating social justice; indeed, by 2009 a comparative bounty of creative outlets were being established as institutions, primarily churches, rebuilt themselves and began offering cultural activities including musical training and performance opportunities to young people. As such projects gained traction, the familiar divide between musicians became ever more deeply entrenched: rappers and hip hop artists identified more fiercely as political activists, positioning themselves as conscious and even militant, in comparison with their peer R&B artists, whose songs were apolitical.

The effort to assert the sociopolitical relevance of rap music coupled with political events in 2006 led to the final musical development I want to take up in this section. Specifically, 2006 was the year of the first democratic elections in the Democratic Republic of the Congo and was, as such, a volatile year for a nation that was already politically precarious. Within the previous five years, Congo had experienced the assassination of President Laurent Kabila (January 2001), who was succeeded by his son, Joseph Kabila, who assembled a volatile transitional government from 2003 to 2006, tasked, among other challenges, with preparing the nation for its first elections, which were held in July 2006. On one hand, election year was a time of optimism as citizens and international monitoring bodies advocated electoral transparency; on the other hand, the rampant ongoing corruption and political disillusionment left large portions of the population extremely agitated. This political polarity was mirrored by the musical output of the year. Musicians were divided; some used their popularity to support political candidates and parties, and others mobilized against political abuses through song. Not surprisingly, the rappers in Goma fell into the latter category; indeed, the songs from this period reveal the growing interweaving of music with political protest. One potent example of this trend is rapper Emma Katya's hit song "Revolution" ⊙ (written in 2006, recorded in 2008), which includes these verses:

REFRAIN:

I'm on a mission ready for revolution
Je suis en mission prêta pour la révolution
I'm on a mission ready for revolution
Je suis en mission prêt pour la révolution

CHORUS:

I'm on a mission ready for revolution
I'm on a mission ready for revolution
I'm on a mission ready for revolution
I'm on a mission ready for revolution

VERSE 1:

Affaire sur terre
non seulement ils veulent ta peau
tu promotions la corruptions
encore une fois des coups de balles
des cries des victimes
j'en aie ras-le-bol
les droits bafoués
les lois ignorés
changement des constitutions
c'est la démocratie acquis aux démocrates
un pour tous
tous pour les caricatures dictateurs
c'est sure
c'est fait pour le futur
écoute ce rap conscient
et sois conscient
c'est toute une générations qui succomber
globalisation capitaliste
politiques
politricks
pour situé l'Afrique
si l'Amérique repose sur le pacifique . . .
total confusion politique
pour politricks capitalistique
j'ai conclu c'est la globe à frustration
à qui la question
nous sommes sous oppression

VERSE 1:

On the ground
not only do they want your skin
forced to promote corruption
once again bullets fly
victims cry
I'm fed up
our rights undermined
our laws ignored
changing constitutions
this democracy sold by democrats
one for all
all for the caricatures of dictators
one thing's for sure
this is our future
listen to this conscious rap
and be conscious
a generation sacrificed
globalization of capitalists
politics
politricks
if to build Africa
America lay buried in the Pacific . . .
total confusion in politics
for capitalist politricks
I see the globe in frustration
no one to question
we are under oppression

REFRAIN:
I'm on a mission ready for revolution
Je suis en mission prêta pour la révolution
I'm on a mission ready for revolution
Je suis en mission prêt pour la révolution

VERSE 2:	VERSE 2:
Avec l'esprit de Lumumba	With the spirit of Lumumba
le cœur de Kwame Nkrumah	the heart of Kwame Nkrumah
je vais vous libéré l'esprit toujours colonisé	I will liberate your spirits, still colonized
le nom de mon pays c'est pays la guerre	the name of my country is not war
mais plutôt Congo	but Congo
le nom de mon continent c'est pas misère	the name of my continent is not misery
mais plutôt Afrique	but Africa
faites attention mes frères	pay attention my brothers
ils veulent nous oppresser	they want to oppress us
et tout manipuler	and manipulate everything
faites attention mes sœurs	pay attention my sisters
ils veulent nous oppresser	they want to oppress us
et tout manipuler	and manipulate everything
manipuler	to manipulate
manipuler	manipulate

REFRAIN:
I'm on a mission ready for revolution
Je suis en mission prêta pour la révolution
I'm on a mission ready for revolution
Je suis en mission prêt pour la révolution

In Goma's hip hop scene, "Revolution" marks the beginning of a shift by the more radical artists from song as a vehicle of general political critique to song as a more overt agitating force. The combination of first person pronouns with active verbs ("I'm on a mission," "I will liberate," etc.) suggests that Katya's objective as an artist is not only to criticize general political failures, though he does that as well, but also to take matters into his own hands. This shift is identifiable, in retrospect, as part of a larger trend (discussed in the final section of this chapter) that began to move artists' practices and audiences' expectations of hip hop as a genre from descriptive to active in a more pronounced way.

On a broader analytical level, the revolution of which Katya speaks is multivalent. On one level, it refers to the immediate sociopolitical conditions of Congo in general (the rampant corruption, threatened changes to the constitution) and North Kivu in particular (through references to immediate experiences of war), calling for a literal political revolution in the style of pan-Africanist leaders like Lumumba and Nkrumah. On another level, the song represents a sort of mimesis, in which act(s) of revolution parallel act(s) of art making and artistic dissent in conditions of "postcolonial" crisis. On this level, there is dual significance in the creative word play of the lyrics (for example, politics and politricks) and the equally creative social maneuvering required to orchestrate community action in the face of state dysfunction. Finally, in the context of a contrapuntal analysis of the evolution of cultural activism, this song also functions as a heuristic point of entry in that its very existence comments on its inherent function as an act of political protest; indeed, there is a convergence of micropolitical acts in "Revolution" (its multilingualism, the material conditions of its production and circulation, its dual existence as a product and avowal of Yole!Africa) that collectively map, for the attentive listener, the specific history and agency, both collective and individual, that define hip hop music in the east of Congo.

ON IMAGE AND THE EMERGENCE OF RADICAL AESTHETICS

Thus far I have made a case for reading hip hop music in Goma as part of a politicized cultural landscape and youthscape. But that case would be radically incomplete without parallel consideration of the evolution of practices of visual representation that are equally central to current trends within cultural activism in the east of Congo. Indeed, as songs like Emma Katya's "Revolution" illustrate, local artists in Goma were reflecting on how to catalyze a cultural revolution of any material significance. This was a debate that engaged aspiring musicians and aspiring filmmakers alike, all of whom were growing adamant that global awareness of local perspectives was (and is) a necessary prerequisite for meaningful sociopolitical change. Ultimately the consensus was that this meant taking ownership of the technologies and distribution avenues for still and moving images.

In the political ethos of the years between 1995 and 2010, taking ownership of image production was an overtly dangerous act that requires significant political and historic contextualization. At the time, the region was suffering a crisis of representation that musicians, limited by linguistic barriers and challenges of distribution, could not address on their own. During the same years when young people were busy building a hip hop music culture in Goma, other sociopolitical forces were establishing strategies of representation nationwide that were palpably suffocating them. Starting in 1997, when rebel leader Laurent Kabila and his army overthrew Mobutu (along with his regime of authenticité), Mobutu's restrictive policies regarding audio and visual documentation were replaced by newer strategies. As early as 1997, rebel groups began to operate their own radio stations, then cameras, then eventually their own television stations as means of extending their reach. During the years 1997–2003, when the east of Congo was embroiled in the First Congo War (August 1996–May 1997), immediately followed by the Second Congo War (also known as the Great African War or the African World War, August 1998–July 2003), many of the rebel groups had international support from countries in the West and, in addition to arms and military training, received encouragement to document and promote their struggle through audiovisual media. At the same time these wars played out in the east, the struggle for power in Kinshasa also manifested in distinct representational strategies. As Joseph Kabila fought to establish himself as president and to boost his popularity in preparation for the elections, he too turned heavily to audiovisual forms. Thus, by 2006 Congo had a vibrant, if propagandistic, television culture controlled by sparring rebel groups, an unstable national government, and privately owned religious stations that positioned God and Divine Truth on the side of a revolving cast of armed leaders.

Outside Congo, global awareness of the nation was also shaped by media representations. What sporadic international media reporting there was of the escalating violence in the east or of the political melodrama in the west conformed to stereotypical Western depictions of Congo (and Africa) as a heart of darkness rife with savage brutality, impetuosity, and unbearable suffering. As the death toll in Congo rose above six million, documentary filmmakers also began to turn their lenses on Congo in an effort to raise appropriate awareness and outrage in the West about a war that was seemingly invisible, despite nearing the death toll of World War II. (I am referring to such documentaries as Journeyman Pictures' *Congo's Tin Soldiers*, 2006; Lisa Jackson's *The Greatest Silence*, 2007; Perlmutt, Walker, and True's *Lumo*, 2007; Susan Schulman and Elliot Smith's *Congo: Knowing the Enemy*, produced for the *Guardian*, 2009; Kavanagh, Krauss, Biagiotti, and Rezvani's *Rape as a Weapon of War*, for World Focus, 2009; among many others.) Collectively, documentary films and news reports did make headway in bringing much-needed international attention to certain aspects of the situation in Congo; yet, whether motivated by the desire to humanize the conflict by telling individual stories (as was the case for many documentarians) or by the commercial requisite to meet voyeuristic norms (as was the case for most mainstream reporters), documentaries and news reports alike focused on the most sensational aspects of the conflict, such as victims and perpetrators of rape, forced conscription of child soldiers, and the greater ethos of terror.

This international focus on suffering and on violent warlordism via representational media had a number of palpable effects on Congolese on the ground. For one thing, in all of these representations, they were perpetually cast either as proverbial bad guys or as de facto victims, which limits their agency in the global imagination to two possibilities: it creates caricatures of those who commit brutal acts of violence and destruction while reducing the remainder of the population to powerless victims. In the case of Congo, as with most conflict or disaster regions, heightened global focus on the plight of certain categories of victims (whether women, children, or those afflicted with illness) led to a wave of well-intentioned interventions by international NGOs. Unfortunately, although the majority of advocacy efforts were fueled by genuine horror at the violation and misery of Congolese and by a genuine desire to alleviate suffering, the approaches many NGOs took ultimately undermined local agency and fostered dependence, in part because, when studying the story and images of Congo championed in mainstream Western media, these organizations and their Western donors were (and still are) in the deadly habit of conflating innocence with helplessness.

Another side effect of Western representations of the Congo conflict was (and still is) demonization of those Congolese in positions of power, often through allusions to "ethnicity," which is a popular catchword that masks other issues. In Congo the mainstream Western media's focus on ethnicity is an insidious and historic tactic that simultaneously situates conflict as the inevitable result of a long and impenetrably complex history of unresolvable local problems, while also obscuring the integral role of Western nations that support rebel groups and opposing regional governments on the basis of their own financial interests in the nation's resources. Some analyses trace this dynamic back to the Belgian King Léopold II's ownership of the Congo Free State—during which he masked his plundering of ivory and rubber behind rhetoric of uplifting (ethnic) savages—through the current frenzy for mineral wealth, which continues to be covered as an "ethnic" war despite the many more-significant geopolitical factors fueling the conflict.

Equally prevalent in Western coverage of Congo is the term *corruption*, which, notably, is used to describe only African leaders and never their Western counterparts. There are, of course, rampantly corrupt leaders in Congo, but this is equally true of Western nations, even if Western media outlets prefer to use other language to describe the behavior of their own leaders. Between allusion to ethnicity and allegations of corruption, what was—and still is—in fact an economic conflict over coveted natural resources such as gold, diamonds, tin, copper, cassiterite, tantalite, coltan, and oil (to name but a few), was—and still is—marketed to the world as an immensely complex ethnic war with little mention of the multinational corporations benefiting from and supporting illicit extraction of minerals. Ethnic identity is indeed a characteristic of the populations involved in the war, and corruption is part of the region's political climate, but disproportionate media focus on these terms obscures the more pressing causes of and potential solutions to the conflict, which would require Western accountability on an economic level.

A third consequence of both local and international representations of Congo was their negative psychological effect on young people in the country. If the focus on victimhood and savagery limited the possibilities of Congolese agency in the minds of Westerners, it also prevented those who were the (ostensible) subjects of the images from imagining alternatives, whether to the situation itself or to how their stories were and were not being told. The versions of Congo's story circulating at home and abroad were either pro- or anti-government propaganda, or religious proselytizing, or complex analyses that veiled Western self-interest behind sensationalist rhetoric. There was little that inspired local recognition—to say nothing of pride—in this barrage of negative images in which corruption, suffering, and disempowerment were presented as the only options for Congolese.

Yet despite bitter disputes among locals about the (in)accuracy of such representations, their impacts were palpable: enlistment in various rebel armies was growing, political participation was becoming more agitated, religious fervor was spreading, and there were a rash of international NGOs arriving to save Congolese victims of one variety or another. Indeed, the power of audiovisual representation was clear even if the content was under dispute. But Congolese who were not inclined to join an army, a political party, or a church and who did not appreciate being solicited as recipients of Western do-goodism did not have access to audiovisual technologies and had few resources if any with which to tell a different version of the story. There was no critical mass with the skills and technologies to document, for example, the growing hip hop scene or the burgeoning local concert culture. Yet it was ever clearer to all involved that precisely such a local media of proximity was necessary if a greater variety of voices from North Kivu were going to gain any real traction.

This was, to reiterate, a time when it was extremely rare in North Kivu to see cameras in the hands of Congolese, save those wedding photographers cobbling together a living by documenting family celebrations with outdated equipment. Indeed, when Petna returned from Kampala in 2007 with his new professional camera and kit, his frequent entanglements with law enforcement proved that having a camera was still a risk and a liability. Once again, he was the first Congolese to own such equipment in the region, but even though this was a source of pride and curiosity for much of the population, for the state and its officials his camera was still perceived as a threat. Despite securing the necessary filming permits and following all official protocol, including registering with every police substation in every neighborhood where he filmed, Petna was harassed and arrested frequently. Some of these encounters are nearly comical in retrospect, such as the heated altercation with angry and bewildered security officers who were convinced Petna was uploading live images of them to an invisible satellite via the boom microphone on the end of its extension pole. In some confrontations with officials, he talked his way out of trouble by reasoning that, since all images are subjective, for reasons of accountability as well as aesthetic sensibility, images shot by a local filmmaker in fact do greater justice to the state than images commissioned and shot by foreign media outlets that prioritize their own, often commercial, interests. In many instances this reasoning, however sound, failed, and instead of leading to new partnerships between law enforcement and civil society, it resulted in confiscation and destruction of tapes (then later memory cards and hard drives) full of images.

When officials did recognize the potential value of local coverage of local issues, they often commanded Petna to bring his equipment and film the action on the physical frontlines of various wars. Like revolutionary filmmakers working in similar circumstances around the world, Petna quickly developed subversive filming techniques to navigate these precarious conditions. For example, he modified his camera to conceal any visual indication of when he was filming and often dangled it seemingly carelessly by his side as if it were switched off so as not to draw excess attention to it during heated negotiations with armed leaders. At other times he would set his camera on a tripod and then ignore it completely while he started a conversation with his guide so that people would not realize he was filming. He also established safe houses protected by "comrades" in Europe to whom he would send his most controversial footage to ensure its protection— and his own. Perhaps his most radical strategy was to train and then eventually hire a second cameraman to follow him with an inconspicuous handheld camera to document his entanglements with officials when shooting in the streets.

This was the beginning of the larger project of developing a cinema of proximity in Goma. After being alone and without a mentor on the literal and metaphorical frontlines of the various wars—both those over resources and those over rights to tell local stories—Petna, like other practitioners of Third Cinema, recognized that the only way to support a substantive revolution of representational practices was to develop a critical mass of film technicians, amass an arsenal of equipment, and cultivate an audience for local films. Having developed, through experience, strategies for navigating Goma's volatile and unstable political state with a camera, he wanted the aspiring filmmakers he mentored to benefit from his experiences and to minimize the risks they faced as he ushered them into the practices of revolutionary cinema. To this end, he created a new program at Yole!Africa called Alternative to TV (ALT2TV), a simultaneously practical and ideological project that aims to cultivate a conscious media of proximity in North Kivu. In late 2006, ALT2TV began with a photography project, which taught young peopl how to use cameras and encouraged them to document the first elections in Congo. This project, which in its first iteration was associated with Sarah Vanagt's documentary film *Silent Elections,* introduced a parallel visual component to the rappers' struggle to develop a culture of resistance in the east of Congo. Nearly a decade later, ALT2TV is an established project that continues to advance a local agenda of social justice.

Practically, ALT2TV includes training for aspiring filmmakers in all aspects of preproduction, production, and postproduction and culminates in public screenings and discussions of student work. Initially the program included three month-long intensive workshops every year, but as ALT2TV grew in popularity, in 2011 the program shifted to include ongoing trainings throughout the academic year with additional intensive workshops in January and July. Figure 1.3 depicts an ALT2TV workshop with Petna in 2010, which focused on documentary film production. Since the beginning of the program, workshops have had thirty to fifty participants competing for the sixteen to twenty seats, and the ongoing courses currently include eighteen to twenty-two participants in each of the beginning, intermediate, and advanced classes; the gender balance of the aspiring filmmakers, which was 100 percent male at the beginning of the project, is now 3:1 male to female as a result of Yole!Africa's efforts to address gender imbalance (discussed further in Chapter Four).

FIGURE 1.3 Alternative to TV Workshops 2011. Photo courtesy of Yole!Africa.

The genres and thematic foci of the short films produced during the workshops and courses range widely, including fiction films and documentaries on all manner of subjects. What is constant is the core ideology of the project, which stresses the importance of controlling one's own image. Like many revolutionary aesthetic projects, ALT2TV encourages students to understand control of image as a narrative project as well as a technical one. This means constructing culturally relevant modes of storytelling alongside mastering the technical issues, such as setting the camera properly to film black skin with nuance, that liberate filmmakers from the camera's hegemony of whiteness. It also means replacing deeply internalized foreign representational practices with appreciation for local realities and developing strategies to navigate film production in a war zone. Of all of these obstacles, it was the project of teaching youth to recognize the value of their own local stories that was the biggest challenge when ALT2TV began.

In the wake of the popularity of American films, which were beloved in Goma at the time, students enrolled in early ALT2TV workshops with fantasies of becoming the next James Cameron or Steven Spielberg. This phenomenon is, of course, common among young people the world over who are conditioned by Hollywood, but in Goma the zeal for American cinema was distorted by an absolute lack of awareness of any African, not to mention Congolese, filmmakers (save their local hero Petna) or of other global traditions of revolutionary cinema.[14] Thus the youths' ardor for Hollywood was not just appreciation of the drama and craft of the productions, but a deeply entrenched belief that Hollywood's was the *only* acceptable approach to filmmaking, that white actors made films valuable, and that American (or on occasion European) stories were the only ones worth telling. In the early years, students of ALT2TV literally did not recognize that there were a wealth of stories surrounding them that they could, with culturally relevant narrative structures and with minimal resources, turn into powerful films.

Thus, in the early years ALT2TV was a kind of counteroffensive against the role dominant representations had assumed in the Congolese imagination. It was (and still is) a project that conformed to the theories put forth by revolutionary filmmakers Solanas and Getino in their early manifesto on Third Cinema, stating that

The decolonization of the filmmaker and of films will be simultaneous acts to the extent that each contributes to collective decolonization. The battle begins without, against the enemy who attacks us, but also within, against the ideas and models of the enemy to be found inside each one of us. Destruction and construction. Decolonizing action rescues with its practice the purest and most vital impulses. It opposes to the colonialization of minds the revolution of consciousness.[15]

But just how does one initiate a revolution of consciousness in practical terms? According to Petna, imagination is the answer. His diagnosis of young people in Goma at the time ALT2TV started was that

> Youth in Congo believe what images have taught them to believe—they believe they are poor because they have been shown they are; they believe they are helpless because all the films about their lives are about victims. If you tell them to send a photo of themselves to relatives they dress nicely and go to the fanciest resorts to photograph themselves so they look European because they think that makes them look valuable, but if you tell them to take a picture of Africa they go to the slums because that's what they think Africa looks like. They don't realize that Africa looks as many ways as they can imagine.[16]

Petna's focus on cultivating imagination is consistent with the ideology of revolutionary art the world over, but it is not so easily put into practice in a postcolonial, postdictatorial war zone. In Goma it was a slow and subtle process of young people learning to see and hear differently, and then developing the skills to manifest an alternative perspective in material form. For musically inclined youth, hip hop was the ideal forum as it was divorced from the legacy of colonial domination and provided a sense of global unity between populations fighting for liberation; but for aspiring filmmakers the task was more complicated, as Goma was not yet part of a network of radical filmmakers at the time. Thus developing alternative modes of storytelling was not a matter of borrowing from similar geopolitical situations (present or past), but of turning to other local sources of inspiration and figuring out how to translate them into the medium of film. This process required constant negotiation and was not without its frustrations for students, as it challenged them to look at the details of their daily life in a new way.

Challenging young people to develop alternative modes of storytelling was also central to Petna's strategy of minimizing the risks for them of learning and exercising filmmaking skills. Having been exposed to physical brutality for documenting interactions with his camera, by the time ALT2TV was gaining momentum Petna had developed an approach to filmmaking and to teaching that was rooted in deep critical reflection and inquiry. His priority for his students was that they approach filmmaking as an exercise in thought, using strategy to prevent confrontation whenever possible. He also insisted to his students that filming, when deployed creatively, could in fact galvanize rather than alienate the community if the filmmaker could frame her or his project as a question and inspire community members to implicate themselvesin seeking the answer(s). To help students develop the skills with which to approach filmmaking in this fashion, Petna often set his students riddles.

A relevant example of this comes from an ALT2TV workshop in 2007, when Petna challenged his students to find a creative way to make a film about police corruption, which was a heated topic of discussion in the city. They were very keen on the idea but had, at the outset, a grandiose and Hollywood-esque vision of the film, until their instructor reminded them that filming police activity was illegal, strictly enforced, and extremely dangerous for professional foreign journalists, let alone for students without the security of having an established name or international reputation or passport to protect them. At first, the students saw in this local reality proof that filmmaking in Goma was, if not impossible, far inferior to filmmaking in the (imagined) West, but with time they came to realize that the very obstacles they face are stories in and of themselves. This led to an array of creative ideas for a film that, though less sensational, would be much more relevant. Perhaps the most creative solution was to make a cinematic profile of the widow who sold peanuts next to the entrance to police headquarters, which would allow them to capture all manner of suspicious police activity in the background of their shots without ever drawing attention to the presence of the camera or being harassed. As this idea gained momentum, the students recognized an unexpected value in making a portrait of a familiar local woman in whose life local audiences could see themselves and whose critiques of sociopolitical issues, including the police brutality and corruption she witnessed every day, gave voice and context to local opinion in an empowering way.

For many of the students, this exercise triggered a minute shift in perspective. In later conversations, some identified this as the moment they began to recognize that their power and authority lay in valuing their own stories over attempting to replicate Hollywood. Focusing on their own stories positioned them as the experts on their own reality and, to the extent that they were (and continue to be) able to construct representational approaches that prioritize their experiences, allowed them to claim the power of audiovisual technologies. From a theoretical standpoint, this minute shift in perspective has the potential to liberate the creative imagination from the hegemony of foreign representational styles, or as Fanon has said, to "trigger a change of fundamental importance in the colonized's psycho-affective equilibrium."[17]

Of course, there were other students who were not so quick to accept that cultivating their imagination was a radical activity. Citing an imagined alignment with global revolutionary icons such as Che Guevara (whose image was popular on T-shirts, but whose history was only vaguely known), some students argued for a vision of revolutionary filmmaking as a necessarily confrontational and aggressive practice of didactic denunciation. This clash of opinions was an important formative part of ALT2TV that directly contributed to the evolving cinematic aesthetic of dissent in Goma. This is particularly evident in the short film *Tuko Tayari* (2007), which was one of the earliest films to come out of ALT2TV and which grew, literally and metaphorically, out of an accident.

With no intention of shooting footage that would actually be used in a film, a group of ALT2TV students were participating in a workshop on filming techniques. As they were conducting an exercise in the streets of Goma, a motorcycle taxi ran over a child directly in front of the camera. At the time, there was little public confidence in the honesty or competence of police to handle matters such as traffic accidents, and consequently the common practice was for surrounding bystanders to administer justice as they saw fit. A series of mob riots that resulted in severe beatings, burnings, and deaths of motorists had conditioned drivers—especially those with agile vehicles like motorcycles—to attempt to flee the scene of an accident as a reflex of self-defense. However, in this case, instead of reacting with violence, the crowd detained the driver and tended to the child, and the motorcyclist, instead of trying to flee, agreed to take the child to the hospital with a group of witnesses from the scene. It is impossible to know whether this accident would have been among the comparatively rare situations in which both the driver and the bystanders followed such protocol, but the frequent demands by the crowd to keep the camera rolling suggested to the young people that the reactions of all parties were linked to the powerful presence and enforced accountability of the camera.

After the adrenaline of capturing the accident and its aftermath began to subside, the thrill of abetting justice faded into the unexpectedly difficult question of what to do with the images. It quickly became clear that the group wanted to make a film about the incident, but figuring out what story to tell was a difficult negotiation. On one hand, there was much precedent for maximizing the shock value of violent images of the region, and for some participants the opportunity to contribute to this trend represented a kind of currency of belonging that they argued would align them with and raise their value in the eyes of potential Western viewers. These students lobbied for the group to make a short film about the insurmountable perils of childhood in the east of Congo and proposed, in addition to the accident, to document rape victims, child soldiers, and other atrocities made popular by foreign films and news reports. Others in the group could not reconcile the idea of focusing exclusively on treachery with the theoretical and ideological concepts of Third Cinema they were learning in ALT2TV, where they were grappling with the relationship between audiovisual representation and (neo)colonialism. (Popular among the students at the time was Solanas and Getino's assertion that "mass communications are more effective for neocolonialism than napalm"[18]). This group argued that the footage of the accident provided a perfect opportunity to counter the dominant representational norms, and to that end they proposed a film about the power of the presence and local control of a camera in a conflict zone, which would feature their own revolutionary actions towards decolonizing representations of Congo.

A temporary deadlock ensued, in which the groups accused one another of either perpetuating voyeuristic practices that perpetuated the System of neo-colonial domination (or, as the students put it, "selling out") or propagating a style of didactic self-congratulatory filmmaking that would alienate any potential audience for future works ("not selling at all"). Beneath the surface of their polarized opinions lurked the common dilemma facing activist filmmakers: Is it better to make a film that appeals to a larger audience even if it requires ideological compromise, or to remain unwaveringly loyal to one's principles at the potential expense of popularity? Unwilling to compromise either ideals or cinematic appeal, they began to grapple, in earnest, with developing an alternative aesthetic. When they turned to Petna for guidance, he responded with an adaptation of traditional wisdom he himself uses as a guide: *no matter how horrific the realities we face might be, if we make films with our mind and not just with technology, we can tell any story—even the most horrific—in a way we could show our grandmothers with pride.* Though abstract, the students eventually interpreted this advice as (1) a reminder that Congo already has established and valuable modes of story-telling and (2) encouragement to calibrate their narrative structure and aesthetic palette to their own audience, rather than an imagined Western one. With this in mind, the students eventually landed on the idea to incorporate the footage of the accident into a film that simply represents a day in the life of a young person in Goma.

On one level, the resultant film, *Tuko Tayari,* [▶] which literally means We Are Ready, is just that: a film that shows the range of daily activities taking place in Goma. *Tuko Tayari* follows an anonymous young woman in a flowing orange blouse and sunhat as she makes her way through scenes of young people leisurely shooting pool with marbles on a miniature homemade table; images of Goma's lively urban traffic mechanically directed by uniformed police officers perched in watchtowers; portraits of the beautiful architecture and murals of the lava-stone Saint Joseph Cathedral; endearing clips of young children performing traditional music and dance on a busy street corner; a survey of the luxury SUVs, motorcycles, colorful public buses, lorries, pedestrians, and locally constructed *chukudus* (wooden bicycles for transport of goods) that make up Goma's traffic; an outdoor tae kwon do competition with bleachers full of parents eagerly cheering their children on; and the unique balance of glamorous high-rise buildings next to lean-to shacks, billboards, cell towers, and lava-engulfed streets that make Goma distinct. Most prominent in this urban portrait are scenes of Gomatriciens playing soccer in various locations, from impeccably manicured pitches to abandoned buildings, to lava fields. The circumstances of their games differ dramatically; some involve uniformed players under the critical scrutiny of professional coaches, others include barefooted children shooting handmade balls at goals marked by piles of stone, and still others are start-up games that include miscellaneous children returning from school, sporting their blue and white uniforms and carrying backpacks full of books.

On another level, *Tuko Tayari* represents a subtle but important challenge to the majority of depictions of Congo that were available at the time. Despite the deep familiarity of the film's scenes to anyone who lives in (or has ever visited) Goma, filming the city's daily happenings without focusing on a rebel invasion or volcanic eruption was novel in 2007. Against the backdrop of films that position Congo exclusively as a place of exploitation, suffering, and death, *Tuko Tayari*'s scenes of modernity, positive potential, and family unity draw important attention to the wide range of human experiences people in the east of Congo share with their global peers. In the absence of exaggerated portraits of villains, victims, and (foreign) heroes, this film attempts to carve out a space for Congolese to recognize their own worth as cinematic subjects and to be recognized by the wider world as complex and three-dimensional human beings.

In addition to affirming the humanity of Congolese people, *Tuko Tayari* accentuates Congo's participation in globally celebrated events by focusing on soccer. At the time, Congo was deeply immersed in qualifying to be one of the five African teams in the 2010 FIFA World Cup. As one of the four highest-ranking African teams in FIFA's 2003 world rankings, there was tremendous enthusiasm among the population for the potential of their team to make the cut. In the absence of international media coverage of Congolese soccer, *Tuko Tayari* depicts some of the many positive actions and aspirations inspired by football fever (as it was commonly called) in the east of Congo. For example, early in the film there is a scene in which the boys playing barefoot soccer on lava fields explain with pride

FIGURE 1.4 *Tuko Tayari* Soccer Sequence.

how they organized themselves into a league, voluntarily taxed themselves 10 Congolese francs each (at the time of filming, one U.S. dollar was worth roughly 500 Congolese francs) and created their pitch with the intention of someday growing up to be as well respected as the rising local striker Mputu Trésor.[19] This scene, depicted in Figure 1.4 (left frame), is juxtaposed with another (Fig. 1.4, right frame) that depicts professional coaches rigorously drilling aspiring players in the spirit of creating future national stars.

By editing the aforementioned sequences together, *Tuko Tayari* does more than just document the enthusiasm for soccer in the east of Congo; it also offers a subtle critique of the space carved out for Congo in the global imagination. This is perhaps most evident toward the end of the film, when, after a shot of intense professional training, the scene cuts back to the children playing on their lava pitch while the professional coach's voice continues to narrate the action as a shirtless boy dribbles down the pitch and then dives onto the lava to shoot the winning goal. The superimposition of the coach's instructions, critiques, and enthusiastic encouragement onto images of anonymous children performing unnoticed feats of athleticism with all the visual accoutrements of "poor Africans" forces competing tropes of Africa (land of star athletes vs. land of poverty) into the same frame. Read critically, this editorial choice suggests an intentional correction of the tendency for Congolese achievements to go unreported, or when reported, for them to be treated as somehow separate from the daily lives of the masses. The contemporaneity and recontextualization of these images of Congolese people with the simple assertion of Congolese humanity does much to suggest that Congo, like all of Africa, can indeed look as many ways as youth—or any interested viewer—can imagine.

In addition to the narrative strategies the students developed in making this film, there are also aesthetic factors to consider, including *Tuko Tayari*'s treatment of the motorbike accident, which bookends the film. After brief credits, the

FIGURE 1.5 *Tuko Tayari* Accident Sequence.

opening scene of *Tuko Tayari* fades in with a long shot of a three-way intersection in Goma visible in Figure 1.5 (left frame), showing vehicles and people fluidly navigating the space. A young boy is almost fully across the street, when a motorcycle appears from behind a parked car, hits the child, and drags him a short distance on the ground. The child's belongings go flying, but he scrambles to his feet and begins to stagger out of the road. As he does so, the realist image of the child is corrupted by other shots of the scene from different angles and points of view, staggered and layered in such a way that they collectively create an abstract but discernible matrix of colors and shapes that simultaneously veils the specificity of the child's pain while capturing the responses to the scene from multiple people. Figure 1.5 depicts this sequence: the center frame shows the extreme abstraction and the right frame shows the reemergence of the child's face (left upper third of the image) as well as the bodies of the surrounding crowd (on the right side and top). As the image returns to realism and the sounds of traffic fade back in, the camera focuses on the boy as people stoop to help him stand. His face is bleeding and he is crying, but instead of zooming in on his suffering, the picture begins to skip like a scratched disc as it migrates back into abstraction. This time the competing colors and shapes disintegrate into the inverted blacks and whites of film negative, as the scene replays in reverse, beginning with the child reclaiming his belongings, righting himself, and backing away from the scene of the accident. Then the image fades through sepia tones to an angry red and finally to black.

The opening sequence lasts only one minute before it yields to other vibrant scenes of daily life in Goma, but in that minute it makes a strong aesthetic statement about framing and consuming images of suffering. In its effort to strike a balance between realism and abstraction, it clarifies the specific events that took place while actively avoiding voyeuristic precedents. The result is the kind of mesmerizing beauty film scholar Frank Ukadike describes when he says, "artistry renders some of the mesmerizing sequences of [suffering] too ethereal or attractive for the viewer, but it is this enchantment that also compels the viewer to examine, confront and contemplate the real images behind the illusion."[20] In this case, contemplating the real images of the accident naturally triggers empathy for the child, but their ethereal treatment prevents that empathy from being contaminated with pity. This is in part because the layered images create the realistic illusion of depicting the scene from the child's point of view, which puts the viewer in the emotional state of experiencing the violence of the impact rather than perpetrating the violence of looking.

Indeed the abstract beauty of the layered images invites the viewer to look closely at what is happening without defaulting to disgust or guilt over her reaction. Thus, when later in the film the image of the barefoot soccer player beings to skip and morph after he scores the winning goal on the lava field and the whistle of the coach becomes indistinguishable from that of the traffic police officer, the viewer is preconditioned to witness the accident and its aftermath as the documentation of a community, like any other, responding to a problem. The film ends with a return to the scene of the accident, fading through the familiar abstraction into realism at the moment when bystanders pick the child up, identify the motorcyclist who hit him, negotiate his transportation to the hospital, and send someone to alert his family. Although the scene is lively, even chaotic, there is nothing savage about it; this is merely one thread in the greater fabric that collectively shapes the capital city of North Kivu province.

Together the narrative and aesthetic decisions in *Tuko Tayari* represent an important evolutionary step in the development of a cinema of proximity in Goma. In making this film, the young people began to reconcile various ideas about filmmaking, revolutionary activity, and their own local realities. By grappling with questions of framing, narrative arc, and editing, they began to familiarize themselves with the mechanics of cinematic imagination, which, for all of them—including the initial skeptics—brought the connections between creativity and social impact into relief. Clearly, portraying a traffic accident is an entirely different matter from representing a war, but there was significant overlap in the underlying questions of how they wanted to tell their story once they felt ownership over it. The cumulative impact of *Tuko Tayari* on the students who participated in creating it is one small piece of evidence in favor of the notion that the revolutionary potential of filmmaking is as much about fostering creative imagination as it is about capturing specific content. It is also a reminder that, beyond the obvious sites of violent conflict, every street is a frontline in a global mediascape in which people do not have the power to tell their own stories.

Of course, developing the skills with which to tell one's own story is not the same as having the power to reach the desired audience for one's story. For all its aesthetic and ideological innovation, *Tuko Tayari* simply did not have much pull beyond immediate local audiences. Thus even though the impact was positive on the young people who created it and on the audiences who saw themselves in it, the film held limited appeal for anyone else. There were a number of obvious problems. First, at the time there were no established means of distributing films from Goma (it was not simply a matter of uploading the film to YouTube and then sharing it on Facebook). Second was the fact that the film was never translated into a dominant global language such as French or English. Third, the universal reality is that (radical) documentaries cannot compete with commercial films for popularity anywhere. And last but not least is simple fact that beyond the standard difficulties of getting student films screened films by unknown (African) authors are extremely hard to market without European or American backing. But despite all of these obstacles, some young people began to insist there was a market for progressive and socially conscious films from the continent because it was the same market their peers were beginning to tap into with hip hop music.

Like the musicians, the aspiring filmmakers were eager to share their art with larger audiences. After releasing *Tuko Tayari* they realized that part of the limited appeal of the film was its poor use of music, which, for better or worse, remains one of the strongest potential "hooks" that attract foreign audiences to African films. Indeed, *Tuko Tayari*'s score is extremely sparse; it includes a disorganized series of synthesizer effects designed to enhance the drama of the story but that have little, if anything, to do with the vibrant musical scene of Goma. In reflecting on this, the film students recognized the potential power of collaborating with musicians in order to augment the potency of their films; simultaneously the musicians recognized that without a visual component to their music, they too were limited in their reach in a market that was becoming saturated with music videos.

INTERSECTIONS

It was, tellingly, the mutual realization by musicians and film students of the limitations of either medium in isolation that inspired the model of artistic collaboration that shapes the current approach to cultural activism in Goma. By 2008, filmmakers and musicians were all cultivating distinct artistic styles, mastering technical skills, and eager to promote their works beyond local audiences. By this time Yole!Africa was also firmly established in Goma; simultaneously, Petna's international career as a filmmaker and high-profile activist was flourishing. Politically this was a time characterized by a massive influx into Goma of international humanitarian and charitable actors intent on intervening in the "aftermath" of crises. In short, there was a critical convergence of practical, ideological, and sociopolitical factors that propelled the next cultural innovations among artist-activists in North Kivu.

Specifically, in 2008, Yole!Africa expanded ALT2TV into a program that served both film and music students and actively encouraged collaboration between them. The successful collaborations from this period began to attract international attention and, for the first time, introduce artists (besides Petna) from the east of Congo to global audiences as well as bring their fight for social justice onto the world stage. The remainder of this chapter is an analysis of two of these early collaborations. I discuss them both at some length first for what they reveal about the convergence of aesthetic practices that were previously evolving in isolation from one another, and second because they represent the earliest moments when local voices began to emerge as important in the larger counterpoint between global actors invested in the east of Congo.

The first film to fully capitalize on the collaboration of musicians and filmmakers was *Ndoto Yangu* (2008) [▶], a short film that has music as its subject. The narrative is a profile of the life and aspirations of Eric Balume aka DJ Fonkodji, a fifteen-year-old musician who was popular at Jam Sessions and whose ambition was to become a professional music producer (an ambition he has since realized). In addition to the overt narrative, *Ndoto Yangu* also exposes many of the other intersections that were developing between music and film in Goma at the time. It is thus a literal example of the convergence of music and film in a fixed cultural product, but it is also a record of a moment in time in which the larger dynamics become visible that were developing between various agents working to establish art as a vehicle of advocacy in North Kivu.

From the beginning, *Ndoto Yangu* fundamentally integrates music into its narrative style. The opening credits are accompanied by the beginning of a popular hip hop song, "l'heure a sonné," by the local group Cogito Ergo Sum, which includes a solo male voice rapping:

Au lieu de réaliser	Instead of acting
ils sont encore dans les processus	they are still in the process
dans leur discours	in their discourse
bitu mingi balitu promises	of making many promises
mais aujourd'hui le bus	but today the bus
est un mettre de terminus	is one meter from the station
chaque jour dans nos quartiers	every day in our neighborhoods
les coups de balles	bullets fly
on se demande	and we ask ourselves
si le quatrième heur est libre	if the fourth hour is free
ou c'est le début de grand vacance. . . .	or if it's the beginning of the holidays. . . .

You said again you will provide reasonable houses safe water, stable electricity ...enough, opportunist time is up, opportunist

FIGURE 1.6 *Ndoto Yangu* Jam Session.

The credits continue through these words, and with the penultimate line the musical accompaniment to the song (bass, guitar, and djembe) enters while the image fades in on a wide shot of Goma's central intersection with cars, motorbike taxis, and pedestrians bustling through the city. Just as two women find a break in traffic and begin to cross the road, the sound of the music changes from the clarity of a studio recording to a live performance of the same song; the film cuts to Cogito Ergo Sum performing outside at a Jam Session, depicted in Figure 1.6. Rappers Soka and Piedestal occupy the elevated wooden stage with Innocent Balume playing djembe in the background. Behind them a banner advertising Yole!Africa's partnership with the Dutch-based cultural organization Baobab Connections hangs from the lava-stone wall. To the side of the stage is the tech booth, a modest table with electronic mixers, cables, and backup mics neatly organized by DJ Fonkodji, who serves as the Jam Session engineer. There are roughly one hundred people in the audience, some seated, others standing between the narrow walls of Yole!Africa's old compound. While the film cuts between shots of the band and the audience, which is clearly enjoying the performance, the song continues:

vous avez promis	you promised
que vous allez construire des bonnes routes	that you would give us good roads
vous parlez	you spoke
comme si vous avez raison	with such confidence
et pourtant c'est une trahison	but all we see is betrayal

encore vous dites que	you also promised
vous allez nous construire	that you would build
des maisons présentable	us reasonable houses
nous assurer l'eau potable	bring us potable water
et l'électricité stable	and stable electricity
démagogue	demagogue
l'heur a sonné	time is up
l'heur a sonné	time is up

The opening sequence of *Ndoto Yangu* is significant on multiple levels. Most obviously, it provides a summary of the local musical activities taking place in Goma in 2008, including the recorded and live performance opportunities for local groups such as Cogito Ergo Sum. The brief shots of the crowd also establish that the audience for local hip hop music is growing beyond the expected mixture of groups' peers and age mates to include older and obviously privileged individuals, many of them foreign (mostly white) NGO employees. On another level, the use of "l'heure a sonné" in particular indicates the increasingly deep engagement with local issues that was developing in hip hop music by 2008. This song was written in response to the newly elected president Joseph Kabila's inaugural speech in 2006, in which he announced "*la fin de la récréation*," which literally means "the end of recess."[21] This phrase came to signify Kabila's claim that the government was finally going to enforce significant measures to bring an end to the lawlessness, inaction, and corruption that had come to characterize Congo and its governing bodies. However, nearly two years after Kabila's promises, songs like "l'heure a sonné" (released in 2008) challenge the government outright and reflect people's dissatisfaction with the lack of results. The title of this song means time is up (lit. the bell has rung); the lyrics subvert Kabila's own terminology of the school calendar to accuse him of broken promises, negligence, and incompetence. In the portion of the song that accompanies the opening credits of *Ndoto Yangu*, Cogito Ergo Sum questions whether after recess the fourth period, which is supposed to be dedicated to rigorous study under the supervision of a qualified instructor, is simply a free-for-all or, worse still, under Kabila's presidency, in fact the beginning of the summer holidays, during which time people should expect nothing at all from the government.

During the final iterations of the chorus of "l'heure a sonné," *Ndoto Yangu* cuts to a medium shot of a street in Birere (a comparatively poor neighborhood, sometimes categorized as a ghetto, on the northeast side of Goma), where a woman and her children look briefly at the camera as they make their way between small

FIGURE 1.7 *Ndoto Yangu* Birere Sequence.

wooden houses. The driving beat of the song is still audible when Fonkodji walks into the frame and introduces himself by saying, "I feel at ease when I am playing music. If I don't play music I feel like I have a debt to pay."[22] As he continues walking, the camera cuts to a bird's-eye view of his two brothers, Prince "Agakahn" and Innocent Balume, sitting in a small outdoor space between two wooden structures lined with jerry cans, playing and singing an homage they wrote to their mother.[23] As Fonkodji enters the shot, he takes the guitar from his elder brother Prince, and after introducing everyone to the camera, they begin to sing together (Fig. 1.7, left and center frames). This shot is followed shortly by another (Fig. 1.7, right frame) in which Fonkodji is surrounded by a group of five brothers and cousins, playing what they call a "forged" guitar (a plastic bottle with a wooden stick placed in the neck to form a fingerboard, fitted with makeshift strings twisted from strands of cloth and plastic flour sacks), beating on an empty tin can, clapping and singing together.

The following sequence of the film introduces the viewer more intimately to Fonkodji's life. There are shots of posters of his local heart throb and his musical inspiration, the Congolese singer-songwriter Lokua Kanza, that adorn his bedroom walls; frank and endearing close-ups of him describing his timidity with girls; excerpts of him performing at a Jam Session. In this sequence, Fonkodji also explains his dream of becoming an international music producer, which, with his access to digital technology, he believes he can realize within ten years. As he tells of his dreams and aspirations, the soundtrack of forged guitar music, clapping, and vocal harmony continues behind scenes of Fonkodji recording Piedestal singing into a microphone in Yole!Africa's modest sound studio. Finally, this sequence cuts to a shot of Fonkodji leaning against an exterior wall of a wooden house, holding his guitar and speaking directly into the camera, telling of his biggest fears:

What I fear most in this world is war, because when I look at the way many young people are dying I get very scared. To look at terrorist attacks, at the way people are killed ... people of my age engaged in the army while they are still very young, while they are still so vulnerable. . . . It scares me, I really fear war. I really fear war.[24]

If I could change something in my country,
that would be the "change of behaviors"

FIGURE 1.8 *Ndoto Yangu* Recording Session.

As Fonkodji talks about young people engaged in the army, the film depicts him in the studio adjusting a microphone in preparation to record. There is a subtle but significant visual metaphor embedded in the correlation of his actions with his words that suggests Fonkodji, like his peers in the army, is deeply engaged in the region's struggle for justice, even if he, as a musician, has chosen to arm himself with a microphone in lieu of a machine gun. The fact that this metaphor is conveyed through the editorial choices of a film-maker adds another layer of meaning, which in turn suggests that, like the musicians, the filmmakers are armed with their cameras and are doing their part to subvert the negative stereotypes associated with youth in the region and bring greater global awareness to the wide range of realities that coexist in the east of Congo.

Lest the subtlety of this visual metaphor be lost, the closing sequence of *Ndoto Yangu* is overt in grappling with the role of art in Congo's fraught social context. The scene is of Fonkodji in the recording studio, speaking into the camera of his hopes for Congo:

If I could change one thing in my country I would change the artistic men-
tality. I don't see how an artist can sing about women or politicians for
long when people are dying of AIDS and there are massive human rights
violations—all these things are truly terrible. The artist must recover his
role and his role is to act as spokesperson of the community. For example,

the song I'm producing now is the kind of song to encourage. I wish all artists in Congo would talk about what is on their minds.[25]

As Fonkodji talks from the booth of the studio, Piedestal from Cogito Ergo Sum is recording in the background (see Fig. 1.8). When Fonkodji says "the artist must recover his role," the camera zooms in on Piedestal, whose vocal track slowly fades in as Fonkodji concludes. The final image of the film is of the flickering monitor before which Fonkodji crouches as he works with the digitized audio tracks of "l'heure a sonné," which concludes the film with the lyrics:

Ils ont gagné la coupe	They won the elections,
mais il n'y a pas de rigueur dans l'equipe	but their team is a joke
pourquoi?	why?
parce-que il y a des cafar	because they are cockroaches
qui crache dans la souppe!	spitting in the soup!

Together the content, the music, and the subtleties of the cinematic language of *Ndoto Yangu* create a portrait not only of Fonkodji but of the growing culture of artistic activism in Goma in 2008. The progression in the level of musical critique is clear if one compares Cogito Ergo Sum's direct criticism of politicians in "l'heure a sonné" with the lyrics of earlier songs, such as South Cross's "Expression," that represent Goma's roots of hip hop. Simultaneously, the visual aesthetics of this film suggest that filmmaking too was evolving into a more potent medium of critique. In terms of narrative arc, *Ndoto Yangu* is hardly original; it conforms to the common documentary practice of showing a place through the story of an individual. But through its cinematic language it tackles the challenge of humanizing a young man from Congo while neither overemphasizing nor ignoring the surrounding context of violence, disease, and suffering.

Though subtle, this is an important stylistic technique, evident in a number of places in the film. For example, the scene of Fonkodji and his brothers singing together in Birere remains strikingly neutral, despite numerous aspects that could easily either exoticize the poverty or romanticize the ruralness of "Africa" (the bare earth, the tight quarters, the well-used jerry cans), or exaggerate the celebration of musical talent in poor, underprivileged youth. The camera remains basically static throughout the sequence, without zooming in on any aspect of the scene, leaving the viewer free to focus her eye at will, but also stoically refusing to privilege one aspect of the scene over another.

Thus Fonkodji's story is allowed to simply be what it is without the images implying a clichéd subtext (poor boy overcomes impossible odds . . .) or decontextualizing his story to elicit a generic emotional reaction (admiration, pity, encouragement for the poor African . . .). This neutrality of image is a visual manifestation of the ideology behind ALT2TV, which recognizes that it is essential to control one's own image—especially for populations fighting for liberation. Indeed, the sheer normalcy of a happy family of brothers making music in their home is radical in the sense that, in (post)colonial societies, "the restitution of things to their real place and meaning is an eminently subversive fact."[26]

However, without diminishing the laudable intentions behind an aesthetic of radical subtlety, there are also serious risks to this strategy, especially for films intended for broad audiences. The restitution of things to their real place and meaning is indeed an eminently subversive act, but relying on normalcy to make a radical point assumes a level of cultural awareness and contextual knowledge that the vast majority of nonlocal viewers simply lack. Thus, where local filmmakers might intend to convey subversiveness by not conforming to clichés about child soldiers, rape victims, and destruction, for many foreign viewers *Ndoto Yangu* is at risk of being consumed as just another film confirming the ubiquity of African musical talent. Worse, *Ndoto Yangu* and others of its ilk risk becoming a kind of literature of precedent that foreign filmmakers and organizations can cite when justifying their own cinematic cultural projects. The logic seems to be that, because a respected local organization (in this case Yole!Africa) produces "positive" films or songs, albums, paintings, etc., so should they. Indeed, the danger is that, if local radicalism is not overt, foreign "collaborators" and international NGOs are able to divorce aesthetics from ideology when, inevitably, they try their hand at creating artistic or cultural works. The recurring pattern in foreign projects is that the creation of *products* gets substituted for the essential, but invisible, revolutionary *process* of filmmakers (or musicians, dancers, painters, etc.) transforming themselves as people.

The irony is that this risk increases in direct relation to the artists' success at reaching a wider audience. Unlike *Tuko Tayari*, *Ndoto Yangu* did gain some traction with international audiences. In addition to screenings in Uganda, the United States, and South Africa, a version of the film was adapted for the Dutch Metropolis Television station into an episode that aired on European television and was featured in their online series. This was because Petna was a regular correspondent for Metropolis, who produced multiple episodes for the station annually. Through this connection, films from ALT2TV began to circulate much more widely, which was empowering for young people in Goma in that their voices and work were being recognized, but it also exposed them to a whole new series of challenges that would become clear only over time.

One of the results of the greater visibility of the products of ALT2TV was that, for the first time, Western audiences started to take hip hop seriously as a cultural force associated with movements of social justice in the east of Congo. (Previously the default expectation for music production in Congo was calibrated to "world music" or Afro-pop, which were the genres of choice for international organizations attempting to convey information to locals through music.) This is in part because there was more hip hop coming out of Goma by 2008 and in part because the ever more successful collaborations between local filmmakers and local musicians were resulting in hip hop music videos that were beginning to gain international attention.

This trend built significantly more momentum when rapper Emma Katya's song and music video "How Long?" ⏵ was one of three winners of the 2010 Fair Play Anti-Corruption Youth Voices award.[27] Organized annually by Jeunesses Musicales International (JMI) and the World Bank Institute under the initiative of the Global Youth Anti-Corruption Network, the Fair Play competition gives socially conscious musicians from around the world a platform to share their critiques with a global audience, and in so doing it aims to connect music to sociopolitical change in a public way.

In the case of "How Long?" winning the Fair Play award was significant on multiple levels. It was both an affirmation of how much hip hop from the east of Congo had advanced and a turning point for the genre in the eyes and ears of international audiences invested in Congo. The music weaves together digital instruments (rhythm section, faint auto-tuned backup vocals) and acoustic instruments (guitars and voices) in a medium-tempo groove that draws equally on hip hop idioms and the rich lyrical phrases of Congolese folk guitar. Its minor key casts the piece as more reflective than aggressive, as does the quiet strength of the vocal style. But the gentle beauty of the music does not diminish the force of the lyrics, which paint a vivid picture, through rap (verses 1 and 2) and song (verse 3 and chorus), of the struggles in the east of Congo and beyond. Following the precedent in hip hop to address the intended audience, Katya starts the song by saying:

> To all my people struggling for peace,
> You know what I'm saying—
> We going to keep it up, the struggle continues. . . .

His use of English and the obvious African American inflection of his pronunciation and vocal rhythm alert the listener immediately to the fact that he is speaking to a global audience and aligning himself with a global tradition. Indeed, with this song Katya asserts himself and his fellow musicians from Goma as powerful contributors to global Black musical traditions in general, and political hip hop in particular. The remainder of the lyrics are as follows:

Verse 1 (Emma Katya)

Mon regard, pleine de tristesse	My look full of sadness
stress c'est la peur	stress and fear in my dreams
mes rêves c'est d'appuyer sur la gâchette	is to pull the trigger
car la haine se fait voir dans son regard	for his hate is visible in his eyes
il a pris mon identité	he has taken my identity
il a tué mon entité	he has killed my entity
Je ne sais où me situé	I don't know where to put myself
Ma vie est un cauchemar	my life is like a nightmare,
C'est pas si je viens de Goma	It's not to say that if I come from Goma
Que mon cœur et fait de pierre	that my heart is made of stone,
Mon destin de vivre des misère de guerre	my destiny is not to live the misery of war;
Je pleur, je crie	I cry, I scream
Pour que la miser s'arête partout en Afrique	for the killings across Africa to cease,
Esperance de vie baisses	life expectancy falls
On est réfugié	we were refugees,
On n'est pas né pour ça	we weren't born for this,
J'ai pas choisi aussi	I didn't choose it,
c'est pas la raison de rester	it's not a reason to stay
dans la berceau de l'ignorance	in a cradle of ignorance,
Il nous faut la solution	we must have a solution
face à la souffrance	in the face of suffering
c'est comme si nous sommes dans la prison	it's as if we are in prison
qu'est qu'il nous font voir à l'horizon	what are they making us see on the horizon

Refrain (Maisha Soul):

How long would you let me cry?
How long would you let me die?
How long would you wipe my tears away?

Verse 2 (Ndungi Githuku)

How long shall we cry for?
How long shall we wail for?
How long shall we complain for?
I have shed these tears before
I have heard these same cries
from dusk to dawn
What is worth dying for
is also worth living for
I have refused to be saddened
by your tricks and lies like before

Sita ya lia haya machozi tena na
sita taka huyu uchungu tena na
pamoja tushikane twende mbele na
twende tuezeke nyumba yetu tena naa
kama vile jua huchumoza kila asubuhi
ni lazima nipate haki yangu sasa
sasa

I won't cry these tears again
I don't want those machine guns again
together we cooperate and go forward
we complete our house together
if the sun rises every morning
I must have my rights now
now

Refrain (Maisha Soul):

How long would you let me cry?
How long would you let me die?
How long would you wipe my tears away?

Verse 3 (Prince Agakahn)

Oui, je suis un point dans la bout
Oui j'ai pas de force comme vous

Mais quand même je suis humain
comme vous
Ne me traite pas comme un animale (2)
J'ai besoin de vivre comme vous

yes, I am a spot in the mud
yes, I don't have the same power as
you
but am human just like you.

Don't treat me like an animal (2)
I deserve to live just as you

Spoken in the background by Emma Katya

Toi meme tu sais
pourquoi ceci, pourqoui celà
pourquoi tous les jours c'est la merde
la guerre tous les jours, pourquoi?

Yourself, you know it
why this here,
why always this shit,
every day war, why?

Refrain (Maisha Soul):

How long would you let me cry?

How long would you let me die?

How long would you wipe my tears away?

The vivid descriptions of suffering and agency in "How Long?" are fairly consistent with trends in conscious east African hip hop at the time.[28] Arguably what gives this song much of its potency is the ambiguity of its open-ended use of the word "you." Lines like "It's not to say that if I come from Goma that my heart is made of stone/my destiny is not to live the misery of war" or "I scream for the killings across Africa to cease" make the material conditions and circumstances of the song unmistakable, but it is not clear whether lines like "I don't have the same power as you/but am human just like you" are addressing Congolese politicians or foreign entities. Similarly, the questions "how long would you let me cry?/How long would you let me die?/How long would you wipe my tears away?" are as relevant to local politicians as they are to every member of the international community with enough privilege and technology to be hearing the song and watching the video.

Compounding the lyric content, the music video for this song further exacerbates the ambiguity of "How Long?" in two ways. First, with every iteration of the refrain the performers speak and gesture directly into the camera with no indication of whether their words are intended for a specific audience or they are suggesting that everyone watching is implicated (see Fig. 1.9, left frame). Second, at the very end of the final iteration of the refrain, the video shows two white Land Rovers of the International Red Cross driving away from the camera through the streets of Goma (Fig. 1.9, right frame). On the surface, this image might suggest that help has finally arrived, but more seasoned connoisseurs of Goma's particular brand of irony might well see in this image a cynical statement about the questionable practices of the abundance of NGOs in the region, as the vehicle of this

FIGURE 1.9 "How Long?" Music Video Sequence.

globally trusted organization drives *away* from the issues the local populations are fighting to make the world recognize.

In addition to signifying on the lyrics, the music video for "How Long?" also enhanced the impact of the song by introducing the east of Congo to the world in a new way. Of course, as a product of ALT2TV the video breaks the convention of focusing on images of suffering and instead contextualizes the region's devastation with frequent visual references to global (ir)responsibility and local agency. On another level, the professionalism of the recording and editing of both the music and the video confirm to the world that Goma has a formidable cultural scene with competent local artists and producers. Beyond that, the presence of familiar figures like Agakahn, Fonkodji, and Innocent, who are featured singing the chorus and playing the guitar, humanizes Goma by allowing the world to see and hear the stories of individual people who are growing and changing. Collectively these are powerful indications of the progress of musicians and filmmakers in developing the skills and assuming the power to tell their own stories.

Finally, for my own theoretical purposes, "How Long?" also serves as compelling evidence of the increasingly powerful convergence of music and film in cultural activism in the east of Congo. In this piece the counterpoint between art and politics, between global forces and individual voices, and between various mediums of expressions all intersect in a way that suggests that the relative importance of artistic resistance is measurable in terms of external and internal transformations alike. Where the former is concerned, "How Long?" is a striking benchmark against which to measure the material progress of artistic production in Goma, from the early days when access to musical technologies was a condition of genocide and migration. With regard to internal transformation, "How Long?" is proof that by imagining themselves engaged in something other than war, a critical mass of young people are actively creating precisely that possibility for themselves, which is a crucial component of the mechanics of social change. And the selection of "How Long?" by the Fair Play jury, the reception of *Ndoto Yangu* by audiences of Dutch National Television, and the rising international careers of many of the individual artists from Yole!Africa are all evidence that theories of artistic radicalism are being put into practice in North Kivu, that students are embodying their understanding that "revolution does not begin with the taking of political power ... but rather begins at the moment when the masses sense the need for change and their intellectual vanguards begin to study and carry out this change through activities on different fronts."[29]

Reading contrapuntally the tumultuous and specifically local history of hip hop music and early film production in the east of Congo suggests that revolution is as much a process as a historical moment. From this perspective, the forgotten efforts of South Cross and White Beret were as important a step toward social justice as the celebrated achievements of "How Long?" and *Ndoto Yangu* in that the former instigated the movement that the latter brought to global attention. Further, this reading illustrates that awareness of the history of artistic development in the region is a necessary prerequisite to understanding the significance and meaning of "local voices" in the current global cacophony of Congo activism. Indeed, despite the success of many of the examples in this chapter, the fact remains that local voices continue to be radically overpowered and manipulated by their global peers in dialogues about what is and is not best for the east of Congo. This is why, for many artists, storytelling remains a matter of survival.

NOTES

1. AbdouMalik Simone, *For the City Yet to Come: Changing African Life in Four Cities* (Durham, NC: Duke University Press, 2004), 4.

2. Edward Said, *Culture and Imperialism* (New York: Vintage, 1994), 66.

3. Carl Dahlhaus, "Counterpoint: 12. The Term Counterpoint after 1600," *The New Grove Dictionary of Music and Musicians*, Vol. 1084, ed. Stanley Sadie (New York: Macmillan, 2001), 561.

4. Sunaina Maira and Elisabeth Soep, eds., *Youthscapes: The Popular, the National, the Global* (Philadelphia: University of Pennsylvania Press, 2005), 1.

5. Dyna Icy (founding member of South Cross and former rapper), in discussion with the author, September 2014, via Skype.

6. Edward Soja, *Postmodern Geographies: The Reassertion of Space in Critical Social Theory* (London: Verso, 1989), 11.

7. The only remaining copy of this video is thought to be in a private archive in Amsterdam but may well be lost.

8. This refers to the French military song "C'était un jeune marin," about a young marine returning from war looking for his beloved beautiful Adèle. The song, which was taught in Congolese schools, was also used in France for army recruitment.

9. Tsitsi Ella Jaji, *Africa in Stereo: Modernism, Music, and Pan-African Solidarity* (New York: Oxford University Press, 2014), 195.

10. The name Empire Z (pronounced Empire Zed) is a plea for national unity in Zaire in the aftermath of the AFDL war. The name asserts the youths' desire that the population remain unified by virtue of their shared *Zariois* identity.

11. This name is a play on words that simultaneously signifies on chrome as an indicator of quality and an indicator of time, and signifies on drums as a traditional means of communication, including, by extension, emcees; the title thus means modern communicators of high-quality/modern drums of urgency.

12. At the time Ellen Lammers was studying anthropology at the University of Amsterdam; she was later instrumental in founding Yole!Africa and establishing the cultural center as a legal entity.

13. Lexxus Legal (rapper) in conversation with the author, July 2011, in Kinshasa, DRC.

14. In 2007, the Congolese filmmakers of repute included Mweze Ngangura, Balufu Bakupa-Kanyinda, Kibushi Ndjaté Wooto, Zeka Laplaine, Monique Phoba, Djo Munga, and Petna Ndaliko Katondolo.

15. Fernando Solanas and Octavio Getino, "Towards a Third Cinema," *Tricontinental* 13 (1969): 17.

16. Petna Ndaliko Katondolo (filmmaker) in conversation with the author, September 2013, in Chapel Hill, NC, USA.

17. Frantz Fanon, *Wretched of the Earth* (New York: Grove Press, 1961), 148.

18. Solonas and Getina, "Towards a Third Cinema," 4.

19. *Tuko Tayari*, 0:03:25–0:04:40 (Yole!Africa, Alternative to TV, 2006), Yole!Africa archive.

20. Frank Ukadike, "African Cinematic Reality: The Documentary Tradition as an Emerging Trend," *Research in African Literatures* 26, no. 3 (1995): 91.

21. This speech was delivered on Dec. 6, 2006, shortly after Kabila was sworn in as president.

22. *Ndoto Yangu*, 0:00:55–0:01:16, *Alternative to TV* (Alkebu Productions, 2007), accessed October 10, 2015, http://metropolistv.nl/en/correspondents/petna-goma/balume-15-years-old-and-already-a-producer.

23. The repeated chorus of the song is *"o zalaki pembeni nangayi tango nyoso/cadeau kitoko opesangayi bomoyi"* ("You have always been near me/the best gift you have ever given me is life").

24. *Ndoto Yangu*, 0:04:32–:52.

25. *Ndoto Yangu*, 0:05:08–:58. Italics mine.

26. Solanas and Getino, "Towards a Third Cinema," 9.

27. Other winning songs were "Let's Stop Corruption," by Mifilika of Malawi, and "I'm Defending," by the Palestinian group I-Voice in Lebanon. http://www.iamic.net/international-news/fair-play-anti-corruption-youth-voices-winners. New link: http://youthaward.org/winners/fair-play-anti-corruption-youth-voices

28. I am referring to such groups as the Tanzanian X-Plastas, the Ugandan artists Babaluku and Sabasaba, and the Kenyan group Kalamashaka/Uko Fulani Mau-Mau and GidiGidi MajiMaji.

29. Solanas and Getino, "Towards a Third Cinema," 2.

History will one day have its say; it will not be the history taught in the United Nations, Washington, Paris or Brussels, however, but the history taught in the countries that have rid themselves of colonialism and its puppets. Africa will write its own history, and both north and south of the Sahara it will be a history full of glory and dignity.
PATRICE EMERY LUMUMBA

2

RE-MEMBERING CONGO

THERE IS A war in Congo being fought over mineral resources, but there is also a war being fought over history, over what and how people remember.[1] This is a war in which history is not a matter of the past but a matter of the present. And it is urgent. It shapes the self-perception of local school children, justifies the policy decisions of geopolitical leaders, validates global campaigns of action, and exonerates complacency. Many before me have pointed out that preserving history is a practice of politicizing memory, sculpting it into the service of ideology, and staking ownership over Truth; that it matters which stories one learns, what one remembers. In the east of Congo, as in many conflicted regions, this is not a theoretical statement but a very literal one. In this conflict, history is as much the frontline as any physical battlefield; it is through enforcing official versions of history that powerful Western nations continue to dominate Congo, and it is in reviving alternative histories that resistance movements gain traction.

Indeed, everyone—from the most powerful transnational entities to the mildest individuals—with a stake in Congo must adopt a version of the nation's history that is congruent with their interests. Although many assertions of history are extremely subtle, they mark pedigrees of belief that continue to have material consequences—physical, economic, political, and cultural—on Congolese populations. This is evident in major geopolitical transactions and also in the smallest of examples. For instance, the Lingala word *monsenzi* (and its Kiswahili equivalent *mushenzi*), which is bandied about as a mild insult between Congolese, has been so thoroughly adopted into the fluid vocabularies of local languages that few people pause to trace its etymology back to its origin in the high colonial era, when Francophone Belgian officers would refer to Congolese as *"mon singe"* (my monkey) to dehumanize them. Equating Congolese to monkeys was not a superficial insult; at a time when scientists and anthropologists were hotly debating where Africans belonged on the evolutionary spectrum from primates to humans, referring to Congolese as monkeys was a calculated statement that justified oppressive systems of governance and education designed to control "lesser beings." Originally it was schoolmasters who institutionalized this word as the epithet with which to reprimand students for failing to properly adopt Western customs or for attempting to reject aspects of European culture. Teachers regularly humiliated Congolese students, calling them monsenzi or mushenzi for anything from the despicable offense of failing to use Western eating utensils (or toilets) properly to the cardinal sin of muddling French pronunciation. The effects of this practice were many. Among other things, it formalized imitation rather than independent thinking as the default mode of education, and it celebrated flawless mimicry of whiteness as the highest measure of value.

This is a self-perpetuating system. Through corporal punishment and subtler means (such as use of terms like monsenzi), the colonial education system enforced in generations of Congolese the desire to defend Belgian values, and by extension Belgian accounts of Congolese history as proof of their unwavering allegiance to Western ideals and hence of their own worth as human beings. This system also peremptorily invalidated (and continues to invalidate) alternative narratives by placing any and all oppositional texts outside the official canon and discrediting their revolutionary producers, such as Frantz Fanon, Wamba dia Wamba, and Cheik Anta Diop (to name but a few) as mentally unstable. Thus, in Congo the war over history does not look like a war; it looks like the "development" of a postcolonial state, while the actual conflict, rather than being grounded in history, is deemed nearly exclusively a humanitarian problem. But as David Rieff suggests, "By calling some terrible historical event a humanitarian crisis, it is almost inevitable that all the fundamental questions of politics, of culture, history, and morality without which the crisis can never be properly understood will be avoided."[2]

This chapter grapples with those fundamental questions about politics, culture, history, and morality that are critical to local cultural activists in the east of Congo. Its point of departure is history, specifically how interpretations of history substantiate current paradigms of action—and thus inform politics, culture, and morality—for a range of actors in Congo that includes geopolitical leaders, regional politicians, UN bodies, NGO personnel, civil society actors, and, of course, local artists. For its part, Yole!Africa has developed a curriculum of popular history that is tethered to Lumumba's insistence that liberation from colonialism is necessarily rooted in African accounts of history. In this chapter I am particularly concerned with the specific interpretations of history that emerge from this curriculum as they shed light on important ways of curating and contesting memory. Accordingly, this chapter is a metaphoric recreation of Yole!Africa's curriculum of popular history, which charts major episodes in Congo's development as well as interrogating the ongoing and controversial politics of representing the nation's history. In short, it captures the process by which dominant histories—or, to quote Lumumba, those taught in the United Nations, Washington, Paris, or Brussels—are being reclaimed and recast by youth in the east of Congo. This process, to my reading, is equally evident in the transformation of historical knowledge (meaning specific content) and in the transformation of modes of engaging with history; indeed, the restoration of glory and dignity predicted by Lumumba is inextricably tied to a shift in pedagogy that equips young people to engage critically, rather than passively, with ideas. In this context the act of asking questions is an embodied—and radical—(re)claiming of agency that disrupts not only the narration but also the behavioral implications of dominant history, encoded as they are in the plethora of details, like my previous example of monsenzi, that collectively shape identity in postcolonial spaces.

In terms of both form and content, my intention is that this chapter unfurl a historical narrative of the past through the present as it is in the process of transforming and being transformed by cultural activists at Yole!Africa. The chapter begins with a brief prologue outlining prominent analyses of the current conflict and explaining the origin of Yole!Africa's curriculum of popular history; the remainder of the chapter is divided into five "acts"—Léopold II, Belgium, Lumumba, Mobutu, and the Next Generation—each of which interweaves historical information and theoretical analysis of a film with ethnographic analysis of their effects on aspiring artist-activists at Yole!Africa. The content of this chapter combines ethnographic research and critical analysis. Specifically, from 2010 through the time of writing, I observed and participated in film screenings and post-screening discussions at Yole!Africa, and conducted follow-up interviews with participants in Yole!Africa's curriculum of popular history. Subsequently I incorporated the findings of this ethnographic research with my ongoing study of film theory. My rationale for offering such extensive analysis of the films in this chapter is that they are among the most highly esteemed and influential works for artist-activists training at Yole!Africa. The films discussed in this chapter are the core of an emerging canon (of sorts) of activism in Goma, one that is formative of the current works (discussed in Chapters Three and Four) being produced by militant artists, which grow out of deep experiential and analytical engagement with these films. Thus familiarity with these films and the interpretations of history they elicit from young audiences is critical, even imperative, prerequisite knowledge for understanding current paradigms of cultural activism in Goma.

PROLOGUE

I opened this chapter by stating that the dual wars over resources and history in Congo are equally urgent. They are also inseparable. In Congo the crisis of history is most immediately evident in the widely varying explanations of the current conflict; indeed, although there is (some) consensus about the symptoms and the statistics of the problem, there is no agreement on the cause. Scholars, journalists, NGOs, and transgovernmental as well as intergovernmental organizations all agree that the conflict in Congo is astronomical; that more than six million people have been killed, that more than one million women, children, and men have been brutally raped; that millions of people have been forcefully displaced from their land into disease-ridden IDP camps; that hundreds of thousands of children have been forcefully conscripted into rebel militias; that this is a dire crisis. What few agree on is how, exactly, this happened, and yet prescriptions to remedy the crisis are wedded to diagnoses of its root cause, which are in turn shaped by conceptions of its origin. In short, solutions to immediate human needs in Congo are directly tied to concepts of the nation's history.

And concepts of Congo's history are abundant. Scholars, journalists, governmental and nongovernmental analysts, and experts all assert evidence for conflicting stories. Among scholars there are three primary schools of thought. The first grounds Congo's present problems in the nation's fraught past and focuses analyses on issues of state collapse. Scholars of this school argue that the current crisis "represents a superimposition of an overdeveloped extractive, and predatory state upon the vestiges of traditional societies and an ethnic mosaic."[3] Further, that, given this country's exaggerated history of violence, greed, and manipulation as the personal property of King Léopold II, as the colonial holding of Belgium, and later under the dictatorship of the neocolonial puppet Mobutu, the current crisis was neither sudden nor unlikely. This historical perspective suggests that cycles of dysfunction are continuously perpetuated by the nation's fundamentally faulty inheritance: "The form of nondevelopmental authoritarianism he [Mobutu] practiced certainly reflected the incapacities of Congo's administrative inheritance, but it also made it likely that his successors would have little prospect of sparking a more virtuous cycle of development and liberal reform."[4]

Scholars from a second school of thought claim that historical roots are less to blame than current economic demands in the era of globalization. Proponents of this perspective foreground the negative impact of international policy changes on the stability of African states, with Congo as a prime example, and cite the rapacious nature of Western corporate dealings with nonstate actors, including warlords, for natural resources the continent over as potential catalysts of warfare (in traditional and various alternative forms) and state collapse. Critics of this trend label the Congo crisis "an emergent ideology that shuns regulation and collective management of social problems on the continent."[5]

A third school of thought positions Congo's crisis not as a matter of internal state collapse, but of external intervention. This perspective draws attention to the questionable motivations of prolonged foreign intervention in Congo, like that of the United Nations, which has undermined the development of a strong state. Citing the parallel infrastructure the UN has created for military action, travel, communications, governance, and food stability, scholars in this camp insist that "whatever activities the state might undertake in building a national consciousness have been indisputably disrupted," which has destroyed all institutions that would otherwise cultivate a cohesive national consciousness.[6] Further, in the absence of of a strong national consciousness, foreign entities can continue to manipulate Congo and retain easy access to mineral resources by supporting warlords and antagonistic regional identities among the population.

Then there is the official perspective of the Congolese government, and to a large extent the UN Peace Keeping Mission to Congo, which tends to focus on specific military actions of each of the implicated armies and rebel groups rather than investigating the origins of the problem(s). Similarly, the vast majority of what James Ferguson calls "transnational entities"—including international NGOs—prioritize strategizing around specific results of the conflict over understanding its history.[7] Thus they focus on issues such as lack of hospitals and schools, violations of international law, increased sexual violence, or the forced conscription of child soldiers. Attention to these problems is necessary, but in their current application the resultant strategies to address material problems divorce specific history from contemporary circumstances in dangerous ways. This creates an opening for foreign activists—specifically those activists from countries that, historically and presently, most benefit from Congo's resources— to ignore Congo's particular legacy and focus on generalized critiques of the depravity of human nature. Ultimately this line of reasoning breeds arguments that the crisis is not specifically Congolese or even African, but rather a reflection of the human vice to be found buried next to coveted minerals in any region on the planet, and by extension that well-intentioned compassionate individuals can—and should—intervene in what is a situation of fundamental human greed. Political scientist John F. Clark sees in this trend worrisome signs that "a cynical kind of international 'triage' is now being practiced that has written off the possibility of real African development . . . while simultaneously insisting on African openness to Western business."[8]

Finally, there are the local populations, whose explanation of the conflict is that it is "political." Notably, in Congo the term refers not to politics per se but rather to the practice of being dishonest and unaccountable. Indeed, when people claim the conflict is political, further questioning reveals they mean it is an effort to cover up lies, though the nature of the lies or the people ostensibly covering them up is not consistent from one person to the next. This diagnosis is particularly interesting as it allows many of the official analyses to be true simultaneously. But the diagnosis is also dangerous because it allows interested parties—whether governing bodies or international NGOs—to cite locals as supportive of their respective positions without offering proper cultural translation of the intended meaning behind the word *political*.

These are the most common explanations of the Congo conflict. But there is another perspective, held by more militant Congolese activists, who insist on rehistoricizing the current conflict so as to address its deeply pervasive—and deeply internalized—roots.[9] These individuals agree with many of the factual claims put forth by the scholars, analysts, governments, and international NGOs addressing the present problems, but see in these problems symptoms of a deeper syndrome of ongoing mental colonization that afflicts the underlying social, economic, and governmental structures of Congolese society. From this perspective mental colonization is a material reality that effects decision making at the national, regional, local, community, and family levels. This is an active colonial legacy that ties the current conflict to the past through the ongoing conditions of oppression and hierarchy. Militant activists align the continued belief on the part of Congolese in the (imagined) superiority of the West with what they argue is a continued assertion by many Westerners of a deeply embodied, if unconscious, entitlement that is self-righteous and shirks accountability. Activists of this ilk fiercely criticize allusions to globalization that are not also accompanied by concrete discussions of global responsibility, arguing that international policy changes that destabilize African states are nothing new, and are certainly not unique to Congo. Similarly, they argue that grounding Congo's present problems in a history that foregrounds ethnicity is just another example of the long-standing practice of hiding Western economic interest behind sensational narratives of ethnic identity that show little progress from the era of King Léopold II.

From this perspective, there are indeed pointed parallels between the brutality of Léopold II's quest for rubber and ivory in the Congo Free State with the present frenzy for coltan and oil in what the West terms the Free Market, both of which evoke(d) ethnicity as a diversion from economic motivations and both of which call for humanitarian intervention from the West. To militant Congolese activists, this pattern begs the question: If, as history has confirmed, Léopold justified his actions with humanitarian rhetoric of benevolence and uplift, what does the current humanitarian rhetoric (of benevolence and uplift) obscure? And what version of history must be evoked to change this perpetual cycle?

As the result of an effort to address these questions on an organizational level, Yole!Africa began to create a curriculum of popular history in late 2010. At the time, the center was in the process of implementing some significant changes as it attempted to shift from a guerrilla operation to becoming a stabler organization. In 2007, Petna had stepped down as director, stating that he wanted Yole!Africa to be run by and for youth (an age category he was rapidly outgrowing) and that the center would benefit from a fresh leadership perspective. In theory this was a welcome idea, but when Sekombi Katondolo (Petna's younger brother) was appointed as the new director, considerable animosity developed in the local community. There were critics who dismissed Yole!Africa as a "Katondolo family thing," some of whom went so far as to link family to ethnicity and criticize the organization for favoring Nandes. There were other critics who disapproved of the new direction Yole!Africa took under Sekombi's leadership, complaining that as he elevated the center's profile through collaborations with international NGOs, Yole!Africa's core ideology was undermined. Over the course of two years, tensions escalated. Yole!Africa became more visible on the international radar owing to its new partnerships with NGOs, yet while the center continued to serve as a gathering space for local youth and to support art and creativity in the community, it was no longer perceived by locals as a space to cultivate Lumumbist liberation ideology. 2010 was a pivotal year, during which Sekombi was asked to resign and Yole!Africa was forced to recalibrate its identity as an organization. To support this process, Petna returned to Goma and, with the urging of the most vocal critics, created a leadership circle for the center that included himself as interim director, Olivier Lechen as consultant, Ndungi Githuku and Excellence Juma Balikwisha as advisors, Ganza Buroko as administrator, Stella Ramazani as coordinator, and myself as a scholar.

It was during the painstaking process of rebuilding trust with the community and exploring new models of leadership that the idea for a curriculum of popular history took root. Specifically, as we searched for examples of ethical leadership in Congo's recent history, it became clear that the challenges Yole!Africa was facing as an organization mirrored those of Congo as a nation, albeit on a much smaller scale. The reflex to mistrust familial ties, the haste to cite ethnicity as a source of conflict, the deep suspicion of Congolese ability to advance: all these dynamics surfaced around Yole!Africa in ways that were uncannily similar to the heated debates, past and present, surrounding national politics. Following the traditional wisdom that states one must know one's past in order to take prudent action in the future, the leadership circle of Yole!Africa began, in earnest, to explore the past. And what started as an effort to trace an organizational chain of events turned into long debates stretching back to the Kongo Kingdom in the fourteenth century. To our surprise, the process of debating history—of reframing it and seeing its contemporary relevance—began to transform animosity into cooperation as each of us had the opportunity to recognize how we are formatively shaped by the past.

This process was further fortified in a series of public forums, in which members of the community were invited to air their grievances about Yole!Africa. In the initial forum, emotions ran high for certain artists, both established and aspiring, who expressed bitter disappointment over Yole!Africa's perceived failings. In subsequent forums, the force of the artists' anger began to subside as they acknowledged the immense challenges of creating a functional organization in a dysfunctional state. But as diagnoses of the state's dysfunction reached further and further into the past, two things became clear: first, that official (rather than popular) history was accepted as Truth by the larger community, and second, that participating in popular (rather than official) history was transformative, in the way Teshome Gabriel suggests when he writes

> Popular memory . . . considers the past as a political issue. It orders the past not only as a reference point but also as a theme of struggle. For popular memory, there are no longer any "centres" or "margins," since the very designations imply that something has been conveniently left out. Popular memory, then, is neither a retreat to some great tradition nor a flight to some imagined "ivory tower," neither a self-indulgent escapism nor a desire for the actual "experience" or "content" of the past for its own sake. Rather, it is a "look back to the future," necessarily dissident and partisan, wedded to constant change.[10]

After reflecting on this phenomenon, the leadership circle of Yole!Africa proposed a curriculum of popular history to mark the organization's reconnection with its founding ideology. As I have witnessed and participated in the development of this curriculum, I have come to see it as a manifestation of Ngugi wa Thiong'o's famed metaphor of Isis faithfully scouring the Sahara for the dismembered body parts of Osiris, which she must ultimately re-member in order to bring him back to life. Yole!Africa's engagement with popular history in Congo was (and still is) an expression of the impulse to move from fragmentation to wholeness (to borrow from Ngugi). Unfortunately, the metaphor of dismemberment is painfully pertinent in this nation in which generations of people were physically dismembered by King Léopold II's brutal Force Publique, where Lumumba's body was dismembered by Belgian soldiers, and where histories are still symbolically dismembered through erasure and distortion. In a very literal sense, attempting to revive popular history in the east of Congo is tantamount to bringing generations of dismembered stories back to life—and the prospects for success are roughly equivalent to Isis' chances of finding every precious piece of Osiris' mutilated body.

Clearly no mere mortal can undertake such an immense project single-handedly. For its part, Yole!Africa's contributions to advancing popular history in Congo have been to acquire, curate, and produce a growing collection of films that tell alternative versions of history, and to screen them in forums that both allow audiences to discover new historical facts and also provide a potent canvas against which to hone their skills of criticism and inquiry. The center's focus on fostering critical thinking skills through historical study challenges young people to purge embodied (historical) practices of imitation and noncritical memorization and to recognize that revolutionary ideology must be equally concerned not only with *what* one consumes but with *how* one consumes it. Thus screenings at Yole!Africa are often lively iterations of what scholars of Third Cinema term the film act, in which the projection of a film catalyzes transformative discussion—even action—that interrupts and extends beyond the screening itself.

Such is the ideal of Yole!Africa's curriculum of popular history: to trigger the revolutionary transformation of young people from subjects to agents of history. But such ideals are, of course, encumbered by mechanical impracticalities. Indeed, screening films in the east of Congo is not so simple since there are no functional movie theaters. Like its global comrades in revolutionary cinema, for years Yole!Africa screened films in all manner of conditions, often with jury-rigged projectors hooked up to car batteries projecting shaky images onto stretched cotton bed sheets. Over time, conditions improved; the center acquired a large blue-and-white striped canvas tent that became a cinema house complete with makeshift bleachers, a gas generator, and even a rickety popcorn machine, and eventually this equipment was further upgraded to include a full-size inflatable screen for outdoor screenings during the dry season and powerful speakers capable of overriding the noisy drone of the generator. Although, by

FIGURE 2.1 Yole!Africa Cinema Events. Photos courtesy of Yole!Africa.

local standards, such screening conditions are comparatively luxurious, watching a film in the east of Congo still requires significantly more effort than swiping a finger across the touchscreen of a tablet. Indeed, when people come together to watch films in these circumstances, there is a palpable sense of the significance of the act. Figure 2.1 depicts various film screening scenarios at Yole!Africa: on the left is an indoor screening inside the tent with the screen built from wood covered by sheets, in the center the technical console and bleachers are visible, and on the right is an outdoor screening with the inflated screen.

For such screenings, anywhere from 30 to 150 young people gather together in the compound of Yole!Africa, where vibrant murals of Angela Davis and Frantz Fanon (depicted on the front cover of this book), Nyiabingi (Congolese heroine discussed further in Chapter Four) and Lumumba adorn the exterior and interior walls. If the political situation is calm, they might sit outside in the open waiting for the sky to darken so a screening can begin, and if the political moment is volatile and early curfews are in effect then they will likely be helping hang dark fabric over the windows of the tent to block the light for an afternoon screening. Eventually, once fuel for the generator arrives, everyone settles in for a film. These screenings and the debates that follow form the core of the center's curriculum of popular history. It is in this space, surrounded by the likenesses of radical liberation activists, that young people, sometimes for the first time in their lives, begin to ask—and seek answers to—questions about their own identity. It is in this space that words like monsenzi, and the complex history that generated them, are repoliticized through a pedagogy of inquiry and critical reflection. It is in this space that young generations begin to dismantle the hierarchy of rote memorization and mimicry and recognize the power of questioning Truth.

There is a popular Swahili proverb that says *Mpaka siku simba atakuwa nawakumtetea, historia itakuwa yakumsifu muwindaji* (history will always glorify the hunter until the lion has his own griot), which is to say that there is always another side of the story—even, or indeed, *especially*, of official history. This is the aim of Yole!Africa's curriculum of popular history, to tell another side of the stories that hold so much power over Congo. Learning these stories is important for young people as they seek to make sense out of their nation's impossibly complex circumstances. Indeed,

I have witnessed radical transformations in them as they encounter and internalize accounts of the past that expose the vital stories omitted from the official historical record. In some cases they transform from disinterested passive observers of their sociopolitical conditions to passionate advocates for their communities as they assume new facets of both the pride and the burden of being Congolese. This manifests in all manner of ways; many of them replace foreign idols (like Arnold Schwarzenegger) with newly discovered Congolese heroes and heroines, stating (in so many words) that learning about local role models gives them an example of local activism whereas identifying with foreign idols is a form of escapism or even a rejection of self. This is the urgency of learning popular history.

But the impact of studying alternative histories is not exclusive to Congolese youth; it is relevant to each and every one of us who has a stake in Congo. Despite my own scrupulous study of the nation's history and my deep engagement with alternative texts, I for one was forced to rethink many of my ideas in light of the perspectives presented by the young people in postscreening debates and interviews. Indeed, my perceptions of Congo—its past, its present, and its future—are indelibly shaped by countless heated debates between youth in Yole!Africa's makeshift cinema hall. Recalibrating my own understanding of Congo by listening to them gave me a glimpse of how Congo's history might be told by the proverbial lion's griot. For me, this vantage point shifted, permanently, how I engage in the nation's current struggle; it revealed for me hidden sources of pain and of pride that I now navigate with greater respect, and it taught me the difference between subtle phrases and gestures that can conjure, in an instant, specters of the heroes or villains who continue to animate the nation's psyche.

The lessons I learned are many and they have changed my vocabulary. For example, I now understand that to "use" art for social ends evokes Mobutu's regime or propaganda whereas advocating transformation *through* art suggests a Lumumbist paradigm; that to conflate "officials" with "authorities" strips community members of their own rightful agency; that when foreigners come to "teach" they exert a kind of paternalist dominance, reminiscent of (neo)colonialism, which precludes mutual "exchange" and enforces notions of Western superiority. I have also learned invaluable lessons about the importance of going to diverse sources to gather information, about listening without preconceived ideas or bias, about resisting the impulse to assign dismissive labels or the reflex to avoid or dismiss uncomfortable truths. In short, bearing witness to the transformative process of re-membering history has conditioned how I hear, how I think about Congo, and how I think about activism as a practice. The following vignettes are thus intended to provide a glimpse of Congo's story from a point of view that distilled, for me, the indelible link between history and sustainable sociopolitical change.

ACT I: LÉOPOLD

Although for centuries the vast land known as the Kongo Kingdom was a thriving and prosperous empire, the momentum of Western history dictates that the real story of Congo begins with its "discovery" and rule by Europeans. Allegiance to official versus popular versions of history often leads historians to disagree on the details of interactions between the Kongo Kingdom and Europe from 1483 (when Kongo was "discovered") to 1884 (when it was claimed by Belgium), but there is near unanimous agreement that the story of corruption and war that plagues contemporary Congo began with the rule of King Léopold II. In short, the story of Congo that popular historians aim to re-member begins with subjugation, slavery, and greed.

From 1884 to 1908 Congo, which was ironically called the Congo Free State at the time, was the private personal property of Léopold II. Although he never once set foot in Congo, his personal ownership of the land meant that he was not subject to any international laws or regulations restricting his rule. At the time, the international laws were decidedly in favor of white Europeans over Africans, yet there were certain measures in place to limit the cruelty of colonial practices. However, Léopold II was exempt. He was permitted, with complete freedom, to plunder the vast wealth of the land and people with the most brutal methods in the history of colonialism. His private police, the Force Publique, was, for instance, encouraged to cut off the hands and feet of slave laborers—and their children—and create piles of the dismembered limbs in the center of villages as a reminder to workers of the importance of meeting daily quotas.

From an economic perspective, his tactics were brilliant; Léopold II was able to turn the most lucrative resources of Congo—the ivory, rubber, gold, copper, and, of course, slaves—into a vast personal fortune. But from a popular Congolese perspective, his rule was devastating and instigated cycles of corruption, plunder, and an ethos of terror that continue to afflict Congo today. Indeed, what was, until more recently, left out of the story is that the death toll of Léopold II's greed is conservatively estimated to have cut the population of Congo at least in half, which amounts to more than ten million deaths and represents the deadliest colonial regime on the continent of Africa.[11]

Discovering, concretely, the atrocities committed in Congo under Léopold II often incites rightful outrage from people, in Congo and the West, whose previous reflections on the subject were shaped by vague or exotic discussion of colonialism in secondary school. In recent years a growing number of historical studies and documentary films—including Adam Hochschild's book *King Leopold's Ghost* (1998), Peter Bates's documentary film *White King, Red Rubber, Black Death*

(2003), and Pippa Scott and Oreet Rees's documentary film *King Leopold's Ghost* (2006)—have brought increasing popular attention to the horrors of colonialism in Congo. These sources, which play a critical role in uncovering another side of Congo's history, feature prominently in Yole!Africa's curriculum of popular history. But the curriculum also encourages equal focus not only on the explicit content of historical narratives but also on the underlying dynamics and patterns that so often get overlooked in the emotional experience of discovering new truths. Thus the atrocities committed in King Léopold II's Congo (for example), instead of being the sole point, become an informative context in which to consider the perpetuation of mechanisms that allow similar activities to continue. One film that regularly catalyzes particularly potent discussions of this nature at Yole!Africa is Francis Dujardin's 1999 documentary *Boma-Tervuren, Le Voyage (de juin à septembre 1897)*.

Boma-Tervuren chronicles the history of 267 Congolese subjects who were forcefully extracted from the city of Boma (a major port city in Congo that exported slaves) and sent as an exhibit to the 1897 World's Fair in Tervuren, Belgium, where they were displayed, studied, and filmed for more than six months. By interweaving original historical images and narratives of the horrific events that befell the Congolese with contemporary interviews of their descendants, this documentary allows the present generation of Congolese, who are represented in the film by a writer, a historian, and a self-proclaimed "descendent of Léopold II's slaves,"[12] to collectively piece together and publicize the "horrordom"[13] of this forgotten history. Despite the passing of a century between the World's Fair of 1897 and the filming of *Boma-Tervuren* in 1999, there is an undeniable power in living Congolese interacting with the same technological apparatus (the camera) in the same physical spaces (the National Garden at Turveren, the port of Anvers) to amend the story of their ancestors.

The opening sequence of *Boma-Tervuren* quickly establishes a cinematic aesthetic, common to historical documentaries, that brings the past and present into dialogue. The film begins with a visual collage: recent images of manicured historical sites such as the museum at Tervuren (which is still dominated by the sculptures erected by Léopold II) juxtaposed with grainy black-and-white footage of Congolese men vigorously rowing a *pirogue*[14] up the Congo river; and still photographs of nursing mothers, young children, working men, musicians, fishermen, families, and communities whose lives were forever changed by this voyage. The sequence concludes its journey through space and time with a full-color shot that brings the viewer to the busy port of Anvers in the present, where a well-dressed Congolese man waits on the dock, watching the coming and going of ships as if in preparation to greet the ghosts of his ancestors a century after their physical arrival.

The arrival of the camera at the port of Anvers, which is one of Europe's largest and was a primary point of arrival for ships coming from Africa, mirrors the physical arrival of the 267 Congolese bound for the World's Fair in 1897. From there they traveled across land to Tervuren where, from May 10 to November 8 they were housed in the Palace of the Colonies, which was, notably, part of a larger zoological (not anthropological) exhibit that included only one colony, the Congo Free State. They were stationed in a traditional Congolese village that was recreated with precision in a depression in the earth that allowed the 7.6 million spectators from the twenty-seven participating Western countries to view, from above, every intimate detail of "Congolese life." By Belgian accounts, the Congolese Village was conceived as an educational space in which King Léopold II could introduce emissaries from the heart of darkness to the Belgian population as anthropological proof of the superiority of civilized nations over their savage peers.[15]

Needless to say, with nothing more than their traditional attire designed for tropical weather, few of the Congolese survived the harsh Belgian climate; nor were they immunized against the flood of foreign diseases that swept through their village as spectators threw peanuts and other discarded items at them to compare their reactions to the neighboring exhibit of monkeys. But according to their descendants, worse than the physical suffering or death was the lasting effect of the insatiable and invasive voyeurism of the West. This seldom-articulated point is made particularly poignant in a medium shot (depicted in Fig. 2.2) of Congolese writer and professor Ngandu Nkashama Pius, speaking directly—and unscripted—into the camera:

> All cultures are made to look at others. The question of the other is at the heart of all our lives. But when I imagine that I am one of the Congolese in 1897, I am in the same place where I am now, and you, a Belgian here in front of me, I realize that you force me to behave as you do in order to recognize me at all, as evidence that I am even a human being. You force me to dress, talk, eat, sleep, *breathe* as you imagine I should. My real life does not interest you at all. What is important is the image you want to create of me; it is this look that kills. This way of looking at the other is a permanent violation [lit. rape], it is a homicide—a cultural homicide. They came, *I* came from my home, already cursed by the weight of history.[16]

In screenings at Yole!Africa this passage often elicits spontaneous applause and vigorous head-nodding from audience members who relate all too well to such

FIGURE 2.2 *Boma-Tervuren* Still.

violations of look and image. Efforts to parse their emotional reaction to this statement reveal disturbing similarities between this historical rebuke and their own daily experiences. But there is also enthusiastic praise for Ngandu's ability to articulate this dynamic, a palpable sense of validation, and optimism that others (meaning Westerners) might learn from his words. The collective analysis is that Ngandu's reflection interrupts the comfortable psychological distance that so often exists between contemporary viewers and historical content and makes clear that deadly ways of looking are not a thing of the past, are not relegated to the historic violence committed against 267 individual Congolese by long-dead Europeans, but that this practice continues in the present. And that everyone is implicated. As soon as Ngandu addresses the camera (as an object), the person operating the camera (as an individual agent), and the spectator (as a critical mass), he transgresses the two-dimensionality of the screen and begins to interact directly with the audience. By disrupting the imagined barrier between himself and the viewer, he transforms himself from an object of another's gaze to the subject of his own discourse. Thus, when he conflates the *regard* of historic fairgoers with that of the contemporary Belgian cameraman, not only do his words transport the viewer through time via the fixed perspective of the lens, but he implicates all of us in the permanent violation and homicide that continues to inform so many visual practices through which we consume the (Congolese) Other.

Although the content of the text is potently critical, many students also appreciate how the cinematic language of the sequence works, symbolically, to foreground possibilities of creating a powerful heterobiography even out of such deeply painful material. Heterobiography, as defined by Teshome Gabriel, who coined the term, is a "multi-generational and trans-individual or symbolic autobiography where the *collective* subject is the focus."[17] True, on the surface this scene depicts nothing more than a man sitting in a park, but closer analysis reveals deep significance to the image. Not only is Ngandu sitting in the National Garden at Tervuren, which was the site of his ancestors' brutal history, he is seated in front of a stream that flows away from the camera throughout the scene. The relative stillness of his body compared to the perpetual motion in the background brings to mind philosopher Gilles Deleuze's theory of depth of field, which, he suggests, "creates a certain type of direct time-image that can be defined by memory, virtual regions of past, the aspects of each region. This would be less a function of reality than a function of remembering, of temporalization: not exactly a recollection but 'an invitation to recollect.' "[18]

The continuous recession of water from foreground to background is indeed a function of temporalization as it symbolically transports the viewer from present to past, creating a temporal bridge that foregrounds the transience of an individual human life, while simultaneously providing a metaphor of the transgenerational continuity of story, myth, and belief. And if the symbolism were not clear enough, the medium by which the viewer travels through time is water, which has its own cultural and historic significance both as the literal means by which the original Congolese were transported to the World's Fair and as a metaphoric invocation of middle passage imagery. Thus the movement of water through the background of the scene both defines depth of field and also serves as a conduit and bearer of memory that connects the suffering of the Congolese at Tervuren to the peoples of Africa around the world; further, it extends, with the invitation to recollect, the real possibility of a collective, or hetero-, biography.

Together the spoken critique and the cinematic language provide potent fodder for alternative historical narratives, but this passage, indeed this whole film, is also telling another important story. Astute students of popular history recognize the critical connection between Ngandu's discussion of the power of the gaze, the cinematic language of the film, and a larger critique of the very history that first brought camera technology to Congo. Indeed, at the same time *Boma-Tervuren* chronicles the history of the 267 Congolese taken to the World's Fair, it is among the few documents (written or cinematic) to chronicle Congo's early encounters with mechanical images. Whereas in other parts of the world (most prominently the West) mechanical images were introduced as tools of documentation and tools of creative expression or even entertainment, in Africa they were from the outset strictly political and represent one of the most insidious means of control, manipulation, and domination.

Numerous traces of this history are visible in *Boma-Tervuren*. The archival images showing the Congolese Village at the World's Fair are excerpts from the footage commissioned by Léopold II for the anthropological study of Congolese. This footage, which was eventually compiled into a collection of films under the title *Les Congolais à Tervuren*, was central to scientific efforts to pinpoint the evolutionary limitations of Congolese and to explain their inferiority to Europeans. For decades this footage was also a celebrated centerpiece of anthropological education in various European countries and was, as such, a common means through which Westerners were introduced to Congolese.

In addition to the images taken in Belgium, *Boma-Tervuren* also subtly introduces students at Yole!Africa to another important aspect of Congo's early encounter with mechanical images. All the portraits in the opening collage (and in later sequences) are from early photographs taken in Congo. Although the film does not go into this history in great depth, it provides a point of departure for inquisitive viewers (like many of the students and myself) to discover that, starting in 1897 with a photographer and film director named Weber, King Léopold II sent numerous expeditions of cameramen both to gather images of wild Congo to bring back to Belgium and to project inspiring images of Belgium—palaces, ships, libraries, royalty—for Congolese subjects. There were many objectives of this activity. For one thing, projecting images of Belgian technologies was a way to demonstrate, unequivocally, to Congolese the superiority of Europe to Africa. Another aim was for King Léopold II to substantiate his flourishing philanthropic efforts in the eyes of Belgian citizens and to justify the lavish monuments he built in his own honor throughout Belgium. To this end he frequently demanded photographs of the railroads, road networks, and various structures he was building (with slave labor) across Congo. Simultaneously, the Catholic Church, which was pivotal in pioneering cinema productions in Congo, had numerous missionaries stationed in the Congo Free State, many of whom returned to Belgium with photographs to substantiate their stories of the inspirational effects of Christianity on savages.

From a historical perspective, the introduction of cameras in the Congo Free State in 1897 not only represents an extension of King Léopold II's gaze across the Atlantic; it also represents the most powerful tactic in his campaign to position himself as an altruistic leader. Indeed, with the benefit of hindsight it is easy to condemn Léopold II as one of the most despotic leaders in history. But at the time he was perceived as a ruler of unparalleled benevolence. And his savvy use of images played a crucial role in his ability to create and sustain this illusion. It was through images that he elevated Europeans (particularly himself) to the status of demigods in the psyche of the Congolese and through images that he permanently cast Congolese as primitive savages in need of uplift in the minds of Europeans and Congolese alike. The rhetoric and aesthetics of philanthropy have evolved substantially since Léopold II's era, but the seed he planted through his use of images retains its potency. Indeed, from a Western perspective, in which images are a fundamental part of positive self-perception and affirmation, it is all too easy to forget that in Congo images are at the core of a long history of self-hatred, violation, and degradation.

But if the relationship between philanthropy and image in Congo began with Léopold II in 1897, the same year also marked the beginning of the relationship between image and resistance, when the British journalist Edmund D. Morel witnessed the atrocities being committed in Congo and mounted a campaign of dissent in the form of the Congo Reform Association (CRA). Morel was not the first to try to raise international outrage about Léopold II's practices in Congo. In 1890 a Black American soldier, journalist, lawyer, preacher, and historian, George Washington Williams, had already exposed the atrocities being committee in the Congo Free State to U.S. President William Harrison and more than a dozen of the most powerful European and American newspapers, in his *Open Letter to His Serene Majesty Léopold II, King of the Belgians and Sovereign of the Independent State of Congo*. Although this document was meticulously researched and proved in retrospect to be accurate and reliable, it made little headway in bringing an end to Léopold II's regime in part because it relied solely on written documentation and could therefore be dismissed.[19] By contrast, Morel centered his campaign, which journalist Adam Hochschild calls "the first major international atrocity scandal in the age of the telegraph and the camera," on images. He was a master of technology and capitalized on its power: "A central part of almost every Congo protest meeting was a slide show, comprising some sixty vivid photos of life under Léopold's rule; half a dozen of them showed mutilated Africans or their cut-off hands. The pictures, ultimately seen in meetings and the press by millions of people, provided evidence that no propaganda could refute."[20] And it worked; through pressure from the CRA, in 1908 Belgium was forced to buy the Congo Free State from King Léopold II. Although Belgium did establish formal colonial control over the territory, little changed in the daily lives of Congolese; but having solved the problem on paper, the CRA and the international community turned their efforts to other projects.

The CRA's choice to accept Belgium's oppressive colonial practices vis-à-vis Congo was due, in part, to the irony that, though he objected staunchly to the exaggerated violence of Léopold II's tactics, Morel was not opposed to colonialism (or slavery) in principle. Thus even though his efforts on behalf of Congo indeed established a potent tradition of resistance, it is not a tradition built on liberation ideology or Congolese autonomy but on the power of Westerners to undertake projects on behalf of Congolese. I point this out not to disparage Morel's legacy but because this represents an important moment in the history of activism and provides a potent lesson for those of us interested in forging new paradigms of advocacy. Without careful critical scrutiny, it is tempting to analyze the story of (heroic) Morel fighting (despotic) Léopold II within the facile yet popular Western construction of life—especially in Africa—as an epic, if one-dimensional, tale of good guys versus bad guys (alas, the short film "Kony 2012" comes to mind as a contemporary iteration of this trend). By contrast, to celebrate Morel's activist efforts from the perspective of popular history in Congo is to commend his introduction of mechanical images as vehicles of resistance while also recognizing the many ways in which his very approach was prescient to the ongoing Western tradition of self-congratulatory, and well-documented, actions taken *about* or *for* Congo rather than *with* or better yet *by* Congolese. It clearly would have been impossible for any Congolese group at the time to achieve the same results as the CRA, but this history nevertheless sets a pattern for a strain of activism that conflates fighting *against* domination (in this example, Belgium) with fighting *for* liberation (in this case, Congo).

Yet despite its limitations, this tradition of resistance remains extremely important and has continued to inspire many positive political, ideological, and cinematic actions from the West, including the production of films like *Boma-Tervuren*. *Boma-Tervuren* revisits history with the willingness to reveal certain unflattering truths about Belgium; through its content, cinematic language, and particularly its use of music, it also offers a sort of apology. This is clearly evident on a physical level when Dujardin orchestrates the excavation and reburial in Kinshasa—complete with traditional funeral—of the remains of the Congolese who died at the World's Fair in 1897. This gesture is one of penance and an effort to grapple with the ongoing implications of present-day Belgians in Congo's past. As critic Phillipe Simone points out:

> No one today has the right to doubt that colonization of the Congo was a nauseating story of civilized barbarism, a regime of terror that still sticks to our life as a cankerous, unhealthy miasma that is still being felt. Yet, many people prefer to turn the page, ignore Belgium's responsibilities in a willful act of forgetting, and deny again and again that the blood of the Congolese, which continues to shape their identity in so many ways, has its roots in Belgian soil. . . . *Boma-Tervuren* sets the record straight and brings an end to the practice of amnesia, insisting on the direct link between the "early days" of the colony and the present moment.[21]

Simone's analysis draws attention to another important social function of the film, namely that of reclaiming Belgian responsibility for Congo's past. From this vantage point, Dujardin's efforts to reposition contemporary Congolese in the larger historical narrative of their ancestors directly parallels his efforts to find his own place in the larger historical narrative of his predecessors, including the perpetrators of colonialism and the pioneers of resistance. His choice to undertake this exploration through film signifies on the dual function of the medium—historical and current—as a force of oppression and liberation.

What is perhaps most striking in Dujardin's stance is the thread of penance and atonement that weaves through the film. *Boma-Tervuren* lays bare the role of Belgium in dismembering Congo, and it also suggests that Belgium can play a part in the painstaking task of re-membering Congo. This suggestion is particularly audible in the musical score of the film, which begins and ends with Gregorio Allegri's "Miserere." The music and the text of this piece set the tone for the remainder of the soundtrack and, to some analyses, sum up its objective:

> Have mercy upon me, O God, after Thy great goodness/According to the multitude of Thy mercies do away mine offences/Wash me thoroughly from my wickedness: and cleanse me from my sin/For I acknowledge my faults: and my sin is ever before me.[22]

Even for viewers who do not understand the text or the context of this piece of music, the stark contrast between the timbre, harmonic, and melodic elements of this Gregorian chant and the grainy footage of colonial-era Congo situates the film immediately as one in which Europe is undeniably the penitent.

The remainder of the musical score takes its cues from this striking piece and relies primarily on Western instruments and European harmonic and melodic practices. Where indigenous African timbres are invoked, it is within the confines of a predominantly Western sonic palette that features a low synthesized drone spontaneously accompanied by splashes of eerie, percussive sounds. In short, the indigenous musical gestures function as exoticizing flavors, but they do not have their own structural integrity. The result is an underscore that interrogates the past by fluctuating between a transspatial, transhistorical soundscape and the extremely literal soundtrack of Belgian mourning.

Designating music as a vehicle of penance is no accident. The film overtly acknowledges the universal centrality of music in rites of mourning and healing, both Belgian and Congolese. In addition to the bookends of Allegri's "Miserere," which, for the sake of argument, I will call an indigenous European song, *Boma-Tervuren* also includes an indigenous African song during the collecting of earth and metaphoric ashes to bring back for burial in the homeland. At the cemetery in Kinshasa where the symbolic dead are being reburied surrounded by a crowd of mourners, a woman comes forward and offers a brief ululation, which gives way to the only traditional song in the film. Accompanied by a single percussive rattle, the gathered sing:

Que l'avion descende/qu'on nous enterre au pays/parce que ici en Belgique/nous avons été déshonorés/et traités comme des singes. (répète).
[trans.: Let the plane descend/so we can bury you in our own country/because here in Belgium/we have been dishonored/and treated like monkeys. (repeat)][23]

Musical and cultural scholars of Africa recognize the consistent pattern within funeral rites across the African continent (and arguably, globally), in which music is, without exception, central.[24] In most accounts, mourning is a somber celebration of a rite of passage, but according to Ngugi, "it is also a memory, a re-membering of the ancestors, an honoring of the heritage they have left to the living. It is a closure and an opening to a new relationship of being."[25]

For Dujardin, honoring the heritage his ancestors left him means grappling with their part in forcing 267 innocent Congolese to come to Belgium as zoological specimens, to say nothing of benefiting from the wealth plundered from Congo at the cost of ten million Congolese lives. Rather than make the popular claim that he personally did not participate in that history and is therefore exempt from responsibility, his film suggests that the heterobiography of Belgium must include ownership of the now-unpopular actions of generations past. And the role he casts for Belgians—indeed for Europe writ large—is self-reflection. Collectively the content, the cinematic language, and the musical critique in *Boma-Tervuren* intimate that the part Belgium can play in re-membering Congo is to reverse the critical lens and engage in self-scrutiny.

The sincerity with which Dujardin attempts to fulfill his own prescription could indeed be said to open a new relationship of being among many audiences at Yole!Africa. But if Belgium's role in re-membering Congo is self-reflection, this film does little—and rightly so—to suggest the role of Congolese in the project. Instead it leaves audiences with burning questions about a history that was previously entirely unknown to them. For example, toward the end of one lively post-screening discussion of *Boma-Tervuren* at Yole!Africa, a young man stood up and said, with evident passion, "I have seen in this film that there are still statues all over Belgium honoring King Léopold II, which, to me, is like Germany keeping statues of Hitler. If there were statues of Hitler in Germany, would Jews risk their lives to go there? What does it say about Belgians that they still honor their own Hitler? And what does it say about Congolese that we risk everything to get to Belgium?" This intervention was met with rowdy applause followed by a long silence. Clearly any attempt to respond to this question would be complicated at best. But, arguably, as important as any potential answer is the *act* of posing the question, particularly for people shaped by an educational system that enforces rote memorization with no critical inquiry.

According to Deleuze, "The political task of cinema is to contribute to the invention of a people, and the time-image is what enables this possibility, because it allows for linkages and relinkages among ideas."[26] Time and again, screening and discussing *Boma-Tervuren* triggers new linkages and relinkages among ideas, and even—indeed especially—when these linkages result in questions (more than answers) they contribute to the larger process of mental decolonization. At the same time, the assertion that the political task of cinema is to contribute to the invention of a people requires profound scrutiny in light of the role cinema played—and continues to play—in oppressing the people of Congo. *Boma-Tervuren* introduces the early history of this tradition under King Léopold II as well as the importance of locating contemporary representational practices in a deep understanding of the practices of the past. Understanding and seeing the continued relevance of the many subtexts of *Boma-Tervuren* triggers among many burgeoning cultural activists at Yole!Africa a burning desire to fill in more of the gaps left by official versions of history.

ACT II: BELGIUM

In 1908, which marked the beginning of Congo's formal colonization by Belgium, the Congo Free State became the Belgian Congo. With the power to rule, the power and technologies to document official history were passed from the hands of King Léopold II to the Belgian government. This was a complex era during which any gesture toward popular history by Congolese was strictly censored by Belgium. Thus the official record exclusively honors the proverbial hunter. To probe this history Yole!Africa screens Tristan Bourland's 1996 documentary *Matamata and Pilipili,* which revives the story of the Belgian missionary and film fanatic Albert Van Haelst and with it his work in Congo during the 1950s on roughly twenty episodes of a comic series. The series, bearing the same title, features two Congolese buffoon characters often equated with Laurel and Hardy (mostly because one is tall and thin and the other short and rotund) and was beloved by Belgian and Congolese during its heyday.

The humor in the *Matamata and Pilipili* series was consistent with the slapstick influences of the time. Even today the antics of the two incite genuine laughter as, for example, in their illiteracy they go to great lengths to hide from the police in the very chest labeled for delivery to the head commissioner, or when, in an effort to combat illiteracy, Pilipili decides to read the newspaper while pushing his son's stroller through town, without noticing that, when he stopped to scrutinize an unfamiliar word, his son crept out of the stroller and a curious white child took his place. It is nearly impossible not to chuckle at the astonished vexation of his wife when, unbeknownst to Pilipili, he returns with an angelic Belgian boy in lederhosen.

But in addition to the surface innocence of the humor, the jokes in the *Matamata and Pilipili* series are based on the common derogatory conceptions of Congolese as lazy, uncouth, ignorant, and of course inherently inferior to Belgians. The series was certainly not worse than other films of its era, but even as they are grudgingly swept up in the comedy, many young people at Yole!Africa are chagrined that the series was so popular in its time. "Why?" they frequently demand, "would Congolese be so pleased to see disparaging images of themselves?" The answer is simple: they were starved to see *any* images of themselves. This realization sparks in many students of popular history a curiosity about the politics of film production and distribution in the colonial era. Their motivation to study this period is often their own discomfort when they notice that, despite the evident aesthetic differences of the era, the buffoonery of Congolese in foreign representations has not in fact diminished; nor has the delight with which people, from Congo and the West, consume degrading images of Africans in the name of entertainment (or uplift).

Bourland's documentary sheds light on some important aspects of this dynamic by pointing out the complex interweaving of colonialism, Catholicism, and the history of cinema in Congo. But in order to fully grasp the nuance and the stakes of this history, it is important to revisit its origins. Any student of African cinema will point to the distinct national agendas that formed different approaches to film production and dissemination in African colonies. What was, for the British, a project of civilizing and moralizing, was, for the French, a project of enculturation, and for the Portuguese a project of commercialism and pornography.[27] For the Belgians, the initial objectives of cinema in Congo were mixed: film was a tool through which to disseminate colonial and religious propaganda (in both Congo and Belgium), civilize savage natives, and thereby consolidate psychological and behavioral control over the colony.

The intricate political engagement with film in Congo is evident both in the material evolution of facilities of production and dissemination and in the ever stricter laws of censorship. By 1909, commercial cinema houses were established in Boma (which was the capital from 1886 to 1920) and Léopoldville and plans to erect further theaters were in the works.[28] These movie houses were designed for white Western patrons, but in the early years Congolese exclusion was not absolute. In addition to the permanent cinema houses, the Belgian government and the Catholic Church supported numerous mobile cinema units designed to introduce Congolese audiences to moving pictures and to the glories of Belgium and of God. An excerpt from *La Tribune Congolaise et la Gazette West Africaine* published in Anvers, Belgium, in December 1908 frames this mission by claiming that, despite what were considered King Léopold II's "generous investments" in the Congo Free State, "Something was lacking from our black brothers that prevented them from being truly Belgian. Ignorance of cinema!" the conclusion: "They shall learn it."[29] This statement exposes, among other things, the underlying ideological relationship between Belgium, Congo, and cinema as one in which information flows unidirectionally and is determined exclusively by Europe.

As the Belgian government and Catholic Church continued to invest in cinema in Congo, censorship and control of image became matters of urgent preoccupation for both entities. In 1917, the existence of well-equipped theaters that allowed Congolese spectators prompted the governor general to publish an ordinance regulating film projection in Congo. In the preface to the ordinance he suggests that "the character of certain films is dangerous to public order in a country whose population is strongly susceptible to falling under the influence of spectacles we might present."[30] This ordinance became the foundation for creating the official regional censorship commissions as well as stricter laws regulating film projection in Congo.

Originally, the stated mission of the censorship commissions was to limit Congolese access to those films proven to promote (Belgian) moral values, (European) education, (Christian) religious beliefs, and (civilized) hygiene. Although the Belgian government decided not to suppress Congolese access to films entirely, there was strict and unanimous recognition of the importance of censoring any film or scene with even the slightest reference to white vulnerability. This included any scene in which a white character was on the losing end of a debate or competition (to say nothing of a fight), as well as any scene depicting scantily clad or affectionate white women. For example, in response to the enthusiastic reception of Charlie Chaplin films among Congolese, the censorship committee published a brochure indicating that, even in the context of comedy, Blacks should never be exposed to images depicting whites being kicked, or falling down. Furthermore, they added, "Blacks here call Charlie Chaplin 'Charlot Kawayawaya,' which means 'clown [lit. vagabond].' No White should ever be the clown of a Black, not even on the big screen."[31] Instead, the censorship committee insisted,

We must program for them a judiciously chosen set of films about King Albert, the Queen, the princes, the principal monuments of Belgium, a parade of troops, views taken on the 1st of July (colonial day), the launching of boats, scenes of aviation or of some European studies, and other images that support White superiority. To facilitate understanding, . . . a "specially trained" Black clerk should briefly explain the various sets of images in simple terms understandable by all the Black spectators. All other films can only harm the prestige of Europeans and in Congo; the prestige is already tottering.[32]

This statement exposes not only the core objectives of Belgium's colonial film policies in Congo, but also the intentionality with which the Belgian government used film as a tool in its regime.

However, even these restrictions were not exercised strictly enough for some critics. In response to a handful of "educational yet comic" Belgian films, which included a laughable Belgian "fool" character, Anton-Johan Wouter Harloff published a brochure, "L'influence pernicieuse du cinema sur les peuples d'Orient" (The Pernicious Influence of Cinema on Oriental Peoples), which was printed in Aras, France, in 1934, stating:

One of the impediments to the progress of colonization, which ought to be fought with the cooperation of the colonial governments, is the negative influence exerted by cinema. It is not only an evil, but a real social danger for the colonies. Indeed, cinema has deplorably undermined the respect for the West, on which rests the foundation of civilization in the colonies.[33]

The Belgian government took this admonishment seriously, and on May 1, 1936, the censorship commission published regulations significantly tightening restrictions on Congolese access to films—moral, educational, or otherwise. In 1945 this regulation became a legislative ordinance prohibiting, a priori, Congolese spectatorship of films unless approved directly by the controlling commission. This restructured commission, headquartered in Brussels with two branches in Congo (in Léopoldville and in Elizabethville), was granted power equivalent to that of the judicial police. The commission categorically refused any film that included scenes of questionable moral value, public disorder, fights, brawls, death, or intimacy. (This commission also marked the beginning of the ongoing dynamic in which authority over issues of Congolese cinema production, dissemination, or content is located in Europe.) As censorship grew ever stricter, public movie houses became completely segregated, with separate establishments, films, and practices for Africans and Europeans that were extreme enough in their implementation to be referred to later as cinema apartheid.

The expanding Nazi occupation of Europe was a significant factor in a number of decisions made by the commission, which was categorically opposed to any Congolese being exposed to the idea of Belgian defeat or weakness in any form. This led to strict censorship of a number of films. For example, in the early 1950s the committee cut out two scenes from MGM's *The Siegfried Follies*: one in which two white women quarrel with one another, and the second in which one of them sings a love song. The reason cited for removing the latter scenes was the limited intelligence of Congolese audiences, who might mistakenly assume the love song was dedicated to the lone Black man sitting obscured in the back of the bar and therefore suffer the illusion that love between whites and Blacks was possible.

In addition to leading to extreme cultural segregation, the justifications offered by the censorship committees regarding the intellectual capacity of Africans to consume film also contributed to the origins of certain stylistic elements that have come, rather alarmingly, to be associated with "African cinema." For instance, the oft-cited natural predilection for slow-moving films might indeed be a function of indigenous precolonial African modes of storytelling, as certain scholars have claimed, but it might also have more insidious roots. It is hard to imagine that the reports and subsequent production strategies of this formative era in the development of cinema did not have lasting aesthetic effects. Take, for instance, the investigative report conducted to determine suitable films for Congolese and published in 1944 by Willy Pitzele, who was the first proprietor of a cinema house for Congolese, which stated that "Congolese fail to follow the plot of films, the sequence of images being 'too fast for their understanding.' Congolese prefer short comic films over films of half an hour; they should be similar to those films suitable for European youth: action movies with simplistic scenarios."[34] Like others of its ilk, this report reflects the commonly held colonial conviction that, regarding intelligence and attention span, Congolese, like all Africans, are essentially overgrown, slow children. Such reports served as the basis for production and distribution tactics in the Belgian Congo and demonstrate (in retrospect) that the dominant cinematic aesthetic practices are built on the "scientifically proven" belief in the inherent inferiority of Congolese.

Matamata and Pilipili was, of course, shaped by these larger forces regulating Congolese cinema, yet at the same time the series also contributed in turn to the evolving stylistic practices and aesthetics that represent Congo. *Matamata and Pilipili* was unique in its prominent inclusion of Congolese actors; prior to this series Congolese were featured either in anthropological studies of primitive peoples or as incidental subservient characters in films glorifying whites.

As such, these short films were beloved by Congolese and met a real need among local audiences to see people to whom they could relate on the big screen. But at what cost? *Matamata and Pilipili* had the dual effect of humanizing Congolese to a certain extent while also, through the veneer of humor, masking and thereby further entrenching extremely racist beliefs and practices.

Bourland's documentary exposes the lasting effects of this series to be both amusing and deeply disturbing. In making this documentary not only did he restore the historic film reels made by Van Haelst in the 1950s, he also projected them for contemporary audiences in Belgium—including a group of former colonial officers and a group of Congolese—and documented their reactions. There was, for both audiences, general amusement over the films as well as significant nostalgia, which often surprises contemporary audiences. Indeed, during screenings of Bourland's documentary, audiences at Yole!Africa find themselves too laughing inadvertently at the humorous antics of the original series, but there is no such levity when it comes to discussing the filmed responses of their contemporaries. In passionate terms, the youths rail against the blatant racism, which, though clearly outdated, still stings in its undeniable similarity to their own present-day experiences (for example, at one point a matron of the church reminisces: "He [Van Haelst] always said the Blacks were born actors. They could sit around all day holding palavers no problem. But as for doing something good, that was another kettle of fish").[35] At the same time, the comments delivered by the Congolese in the film provide a frustrating but informative example of the insidiousness of mental colonization, which is also familiar (in response to an episode featuring Matamata very drunk, one Congolese gentleman in the audiences says, "getting drunk is not good . . . to such an extent that when my cousin came and told us (we were ten at the time) that they found a drunken White man, we couldn't believe it—we thought only Matamata could get drunk").[36]

The discomfort of witnessing such deeply ingrained behaviors of externalized and internalized racism also serves, for many young people, as a window through which they begin to feel implicated in an important historic period in the development of their country. As the medium through which this realization comes is film, there is often significant criticism of the role of film in perpetuating the very problems they continue to face. The most astute youth note, with mounting anger, that the evolution of film production in and about Congo mirrors the evolution of justifications of racism, first in the name of civilization and later in the name of humor. Equally disturbing is the flourishing legacy of mental colonization that conditioned Congolese not only to accept—and later perpetuate—such representations of themselves but to join in the laughter at their own expense.

These lessons, though bitter, are a valuable reminder for aspiring artists and cultural activists that during the colonial era film was a tool, and that, even when well disguised as entertainment or education, it was a potent means of domination and control. That the control exerted through film was both behavioral and psychological points to the direct connection between cinema and mental colonization in Congo (and beyond). What is often most deeply unsettling for audiences of Congolese youth is the undeniable role of the church in fostering racism and oppression. Prior to watching this film, many perceive the forces of religion, politics, and cinema as separate, but when they come to recognize the cooperative relationship between the church, colonial government, and cinema as a propaganda machine, emotions often run high. As one student articulated in a state of semishock, "all of colonialism was a lie, everything I've ever been told—about myself, about my family, about my history—all of it was a lie. And to think they are still laughing at us because we didn't know. . . ."

ACT III: LUMUMBA

It is no small task to summarize the events surrounding independence in Congo. According to official history, Belgium granted Congo its independence on June 30, 1960. According to popular history, Congo won its independence on that date. Regardless of disagreements over the agency behind this event, all accounts agree that Patrice Emery Lumumba was the first prime minister of the newly renamed Republic of the Congo and that he was assassinated on January 17, 1961, only three months after his official inauguration in September. Not surprisingly, the reasons given for his assassination differ dramatically. According to Belgium and other Western nations, Lumumba was a radical extremist who was assassinated as a result of ethnic fighting that proved both the inherent savagery of Congolese and the continued need for Belgian rule. From a popular Congolese perspective, Lumumba was an unparalleled hero who was willing to sacrifice his life in the fight to rid Congo—and Africa—of foreign domination in *all* its forms and who was consequently killed by orders from Belgium, the United States, and Great Britain, which wanted to maintain control over Congo's resources, including the uranium that was used in the atom bombs dropped on Hiroshima and Nagasaki.

In the context of this fraught history, it is as enlightening to interrogate the means and motivations of telling these conflicting stories as it is to search for absolute Truth. There is, of course, ample documentation substantiating the Belgian version of events, but in the story of Patrice Lumumba the silences often yield the greatest insights. In the introduction to his book *The Assassination of Lumumba*, Belgian historian Ludo De Witte makes this point with force:

Few events in recent history have been the target of such a ferocious campaign of disinformation as the war waged by the Belgian establishment against the first Congolese government of Patrice Lumumba. . . . This dark episode was suppressed for almost forty years, hidden from the history books. For fear of losing prestige, funding and other facilities, nobody has dared undertake a serious analysis and describe the Congo crisis as it really happened. No politician has taken the initiative of subjecting Belgium's Foreign Ministry archives to careful scrutiny, or requested a debate or parliamentary inquiry on the subject. On the contrary, once Lumumba's government was ousted, an attempt was made to deprive the Africans of the true story of his overthrow: not only had Lumumba been physically eliminated, his life and work were not to become a source of inspiration for the peoples of Africa either. His vision of creating a unified nation state and an economy serving the needs of the people were to be wiped out. In an attempt to prevent another Lumumba ever appearing again, his ideas and his struggle against colonial and neo-colonial domination had to be purged from collective memory.[37]

The remainder of De Witte's text provides detailed historic research irrefutably proving the involvement of Belgium in Lumumba's assassination. Although the impact of this book was significant and even forced the Belgian foreign minister, Louis Michel, to issue an official apology from Belgium to Congo in April 2002, this text has not been integrated into the Congolese history curriculum; nor is it readily available in Congo. Thus even though this research contributes substantially to efforts to construct a popular history around the story of Lumumba, it is not yet a popular history that actively reaches many Congolese youth.

Yet for many young activists, learning about Lumumba's life and legacy is a pivotal moment that forces them to grapple with important questions, including the differences between and consequences of engagement versus activism versus militantism. For more radical organizations such as Yole!Africa, Lumumba's ideology of autonomy, unity, and local value is fundamental to their vision of sociopolitical strategies in Congo. But Lumumbist movements must, by definition, actively include youth, which is particularly challenging since Lumumba's story has been so thoroughly misrepresented in official curricula and purged from collective memory to the extent that many young people in Congo have never heard of him and the majority who have believe he was a truculent and impulsive leader with little legacy other than his record of inflammatory speeches and ethnic turmoil.

That is the official story of Lumumba as told to Congolese students—when it is told at all. It is not surprising then that encountering an alternative version of this particular history is, for many young Congolese, both shocking and transformative. At the same time, introducing Lumumba's side of the story has the potential to incite reactionary anger as much as inspiration. To navigate this precarious balance, Yole!Africa approaches the story of Lumumba and of Congo's independence as an opportunity for students to become active in re-membering their own history. One of the most potent texts in this process is Raoul Peck's 1990 creative documentary *Lumumba: La mort du prophète* (The Death of the Prophet), which Yole!Africa screens regularly. This film provides important factual information about Lumumba's life and death that is omitted from the Congolese school curriculum, while also advancing a cinematic strategy that serves as a metaphor to the selective narration and erasure that define Lumumba's life, assassination, and legacy. *La mort du prophète* has a distinct aesthetic that juxtaposes disparate styles and footage sources, including ambient shots of Brussels in 1990, abstract portraits of people seemingly unrelated to Lumumba's story, archival video footage and stills, and abstruse experiments with light and void. This visual language brings obvious attention to the medium of film itself as the means of transmission of Lumumba's story and invites viewers to reflect on the process and meaning of visual technologies in narrating history.

La mort du prophète also advances narrative strategies that prioritize popular memory over official versions of history and foreground culturally relevant transgenerational practices of transmitting oral history that stand in stark contrast to official means of documenting the past. Through a series of vignettes that begin "*ma mère raconte . . .*" (my mother told me . . .), the film pieces together the story of Congo as Peck recalls hearing his mother tell it, from King Léopold's rule of the Congo Free State and establishment of the Force Publique, to the brutal impact of colonialism and missionaries, the history of forced labor, the deadly laying of the railway, and the overall bloodshed of the conquering of the Congo. The language of these stories is reminiscent of the fanciful prose of folktales or fables, but, even if it is only human to want to dismiss the horrors of Congo's history as fictional, Mother's stories are corroborated by historic images and contemporary interviews, leaving the viewer no choice but to accept the veracity of her gruesome tales.

By contrast, *La mort du prophète* casts suspicion on the ostensible neutrality of Western journalism and demonstrates the power of film not only to accurately document reality but also to selectively construct truth. Peck does this through the very techniques said to ensure narrative objectivity, such as interviews with expert witnesses. For example, after introducing the content and approach of the film, there is an edited sequence of interviews conducted with prominent international figures who participated in Congo's independence and the journalists who represented it in text and image. This three-minute sequence begins with a confident statement by Louis Willems, who was active in Belgium's Belga News Agency in 1960, asserting that "Belgium is a very advanced democratic country with regards to open information and public opinion." Willems's claim to transparency is followed immediately by an admission from Jacques Brassinne, who was Belgian ambassador in Léopoldville in 1960, acknowledging "all the major press agencies originate in the West, therefore they're tendentious without realizing it." The doubt this comment casts on the objectivity of the Belgian press is further inflamed by Pierre Devos's reflection on his experience as an international reporter in Congo in 1960: "Belgian journals supported Belgium's presence in Africa . . . [as a journalist] you cannot support somebody who advocates Belgium's departure from the colony." And as proof, the sequence concludes with the testimony of Jean Van Leerde, a Belgian pacifist and friend to Lumumba who was physically present in Congo throughout the independence period, who confirms, "the press completely misrepresented what happened at the time . . . yet it's true, this image will always remain."[38]

Through the words and moving images of reliable Belgian figures, Peck makes the point that Belgium's own agenda rather than the quest for factual information was at the root of its reporting strategies about Congo. This sequence exposes in Belgian representations the very subjectivity of which they accuse Congolese and, in destabilizing the privilege of journalistic text as harbinger of Truth, confirms that Belgium's account of independence in Congo is in fact a fictitious rather than official history. The reliability of official history deteriorates further when the film later reveals that the stories Peck's mother tells are based on classified information that was available to her through her position as secretary to the mayor of Léopoldville (later renamed Kinshasa). That the information Mother delivers through methods reserved for popular histories ultimately proves more factual than that provided by official channels creates a tension between modes of storytelling and perceptions of truth through which Peck actively advocates alternative narrative strategies. This sequence—indeed the entire film—places the destabilized notion of representational objectivity in direct dialogue with orality and confirms that the truth surrounding Congo's independence and the assassination of Lumumba is audible in unexpected ways.

Although the privilege *La mort du prophète* gives to oral communication is a direct challenge to traditional Western approaches to history and education, it is deeply familiar to Congolese youth and has led some particularly astute viewers at Yole!Africa to scrutinize not only the spoken soundscape of the film but also the other sonic elements, especially music. From a local perspective, music plays a prominent role in guarding popular histories and is inseparable from any other component of orality. The assumption is thus that the music in this film, though sparse, is as central to the film's agenda as the narrative or visual choices and must, on analysis, provide greater insight into the story it tells about this nebulous moment in Congo's history.

The first music audible in *La mort du prophète* is the immensely popular Congolese song "Independence Cha Cha," which describes the roundtable talks that took place in Brussels in January 1960 during which the date was set for Congolese independence. Musically this song incorporates instruments and rhythms from the African diaspora (particularly Cuba in this case) and reflects the popularity of transnational musical influences that were at the time linking the continent to the growing Black Pride movement through circular patterns of physical and cultural migration.[39] The lyrics reflect the hope and buoyant optimism that characterized the era of independence, when, en masse, people were convinced of a better and brighter future with a little hard work. The refrain also states, in no uncertain terms, that the agency behind Congo's independence movement was entirely Congolese:

Indépendence cha-cha tozui e	Independence cha-cha, we've won it
Oh! Kimpuanza cha-cha tubakidi	Oh! Independence cha-cha, we've achieved it
Oh! Table Ronde cha-cha ba gagné o	Oh! The roundtable cha-cha, we've pulled it off
Oh! Dipanda cha-cha tozui e.	Oh! Independence cha-cha, we've won it

This song was most famously performed (and in most accounts also written) by Joseph Kabassale Tshamala, popularly known as Grand Kallé and considered the father of contemporary Congolese music, and his band L'African Jazz. The significance of this song extended well beyond Congo. Indeed, "Independence Cha Cha" is not only known as the independence anthem of the Nationalist Movement of Congo but, with the celebration of independence in sixteen other African countries in 1960 (Benin, Burkina Faso, Cameroon, Central African Republic, Chad, Congo Republic, Cote d'Ivoire, Gabon, Madagascar, Mali, Mauritania, Niger, Nigeria, Senegal, Somalia, and Togo), became the independence anthem of Africa.

Although the optimism of the independence era has faded over the generations since 1960, the popularity of "Independence Cha-Cha" has not. Thus it is significant to Congolese viewers of all ages that the images accompanying this song in *La mort du prophète* are of the museum at Tervuren in Belgium, which houses the world's largest collection of Congolese artifacts. The first iteration of this song accompanies a scene that starts with the camera slowly panning over specimens dating back to Léopold II's ownership of Congo, as an invisible narrator muses:

> What is there left to say about a 30-year old murder? There are memories that are better forgotten. For the executioner as well as for the victim. And then, the assassin is often not who we thought. There are many ways of killing someone.[40]

In lieu of a verbal answer to this puzzle, Peck allows the music to make the point: when the full band hits the first musical break of "Independence Cha Cha" the film cuts, in rhythm, to the gaping eternally silenced roar of a hippopotamus, frozen forever in its ferocity; then to a lion preserved midbreath in transplanted African grasses; and then to pelicans midwing in a bucolic panorama, their flight cut short by the awkward barrier of the ceiling. The next musical hit cuts to a low-angle shot of an lifesize sculpture depicting an African man whose features are distorted (either by a failed artistic rendering of anger or by a visual manifestation of the racism that likens Africans to primates) and whose powerful raised fist grips a large stone. With the final musical hit of this sequence inside the museum, the camera lands on the bare breasts and face of the young woman whose pleading supplicant effort to escape her savage tormentor forms the other half of the famed sculpture.

Clearly, "Independence Cha Cha" is incongruous, lyrically and musically, with the images and history of Tervuren. The hopefulness of the era's soundtrack renders the images of its failure all the more poignant and disturbing; the perfect synchronicity of the contagious dancelike quality of the music with the static images of exoticism and horror makes of this buoyant song an agitating rather than celebratory factor. Cinematographically, the result is startling dissonance, a deep disillusionment that is both visible and audible. Psychologically the effect of "Independence Cha Cha" in this scene is the inverse of the musical scoring in *Boma-Tervuren*, namely the auditory imposition of Congo on the physical space of Belgium (as opposed to the Allegri "Miserere" behind scenes of Congo). Overlaying a Congolese soundtrack on the vaults of Tervuren speaks to the film's theme of offering a Congolese critique of Belgian actions, yet simultaneously it also riffs on transnationalism vis-à-vis Belgium (vs. the Black Atlantic world) in a particularly disturbing key. Whereas the Cuban influence in Congolese music is a source of pride, dignity, and affirmation, this placement of "Independence Cha Cha" evokes from the attentive spectator a sober acknowledgment of the undeniable transnational flows of experience via Belgium that continue to mediate Congolese existence.

FIGURE 2.3 *La mort du prophète* Still Sequence.

The musical critique of the relationship between Belgium and Congo continues in a later sequence, represented in Figure 2.3, that challenges notions of civilization and savagery in the story of Lumumba. After outlining the key events that led to Lumumba's assassination—including his arrest while trying to cross into Kinsangani, Mobutu's refusal to protect him, and his transport by air, during which he was tortured by members of the Force Publique—*La mort du prophète* incorporates a montage of historical images (center frame of Fig. 2.3) depicting Lumumba's attempt to escape house arrest and rejoin his supporters in the north as the invisible narrator forewarns the viewer that Lumumba's effort will be thwarted when Mobutu's soldiers deliver Lumumba into the hands of his assassins. The final image in this sequence shows Mobutu's fleet of automobiles being deployed to arrest Lumumba. Behind this final image the soundtrack includes a smattering of civilized applause that begins well before the film cuts to a lavish black-tie dinner hosted in an ornate palace in Brussels (right frame of Fig. 2.3). The practice of introducing the sound of an impending cut before the image itself is, of course, standard practice in documentary film editing, but critical scrutiny of this scene raises questions about the intended recipient of the applause: the pianist and baritone taking the stage amidst the standard sounds of orchestral tuning, or Mobutu's soldiers, who secured Belgium's neocolonial dominance over the wealth of the Congo. This moment passes quickly; indeed it would pass unnoticed except for the music that retrospectively—but insistently—ties it to what follows.

The subsequent scene begins with a medium shot of snow falling as an anonymous member of Peck's crew films in the streets of Brussels, and the invisible narrator speaks: "The Holocaust was not a matter of economics. That made everything much clearer. The old, civilized Europe was killing, meticulously, its own elite. For each death, the sadness remains the same."[41]

Behind these words, an orchestra plays a sustained note, which was initiated when the musicians came on stage in the palace scene and which, in deference to the images and the narrator's voice, became nearly inaudible. When the narrator finishes, the sound crescendos into Leporello's early aria from Act One of Mozart's opera *Don Giovanni*.

There is no way of knowing for certain whether this was in fact the aria delivered at the palace in Brussels depicted in the preceding scene, but regardless, Peck's choice of this particular musical excerpt is an ironic musical critique of the "meticulous civilization" for which Europe prides itself. In its original context, this aria is set outside the palace of Don Giovanni, who is renowned as a scandalous womanizer. When he recognizes Donna Elvira (a woman he recently seduced and then spurned) as the woman he is flirting with, he shoves his servant, Leporello, between himself and the unsuspecting woman, ordering his servant to offer an excuse as he hurries away. As Leporello attempts to console Donna Elvira, he unrolls a list of Don Giovanni's conquests, rattling off their number and their countries of origin: 640 in Italy, 231 in Germany, 100 in France, 91 in Turkey, and 1,003 in Spain.

Read critically, this aria ties together the preceding images and adds a subtext to the docile white-gloved applause at another triumph of the great philanderer whose list of conquests spans the globe. It is significant that this aria is generally considered comic, which does not speak favorably about "civilized" opinion of the consumption and disposal of women—or perhaps any beings perceived as inferior by Western powers—for the pleasure and benefit of a hero. Indeed, whether the elite of Belgium were applauding Don Giovanni or Mobutu is of little import. What matters is that, from a Congolese perspective, appreciation of either reflects savagery, not civilization.

By calling European civilization into question, this musical moment also reinforces Peck's larger project of aligning the history of massacres in Congo with globally accepted atrocities. The narrator's rumination on the European practice of meticulously killing its own elite is a central theme of the film that recurs frequently, for example in a shot (left frame of Fig. 2.3) from the front of a train as it moves along a tree-lined railway covered in snow while the narrator contemplates:

Why do these images keep returning to my mind? What have they to do with Patrice Lumumba? With the millions dead, with the uranium of the Congo, with an old greedy king? Is the Holocaust the only unit of measure for the human race? Imagine that there is no heaven, no hell, that there is no explanation for all that. And if there had been no uranium in Katanga to build the bomb for Hiroshima?

This, and other moments, form a sequence in the film that aligns popular histories across time and space and effectively draws on the established acceptance of the Holocaust and other officially recognized atrocities that cannot be erased, to provoke collective engagement with the story of Congo and Lumumba.

The need to validate Congo's story in terms of globally accepted atrocities is particularly urgent because of the absence of images documenting the most critical moments. *La mort du prophète* makes this point unequivocally. It includes a seventy-two-second excerpt of a British newscast reporting (with the drama of a sportscast) the final capture of Lumumba before his death, and then cuts to a medium verité shot of people descending a staircase at the Brussels airport, as the narrator reveals:

> The British Movietone News asked $3,000 a minute for this footage. One gets used to it. Everything passes, the images remain. A Congolese earns $150 a year. Memories of a murder are expensive.[42]

This factual statement of the influence of the hegemonic practices of capitalism on mediating history highlights the challenges of substantiating popular memory in dominant terms. The categorical impossibility of the average Congolese accessing these images puts Mother's oral stories in sharp relief. These two competing modes of guarding the past lend credence to revolutionary theories foregrounding the perpetual and universal fight for popular liberation against imperial domination in any form or disguise.[43]

But fighting for popular liberation is particularly challenging in an environment from which the history and ideology of the most powerful potential role model have been systematically erased. Indeed, for youth in the east of Congo, watching *La mort du prophète* is their first exposure to some of Lumumba's greatest achievements, including the speech he delivered at the official announcement of Congo's independence. The film includes an excerpt from the audio recording of this speech, in which he says

> We have known sarcasm, insults, we have endured beatings, morning, noon and night because we were negroes. Who will forget that a Black was always addressed in the familiar (tu) form, certainly not as a friend, but because the respectful form of address (vous) was reserved for the Whites only?[44]

Exposure to even this fragment of Lumumba's controversial speech motivates many students at Yole!Africa to investigate the context in which he dared deliver these words to an audience that included powerful Belgians. What they discover is that, despite having agreed to deliver a politically tame address following King Baudouin II's officially transferral of governance into Congolese hands, Lumumba was so enraged by the young king's patronizing celebration of the benevolence of Belgium and its wise decision to grant Congolese independence that he scribbled an alternate speech on the back of a scrap of paper. Immediately following the brief excerpt quoted in *La mort du prophète,* Lumumba continued:

> We have seen our lands despoiled under the terms of what was supposedly the law of the land but which only recognized the right of the strongest. We have seen that this law was quite different for a White than for a Black: accommodating for the former, cruel and inhuman for the latter. We have seen the terrible suffering of those banished to remote regions because of their political opinions or religious beliefs; exiled within their own country, their fate was truly worse than death itself. . . . And, finally, who can forget the volleys of gunfire in which so many of our brothers perished, the cells where the authorities threw those who would not submit to a rule where justice meant oppression and exploitation.

After this he went on to explain that Congo's independence was not in fact a gift from Belgium as Baudouin claimed, but an agreement between two equal nations. Eventually, he concluded with the words, "No Congolese worthy of the name can ever forget that it is by struggle that we have won [our independence], a struggle waged each and every day, a passionate idealistic struggle, a struggle in which no effort, privation, suffering, or drop of our blood was spared."

For many students at Yole!Africa, exposure to this speech is a pivotal experience, paralleling De Witte's historic analysis that

> Lumumba has spoken in a language the Congolese thought impossible in the presence of a European, and those few moments of truth feel like a reward for eighty years of domination. For the first time in the history of the country, a Congolese has addressed the nation and set the stage for the reconstruction of Congolese history. By this one act, Lumumba has reinforced the Congolese people's sense of dignity and self-confidence.[45]

The dignity and confidence of many Congolese youth are indeed reinforced by discovering the potent legacy and words of their first national hero. For, when they uncover transcripts of this speech, they are also inevitably exposed to accounts of history that describe Lumumba as an unparalleled hero of the people, who was courageous, discerning, and inspirational. They learn of his sensational rise to popularity, his unfailing confidence that true autonomy precludes neocolonial relationships (and his willingness to say as much to Western leaders). They learn of the passion with which Congolese united in their support of his policies, and of the promise he represented to the African continent when he advocated—and gave his life for—African control over African resources as a prerequisite to independence or development.

But these discoveries also spark in many young people burning questions about their previous ignorance of Lumumba's side of the story. Peck offers one explanation of this phenomenon when, over a black screen that precedes the audio excerpt from Lumumba's famous speech, the narrator says: "The images have been lost. The voice still remains."[46] Peck's choice to include the audio recording and to leave the screen black highlights the fact that all known images of this triumphant moment in which a Congolese gained the proverbial upper hand over Belgium have been destroyed. This is part of what De Witte refers to as the ferocious campaign to eliminate the life and work of Lumumba so as to prevent his becoming a source of inspiration. But as savage as the destruction of this historical record is, it is a comparatively benign metaphor for the actual disposal of Lumumba's body, which, instead of being buried or honored in any way, was dissolved in hydrochloric acid so that, excepting the few teeth his assassins saved as trophies, no trace of his physical remains would ever be found. The act of destroying Lumumba's physical remains was among the most potent signals in the history of colonialism that liberation ideology will not be tolerated by dominant forces; it was also a threat that aimed to permanently extinguish the collective impulse toward activism in Congo.

This is why re-membering Lumumba's story is so radical; it is not only a task of piecing the legacy of a popular hero back together (in a disturbingly literal sense) but also a vital step toward reviving the culture of activism. The magnitude of this is not lost on youth whose daily lives continue to be defined by endless cycles of violence and unrest that are the aftermath of this history. But it is through discussions and critiques of films like *La mort du prophète* that this realization shifts from principle to practice. It is by deconstructing Peck's experimental visual language and his pointed use of music that many young people at Yole!Africa begin to recognize, on an experiential level, the power of storytelling as an act of resistance. And because the very process of engaging in this genre of debate cultivates the selfsame skills of critical thought that were historically forbidden for fear they would empower Congolese, discussions of this nature are not merely intellectual exercises; in themselves, they constitute participation in the practice of dissent. It is at this intersection of personal stakes, critical reflection, and the desire to take action that students begin to see cultural products like films and music as potent—and accessible—channels of activist work that potentially allow every one of them to contribute not only to re-membering the past but to repositioning themselves as agents of change in the present.

This is, of course, easier said than done and, in addition to enthusiasm and critical understanding, requires young people to develop concrete strategies for merging art and activism. In this too, *La mort du prophète* provides a valuable example. One ingredient that often surfaces in postscreening debates as a guiding principle of radical filmmaking is the distinct variety of reflexivity in this film, which foregrounds the value of self-reflection, self-interrogation, and self-articulation in activist practices. This reflexivity is evident in the personal narrative that weaves through the film and informs the viewer of Peck's own experience of grappling with the official versus popular versions of history he learned when, as a child, his family was relocated from Haiti to Congo as part of the international group of middle-class Black professionals who were brought to facilitate the transition to independence. Peck's acknowledgment that, for him, the stakes of retelling Lumumba's story are equally tied to his participation in global resistance movements and to his own personal biography opens, for young viewers, the possibility of a parallel realization, namely that history is personal, that resistance is not an abstract or universal concept but a series of choices made from a point in space and time, and by extension that their own positions in space and time are as valid as any to be the foundation of transformative cultural activism. (The extent to which certain students incorporate this understanding into their art is evident in many of the music videos in the Art on the FrontLine series discussed briefly in Chapter Three.)

This realization, though empowering, also draws attention to the dire importance of fully knowing one's position in space and time as a prerequisite to developing strategies of action. Peck's own experience of being banned by the secret service from entering Congo (then Zaire) during the making of *La mort du prophète* is a salient example of the physical and material circumstances surrounding cultural activism. He chose to make of his extended exile in the Brussels airport an aesthetic language that serves as a reminder that the fear, stringent control, and severe restrictions on film production that the Belgian government initiated during the colonial era were still central to Congo's relationship with cinema in 1990. The very choice to make a film about Lumumba is an effort to reverse the momentum of Congo's relationship with cinema, which traces back to the strict prohibition against training Congolese film technicians in the colonial era and led to the collapse of the culture of cinema in Congo with the official withdrawal of Belgium in 1960. In making *La mort du prophète* Peck aligns himself with the few Congolese perseverant enough to pursue careers as filmmakers in the early years of independence, all of whom were forced to move abroad and only surreptitiously film in Congo when they occasionally returned for what the government took for family visits, and who, even then, faced severe restrictions.

These were some of the conditions that defined Peck's position in space and time during the making of *La mort du prophète*. His awareness of them did not in any way exempt his being restricted by them. Instead he chose to use these restrictions as the foundation of his narrative structure, which attests to the force of creative expression as a mode of activism and is a reminder—or perhaps a warning—that effective activism is best based on realistic rather than idealistic or imagined analyses of one's environment and abilities. And here the logic comes full circle: the attempt to develop a concrete strategy of cultural activism leads directly back to the need to actively study history so as to understand one's position in space and time. In light of this, for the most militant artists working toward a new aesthetic of resistance in contemporary Congo, the study of history does not end with re-membering the life and death of Patrice Lumumba; it also includes investigating what followed.

ACT IV: MOBUTU

From the perspective of cultural activism, Congo's post-independence history contributes directly to many of the challenges the country's current artists face. The period following the official announcement of independence in Congo and subsequent assassination of Lumumba was characterized by disintegration of the transitional government, a tumultuous five-year scramble for power, and then, in 1965, installation of Joseph D. Mobutu as the new leader of the nation. Mobutu, who was the lieutenant general of the army and who had been instrumental in Lumumba's murder, was deeply indebted to the West for facilitating his rise to power and accepted many neocolonial arrangements with Belgium and the United States in order to maintain their support. At the same time, before betraying him, Mobutu was one of Lumumba's closest disciples and was profoundly aware that part of the popular appeal of Lumumba's ideology was its congruence with the overriding ethos of the independence era continentwide. But where for Lumumba culture was a means of actual liberation, for Mobutu it was a way to create the illusion of independence while in fact exercising strict control. In the absence of adequate practitioners, equipment, or screening facilities that would allow him to exercise this kind of control through cinema, Mobutu turned to other art forms, most prominently music. Thus, discussions of this period in Yole!Africa's curriculum of popular history focus on practices and politics of music making. The approach the center takes to this material includes two components: first, discussion of the lives and circumstances of popular Zairian musicians based on screenings and debates of Olivier Lechen's 1992 documentary *Rumba: deux rives au meme tempo*; and second, in-depth historical analysis of the formative aspects of music production in the era of Mobutu's dictatorship. This latter component is my focus in this section as it is the foundation on which activist musicians in Goma begin to decipher the direct connections between contemporary music productions in the age of humanitarianism and their historic precedents.

Historically, music played a pivotal role in shaping contemporary Congo, a role that is an essential component of study for anyone aspiring to engage in social or political action in or on behalf of Congo. During his rule (1965–1997), Mobutu catalyzed the destructive trend of disguising political manipulation beneath a musical façade that played on the romantic association of African music with popular resistance or empowerment and the vague assumption that "traditional" songs are, by default, expressions of autonomous local views. There are some factual roots that connect music to resistance in Congo; thus Mobutu's allusions to the revolutionary power of music were not entirely fictional. Historically in Congo, as in other colonial territories, music provided one of the only avenues through which local populations could criticize or complain about colonizers without being understood or punished. Historians and ethnomusicologists have also demonstrated that genres such as Congolese rumba (sometimes called *Rumba Lingala*), played a unifying, if subtle, role in the fight against colonialism and were, as such, perceived by the population as indigenous means of resistance. Many popular Congolese songs produced between 1950 and 1960 had, in both their lyrics and their musical styles, increasingly discernable subtexts of resistance. Although there is no record of outright revolt in the music of this period, there is compelling evidence that techniques such as hyperbole, repetition, and indirect speech or proverbs contributed to wearing down opposition to independence and to expressing the desire for freedom from colonialism.[47]

Indeed, by aligning his own musical rhetoric with historically real applications of music to social politics, Mobutu positioned music as the ideal medium through which to appease the population's self-perception as an independent nation while in fact advancing an agenda of domination. Specifically, he was able to capitalize on popular appreciation of the role music played in galvanizing Congolese in the fight for independence, which, combined with the extraordinary popularity of music in Congo, made it the perfect conduit for advancing his agenda. And he used it liberally. Beginning in the period immediately after Lumumba's assassination, when the nation was in turmoil, Mobutu paved his way to popularity with incessant diffusion via national radio of a song praising himself as the only leader capable of bringing order and peace to Congo. "Cinq ans!" (Five Years!), composed by Tabu Ley Rochereau, is an infectiously upbeat and memorable song that became the signature tune played before all news broadcasts. It left Congolese of all generations stuck with this catchy refrain in their minds:

Balobi te mboka Congo etondi na bato.	They say that the town of Congo is full of people.
Batata, bamama na bana bobima libanda,	Father, mother and children, come out into the open,
toyokana, tobongisa mboka.	let us agree together, let us put the town right.
Cinq ans! Cinq ans! Mobutu akotomisa Congo.	Five years! Five years! Mobutu will set up the Congo
Cinq ans! Mbula ya mitano (i), biso tokoyokana.	Five years! By the fifth year, we shall agree together.
Cinq ans! Mulamba akokumba gouvernement	Five years! Mulamba will carry the government.
Cinq ans! Mbula ya mitano, biso tokoyokana.	Five years! By the fifth year, we shall agree together.[48]

Of course, the frequency of diffusion of this particular song decreased as Mobutu shifted his mode of governance from democracy to dictatorship. However, his effective use of music as a means of social control continued to rise in various forms throughout his thirty-two-year rule.

One of Mobutu's signature cultural contributions was the regime of authenticité, which began in 1971. Authenticité stemmed from a politics of cultural recovery of the kind that was popular in postcolonial nations around the world. In the case of Congo, efforts toward cultural recovery were modeled on Mao's cultural practices in China and, as such, proved to be as much an insidious mechanism of dictatorial control as a source of renewed identity. Although Mobutu himself struggled to offer a consistent verbal or written definition of it, he regularly evoked authenticité when justifying state mandates and economic strategies; indeed, despite the absence of a concrete definition, the effects of authenticité are readily visible.[49] In practice it dictated rejection of Western cultural influence in favor of African practices. This included renaming places (Congo became Zaire, Léopoldville became Kinshasa, Stanleyville became Kisangani, Lake Edward became Lake Mobutu, etc.), renaming people (Joseph Mobutu became Mobutu Sese Seko Kuku Ngbendu Wa Za Banga, and all Zairian citizens were commanded to replace Western names with African names), imposing an "authentic" African dress code designed by Mobutu himself (men were required to wear *abacosts* and women could no longer wear pants), and the return to an "authentic" African paradigm in all aspects of cultural production.[50] Figure 2.4 is an example of the spectacles performed regularly under the regime of authenticité.

In a macabre twist on the emerging popular theories of the era that celebrated the powerful relationship between culture and the construction of national identity, Mobutu actively integrated music and dance at the center of his regime of authenticité through state-mandated performances and exhibitions that were called *animation politique*, an example of which is visible in the figure. By the 1980s cultural ensembles under animation politique included as many as five hundred performers (never fewer than fifty) and regularly presented mandatory spectacles lasting three or four hours that included elaborate costumes, choreographies, musics, and plots. These spectacles, which he justified as a necessary part of the project of liberating precolonial African cultural practices from the lasting grip of colonialism, created in Congo a questionable new repertoire of "traditional" songs and dances overtly praising Mobutu and his political party.

He also introduced a law obliging all Zairian citizens to sing prescribed patriotic songs daily in all public or private institutions and with the arrival of any state dignitary. Failure to comply, or worse still, outright opposition, was met with severe consequences. There is the infamous example of a tenured and celebrated professor of political science at the University of Kinshasa, whose opposition to Mobutu earned him a week in confinement, where he was treated with deference and accommodated in luxury save being subjected to the perpetual repetition of political songs. When, after his release, he was overheard humming the songs of praise for Mobutu that were permanently imprinted in his mind after seven days of uninterrupted repetition, he began to lose credibility as a real opponent to Mobutu's regime, and eventually he was dismissed in the public eye as an imposter and his criticisms and opposition ceased to be a threat to the regime. If nothing else, this demonstrates the degree to which music was integrated into Mobutu's politics. Indeed, beneath the ever-rising grandeur of animation politique, creativity was strictly legislated in a way that eroded any optimism about cultivating national culture as music— "traditional" and popular—solidified into a central component of Mobutu's propaganda machine.[51]

Using music as a tool to consolidate power required enforcing strict control over artists. For this Mobutu introduced watchdog figures under the auspices of the Mouvement Populaire de la Revolution, who worked through UMUZA (l'Union des Musiciens Zairois) to monitor musical activity in Zaire. Like all branches of law enforcement created by Mobutu, UMUZA imposed extremely restrictive rules regarding every aspect of culture production. Songs were reviewed and censored for use of "nonauthentic" instruments and musical idioms, and a special official visa was required from UMUZA for musicians to perform, record,

FIGURE 2.4 Zaire president Joseph-Desire Mobutu Sese Seko. Photo by Jean Tesseyre/Paris Match Archive/Getty Images.

or travel. Anyone who disobeyed these rules—or Mobutu's subjective interpretation of them—was severely punished. There are countless stories of artists, like the orchestra SOSOLISO, who went on tour in East Africa without a visa from UMUZA, and were punished with three months in solitary confinement for their failure to produce receipts accounting for every penny spent abroad. This forced the dissolution of their band as rival groups took over their weekly gigs. Still, it was better than the fate of the musicians from Wenge Musica, who were severely beaten by Mobutu's soldiers after failing to praise his son Manda at a public concert and then forced, despite their fresh injuries, to play a private concert praising Manda and eventually to release an album in his honor likening his imminent return to Congo (from Belgium) to Christ's return to Bethlehem.[52] Needless to say, by the end of this their reputation, creativity, and psyche were compromised, to say nothing of the enduring physical injuries they suffered.

In this environment it is not surprising that musicians accepted to become the mouthpieces of politicians. Mobutu set a powerful precedent for this dynamic when he equipped himself with an entourage of musicians for all occasions so that, whether addressing foreign dignitaries or speaking to the masses, he could bring Rochereau or Franco, respectively, to sing his praises in a fashion guaranteed to seduce any listener. In fact, Mobutu never addressed any audience without a musician accompanying him, which solidified a distinct interconnection between music and politics in Congo that continues to this day. It was through songs praising Mobutu that he elevated his popularity in the eyes of the population, through songs that he compelled people to support changes in policy, and with songs that he introduced new laws and announced the change to a new currency. Over time this practice elevated the status of musicians in the eyes of the population, who viewed them as having significant power, which led in turn to a culture of politicians promoting themselves through the popularity of musicians. To see the lasting effects of this, one need look no further than Congo's current government, which includes many politicians who are known to the population primarily (and in some cases exclusively) because they paid to have their names sung by popular musicians and not because of any substantive political record.

The close relationship between music and politics in Congo also has an economic component that goes beyond the obvious practice of musicians being paid to compose and perform political propaganda songs. As in many African nations, traditional cultural practices in Congo include the custom of musicians honoring individuals by citing their names in song. Compensation (generally in the form of monetary contributions) is a standard response from honorees and a motivating factor for the musicians, but under Mobutu this traditional practice, called *libanga* in Lingala, took a new shape.[53] What was once a spontaneous gesture by patrons after a musician had already sung their praise became a fixed and for-mally extortive business that was negotiated in advance. Musicians requested money, houses, automobiles, or other goods in exchange for shouting out a poli-tician's name an agreed number of times in a designated song. Depending on the popularity of the musician and the wealth of the patron, prices could range from $100 to $1,000 per iteration of a name. The most popular musicians had multiple patrons (and of course multiple songs) per concert, which made libanga an extremely lucrative practice.[54] But even this represents only a portion of the financial incentive, as demonstrated by the notorious story of the director of Petro Zaire, who was nicknamed "*le grand Lebonais*"; he gave singer Koffi Olomide $10,000 to extend a concert beyond its designated ending time. Not only did this lead the singer to call out his name, but for decades after musicians would shout out "grand Lebonais!" in hopes of generous compensation.

By all standards, a $10,000 tip is extravagant, but beneath the glamour it also reveals another insidious aspect of Mobutu's government. Not only was his regime so corrupt that it led economists to coin the term *kleptocracy*, but in a tele-vised public address Mobutu also famously told the population "*débrouillez-vous*" (which translates, roughly, to "no matter what, find your way"), which was open encouragement for people to fend for themselves when the state failed to deliver on its promises—and for the state not to deliver on promises. For decades public employees were not paid, which forced many to compensate themselves by "bor-rowing" from their institutions' funds. When those quickly dwindled to nothing people had to become more creative still: soldiers used force to take what they needed from middle-class citizens, who then exercised what power they could over the lower classes, often by demanding bribes. This social strategy, known as "*debrouillardaize*," affected artists and musicians like everyone else, forcing them to extort extravagant compensation whenever they could to ward off the ever-impending threat of poverty. As Lechen's *Rumba: deux rives au meme tempo* elegantly depicts, no matter how celebrated—or rich—musicians were when in favor with Mobutu, the majority ended up living in abject poverty, discarded by the politicians they had elevated to glory, and forgotten by their adoring fans.

Under Mobutu and the system of debrouillardaize, a very distinct relationship developed in Congo between art, specifically music, and the political agenda. There were, of course, instances of subversion, but by and large music was a tool wielded, by force or coercion, in service of power. The general population was conditioned to the culture of musicians serving as the mouthpieces of a dictator, and musicians were conditioned to yield artistic autonomy for survival. This was an era in which Mobutu *used* music and, in so doing, linked it in the collective psyche to propaganda rather than free creative expression. The social reflexes he conditioned continue to linger, and indeed they are often triggered by interactions between international NGOs (contemporary representatives of power) and present-day musicians, who remain caught between the conflicting needs of subsistence and expressive autonomy.

ACT V: THE NEXT GENERATION

A central question that arises as students make their way through Yole!Africa's curriculum of popular history is how to create an aesthetic that is not suffocatingly encumbered by Congo's audio and visual history. Clearly the models prescribed by Léopold II and Belgium are not appealing, and Lumumba's vision for Congo has been so thoroughly corrupted by Mobutu's legacy that it does not yield an obvious aesthetic. There is the growing influence of international organizations investing in culture production as part of humanitarian or charitable missions, but critical young people simply see this as a shift from didactic appeals to morality to trendy experiments with software effects, having more to do with marketing do-goodism than crafting meaningful interventions. The challenge youth face in developing an alternative aesthetic is that global activism has become a brand. In Congo the result is that the overt aesthetics that characterized audio and visual representations in the generations from Léopold II and Morel through Mobutu's era have given way to subtler and savvier representational practices that blur the most visible or audible distinctions between cultural actions rooted in domination and those rooted in resistance.

As an organization dedicated to fostering critical inquiry and highly wary of prescriptive methods, Yole!Africa does not offer any concrete solutions to this puzzle. Instead, as a catalyst of further exploration, it added Petna's 2004 creative documentary *Lamokowang* to the later part of its curriculum of popular history. The short film provides meaningful insight to Congolese youth at the outset of their quest to develop a new aesthetic both because it confirms that local narratives and alternative aesthetics can garner international recognition and appreciation (*Lamokowang* has won many international awards) and because of the film's genesis in artistic and intellectual struggles to which aspiring artists can relate and from which they can learn.

As a young filmmaker, Petna was struggling to identify a cinematic mother tongue when he made *Lamokowang*. According to an unpublished interview of him at the time, he was openly grappling with a question: If film was brought to Congo as a means of domination, we know that the images Congolese were conditioned by were obviously destructive, but the cinematic language we have imbibed is also foreign, so what is the parallel for African filmmakers to the efforts by African writers to express ourselves in our mother tongue? The Senegalese filmmaker Ousmane Sembene had obviously already made strides toward answering this when he made the first African-directed film in an indigenous language; but, inspired by the militantism of Sembene's revolutionary inclusion of literal African languages, the present generation of filmmakers is still working to craft an aesthetic language of African cinema that meets the needs of the time.[55] The more radical among them, including Petna, rebut attempts to celebrate the stylistic qualities often associated with African Cinema or Cinema Calabash (including slow development of plots, the penchant for long shots and limited cuts, etc.) first by pointing out that funding, and thus the content, for such films is still controlled by the West, and then by citing Fanon's description of the colonized intellectual:

> The colonized intellectual, at the very moment when he undertakes a work of art, fails to realize he is using techniques and a language borrowed from the occupier. He is content to cloak these instruments in a style that is meant to be national but which is strangely reminiscent of exoticism. The colonized intellectual who returns to his people through works of art behaves in fact like a foreigner. Sometimes he will not hesitate to use the local dialects to demonstrate his desire to be as close to the people as possible, but the ideas he expresses, the preoccupations that haunt him are in no way related to the daily lot of the men and women of his country. The culture with which the intellectual is preoccupied is very often nothing but an inventory of particularisms.[56]

Identifying the "techniques and a language borrowed from the occupier" is particularly difficult for filmmakers since, unlike other expressive mediums such as music, dance, or visual arts, film was introduced during the colonial era and does not have any precolonial roots on which to draw when working toward a renewed but culturally relevant aesthetic. Thus deconstructing the accepted cinematic inventories of particularisms requires creative engagement with every component of the art form. For its part, Lamokowang takes up this project through its experimentation with image, sound, and time.

Suspended somewhere between past and present, situated in an unidentified rural village that is both geographically specific and metaphorically ubiquitous, this cyclical short film does not have a linear plot line in the Aristotelian sense; instead, through avant-garde cinematic language, it cites African rather than colonial traditions as the source of contemporary practices. After a haunting a cappella song accompanying a black screen, a hyperrealistic wind blows the image from blackness into the gritty grays of old 35mm film with vertical lines and flecks of texture commenting on an idyllic pastoral scene: a regal man

FIGURE 2.5 *Lamokowang* Sequence.

(visible in the left frame of Fig. 2.5) with all the identifiable trappings of a noble savage stands stoically, and then dances reverently, with no sound but the wind to accompany the visual rhythm of his movements. The camera positions him in the distance, in the middle distance, and in extreme close-ups so intimate that every crease in his feet and ankles, his fingers and drum, become maps of possible meaning. Then, without explanation, the film cuts to another man, who has the bearing of dignity and importance, calling powerfully into the wind. It is as if his incantation transforms the image of the landscape from its flecked grittiness to a jostled digital vibration of colors and textures. With every reverberation of his untranslated invocation, an abstract wash of blues, greens, reds, and grays super-imposes glimpses of this rural landscape into a jungle metropolis of high-rise tree lines (center frame of Fig. 2.5). And then the film cuts again to a full-color image of a beautiful young woman, clothed in a modest bathing suit, gathering water from the river in a large calabash.

According to its press kit, "*Lamokowang* is a meditation on history, imagination and potential, a renewed Calabash full of questions, reflections and dreams."[57] Though this "meditation" is not didactic in terms of content or narrative, it makes a clear political statement through its use of image and sound. In the most lit-eral sense, physical calabash are a central visual metaphor that runs through the film: in various scenes calabash serve as vessels for fetching water, con-taining dry goods, trapping birds, protecting babies (visible in the right frame of Fig. 2.5), drinking, measuring, and forming numerous musical instruments. Foregrounding calabash as noteworthy indigenous technologies affirms the rich history of innovation in the region and links the spirit of technological advance as much to Africa as to the West. At the same time, the use of calabash is also a visual metaphor asserting a pointed critique of Cinema Calabash as a genre built on a dubious inventory of particularisms. The director's statement for the film says as much:

Cinema Calabasse is a 50 year-old genre of cinema depicting Africa from the perspective of foreigners fixated on the 'exotic,' with plots and characters shackled by clichés. The calabash is the metaphoric reduction of diverse African cultures that came to represent this genre, a genre that depicts both embodied practices and the power of dominant ideology in media, a genre that—historically speaking—has contributed to the oppression of the continent. Yet, the problem is not the calabash itself, or even the media per se; the problem is how to adapt this genre of cinema to present-day reality, how to reclaim the history of images from a perspective that fosters dreams for the future.[58]

In its effort to fulfill this self-assigned objective, *Lamokowang* takes a different approach to the project of re-membering Congo's history: in lieu of offering a portrait of any specific historical event, it grapples with the very cinematic language through which Congo has learned to understand itself.

The film openly quotes the visual language of anthropological film, the documentation of the "noble savage," the realism of feature film, and the verité of observational documentary, each of which aesthetics played a crucial role in cultivating the dominant approaches to representing Africa. But these quotations are choreographed in a way that brings overt attention to film as the conduit of information. As in many revolutionary cinematic traditions, the camera in *Lamokowang* is never static, moving instead as an instrument in the story/dance that imposes itself, and forces the viewer to grapple with its presence through interruptions of texture, color, and view. The viewer is thus not invited to suspend herself in a "real," True, or finite Africa or to lose herself in the manipulations of a story, but rather to recognize that every moment of this Africa—past and present—is mediated, and subjectively so. In short, by subjugating overt stylistic quotations of dominant cinematic practices to digital iterations of revolutionary ideology, *Lamokowang* directly challenges the lingering habit of exoticizing Africa.

The interrogation of cinematic language is also evident in the film's use of sound and music. The music in *Lamokowang* is an obvious indicator of tradition, as evidenced by the drumming (seen but not heard) that accompanies the dance in the opening sequence, and the array of traditional instruments and songs that punctuate the film. However, music is also a deciphering key that forces the viewer to recognize Petna's conception of tradition not as specific actions fixed in time (as promoted in anthropological films of "authentic" African practices) but as ever-evolving lived and embodied practices. In response to a query about his conception of music in *Lamokowang*, Petna responded:

Musically, I am recognizing that tradition is the base of everything, but at the same time, I've never believed that this tradition was stuck. We

[Africans, Congolese] call it tradition because for us it is tradition *now*, and I'm sure my children's children will call practices we think of as new today "tradition" in their time. It's only when we agree on the Western concept of tradition, that is linear instead of cyclical, that traditions become fixed. Music shows the evolution of tradition—how does a tradition become a tradition? According to where a generation is placing itself. But what we learned and what we keep on learning from the West is that tradition has never changed—they want us to believe that. That is my problem with tradition: Western claims that it is fixed and does not evolve. Personally, most of the time I refer to "a live tradition," a tradition which is still living. You're small, you get old, *it* never gets old. Following what they present in the West, it's as if it [tradition] died, we have to go somewhere fixed, like a museum, and read, "oh, *this* is tradition." But I disagree, to me that was a particular scene in how things were evolving. I look at music, life, film, etc. as fontos, one particular frame in cinema and you need twenty-four of them to have one single movement. To me, music is the best representation of this.[59]

Music's function as both source and indicator of the evolution of tradition is evident throughout *Lamokowang*. For example, the incantation in the opening sequence is a sung/spoken prayer in which the speaker's voice appears to have power over the image. The raplike vocal effects of this traditional invocation are undeniable and, in conjunction with the visual effects, conjure an aesthetic that is suggestive of contemporary hip hop while still rooted in Congo's specific history. Another example occurs later in the film, when in a neatly swept courtyard two kneeling women vigorously grind grain into flour between rough stones and riff, with breathlessness and haunting, hocketed melodic play against the rhythm of their work. One woman has a baby tied to her back, and the strenuous thrusts of her grinding motion jostle him about, prompting him to punctuate their song with his cries—or perhaps it is his cries that bring them to sing despite their physical exertion. Either way, their rhythmic vocal improvisations are eerily prescient of the sonic collage of autotuned clips that saturate contemporary hip hop tracks. Perhaps it is going too far to compare the scratching of stone to the scratching of records, but even without this element the combination of sensual yet distorted images with driving yet lyrical music undeniably suggests that traditional musical gestures cumulatively contribute to contemporary genres. Inversely, when the film later depicts a small group of people in a grassy area scratching different-sized calabash on long flat stones in complex interlocking rhythms,[60] or three young men plucking a melody out of a rope strung tautly over a calabash,[61] one cannot help but reflect that what the black and white of the cinematic language insists is old must once have been the latest innovation.

In *Lamokowang*, the focus on tradition as evolving rather than fixed foregrounds a fluidity of past, present, and future that is intrinsic to cyclical rather than linear conceptions of time. Advancing a cyclical theory of time through the fundamentally temporal medium of film is a strategy of locating contemporary techniques of representing Africa in traditional African cosmology without relying on the visual or sonic inventories of particularisms constructed by foreign representations. This is one way in which film, despite its colonial roots, can be as traditional an African expressive medium as any other, without being restricted to the narrative and representational vocabularies either of colonial cinema or of traditional iterations of Cinema Calabash. This point is made with force when, after a lengthy full-color sequence, the film not only returns to black and white but revisits the same footage of the noble savage character dancing against the wind in an isolated field. Only this time, there is no doubt that the lines and dust flecks of old 35 mm film are a digital indication of innovation rather than anthropological "authenticity" and that the subject in question is as modern as the technologies mediating him. Further, having just witnessed a rowdy musical circle gathering with familiar characters from the film drumming, dancing, stomping, shaking rattles, clapping, singing, blowing powerful blasts through hollowed bones, and ululating passionately, we find the conditioned reflex to categorize a traditionally clothed African man dancing in a field as a "noble savage" complicated by the sense of humanity and continuity established by the preceding scenes. Indeed, an attentive viewer might well be preoccupied with questioning the values and motivations underlying dominant methods of representing Africans that conditioned generations of viewers—Western and African alike—to quarantine Africans in a permanent and unchanging past without acknowledging the extent to which that past is the foundation of the global present.

After watching *Lamokowang* at Yole!Africa, one young man shared his analysis of the film as a dream or vision of the lone drumming man in the field. In this interpretation of the film, the character was a warrior preparing to go on a long journey and fortifying himself with the traditional wisdom and technologies of his community. Watching the film from this perspective, the student expressed a new understanding of the degree to which he had been conditioned by stereotypes that suggest Africans are fixed in an eternal past and do not contribute to valuable global innovations. "We didn't stop in the days of feathers and calabash," he said, "we have a history of inventing and innovating and it continues. Africans—Congolese—continue to invent new things all the time." With that statement he rushed out of the tent, calling over his shoulder that he was going to do more research about the technological contributions and innovations that trace back to Africa, and specifically to Congo. (This same young man was later triumphant when he watched Balufu Bakupa-Kanyinda's *Afro@Digital* and learned about the Ishango bones, Congo's ancient equivalent to the abacus, which allowed indigenous populations to calculate complex mathematical equations.)

However exciting, his was an unusual response; generally such analysis is hard to come by after a single viewing of the film. Most postscreening discussions of *Lamokowang* at Yole!Africa begin with exuberant applause followed by utter bewilderment when viewers attempt to articulate *why* they are so moved by the short film. Relative to films like *Boma-Tervuren, Matamata and Pilipili, La mort du prophète* or *Rumba: deux rives au meme tempo, Lamokowang* is abstract to the point of esotericism. But in the project of honing critical analytical skills, grappling with abstraction is a useful activity in the quest to piece daily experience into popular history, particularly as it sparks curiosity in an organic way—especially in young people conditioned not to ask questions.

EPILOGUE

For the youth gathered in the blue-and-white striped tent of Yole!Africa's compound, the lively discussions and debates at the heart of the curriculum of popular history often raise as many questions as they answer (if not more). These questions extend in all directions toward the past, the present, and the future, bringing to mind Said's suggestion that "more important than the past itself . . . is its bearing upon cultural attitudes in the present."[62] To my reading this is precisely what is radical about Yole!Africa's curriculum of popular history: it does not treat the past as a collection of facts or statistics, but as a trigger to cultivate critical skills, to encourage young people to seek answers for themselves, and to cultivate intentional cultural attitudes against a backdrop of conflict.

For those foreign activists expecting revolution to appear in real life as it does in retrospective narrations of history, a motley group of students discussing esoteric films in a rugged tent in Goma might not appear significant. But for those who recognize fostering mental decolonization and developing heterobiography as prerequisites of sustainable sociopolitical transformation, there is no sight more radical. According to film theorist Bill Nichols, "what works at a given moment and what counts as a realistic representation of the historical world is not a simple matter of progress toward a final form of truth but of struggles for power and authority within the history arenas itself."[63] The passionate arguments among previously disinterested students about the ongoing—and personal—relevance of historical moments long past is its own version of a struggle for power and authority within the arena of history. Indeed, young people frequently cite an internal shift of self-perception as the most powerful lingering impact of the films discussed in this chapter. In their own words, they identify the screenings and debates of Yole!Africa's curriculum of popular history as the forum in which they began to see themselves not as subjects of history but as agents of the present, as the forum in which they realize, with full force, that it is not through memorizing official versions of history that they will win power and authority, but rather through the quiet revolutionary project of re-membering their own version of the story. On a global scale, the most powerful lingering impact of this study of popular history is, perhaps, the insight it offers about how to listen to—and heed—the dialogue between voices, past and present, fighting for the liberation of Congo on the front lines of geopolitical conflict and also in global memory.

NOTES

1. Original text: *"L'histoire dira un jour son mot, mais ce ne sera pas l'histoire qu'on enseignera à Bruxelles, Washington, Paris ou aux Nations Unies, mais celle qu'on enseignera dans les pays affranchis du colonialisme et de ses fantoches. L'Afrique écrira sa propre histoire et elle sera au nord et au sud du Sahara une histoire de gloire et de dignité."*

2. Rieff, *A Bed for the Night*, 87.

3. Jermaine McCalpin, "Historicity of a Crisis: The Origins of the Congo War," in *The African Stakes of the Congo War*, ed. John Clark (New York: Palgrave Macmillan, 2002), 33.

4. John F. Clark, "Introduction: Causes and Consequences of the Congo War," in *The African Stakes of the Congo War*, ed. John Clark (New York: Palgrave Macmillan, 2002), 2.

5. Clark, "Introduction," 4.

6. Clark, "Introduction," 8.

7. Ferguson, *Global Shadows*, 90.

8. Clark, "Introduction," 4.

9. I make this claim on the basis of extensive interviews and participant observation work with a number of internationally recognized Congolese activists, including Petna Ndaliko, Samuel Yagase, Balufu Bakupa-Kanyinda, Ray aNsi Lema, Justine Maseka, Balufu Bakupa-Kanyinda, and Kenyan Ndungi Githuku.

10. Teshome Gabriel, "Third Cinema as Guardian of Popular Memory: Towards a Third Aesthetics," in *Questions of Third Cinema*, eds. Jim Pines and Paul Willemen (London: British Film Institute, 1989), 53–54.

11. As Adam Hochschild points out in chapter 15 of *King Léopold's Ghost*, determining the death toll of King Léopold's Congo "requires considerable historical detective work" (225–34). The reasons for this are many: first, no accurate census of African lives was taken until long after the rubber frenzy (which boasted the highest death rate) was over; second, as the mass slayings in Congo were economically driven rather than motivated by the desire to eliminate one specific ethnic group, Léopold's men did not bother to keep accurate records of their

slaughters as the killing of African slaves was considered "incidental." And third, there are four factors that contribute to establishing death count: (1) murder; (2) starvation, exhaustion, and exposure; (3) disease; and (4) a plummeting birth rate, all of which were abundant in Léopold's Congo. According to Hochschild, "the most authoritative judgment today comes from Jan Vansina, professor emeritus of history and anthropology at the University of Wisconsin and perhaps the greatest living ethnographer of Congo basin peoples. He bases his calculation on 'innumerable' local sources from different areas: priests noticing their flocks were shrinking, oral traditions, genealogies, and much more." His estimate is the same as the official estimation of the Belgian government commission in 1919, as the finding published in 1920 by Major Charles C. Liebrechts (top executive of the Congo state administration for most of its existence), and Belgian anthropologist Daniel Vangroenweghe, who worked in a former rubber area in the 1970s. They all suggest that between 1880 and 1920 the population of the Congo was cut "at least by half" (Hochschild, 233). At its most conservative, "at least by half" translates to a minimum of ten million people, making the colonial regime in Congo deadlier than any other on the African continent.

12. *Boma-Tervuren le Voyage (de juin à septembre 1897)*, directed by Francis Dujardin (Cobra Films, 1999), DVD, 0:30:47.

13. Ngugi Wa Thiong'o's term for the Holocausts and mass atrocities that took place in colonial and slave-era Africa. Ngugi wa Thiong'o, *Something Torn and New: An African Renaissance* (New York: BasicCivitas Books, 2009), 59.

14. A wooden canoe often used for fishing.

15. *Boma-Tervuren*, 0:03:21.

16. Original text: "*tout les cultures sont faites pour regarder les autres. La question de l'autre, elle est au cœur de toutes nos existences. Mais, j'imagine moi je suis ce Congolais de 1897, je suis au même endroit ou je me trouve maintenant, et toi tu est belge en face de moi. Tu m'obliges à adopter un comportement que tu voudrais absolument reconnaître à moi pour que je fasse la preuve que je suis un être humain. Tu m'oblige à m'habille, à parler, à manger, à dormir, à respirer même comme tu voudrais que je sois. Mon existence en réalité ne t'intéresse pas du tout. Ce qui est important c'est l'image que tu veux retrouver à moi, c'est ça le regard de l'autre qui tue. Ce regard de l'autre, c'est un viol permanent, c'est un homicide, un homicide culturel. Ils sont venus, je suis venu de chez moi, je suis déjà une pesanteur historique.*" *Boma-Tervuren*, 0:18:13–0:19:26 (translation mine).

17. Gabriel, "Third Cinema," 57.

18. Gilles Deleuze, *Cinema 2: The Time-Image*, trans. Hugh Tomlinson and Robert Galeta (London: Athlone Press, 1989), 109.

19. Adam Hochschild, *King Leopold's Ghost* (New York: Mariner Books, 1999), 102–9.

20. Ibid., 215.

21. Original text: "*Que la colonisation du Congo fût une histoire nauséeuse de barbarie civilisée, un régime de terreur qui aujourd'hui encore colle à notre vie comme un chancre malsain dont les miasmes se font toujours sentir, nul aujourd'hui n'a le droit d'en douter. Et pourtant nombreux sont ceux qui préfèrent tourner la page, évacuer les responsabilités de la Belgique dans un oubli volontaire et dépouiller encore et toujours les Congolais de ce passé sanglant où leur identité présente plonge ses racines et trouve le terreau de ses multiples facettes. ... Boma-Tervuren remet les pendules à l'heure et fait un sort à cette pratique de l'amnésie en faisant le lien entre les 'premiers jours' de la colonie et l'époque actuelle.*" (translation mine). http://www.cinergie.be/critique.php?action=display&id=223.

22. *Miserere, mei Deus* (Have Mercy on Me, O Lord), often referred to as the *Allegri Miserere*, was composed by Gregorio Allegri in the 1630s to the words of the fifty-first psalm.

The English translation is from the 1662 Book of Common Prayer. Eric Blom, ed., *Grove's Dictionary of Music and Musicians* (New York: St. Martin's Press, 1954).

23. *Boma-Tervuren*, 0:45:15.

24. See for example, *Funeral Dirges of the Akan People*, where J. H. Nketia analyzes the importance of music in mourning, marking its central presence in the five stages of honoring the dead among the Akan of Ghana (preburial mourning, including the wake; internment; after-burial mourning; and subsequent periodic mourning), Joseph H. Nketia, *Funeral Dirges of the Akan People* (Exeter: Achimota, 1955), 5; John Mbiti, *African Religions and Philosophy* (Portsmouth, NH: Heinemann, 1990); V. Y. Mudimbe, *The Invention of Africa: Gnosis, Philosophy, and the Order of Knowledge* (Bloomington: Indiana University Press, 1988).

25. Thiong'o, *Something Torn and New*, 58.

26. Deleuze, *Cinema 2*, 224.

27. For a thorough discussion of colonial cinema models in Africa, see Manthia Diawara, *African Cinema: Politics and Culture* (Bloomington, IN: Indiana University Press, 1992).

28. Léopoldville became the capital of Congo in 1920 and was renamed Kinshasa in 1966.

29. Original text reads: "*il manquait quelque chose encore à nos frères noirs pour être vraiment belges. Ils ignoraient le cinema! Ils vont le connaître.*" Convents, 29. Translation mine.

30. Original text reads: "*certains films présentent un caractère dangereux pour l'ordre public, dans un pays où la population est susceptible de subir fortement l'influence des spectacles qu'on lui présente.*" Guido Convents, *Images et démocratie: Les Congolais face au cinéma et à l'audiovisuel. Une histoire politico-culturelle du Congo des Belges jusqu'à la république démocratique du Congo (1896–2006)* (Brussels: Aden Diffusion, 2006), 31. Translation mine.

31. Original text reads: "*Les Noirs ici appellent [Charlie Chaplin] Charlot «Kawayawaya», c'est-à-dire: le pitre. Aucun Blanc ne doit être un pitre pour un Noir, même à l'écran.*" Quoted in Convents, 33. Translation mine.

32. Original text reads: "*il faudrait leur programmer des films judicieusement choisi sur le roi Albert, la reine, les princes, les principaux monuments de Belgique, un défilé des troupes, des vues prises le 1er juillet (journée coloniale), le lancement d'un bateau, des scènes d'aviation ou certains travaux européens, et d'autres images qui soutiennent la supériorité Blanc. Pour leur faciliter la compréhension, . . . un clerc noir «spécialement dressé» devrait expliquer brièvement les diverses séries d'images, et dans des termes assimilables par tous le spectateurs noirs. Tous les autres films ne peuvent que nuire au prestige des Européens et « au Congo, ce prestige est déjà bien chancelant.*" Convents, 33. Translation mine.

33. Original text reads: "*Une des entraves au progrès de la colonisation qu'il serait souhaitable de combattre avec la collaboration des gouvernements coloniaux, c'est l'influence néfaste exercée par le cinéma. Ce n'est pas seulement un mal, mais un véritable danger social pour les colonies. Le cinéma a miné en effet d'une façon déplorable le respect pour l'Occident, sur lequel reposent en majeure partie les fondements de la civilisation aux colonies.*" Quoted in Convents, 37. Translation mine.

34. Original text reads: "*le Congolais ne parviendrait pas à suivre la trame du film, la succession des images étant 'trop rapide pour sa compréhension' . . . les Congolais préfèrent les comédies brèves aux films d'une demi-heure, à condition qu'il s'agisse de films similaires à ceux qui conviennent à la jeunesse européenne: des films d'action au scenario simpliste.*" "*Quelques observations concernant le cinéma pour indigènes au Congo*" in *Revue coloniale belge*, 15.03.1948. Quoted in Convents, 39. Translation mine.

35. *Matamata and Pilipili*, directed by Tristan Bourlard (First Run/Icarus Films, 1997), DVD, 0:21:40.

36. Ibid., 0:27:45.

37. Ludo De Witte, *The Assassination of Lumumba* (New York: Verso, 2002), xix.

38. *La Mort du Prophet*, directed by Raoul Peck (California Newsreel, 2008), DVD, 0:07:44–0:10:32.

39. There is established documentation of the strong relationship between Congolese music and certain musical genres that developed in the African diaspora, specifically in Cuba, where more than 70 percent of African slaves were brought from the Congo River Basin. Specific aspects of these musical retentions include the clavé, which likely developed from the 12/8 bell pattern and later became the rhythmic foundation for Cuban Son and Son-Montuno. Starting in the 1930s, the music of Cuban bands such as Septeto Habanero, Orquesta Aragon, and Septeto Nacional became available in Congo. After the 1932 World's Fair in New York, during which Machito and his Afrocubans, Johnny Pacheco, and Orquesta Broadway performed, Latin music became extremely popular among Europeans some of whom eventually hired bands to accompany them to their colonial posts in Africa. Through these exchanges, Dominican merengue, Martinican beguine, Haitian mering, Brazilian samba, Argentinean tango, and the Cuban cha-cha, bolero, mambo, rumba, and son-montuno all became popular in Congo. However, Congolese musicians and dance bands gravitated most strongly toward Cuban Rumba and son-montuno, genres that clearly retained the strongest and most direct African musical influence. In his article "Congolese Rumba and Other Cosmopolitanisms," Bob W. White argues that "Afro-Cuban music became popular in the Congo not only because it retained formal elements of 'traditional' African musical performance, but also because it stood for a form of urban cosmopolitanism that was more accessible—and ultimately more pleasurable—than the various models of European cosmopolitanism which circulated in the Belgian colonies in Africa." Bob W. White, "Congolese Rumba and Other Cosmopolitanisms." *Cahiers d'Etudes Africaines* 43, no. 168 (2002), 663.

40. *La mort du prophète*, 0:19:26.

41. Ibid., 0:48:54.

42. Ibid., 0:57:58.

43. Epifanio San Juan, Jr., *Beyond Postcolonial Theory* (New York: St. Martin's, 1999), 81.

44. *La mort du prophète*, 0:16:14.

45. De Witt, *Assassination of Lumumba*, 3.

46. *La mort du prophète*, 0:16:11.

47. For more information on this see, for example, White, "Congolese Rumba"; Jesse Samba Wheeler, "Rumba Lingala as Colonial Resistance," *Visual Narrative: The Visualization of the Subaltern in World Music: On Musical Contestation Strategies (Part 1)* 10 (2005), 1–53, accessed Oct. 10, 2015, http://www.imageandnarrative.be/inarchive/worldmusica/worldmusica.htm; Manda Tchebwa, *La terre de la chanson: La musique zairoise hier et auhourd'hui* (Brussels: Duculot, 1996); Jayna Brown, "Buzz and Rumble: Global Pop Music and Utopian Impulse," *Social Text* 28, no. 1 (2010), 125–46.

48. John F. Carrington, "Tone and Melody in a Congolese Popular Song," *African Music* 4, no. 1 (1966/1967), 38.

49. For a thorough and nuanced consideration of *authenticité*, see Bob W. White's "L'Incroyable Machine d'Authenticité: l'Animation Politic et l'Usage Public de la Culture dans le Zaïre de Mobutu," *Anthropologie et Sociétés* 30, no. 2 (2006), 43–63.

50. During this period Mobutu also changed the national anthem from "*Debout Congolais*" to "*Zairois dans la paix retrouver.*" Ironically, despite the regime of *authenticité*,

he kept the national anthem in French instead of any or all of the four indigenous national languages. In terms of harmonic and rhythmic structures and instrumentation, he maintained what music ethnologist Gerhard Kubik refers to as "those musical forms which the colonial government spread in its own and sympathetic institutions," i.e., I IV V I progressions in 4/4 time. See Gerhard Kubik, "Neo-Traditional Popular Music in Eastern Africa Since 1945," *Popular Music, Vol. 1 Folk or Popular? Distinctions, Influences, Continuities* (1981), 83.

51. For more on this, see White, "L'Incroyable Machine d'Authenticité," 53.

52. The song in question is "Tempête du Desert," from *Les Anges Adorables Vol. 1*, produced by Sonodisc, 1994.

53. *Libanga* literally means stone (including gold or diamonds) and colloquially means gig. *Beta libanga (casser le pierre*, or "break stones if necessary to forge your path") was a popular phrase describing life in Zaire. The variation of *Beta libanga* that was used specifically for music is *Ko lancer libanga*, a combination of French and Lingala meaning "to throw *libanga*" or to throw praise, or recognition.

54. For a more thorough discussion of this practice, see, for example, Kazadi wa Mukuna, "The Evolution of Urban Music in Democratic Republic of Congo during the 2nd and 3rd Decades (1975–1995) of the Second Republic—Zaïre," *African Music* 7, no. 4 (1999), 84.

55. *Mandabi*, directed by Sembene Ousmane (Filmi Domireve and Comptoir Français du Film Production, 1968, 2005), DVD.

56. Fanon, *The Wretched of the Earth*, 160.

57. Petna Ndaliko Katondolo, "Lamokowang Press Release," *Alkebu Productions*, 1, accessed October 10, 2015, http://alkebu.org/index.php/film-productions/lamokowang/.

58. Ibid.

59. Petna Ndaliko Katandolo (filmmaker), in discussion with the author, June 2010.

60. *Lamokowang*, directed by Petna Ndaliko Katondolo (Alkebu Productions, 2004), DVD, 0:08:57.

61. Ibid., 0:08:15.

62. Said, *Culture and Imperialism*, 17.

63. Bill Nichols, *Representing Reality* (Bloomington: Indiana University Press, 1991), 33.

Culture eminently eludes any form of simplification.
FRANTZ FANON, Wretched of the Earth, *p. 160*

3

PEACEMONGERS

SOMETIMES CREATIVE EXPRESSION is a matter of survival, but sometimes
it is a currency that cloaks the machinery of power in the guise of art. In the
east of Congo, it is both. The creative energies of pioneering young people in the
early years of Yole!Africa in concert with the critical analytical skills developed
through the study of popular history set the conditions for Goma to blossom
into a vibrant cultural scene with individuals and organizations actively engaged
in all mediums of art making that cumulatively suggest a microhistory of effective local social and political action. Alarmingly, the vibrancy of art making—
specifically in the domains of music and film—in Goma is presented as evidence
by opposing forces crafting contradictory agendas. On one hand, the cultural
scene is proof of a revolutionary impulse made manifest; on the other hand, it
represents an embodied inventory of the most celebrated (and lucrative) buzz-
words in humanitarian fundraising. Thus currently practices of art making in
Goma are caught between revolutionary ideology and the hegemony of capitalism. Globally speaking, this phenomenon is neither new nor unique to the east of
Congo, but studying it in Goma provides a revealing backdrop against which to
examine larger issues of cultural domination and resistance.

The choices artists currently face in Goma are not dissimilar from the choices
outlined by Fanon in his quest to articulate the role of national culture in the
anticolonial struggle. The question this chapter takes up, then, is how the revolutionary project of national culture navigates the era of humanitarianism and
charity. To that end, the chapter consists of three interrelated essays—Art vs.

Aid, Art vs. Advocacy, and Art vs. Activism—that interpret empirical evidence from Yole!Africa in dialogue with global trends of artistic and representational engagement with (and in and about) the east of Congo. The arc of this chapter moves from a discussion of aid, which I limit to humanitarian and charitable aid, to advocacy, which is the self-designated description of the organizations I profile, to activism, which I explore in the full spectrum of its manifestations as I defined them in the Introduction of this book. The empirical evidence presented in this chapter is drawn from my ongoing ethnographic research and from my firsthand experiences as executive director of Yole!Africa during the period covered in this chapter. In the spirit of transparency, I will add that my role in the activities discussed in this chapter was peripheral at best, both in the case of creating Art on the FrontLine (for which I am only the translator of the online videos) and in facilitating the interactions between Peace One Day and the Salaam Kivu International Film Festival (SKIFF). Regardless of the specifics of my administrative tasks at Yole!Africa, what this dual vantage point affords me is a multidirectional perspective on the forces that leave artists in the east of Congo caught in the crossfire between radical artistic traditions and the influx of humanitarian and charitable NGOs.

ART VS. AID IN THE EAST OF CONGO: MUSIC AND HUMANITARIANISM

There is a very curious dynamic unfolding in the east of Congo, where in response to the popularity of local artists humanitarian NGOs are now producing music and films with great frequency. I call it curious because the NGOs in question are primarily equipped to support disaster relief, medical relief, and structural aid—not art production. Yet they are turning to art, specifically to music and film, both to convey information to local populations and to communicate to donors in emotionally powerful forms. The songs produced by charitable and humanitarian organizations are framed as either (1) the most effective way to communicate vital information to illiterate populations about, say, democracy or sanitation, or (2) part of the efforts deemed necessary to rouse the West from complacency about the atrocities taking place in Congo. Both of these are laudable endeavors. But scrutinizing the politics of production behind such projects suggests that art is often an effective façade to mask struggles for power between local communities and international organizations. This dynamic is both specific to the east of Congo and symptomatic of larger issues of power and the commodification of art that increasingly characterizes humanitarian interventions in many fraught parts of the world. The following recent example from Goma substantiates this point.

This example is set against the backdrop of the Congo conflict, in which more than six million people have lost their lives, millions more have been displaced, and hundreds of thousands have experienced extreme sexual violence and other forms of cruelty. I have already outlined, in previous chapters, the horrific characteristics of the war taking place in North and South Kivu; I reference it here not to revisit the exaggerated violence, but to establish the magnitude of this conflict and point out that the stakes of interventions—local and international—are extremely high. For local populations, the stakes of this war are the material ways in which campaigns of action (or the absence thereof) give or block access to education or medicine, support or undermine the development of a strong state, and, on a less measurable but equally important level, foster or suppress local autonomy and agency. It is the third dynamic that is of greatest concern because the autonomy and agency of local populations in war zones can be hard to detect, and harder to quantify, and the presence or absence of local autonomy is deeply tied to the underlying ideologies motivating humanitarian interventions. Even seemingly constructive projects like building and supplying schools in rural areas are complex; from the NGO point of view, this is a valuable service that gives younger generations access to education, but from a local perspective there are grave concerns about dependency, stagnation, and disempowerment when external organizations assume the roles communities pride themselves on filling autonomously. If questions of agency are tricky in concrete projects like building schools, they are exponentially multiplied when, instead of material structures, the commodity in question is art.

There is an experiment I like to do with students in the United States to introduce the pivotal role of the politics of music production into the conversation about culture, war, and humanitarianism in the east of Congo. The experiment goes like this: first I play for them "Sote Tunawe" ⊙, a soulful R&B song with a deep groove that, within moments, invariably has many feet tapping and heads bobbing to the rhythm. After listening to the song, students indicate, with a show of hands, how many of them liked it. Next I play for them "Mazao" ⊙, a powerful hip hop song with a heavy beat and sparse ascending piano riff that adds a touch of moodiness with its minor key. After "Mazao" they weigh in again. Regardless of class size, at least 70–90 percent consistently raise their hands for each song. When pressed, students say their appreciation is for the music itself, as they rarely understand the Kiswahili or French lyrics. Indeed, the songs' popularity with American students makes sense as these are (subjectively) both great songs that are accessible yet distinct in their blend of popular Western idioms with subtle Congolese musical influence. Students' appreciation is likely also influenced by their knowledge that both songs are by young artists in the east of Congo.

Many students see the fact that young people in a war zone on the other side of the world are producing music with a groove that translates to their own sonic palettes as proof that this music is part of a universal language. The noncritical argument for the universality of music that many students evoke goes hand in hand with the popular sentiment that music can "change the world," a sentiment that is, notably, automatically assumed to mean "change the world for the better." I, too, believe that music—like other art forms—is a powerful force that affects human beings profoundly and that making and sharing music is a fundamental aspect of human behavior. What I want to point out through this example, though, is what happens when vague conceptions of music as a universal language are commoditized and put to service in marketing songs and albums that have a material impact on people's lives.

Both "Sote Tunawe" and "Mazao" are the result of a competition organized in February 2013 as part of a project spearheaded by the international NGO Solidarités Internationale, and sponsored by UNICEF. As organizations that work primarily in the fields of disaster relief and human and children's rights, at the time both NGOs were involved with populations in the internally displaced persons (IDP) camps in North Kivu, where an epidemic of cholera was spreading. In an effort to educate local populations about the spread of cholera, the NGOs decided to commission a song. To their credit, Solidarités was aware of some of the negative dynamics that have developed in Goma (as elsewhere) when foreign organizations intervene in art production by "editing" lyrics. They knew that this is often perceived by locals—artists and audiences—as a form of censorship that is disturbingly similar to the dictatorial musical inheritance of Mobutu's era, during which music production was strictly censored and tightly controlled. They were also aware that Goma's cultural scene was nearly destroyed by bitter rivalries and sabotage that developed among musicians competing for the disproportionately large short-term financial benefits of performing or recording for NGOs in years past.

To avoid precisely such dynamics Solidarités requested that Yole!Africa partner in the project. For Solidarités, partnering with Yole!Africa had certain benefits including the credibility, by proxy, that comes with Yole!Africa's reputation for not compromising its values at any cost. For Yole!Africa the partnership posed certain risks, including potential threats to the center's credibility; as an underfunded organization, the only real capital Yole!Africa has is its reputation for unwavering commitment to artistic integrity, which had been threatened by past partnerships with international NGOs that demanded editorial control over artistic works.

In an effort toward equitable collaboration, Solidarités asked Yole!Africa's advice on how best to engage musicians in writing a song that addressed the issue of cholera prevention from a local perspective. Solidarités was prepared to offer a sizable cash prize, recording contract, regional tour, and extensive radio play of the song. For its part, Yole!Africa was tasked with bringing musicians and community members together to discuss the cholera epidemic and, on the basis of that discussion, to explore what role music might have in preventive measures. The idea was that, in dialogue with the larger community, artists would identify the most effective way to speak to the community.

To this end Yole!Africa organized a barazza (traditional community circle gathering) on the topic of cholera. Given the freedom to express themselves, the solution community members saw to prevent the spread of cholera was for citizens and governments of the Western countries whose economies are implicated in the conflict to change their own policies and consumer practices. Their reasoning was that Western organizations should put their efforts into ending their governments' and corporations' support for neighboring countries (Rwanda and Uganda), whose American- and British-backed armies are terrorizing people off their land and forcing them into IDP camps, where cholera then spreads. In short, from their point of view, the best way to stop the spread of cholera was to eliminate the need for IDP camps. The subtext of this discussion was that organizations like Solidarités, UNICEF, and the hordes of other NGOs operating in the region should not invest extensive resources in what the local community criticizes as putting band-aids on mortal wounds, because doing so allows governments and multinational corporations to continue causing the very problems in which NGOs then intervene. In sum, this conversation mirrored Arundhati Roy's criticism that "it's almost as though the greater the devastation caused by neoliberalism, the greater the outbreak of NGOs. Nothing illustrates this more poignantly than the phenomenon of the U.S. preparing to invade a country and simultaneously readying NGOs to go in and clean up the devastation."[1]

From the community's response to the barazza, Yole!Africa drafted a call for artists to participate in the competition that would determine the winning song. The announcement included very specific wording inviting musicians to "express their artistic sensibility with regards to the cholera epidemic." Having witnessed the barazza, representatives of Solidarités were understandably wary of opening the floodgates for political songs and instead proposed that artists focus on the five stages of washing hands that help prevent the spread of cholera. After much negotiating, this was the final announcement of the competition:

FIGURE 3.1 Cholera competition Poster. Image courtesy of Yole!Africa.

Translation: I Play My Role as a Social Communicator
I compose a song about the five key moments
Music competition/Call for submissions from 8–24 February,
2013
Hand Washing: *Before eating, *Before nursing, *Before
cooking, *After using the toilet, *After changing diapers

After selecting eight finalists, a live concert with a jury will
be organized to pick the winner, which will receive a size-
able prize and have his or her song professionally produced
and diffused on all the radio stations in Goma

By this point, both organizations were feeling the constrictions of compromise. Solidarités was trying to honor its intention to collaborate equitably with
Yole!Africa, which was in turn trying to honor its commitment to the artistic integrity of local musicians. Things escalated further when half the songs submitted for the competition were about the irony of focusing on hand sanitation, as if
people's ignorance rather than lack of clean water was the impediment, and the
rest of the songs detailed the larger vision for eliminating the need for IDP camps

and mentioned hand washing, in passing, as a useful interim activity. Confronted with these texts, Solidarités suggested a member of their organization be added to the jury of artists. With this measure in place, a theater group—not a musician—won the competition for their humorous skit, with song, about hand sanitation. To its credit, Solidarités did support the recording of the second-place song. The winning songs were, of course, "Sote Tunawe" and "Mazao," respectively.

At this point in my classroom experiment, I replay both songs for students, accompanied by translations of the first verse of each song.

Sote Tunawe	Let Us Wash Our Hands
Kipindu pindu ni mangojwa mbaya sana	Cholera is a serious sickness
kwani ina uwa na ku tessa watu wengi duniani,	people suffer and even die from it
ila kuna tabia ambazo ninazo weza kutu sahidia	but there are means to avoid the sickness,
ili tuepuke hizo shida, yeeeeeh!	and the suffering from it, yeeeeeh!
Solidarité internationale na UNICEF	Solidarités International and UNICEF
wametueleza toka zamani ngisi gani kujikinga,	have been telling us since long ago how we can protect ourselves,
soouuouuuuh!	soooouuh!
wamoja hufuata	Some people put it in practice
na wengine hupuuzi,	others don't,
sasa leo tena wametushauri	today they are coming to advise us
ili sote kwa umoja na ndani ya masikilizano	so that together we can avoid cholera
tueshimu shuari zamakingo bora,	we should respect their advice
nikwa faida yangu	it is my own interest
na nikwa faida yako wewe,	and it is for your own interest,
Soouuoouuuuuh!	soooouuoouuuuuh!

Mazao	You Reap What You Sow
On vie la voie de nos choix	We take responsibility for our choices
comme on supporte sa croix	everyone has to carry his/her own cross
Quand on vise la gloire on meurt le dents sérés	when you aim for glory you die in pain
Parcours fatal de ma justice	justice is a fatal path
je parle de la RDC	I am talking of Congo

je vie se retombe comme un fils de la guerre—	I live the consequences as a child of war
toujours le même système	always the same system
qui trahissent le peuple	that betrays the people
ils ont truqués les élections	they rigged the elections
et martyrisés nos frères	and martyred our brothers
On vote pour ou contre	whether we vote for or against
l'histoire reste la même	history stays the same
écrire ceux pertes des vies	I've made it my fight
c'est mon combat perdu	to document this loss of life
je fonce,	I insist,
le noir la marque d'héro	Black, emblem of hero
besoin de paix d'égalité	in need of peace and equality
Dénoncer les meurtriers mérite le choix	Denouncing murderers is a choice
du peuples la révolte armée	of the people armed for revolution
de peuples opprimés	of the oppressed
nos terres sont divisées	Our land is destroyed
la loi est a réviser	our laws revised
on manifeste à terre ici	even our demonstrations are being undermined
on meurt à masse nos drapeau sont lèves	Red alert: we are dying in masses
On en a mare de la guerre	we have had enough of war
marre de vos douce paroles	enough of your thoughtful words
qui enterre mon peuple	that bury my people
Je vote le changement	I vote for change
mais pas mes dirigeant	but not for politicians
Mambo ya badilike nami kesho ni tcheke	for all of this to change for a brighter tomorrow
Mambo ya badilike nami kesho ni tcheke	for all of this to change for a brighter tomorrow

Knowing a few nuances of the politics of production (and understanding the lyrics) often shifts students' opinions of these songs. The music retains its sonic appeal, but instead of feet-tapping, head-bobbing appreciation, students are often stoically horrified by the pandering of "Sote Tunawe" and stirred into a mild frenzy by the potency of "Mazao." Their reaction represents, on one hand, the knee-jerk reflex to side with the proverbial underdog out of righteous indignation. But there is also something else going on. The story behind the songs reveals the immense web of complications that go into music production in a conflict region; these are the mechanics of music as a vehicle for social change and they are fraught, in the vast majority of cases, by compromise. In this particular case, both organizations acted with integrity. Indeed, Solidarités's willingness to continue to negotiate and communicate with Yole!Africa throughout the process is, in its own way, a successful example of equitable collaboration, for many organizations would simply have called the project off or sought a less ideologically militant partner at a later date—or both. In this case, the compromise was triggered not by lack of organizational integrity or even by the complexities of cross-cultural collaboration, but by the respective organizations' fundamentally different conceptions of local needs.

Economist Manfred Max-Neef's human-scale development theory offers vital insight into the dynamics at work both in microcosmic examples like the song competition and in larger-scale humanitarian projects. In this theory, Max-Neef identifies nine fundamental human needs—subsistence, protection, affection (or love), understanding, participation, leisure (sometimes translated as idleness or time to reflect), creation (or creativity), identity, and freedom—which he determines are constant across all populations and throughout time; he then differentiates *needs* from *satisfiers*, which, he argues, vary with cultures and historical periods. In this theory, a need is a *state*, not an object; thus food, clothing, and shelter, for example, are not needs in and of themselves but rather satisfiers of the need for subsistence. Max-Neef creates out of axiological needs and satisfiers a grid, called the Needs Matrix, that charts the possibilities of satisfying human needs in terms of the ontological categories of being, doing, having, and interacting. Notably, the Needs Matrix avoids material objects; thus the need of "having" refers to having principles, values, laws, rules, or traditions rather than having material things. The completed Needs Matrix is visible in Table 3.1.

Through the lens of the Needs Matrix, deeper sources of the tensions behind the song competition become clear. Like most organizations dedicated to disaster relief, Solidarité focuses on "meeting vital needs,"[2] which maps onto the Needs Matrix under "having" and "doing" "subsistence." From the point of view of human-scale development, what the local musicians were advocating during the competition lands at the intersection of "being" and "protection" and at

TABLE 3.1

Human Needs Matrix From *Real Life Economics: Understanding Wealth Creation*, edited by Paul Ekins and Manfred Max-Neef. Routledge © 1992, reproduced by permission of Taylor & Francis Books UK

Needs	Being (qualities)	Having (things)	Doing (actions)	Interacting (settings)
Subsistence	Physical and mental health	food, shelter, work	feed, clothe, rest, work	living environment, social setting
Protection	care, adaptability, autonomy	social security, health systems, work	co-operate, plan, take care of, help	social environment, dwelling
Affection (love)	respect, sense of humor, generosity, sensuality	friendships, family, relationships with nature	share, take care of, make love, express emotions	privacy, intimate spaces of togetherness
Understanding	critical capacity, curiosity, intuition	literature, teachers, educational policies	analyze, study, investigate, meditate	schools, families, universities, communities
Participation	receptiveness, dedication, sense of humor	responsibilities, duties, work, rights	cooperate, dissent, express opinions	associations, parties, POW*, neighborhoods
Idleness (leisure)	imagination, tranquility, spontaneity	games, parties, peace of mind	day dream, remember, relax, have fun	landscapes, intimate spaces, places to be alone
Creativity	imagination, boldness, inventiveness, curiosity	abilities, skills, work, techniques	invent, build, design, work, compose, interpret	spaces for expression, workshops, audiences
Identity	sense of belonging, self-esteem, consistency	language, religions, work, customs, values, norms	get to know oneself, grow, commit oneself	places one belongs to, everyday settings
Freedom	autonomy, passion, self-esteem, open-mindedness	equal rights	dissent, choose, run risks, develop awareness	anywhere

* POW=Place of Worship

the intersections of "having" and "doing" with "participation." In short, where Solidarités aims to meet material needs of people in dire situations with food, shelter, and hygiene, the artists were fighting for autonomy, rights, and the freedom to express dissent against a system of oppression. All of these activities are equally necessary. But they do not all trace back to the same motivations. Max-Neef argues that the purpose of any economy is to allow people access to satisfiers so that people can satisfy their own fundamental needs; by extension, protecting human rights means creating conditions in which people's capacity to meet their basic needs is not systematically undermined. This is a notably different prescription from that of many international human rights organizations.

Max-Neef's ideas are the logical extension of a system that sees people as subjects rather than objects, which he calls protagonism of people, and which is the foundation on which the theory of human-scale development grows. No organization can accomplish this alone. But the extent to which an organization supports or undermines the protagonism of people is an important determinant of truly sustainable development. Although scholars and critics usually chart this dynamic through critiques of systems of government, economics, health, education, or human rights, it is also evident in the production of music and art. Yet, unlike the outrage that accompanies news of corruption or of NGO projects that fail to meet the needs of local communities, the politics of production behind songs and musical albums are obscured by the feel-good factor of art, which prevents critical scrutiny by foreign audiences.

On a theoretical level, this corruption of art can be read as a distortion of Lumumba's utopic vision of Congo as a place of autonomy into neoliberal rhetoric deployed to conjure illusions of humanism. This works because the failure of Lumumba's vision of self-governance has not eradicated his vision of utopia; it has only left little space for the utopic to endure in any realm outside of the creative. Art has become a way for Westerners to engage, positively, with Congo, to remedy the social ills of war. But art has also become the vehicle through which to inflict new kinds of domination. At its worst there is, in the production of art by NGOs, unsettling evidence of Robert Stam's suggestion that "the colonialist attitude has moved from obnoxious exteriority—i.e., overt hostility to the third world other—to obtrusive interiority. Now the colonialist probes the secrets of the other without ever relinquishing his own."[3] Indeed, beneath the feel-good factor of music or films, the popularity of medical, structural, or disaster relief NGOs producing art suggests a hierarchy of values in which the integrity of artistic practice is secondary to the practices of more quantifiable fields.

Certainly, if the equation were reversed and artists took to the fields to administer medical aid, there would be immediate outrage and rather serious sanctions.

Local artists have much to say on the topic, for this practice has a much longer and more insidious history in the east of Congo than the recent song competition. To this point the perspective of reggae superstar Mack el Sambo is revelant. As one of Goma's most prominent musicians, president of the North Kivu branch of the Union des Musiciens Congolais (Congolese Musicians' Union), and a musicians who is regularly approached to compose songs for politicians and international NGOs, Mack el Sambo has had ample opportunity to witness the dynamics of music production in Goma. According to him there are a tangle of problems that surround NGO music production, among them issues of power and money, censorship and control, the potency of music as a medium of resistance, and the identity of musicians.[4]

At the core of many of these issues is money. NGOs pay musicians to write and record songs; as such they maintain a certain level of control over the songs and, by extension, over the musicians who write them. One of the most obvious points of contention is the amount NGOs pay a given musician to write and/or record a song. This is by no means regulated and, notably, NGOs are criticized for both overpaying and underpaying musicians. On one hand, when NGOs pay musicians too generously, it creates a temporary and unsustainable bubble that eventually bursts, destroying musicians' individual careers and threatening the viability of the larger cultural scene. This was evident in Goma in the production by the hospital and NGO Heal Africa of a musical album, recorded in 2006, which triggered the disintegration of sixteen of the city's eighteen most popular bands because they later refused to play for less than what the NGO workers briefly paid them for playing private parties. At the same time, when NGOs pay too little, they are accused of undervaluing and disrespecting musicians, forcing them to compromise their artistic integrity for insultingly little financial reward, as was the case when Doctors Without Borders offered a prominent local musician a flat fee of $200 to write, record, and license a song introducing their organization to skeptical locals, without adding any funding for the transportation of band members and instruments or the cost of studio time. The end result for the musician was less than $20 for more than two weeks of full-time labor.

Another complication around money is the practice NGOs have introduced of paying people to participate in activities. This takes many forms, often termed "transport" or "incentive" fees rather than outright payment. The reason NGOs adopted this practice was to facilitate participation by people who live in remote areas and whose presence at a given workshop means their absence from their source of income, which can cause real financial hardship. However, when such incentives are applied to educational or artistic activities, things often get very complicated. Local filmmaker Jack Muhindo (aka TD Jack) explains it thus:

> Since NGOs have arrived here in Goma they have inculcated people with the spirit of money so that for everything people do they want to be paid, which causes a problem for us, the locals, who don't have enough money to pay people. You see, here, if you invite someone to come to a training or workshop you have to pay them. So you give twice. You give the knowledge and the money. And if you say to someone, "listen, come to this workshop, we'll do this, and this," they'll ask for money even as you are trying to help them. That's the big problem.... Recently I participated in a workshop with an NGO that gave us $10 for transport. In Goma where can you go that costs $10? We pay 500 francs [roughly 50 cents] for transport. So why do they give us $10? They call it transport, but morally, it's payment.[5]

This spirit of money, as TD Jack calls it, has far-reaching consequences. For local filmmakers it complicates the prospects of capturing honest encounters in which people are not changing their behavior for monetary incentives. Indeed, such encounters are becoming difficult for filmmakers to come by as potential subjects are now conditioned to demand payment for participating in anything.

But on a deeper level this is a symptom of the erosion of autonomy and collective self-worth. Prior to the arrival of international NGOs, people in the east of Congo paid for education; they were not paid *to be* educated. Paying for education is a literal and symbolic investment in community development that increases citizens' accountability, agency, and the sense of empowerment that comes with providing for oneself. It is the war, not the international NGOs, that disrupted the cycle of agency in supporting education in the region. But in the eagerness of international organizations to meet the pressing needs for school and other educational fees to be paid, they often overlook the disempowerment, dependency, and stagnation that result when people are no longer expected to do the small acts that boost their sense of pride.

Artists—musicians, filmmakers, dancers, visual artists, etc.—also more than ever read NGO incentives as unspoken permission to exert control over artists' work and to censor that work to fit the demands of reports submitted to funders. Frustrated by this dynamic, rapper Bin G says,

> You can't force inspiration. When they [NGOs] come, you know, the majority of Congolese don't have enough money, so when NGOs propose money, you

see? People try to force inspiration, but forcing your spirit, your heart—that doesn't work, it's not good. When people do that they don't see the message [in their songs], they just see the money behind NGOs.[6]

As Bin G suggests, the combination of art with financial need on the part of local communities and financial power on the part of NGOs leads to some complex compromises. This is a small sampling of examples of the ways in which NGO presence in culture production, as in other activities, "interferes with local peoples' movements that have traditionally been self-reliant. NGOs have funds that can employ local people who might otherwise be activists in resistance movements, but now can feel they are doing some immediate, creative good (and earning a living while they're at it)."[7]

If the problem of money is insidious, it is not only because international NGOs have failed to find the right formula for compensation, but also because many of the musicians in the east of Congo think of themselves as artists in a revolutionary sense of the word. Indeed, musicians conceive of themselves and their art as conduits for sociopolitical critique and change. According to Bin G, "an artist is someone who speaks what is in his heart, and above all, speaks the truth. That is rap—to speak what we live."[8] Many of the local musicians, in particular the rappers, share this view. Speaking to the importance of maintaining artistic integrity, in this case on the subject of singing for peace, rapper Fal G says,

Personally I can't sell peace like they [NGOs and musicians who accept to censor their songs] do. . . . You can't just sing any old thing for peace. . . . Myself I sing peace, I don't sing *for* peace because if you sing peace, you sing peace—just peace. But if you sing *for* peace, you can sing absolutely anything, you can scream for peace, etc. and you can also accept to be censored.[9]

There is no dollar amount that can reconcile this self-conception with the organizational constraints of an international NGO. Thus musicians rail against the control NGOs assert, citing the control of artistic content that comes with the power to pay.

Goma is rife with popular wisdom about this dynamic, which is often summed up in the phrase *le main qui donne c'est le main qui dirige* (the hand that gives is the hand that controls). From years of experience working with international NGOs in the region, Mack el Sambo is deeply critical of this dynamic:

When you work for an NGO you are basically a slave because the hand that gives is above the hand that receives. When they pay you they require you to do this, this, and this . . . they censor your words and force you to change your message. . . . And the more money that comes in [to North Kivu] the worse things get. It's like a form of commerce. There are certain local NGOs that profit from war, misery, and suffering by deceiving funders. If the international NGOs would listen to me they would have to ask themselves, Did we go to Goma to change things or did we go there to make certain people wealthy? There are many NGOs, many multinationals, many people who profit from this war. For them the war must continue so they can live. And if the war ever finishes, for them it will be a catastrophe. You need to understand this.[10]

This perspective on the destructive presence of NGOs is not uncommon; many artists in North Kivu rage against the corruption of art (among other things) from the influx of international NGO money into the region. Among others, rapper Emma Katya shares this point of view. Speaking of his own experience participating in an NGO album project in 2006, he says

they [the NGO] said we were allowed to select the song we contributed, that it was a way for us to share our message with the world, but then they wanted to read the lyrics before we went into the studio. I first gave them one song, which they rejected because they said it was "too political." It's a song that criticizes the system that is destroying our lives here—they said they wanted to "heal" things, but they reject the songs we create ourselves that explain why we have problems in the first place. Next I gave them another song but it was the same story. You know? What's really true is that they wanted my music but not my message; yeah, the music without the message.[11]

The sum total of the complaint is that international NGOs do not listen to the messages artists want to convey and instead use (subtle) means of censorship to restrict musicians in writing the songs that are later marketed to funders as authentic expressions of local opinions. Indeed, the album about which Katya speaks was central to Heal Africa's fundraising campaign and was cited as proof that the hospital was collaborating with and responding to local needs. From a local perspective, there is a deep irony in this. Critical musicians are quick to point out that the very justification NGOs use to validate their choice to produce music in the first place is that it is to music, above all, that local populations listen—yet NGOs themselves do not listen to the very people who make this music. Instead they position themselves as gatekeepers of one of the most potent tools of activism and slowly leach it of its power.

But for all their criticism, for many musicians the catch is that, despite conceiving of themselves as artists in a radical or revolutionary tradition, they still need to earn a living. As NGO contracts are by far the most lucrative in North Kivu, there is never a shortage of musicians (or other artists) willing to sign. Indeed, for many musicians, the only conceivable way to make even a partial living through their art is to become the mouthpiece of an international NGO. For those artists who refuse NGO contracts, the chances of independent success are even more limited than in politically and economically stable regions with commercial audiences and established channels of marketing and distribution. Artists everywhere face this dilemma; it is not unique to Congo, or even to conflict regions. But the stakes of compromising artistic integrity to contribute to materials that in turn are central to the very stories and strategies NGOs use to raise funds for humanitarian and charitable projects in war zones come with real consequences.

I do not condemn NGOs, neither Solidarités nor Heal Africa, for turning to music to promote their initiatives. The problem is that they often do so in ways that local artists find contradictory. Analyzing this dynamic through the theory of human-scale development reveals the crux of the matter to be this: most NGOs trace their funding back to the United Nations, the World Bank, the International Monetary Fund, Western governments, and multinational corporations. Therefore NGOs must, by necessity, justify their budgets in terms that are linked to an economy in which the GDP, rather than personhood, is the common denominator. This is why many scholars point out that NGOs are first and foremost accountable to their funders rather than to local population they purportedly serve.[12] However, the rhetoric NGOs use to articulate their activities to donors and local communities frames their interventions in the language of human needs and rights, which creates the impression of focusing first and foremost on the humanity of the people in question. But there is a fundamental disconnect between projects undertaken to serve *people* and projects that must, at the end of the day, fit into an economy of *things*.

From this perspective, the frustrations expressed by artists in Goma are a reflection of the underlying tension between their own conception of interventions as actions that should be directed toward human beings in need and their experiences of working for NGOs in which, despite the politically correct language of equality and collaboration, they ultimately embody margins of profit and loss. Clearly NGOs that function in a capitalist economy, must exercise the fiscal responsibility that allows them to balance their budgets at the end of the year. They must, among other things, make purchases and pay employees. But tracing money through humanitarian cultural projects eventually brings the discussion full circle to the degree to which interventions are materially—not just rhetorically—based on the protagonism of people. In short, the issue is not the use of capital; it is the ideology behind its use. Understanding the politics of production behind music coming out of conflict regions sheds crucial light on the gaping chasm between organizations that prioritize helping people establish the conditions that allow them to meet their own needs and those that prefer to meet people's needs for them. At the core of their frustration with international NGOs is local artists' understanding that, no matter how valuable certain interventions are, approaching humanitarian or charity work from any perspective that does not foster the *autonomy* of local communities has consequences.

To distill such dynamics, human-scale development provides for varieties of satisfiers including violators, destroyers, pseudo-satisfiers, inhibiting satisfiers, singular satisfiers, and synergetic satisfiers. Each category of satisfier denotes how a given action intersects with existential needs. From this perspective, the majority of songs produced by international NGOs are best analyzed as singular satisfiers that address one specific problem without addressing the web of other issues that are inevitably intertwined. In principle there is nothing wrong with this; but in practice, if the rhetoric surrounding a satisfier evokes collaboration, which is customary when working with music in Congo, local artists expect the project to be one in which their creativity, identity, freedom, and participation will be honored. When this does not happen, it confirms to the artists (and to the community at large) that the NGO in question is not actually interested in helping the community secure the conditions in which they can solve their own problems, but rather in exercising control. Thus, when interventions fail, as they invariably do, to live up to the high expectations of locals according to their awareness of the large budgets of international NGOs, bitter rifts develop, and this further undermines the conditions that support people in meeting their own needs.

This is what is at stake when producing music in a war zone. Although on many fronts the cholera song competition was successful, for local artists it nevertheless bears many of the hallmarks of projects that are rhetorically but not materially based on the protagonism of people. To substantiate this claim, the musicians reference the afterlives of the songs. In brief, Solidarités used "Sote Tunawe" in their sensitization campaign, which was a success regarding cholera awareness but was a source of stigma and ostracism for the group that recorded the song. (In discussing the aftermath of this competition it is important to note that since the cholera project Solidartiés has shifted some of its policies in Congo and in early 2016 approached Yole!Africa about a second collaboration, this time to make educational videos instructing local populations on the use of inexpensive water purification tables they now manufacture, which is a recent initiative the NGO developed to

FIGURE 3.2 Art on the FrontLine Poster. Image courtesy of Yole!Africa.

give communities more realistic access to clean water.) "Mazao," in contrast, did not receive any financial compensation, but the community's outrage over the competition prompted Yole!Africa to launch an online series, *Art on the FrontLine*, as a platform for artists to express uncensored dissent (poster visible in Fig. 3.2).

As the title suggests, *Art on the FrontLine* is a critical series that draws attention to the many frontlines of conflict. As an online series, it serves as a platform for musicians, filmmakers, dancers, and journalists from the Great Lakes Region who want to share their stories without censorship. The series features episodes (visible on the companion site to this book) like "Mazao," ⏵ which was the inaugural episode; "Uhaki" (Justice) ⏵, a song that was another finalist from the cholera competition, and its accompanying music video against "glocal" corruption[13]; "Dream Under Fire" ⏵, a short documentary about a local journalist and filmmaker each of whom covered the December 2013 attacks of the M23 from a surprising angle; "Faraja," ⏵ an uplifting documentary about a young entrepreneur who pays his own school fees by renting out his bicycle; and "Agizo ya Lumumba," ⏵ featuring the text of Lumumba's famous poem, which musicians turned into a hip hop song accompanied by a music video.[14]

This is a sampling of the stories local artists choose to tell when given the autonomy to express their own opinions. For the artists this project serves as a synergetic satisfier of an array of needs that fall under "creativity," "freedom," "participation," "identity," and "protection." Unfortunately, between the economic and political instability and the sea of international NGOs introducing money into music production in exchange for control of content, to date *Art on the FrontLine* has not helped musicians satisfy the need for "subsistence" in any materially significant way. But where synergetic satisfiers differ from singular satisfiers is that in failing to satisfy a given need (in this case subsistence) they do not undermine the satisfaction of other needs, whereas singular satisfiers focused on one material outcome (such as hygiene) often inadvertently trample other needs (like creativity, autonomy, participation, or dissent).

As the curator of *Art on the FrontLine*, Yole!Africa recognizes that the proverbial frontline in Congo's conflict includes the literal space of physical battle and the more urbane interactions with transnational entities. Analyzing such interactions reveals that the models of domination that sustained colonial and imperial projects in Africa also undergird many humanitarian projects.[15] In and of itself this argument is not new, but its application to art production adds crucial information to theoretical and practical efforts to mitigate overt violent conflicts as well as subtler power struggles. Whereas in fights for political independence liberation ideologies once proposed culture as a national project in decolonizing efforts, *Art on the FrontLine* is an example of how radical arts centers are now extending this mandate and including culture as a global project. Decolonization writ large is still the aim, but the forces of neocolonialism and neoliberalism have radically reconfigured this project.

The task at hand for artists is thus to renew, in practice, theoretical models of liberation. In *Art on the FrontLine,* efforts in this vein are most evident in applying extant liberation ideologies to digital production. In music videos such as "Agizo ya Lumumba," the juxtaposition of a historic poem by Lumumba with contemporary dance, rap, scenes of local cultural protest, and digital editing techniques follows, in contemporary terms, Fanon's prescription that "by imparting new meaning and dynamism to artisanship, dance, music, literature, and the oral epic, the colonized subject restructures his own perception."[16] In this project, the sonic aesthetic is distinctly global; the rhythms, melodies, and sparse harmonies clearly cite transnational hip hop cultures more than they evoke a specifically Congolese soundscape. What the musicians (and dancers and filmmakers) assert in this piece is their allegiance to conscious underground hip hop movements, including those in the United States, Europe, South America, and other parts of Africa. Thus the perceptions being restructured are many; this piece is certainly part of the larger project of decolonizing the mind of local communities, but it also aims to complicate foreign perceptions of Congo as a place of exaggerated violence and helplessness with concrete images of agency and politically astute local commentary.

It is this sense of global belonging to a powerful body of oppressed populations, rather than to a singular nation, that serves as the artists' barometer of social and political (in)justice. And in an economy overrun by foreign actors—humanitarian and other—their inclination toward the global makes sense. Yet despite the transnational aesthetics evident in the sounds, images, and choreographies, the potency of art remains tethered to the same principles now as it was in the fight for national liberation. Indeed, Solanas and Getino's assertion that "revolutionary cinema is not fundamentally one which illustrates, documents, or passively establishes a situation: rather it attempts to intervene in the situation ... it provides discovery through transformation" is an apt description of the music videos in *Art on the FrontLine,* which intervene both in global perceptions of Congo and in the local politics of art production like those that defined the cholera song competition.[17] Equally relevant is Stuart Hall's suggestion that "cinema is not a second-order mirror held up to reflect what already exists, but that form of representation which is able to constitute us as new kinds of subjects, and thereby enable us to discover places from which to speak."[18] For activist and militant artists in Goma, the combination of economic pressures, comparatively affordable digital technologies, and their identity as global (rather than national) citizens positions music videos more than other forms of cinema as the medium of dissent and self-constitution. But regardless of the medium in which their commitment to autonomy and liberation manifests, art is still both the vehicle and the gauge of sociopolitical change in the east of Congo.

This is where art is in conflict with aid. In their ideals, socially engaged artists and humanitarian NGOs all strive to address social ills, but their respective conceptions of the role of art in remedying problems are fundamentally at odds. Although there is more to say about the wider issues, the main point here is this: in the case of Congo, the fight for artistic and expressive freedom is one of the smaller battles that make up the larger war. At stake in the battle over art are which stories the world hears, who tells them, and how. By extension this influences whether and how the world sees fit to intervene. In short, beneath the universal appeal of music as the mode of delivery, the stories conveyed through songs and music videos are as much about power as about specific content. Thus the final component of my classroom experiment with students involves a discussion of how, when we listen to sound, we must also listen for silence.

There is a wealth of information in the silences in both "Sote Tunawe" and "Mazao." The absence of uncensored local opinion in "Sote Tunawe" obscures the analyses that have the potential to affirm the agency and power of Congolese people; the lack of distribution or promotion of "Mazao" (outside of ideologically like-minded circles) is a silence of its own that reflects the many ways alternative narratives are marginalized. The common denominator is power, not music. Yet music is increasingly the vehicle through which these silences translate, rapidly, into campaigns of action; in this case the options were hand sanitation or Western economic reform.

Both are necessary. But if music is ultimately going to prove viable as a means of sustainable sociopolitical change in any conflict the world over, it seems to me that it must be music produced from—or exposing—positions of power.

ART VS. JOURNALISM IN THE EAST OF CONGO: IMAGE AND PUBLICITY

The challenges that arise at the intersection of culture production, money, and humanitarian crises are not exclusive to music. Indeed, next to the nearly inaudible subtleties of the politics of music production, their visual equivalents are comparatively overt and reveal additional discrepancies in the fundamental orientation of cultural projects in the east of Congo. There are, of course, many similarities in the motivations for and challenges that arise during audio and visual projects. One similarity is that, as with song, image is perceived by both locals and international NGOs as an effective conduit of information for local and global audiences; another similarity is that, in visual projects as with sonic, money and control are at the core of the matter. I include some visual examples to demonstrate specifically how such projects translate to local audiences, many of whom perceive a malicious sleight of hand in simultaneous acknowledgment by NGOs of the power of images and stubborn insistence by the same organizations on maintaining, rather than sharing, control over them.

Like their musical equivalents, many visual projects are framed as inherently positive activities through language that capitalizes on the (real or imagined) universal love of art and creative expression. One recent manifestation of this in Goma is evident in the surge of NGOs offering varieties of art therapy for youth. As a respected method for addressing trauma, art therapy is a meaningful service to offer in a war zone. But even in activities designed for healing there are risks of misunderstanding (and worse) as organizations and communities navigate their respective conceptions of local needs. Take, for instance, the attempt to reconcile the need for "subsistence" with the project of art therapy, in which the drawings and paintings completed by young people during workshops were sent to Europe and America, where they are auctioned and the proceeds returned to participants for school fees. This idea was developed in response to the reticence of some families to encourage their children to participate in art when they could be doing more lucrative things. In monetary terms, this project was a success; it generated school fees for a number of students and confirmed to parents that art is a valuable activity from a psychological and a financial point of view.

However, amid all the celebration of this project as an example of the power of art to have a positive impact on people on the ground, organizers failed to recognize that the control they exercised in selecting which pictures to send for auction had an unintended side effect. The participating children quickly learned that pictures of explosions, guns, fighting, and death were considered more indicative of healing than pictures of happy families or pastoral scenes; thus participants, some of whom had never experienced war-related trauma, began to concoct violent images in order to compete to have their school fees paid (eventually the enthusiasm spread further and children from stable upper-middle-class families also began to conjure stories of war and victimhood to sell to the highest bidder). Although their agency in generating their own school fees is arguably empowering for young people, in the longer run such empowerment comes with a price, or what local artists term a "compromise," that circumscribes creativity to expressions of victimhood that conform to external values. Ultimately, despite the theoretical brilliance of this project, it confused the satisfiers of "creativity" (imagination, boldness, inventiveness, curiosity) and of "identity" (sense of belonging, self-esteem, consistency) with those of "subsistence." Even if we read this as an effort to foster mental health, which is a critical satisfier of the need for subsistence, lingering questions remain about the healthfulness of young people learning to capitalize on experiences of trauma and to market themselves as victims. To whatever extent one might argue for the agency of the youths' subversion of the project or their clever manipulation of the system, it is not a variety of agency that breeds community autonomy.

Questions of visual representation extend far beyond creative or artistic projects. Indeed, this example of the potential problems of introducing art therapy into a conflict region dwarfs in comparison to the industry of visual representation that in Congo, as everywhere, is an uncontestably powerful force. In the east of Congo, as in other places, frustrations about visual representation are not limited to the effects such representations have on campaigns of intervention (as discussed in the previous chapter) but also hone in on issues of control and ownership of the images themselves. This dynamic is one of the most prominent critiques put forth by the Dutch documentary filmmaker Renzo Martens in his provocative 2008 film *Episode III: Enjoy Poverty*, which ultimately suggests that, through their tenacious control and credited ownership of images of suffering, humanitarian organizations in fact capitalize on poverty. Although the film is cynical, even mercenary at times, the discomfort it engenders carves an important space for addressing some of the most urgent questions of representation in Congo.

Cinematically, *Enjoy Poverty* employs a minimalist aesthetic reminiscent of the blurring of fiction and non-fiction (ethno-fiction), realism and trance in Rouchian ethnography. The entire film is shot with a handheld camera and often includes Martens's train-of-thought commentary (and sometimes singing) as he probes the inner sanctum of humanitarian aid. The narrative of *Enjoy Poverty* follows Martens at work on his controversial project of promoting poverty as a resource on which he urges the poor in the east of Congo to capitalize. Early in the film Martens establishes the premise of his argument when he attends a World Bank Conference in Kinshasa. After the Congolese minister of the interior summarizes the proceedings and confirms that the World Bank has pledged US$1.8 billion to Congo, he opens the floor to questions. Martens, who has an official press pass, films himself asking, "What share is this $1.8 billion of the Congo's total revenues? And if it is a high percentage, I would like to know whether the fight against poverty, for which this money is destined, may be an important natural resource for the Congo? Or even *the* most important?" In response, the visibly flustered World Bank director responds, "First of all, poverty is not a natural resource. Poverty is a shared defeat for the entire international community. It is true that development aid brings in more money to the Congo than copper or coltan or diamonds. Even if combined. But it's normal. That's how a postconflict situation develops."[19] In response to this analysis from an official of the international community, the remainder of *Enjoy Poverty* proceeds to question the so-called normalcy of Congo's (post)conflict development.

Clearly this is a challenging task, especially when coupled with interrogating visual representations. In addition to the obvious concerns about the content of images from any war, Martens's encounters with a significant cross-section of populations living and working in the east of Congo suggest that ownership and crediting of images is a more insidious problem than one might think. Critiques of poverty pornography are prevalent enough that they have infiltrated mainstream thinking about the ethics of representing suffering, but it is still uncomfortable to witness the negotiations behind the scenes where such images are created. Sparing no discomfort, Martens includes a conversation he engaged in with two journalists (one French, the other Italian) after witnessing them repeatedly photograph corpses strewn by the roadside in a village ravaged by militias:

JOURNALIST: If you're making this documentary and it's like for news and you think it has a news value, then we pay around $300 per story used. And usually our stories are not more than a minute and a half.

MARTENS: Right. And what kind of stories do you need?

JOURNALIST: Unfortunately, the time they're interested in stories these days is if there is something negative. So usually it has to be a disaster or a humanitarian crisis or dead people, poor people or something. But if they have a nice parade or a carnival, then we are not interested.

MARTENS: I understand.

JOURNALIST: But it's not me, it's supply and demand. It's a market out there.

MARTENS: Huh, it's a market.[20]

That journalists must compete in a capitalist market is obvious, but this scene advances Martens's larger project of bringing the capitalism of visual documentation into uncomfortably close proximity to what many donors (and volunteers) have been conditioned to accept as the altruistic charity of humanitarian work. Later in the film, Martens pushes this point further when he ascertains that, in addition to having all expenses paid, journalists receive fifty U.S. dollars per photograph, compared to local photographers, who make roughly seventy-five cents for the pictures they shoot at weddings and birthday parties. As part of his short-lived one-man campaign to work toward greater representational equity, Martens gives (and films) a semiformal presentation to the locals of the rural village of Kanyabayonga in the east of Congo, during which he says:

> The fundamental question is: to whom belongs poverty? If it can be sold, that means that it is important to know who is the boss, the owner of that poverty. Since it brings in money, donors, even individuals like perhaps my father, who says, "How awful! Look at those photos of children in Africa who can't even go to school, I'm going to donate fifty dollars to this or that NGO." So you are not only beneficiaries of the good will of others, of NGOs like MSF [Doctors Without Borders] or WWF [World Wildlife Fund] and other agencies that come to help you, and then you should be endlessly grateful, no, you are also actors—extremely important actors in this world. Because if poverty is like a gift that creates deeper understanding, you also give it back to the world—to the people who come to visit you. It is something that makes us happy, in a way. There will always be people visiting you, taking pictures, supposedly funding projects. But then it's them that will have the pictures, it's them that will have, let's say, captured your poverty free of charge, while you don't benefit too much. It's a resource![21]

After presenting this analysis, which the Congolese audience receives with a mixture of amused skepticism and tentative curiosity, he sets out to teach local photographers how to capitalize on the suffering of their people and turn their poverty into profit. He instructs them on how best to capture suffering: the visibility of ribs is important when shooting malnutrition; closed eyes, preferably swollen from beatings, are the best for rape victims; it is important that hungry children be surrounded by flies; etc.[22] Martens uses his status as a white journalist to gain the group access to hospitals and IDP camps in which he coaches them and encourages them to compile portfolios of their photographs. Eventually he accompanies the local photographers of Kanyabayonga to show their portfolios of humanitarian photographs to "Fred," the head of the Doctors Without Borders hospital in Goma. Their hope is that Fred will grant them the right to receive a UN-issued press pass, which would permit them to continue the project after Martens's departure and allow them to develop a steady income. After a brief but cordial introduction to Fred, Martens proceeds:

MARTENS: The essential question is, the photographers present here today have noticed that international photographers report on malnourished children, raped women, etc., and that there's more money in this than in parties and weddings. So we'd like to ask you if they too, like the international photographers, can come and photograph inside your hospitals, if possible.

FRED: You're asking if they can photograph us so that they can sell their photos. That's what it boils down to?

MARTENS: Yes.

FRED: (laughs) Does that sound right to you?

MARTENS: Yes, because I . . .

FRED: I'll be careful with what I say here. I'm responsible for my patients, I'm not here to make an exhibit of their misery. I'm not here to use my patients, and malnourished mothers and children in our care, in order for one to make money. I'm not here so that the logo of Doctors Without Borders can be stuck in a photo to make cash. There's no way.

MARTENS: But the international photographers sell pictures too, right?

FRED: No, that's part of communications.

MARTENS: But they sell them too, right? If a photographer from *Libération* or the *New York Times* or whatever comes to cover the Congo, would you deny him access because he's making money?

FRED: No, because he's here to make news, not money. We know exactly why these photos are taken. It may seem shocking to you, but it doesn't shock me.

MARTENS: But the overall problem remains, that those who live in poverty can't benefit from it themselves.[23]

Although Fred's mandate to protect his patients is obvious, his assumption that Congolese documentation of the suffering in their own nation would, by default, be predatory rather than undertaken in service of "news" or "communications" reveals a certain preconception about the possibilities and limitations for Congolese. Clearly it is unethical for any photojournalist to prey on suffering for financial gain, but why, when it comes to Congo (or other African countries), is this a question of national affiliation? Previous sequences in the film already established that foreign photographers make significant profit exhibiting and selling images of suffering outside the realm of news reporting (for example, following the World Bank Conference in Kinshasa there was a lavish reception during which expensive photographs of poverty and suffering taken by European and American journalists adorned the walls and were available for purchase).[24] But from Fred's perspective, what is acceptable, even encouraged, for Western photographers is unimaginable for Congolese. True, Martens's claim that poverty is a resource is outrageous, but beneath the mercenary irony of his actions, this episode makes a compelling case that it is equally outrageous that Congolese agency is perceived as undesirable, even categorically impossible, by officials of one of the world's most prominent and well-respected NGOs.

In *Enjoy Poverty*, Martens positions his exchange with Fred as evidence of his larger thesis that the West's strategic control of representations of atrocity capitalizes on suffering and, through illusions of humanitarian charity, in fact solidifies neocolonial domination of Congo. Framing poverty as a resource is problematic for a number of reasons, but it nonetheless provides a powerful analytic structure through which to question the larger function of the organizations Martens profiles, such as the World Bank, the UNHCR, UNICEF, and Doctors Without Borders, and many others he does not include in this film. Rather than celebrate their humanitarian contributions, *Enjoy Poverty* foregrounds these organizations' roles as transnational entities that rely on strict control and ownership of representational rights to mask capitalist agendas behind a façade of charity.

Martens's focus on the clash between a capitalist economics of image production and rhetorics of humanitarianism calls into question *which*—and *whose*—needs are being addressed through charitable action. One uncomfortable scene that makes this point involves an impromptu interview with the director of an IDP camp in Mugunga. The sequence opens with a shot of women mourning on the newly covered grave of an infant who died of malnutrition. As the camera zooms in on them grieving, it becomes impossible to ignore the logos of UNHCR and UNICEF plastered on every surface in the camp, most prominently the tarps and plastic sheeting that serve as walls, roofs, and ponchos (visible in Fig. 3.3 left frame). When pressed to explain why people do not have the option of protecting themselves from rain without sporting humanitarian logos, the director confesses NGOs want the "visibility."[25] The camera lingers on the director's face, creating an intensity that makes this matter-of-fact statement extremely uncomfortable. Clearly the visibility of humanitarian logos is not intended to suggest that NGOs are responsible (or want credit) for the problems local populations face, but it is also clear that they do want recognition for their contribution

FIGURE 3.3 Enjoy Poverty Sequence.

to alleviating suffering. But Martens's camera offers a rare glimpse of this phenomenon from a point of view shared by many Congolese, who condemn foreign
NGOs for using suffering bodies as sites of advertisement.

The issue of logos (and the hive of related issues of naming, ownership, and
credit it triggers) is tricky in cross-cultural encounters. Citing authorship,
whether by name or logo, is a practice that is so directly linked to the high
esteem Western cultures place on recognizing individual achievement that,
from a Western point of view, it is perceived as an imperative and fundamentally
ethical act. But from another point of view, habitual and prominent placement
of names and logos is a murky practice that, in conflict regions, often makes de-
marcation of achievement indistinguishable from commodification of suffering.
The combination of prominent logos with perceptions by locals that NGOs do
not live up to their promises leads to bitter, yet common, analyses of the conflict
as a material benefit for Americans and Europeans who need a backdrop against
which to celebrate their caring and heroism, and make decent money while they
are at it.

Underlying this criticism is the assertion that many NGOs and the armies of
well-intentioned workers and volunteers they bring with them to global disasters
are, in fact, satisfying their *own* needs for "affection" and "participation," with
"generosity" and "dedication." But rather than *being* generous and dedicated,
the accusation is that many organizations (and individuals) *perform* these qualities in lieu of supporting local communities in fulfilling their own needs. The
result is that working or serving or volunteering in a fraught part of the world
does satisfy the employee's or missionary's or volunteer's need for "identity" by
cultivating "self-esteem," but this does not necessarily (or often) translate into
behaviors that support the protagonism of *other* people. The problem here is not
just that local needs go unmet (or worse) but that performing is for credit and
activism is not. Indeed, the self-interest underlying many organizations promoting activism, charity, and humanitarianism is a subject of vehement contention in Goma, where, to put it mildly, people do not appreciate being the backdrop against which foreigners build their self-esteem, their identities, or their
résumés.

In characteristically provocative style, Martens addresses this dynamic as well; indeed if *Enjoy Poverty* is a critique of humanitarianism, it is also a critique of activism. On the surface, Martens's project of empowering Congolese to capitalize on their own suffering is ludicrous from a Western perspective, but it is a useful, if macabre, parody on the absurdity of many Western projects from the Congolese point of view. To what extent Martens's efforts on behalf of the photographers is satirical remains unclear throughout the film, but, whatever else it says about him personally, his willingness to overtly manipulate the feelings and sacrifice the integrity of those he ostensibly wants to help forces viewers to grapple with uncomfortable questions of privilege, intention, and personal stakes that riddle foreign interventions. By virtue of his status as a white Westerner, Martens has access to European funding, UN-issued press passes, and the privilege to use these currencies to act on his own intentions (however questionable); yet, when inevitably his project fails, the stakes for him prove to be quite low. Indeed, having raised the hopes of the local photographers and exposed them to (and documented their) immense humiliation when they submitted their portfolios to Fred, toward the end of the film Martens simply tells them that the project will "fail," that he is going back to Europe, and that they should go back to what they were doing before he arrived and be content to "continue to take photos of parties and weddings."[26]

If this callous interaction suggests that Martens, like many foreigners intervening in the Congo conflict, has little to lose if anything, the penultimate scene of *Enjoy Poverty* makes the incendiary case that he, like others, in fact has something to gain. The scene, depicted in the right frame of Figure 3.3, begins when he concedes defeat to a plantation worker he had hoped he could help, and, in lieu of offering a sustainable solution to the man's dire situation, simply offers his family a meal. At the end of the meal, Martens gathers the worker's children round and allows them to select humanitarian logos from his ample collection, which he then pins onto their tattered shirts, while thanking them for giving him the footage that will make his film successful. When the family thanks him for the food, he responds, "I thank you too. Because of the labor you provide, almost for free. I think it's almost impossible for your situation to change. You will always have a job with low wages. In Europe we don't want cocoa or coffee or palm oil or coltan or any of that to get more expensive." The camera lingers on the man's disappointed face, then cuts to images of a party Martens has orchestrated in the plantation village to celebrate the illumination of his one lasting contribution to the community: a monumental generator-powered neon sign reading ENJOY please POVERTY (Fig. 3.3 center). After they politely cheer the cumbersome, expensive, and ultimately useless installation, Martens tells the community that he too will offer them nothing in return for their cooperation and participation in his film:

MARTENS: All over Africa there are plantations like this one, where people earn very little. If you are going to wait for your salary to grow so you can be happy, you will be unhappy all your lives.

CROWD MEMBER: We'll gladly accept whatever you can do for us when you get back.

MARTENS: There is nothing prepared.

MAN: There's nothing prepared?!

MARTENS: Nothing.

MAN: Once you go back you can't deliver reports?

MARTENS: I doubt it.

MAN: Why did you come then?

MARTENS: To tell you you'd better enjoy poverty rather than fight it and be unhappy. Do you want to remain unhappy all of your life because of poverty?

CROWD: No.

MARTENS: Then you need to accept things the way they are. Be happy despite poverty.

WOMAN: But if there's change . . .

MARTENS: No, no changes, if you accept what you cannot change you can have a bit of peace in your hearts and minds.

MAN: But will you project the film here?

MARTENS: The film will be shown in Europe, not here. (pause) Experiencing your suffering makes me a better person. You really help me, thank you.[27]

Martens's mercenary irony aside, his willingness to fail publicly exposes many of the insidious subtle dynamics most international NGOs prefer to ignore (if not actively hide). The fact is that engaging in activism does benefit the activist. But rather than acknowledge this or make of it a foundation for exchange and mutual respect, most organizations prefer to downplay potential benefits to activists by focusing on the morally superior values of help, compassion, and courage. It makes sense that organizations and individuals are reticent to foreground the material benefits to themselves of working with people whose lives have been systematically devastated by violent conflict. The very notion of acknowledging benefit goes against the image of selflessness that is strategically cultivated in the language of charity. But where the language of charity calls on virtues, it does so in a way that disconnects the resultant values from the historically and geographically rooted systems that elevated them, in the eyes of a few, to the ideal qualities to apply to the lives of everyone.

Divorcing cultural values from their historic context perpetrates its own kind of violence. It opens the floodgates for armies of well-intentioned people to impose their generosity, help, and courage on others without realizing that, in any configuration of events that lead to manmade problems in the (post)imperial world, those values are inextricably related to power. As many anti- and postcolonial scholars before me have argued, to counteract this trend it is necessary to highlight the relationship between imperialism, which ultimately spawned humanitarianism, and charity, lest zealous do-gooders forget that the popular insistence on "morality" in the West is, in fact, an extension of the same impulse that underlay the imperial project. This impulse, as it was artfully articulated by Edward Said, grew out of the conviction that "the source of the world's significant action and life is in the West, whose representatives were at liberty to visit their fantasies and philanthropies upon a mind-deadened Third World."[28] In the high era of European imperialism, these fantasies and philanthropies were tethered to the expansion of territory; in the postimperial, postcolonial era, the fantasies and philanthropies of the West are conditioned by the distinctly American self-perception as the global "righter of wrongs." The former was justified by a narrative of civilization and uplift, the latter by the rhetoric of heroism. Both mask power. Relevant to the conflict in Congo, though, is the lethal imposition on local communities of fantasies and philanthropies incubated in the illusion that heroism is selfless.

It is quite the opposite; heroism is an exercise of power. Yet, in conflict and disaster regions, where privileged people encounter excruciating violence (often for the first time), "the rhetoric of power all too easily produces an illusion of benevolence."[29] Despite the fact that history has proven, beyond the shadow of a doubt, that the imperial agenda has dire consequences for its human subjects, the rhetoric once evoked to justify imperial projects continues to surface in humanitarian and charitable projects and continues to produce illusions of benevolence. The difference is that the vocabulary of power has been replaced by the vocabulary of charity, with no mention of how charity is an extension of and in service to geographically and historically specific powers. This is the point that Martens makes so potently when, in all sincerity, he encourages people to enjoy their poverty and thanks them for making his life easier and for giving him the footage from which he will benefit materially when he puts his name on the film. For critical viewers of this scene, the discomfort and the public failure of his project offer rich insight into the perversion of language and values that so deeply irks local communities in the east of Congo. Stripped bare, their criticisms are thus: that help, which ought to be an expression of selflessness, has become a staging ground for feats of heroism; that compassion, which would ideally lead to empathy, is a disguise for pity (which exists from a stance of superiority); and that courage, which at its best is the impulse that compels people to take risks on behalf of others, is, in the east of Congo, a thin veneer for greed.

ART VS. ACTIVISM IN THE EAST OF CONGO: MAKING
AND MARKETING PEACE

As in other parts of the world where activists (volunteers, humanitarian workers, etc.) from geopolitically powerful countries come to help without recognizing the fundamental imbalance of power underlying their projects, Gomatriciens are armed with ready criticism of aid. Recognizing the validity of many such complaints, some advocacy organizations have shifted their focus toward taking action in their own country of origin in a kind of reversal of the "liberal internationalism" that lured international NGOs into Africa decades earlier.[30] In the case of Congo, this is a particularly viable option as so many of the countries exporting aid workers and volunteers are simultaneously importing the resources fueling the conflict. Thus there is much work that people genuinely concerned about the well-being of Congolese can do in reforming their own nation's economic and political policies, with no risks of stumbling unintentionally on the psychological landmines of colonial inheritance.

The two most established examples of this kind of advocacy in the United States are Friends of the Congo and the Enough Project's Raise Hope for Congo campaign. Both of these organizations advocate relentlessly at the U.S. policy level, bringing awareness to companies and laws that support unregulated extraction of minerals from the east of Congo as well as encouraging students to petition for campuses, cities, and states to go "conflict mineral free." Both of these organizations also work hard to educate Americans about the conflict and about their own implication in it, to inform a critical mass of globally conscious American citizens who will unite to do their part in stopping the war by eliminating the funding and training of proxy armies in Uganda and Rwanda and by eliminating the demand for the unregulated minerals they plunder.

In addition to a variety of other formats such as websites, press releases, and public appearances, both of these organizations also rely on audiovisual representations to convey their points. For its part, the Enough Project launched an online video series entitled *I Am Congo*, which offers positive portraits of Congolese working actively to address the needs of their local communities. To date, the episodes include profiles of Fidel Bafilemba, "the activist"; Petna Ndaliko, "the artist"; Dominique Bikaba, "the conservationist"; Denise Siwatula, "the human rights lawyer"; and Amani Matabaro, "the community builder (and footballer)." The aesthetic of the videos is contagiously upbeat, with Congolese dance music as the soundtrack and smiling bodies and beautiful nature featured in nearly every shot. The objective of this video series is to introduce to the world positive stories of local life and local agency to work against the dangerous single story of Congo that is so prevalent in the United States. In this the series succeeds (albeit with less radicalism than it could have, had it opted to curate Congolese films on the topic rather than sending American filmmakers to shoot the portraits). Indeed, these engaging portraits, combined with the Enough Project's significant following, have effectively begun to chip away at the stereotypes that homogenize Congo and its people as a place of nothing but victims of war. Experiencing the humanity of Congolese through these videos has inspired many people in the United States, particularly college students, to get involved in Congo advocacy by taking action in their own home towns, which not only leads to viable solutions, but also avoids many of the potential dangers of foreign activism.

As a series dedicated to positive and inspiring portraits, what *I Am Congo* does not do is recontexualize or repoliticize the conflict. By contrast, Friends of the Congo's 2011 documentary *Crisis in the Congo: Unveiling the Truth* takes a historical approach to dissecting the conflict. (It is important to note that my analysis here is of the original 20-minute version of this film released in 2011 not the later 25-minute version, which includes additional footage that compromises the aesthetic of the original.) This film's comparative radicalism is evident in its progress toward reversing the illusions of transparency propegated by the Western world's simultaneous invasive exposure of African ills and celebratory promotion of its own philanthropy (to return to Stam). Indeed, the historical narrative of *Crisis in the Congo* foregrounds Western, and particularly U.S., participation in Congo; ultimately the truth being uncovered (as indicated by the title) is not in fact a universal Truth about Congo, its people or its politics, but rather about the strategic U.S. presence (and absences) therein. In this film, the critical lens is effectively directed inward instead of outward, which creates a strategic inversion in which Congo's bloody history becomes a backdrop for a reflexive investigation of U.S. interventions, actions, and inactions.

In alignment with the explanation of the conflict given by militant Congolese activists, *Crisis in the Congo* traces the present war back to King Léopold II's colonial regime, citing Congo's extreme natural wealth as the source of exploitation by the West for more than 125 years. Through a series of interviews with experts and activists, *Crisis in the Congo* informs the viewer of Congo's vast mineral wealth and the devastation its global demand wreaks on millions of Congolese. Yet, in discussing the savagery to be found in the proverbial heart of darkness, this film maintains its focus on U.S. actions. Early in the film an invisible narrator explains:

> The story of Congo is often overlooked for its complexity. It's a story where boundaries are porous and national identities mean little. Militant groups with ever-changing acronyms are not who they claim to be and neighbors loot and murder while they are praised by the international community. But the death toll is now surpassing that of the holocaust, in part because of the way the United States is involved in Central Africa.[31]

Accompanying this recitation are images of American presidents Ronald Reagan, Bill Clinton, and George W. Bush shaking hands with the African leaders Mobutu (Zaire), Paul Kagame (Rwanda), and Yoweri Museveni (Uganda) respectively. This combination of sonic and visual information prompts the viewer to grapple with the historical journalist Adam Hochschild's pointed question, "Why are people living hand to mouth in one of the most mineral-rich countries in the world?"[32] Cumulatively, *Crisis in the Congo* provides an answer through images, stories, and testimonies of slaughter, rape, and wealth: it is because of the historic and ongoing greed and passivity that taint Western policy.

Foregrounding American participation rehistoricizes the conflict in ways that stand in stark contrast to the habitual references to ethnicity or vague allusions to economics that characterize so many accounts of the war in the West. The narrator states this outright when he says "scenes like this [of massacres and genocides] are often misunderstood as simply the result of an ethnic war, a mistake that only benefits those trying to hide their illegal exploits."[33] Instead of perpetuating this dynamic, *Crisis in the Congo* offers concrete evidence of America's role in the ongoing wars. After contextualizing the "Clinton era guilt" over the genocide in Rwanda as motivation for the subsequent U.S. support of Rwanda in the invasion of the east of Congo, professor and lawyer Gregory H. Stanton, who during his time in the U.S. State Department (1992–1999) drafted UN security council resolutions that created the international criminal tribunal for Rwanda and who later founded Genocide Watch, says:

> So the question is, what role did the U.S. play in this? It was a pretty direct supporting role. I happened to go to Rwanda just before this invasion took place and major shipments of weapons [pictured] were coming in at night to support the Rwandan army; we had placed people in the country who were training the Rwandan army troops; in short, we were supporting the invasion.[34]

Immediately following this statement, the film cuts to archival footage of the U.S.-backed invasion of the east of Congo by Rwanda and Uganda. In the next shot, which depicts the lush banks of the Congo River from an aerial view, the invisible narrator continues to expose the role of the United States in the conflict:

> The reason the United States supported Rwanda and Uganda in their invasion of Congo cannot simply be attributed to genocide guilt. The U.S. had economic and political motivations as well. One reason for our involvement extended back to our support of Mobutu Sese Seko, a dictator we helped install in Congo and supported for thirty-two years.[35]

Cut to an interview of Hochschild, who continues the history of U.S. ties to Mobutu:

> This man [Mobutu] bled his country dry; he extracted even more money from it than King Léopold did in his time. Mobutu had a longer reign and a much more developed economy to plunder. And the United States was deeply complicit in that because we supported Mobutu lock, stock, and barrel.[36]

The anonymous narrator resumes:

> When Mobutu became an embarrassment [because of his despicable human rights record] we helped Rwanda and Uganda overthrow him and install another dictator [Laurent Kabila, pictured] and another [Joseph Kabila, pictured]. Now the Congolese people are victims of a corrupt dictatorial network that receives financial support from the United States. . . .

Here the camera cuts to a wide-angle shot of the White House and continues to zoom in as the narrator continues:

> The role that the U.S. plays in Central Africa is complex. Historically we've maintained influence in the area for access to minerals on which our economy and our military rely. But our connection to Rwanda serves our interests in yet another way. . . . The disciplined and organized armies of Rwanda and Uganda are useful for protecting American interests in Africa. Similarly, friendships with dictators [pictured: Pinochet (Chile), Suharto (Indonesia), Mubarak (Egypt), Museveni (Uganda), and Kagame (Rwanda)] are easier to manage than complex, thriving democracies. For generations the way the United States has been involved in Africa has helped to perpetuate tyranny and dependency.[37]

In the conclusion of this sequence, Maurice Carney, founder of Friends of the Congo, says, "So, when you see these prescriptions coming out of Washington and they say that 'we've tried everything,' that 'we support peace-keepers,' that 'we've had peace talks,' it's usually within the parameters of maintaining the current order."[38] This three-minute sequence achieves a number of things. First, it concretizes the meaning of "Western complicity" that is often alluded to but rarely explained. Defining the role of the United States in the conflict has the effect of demystifying what is otherwise at risk of being perceived as anti-Western conspiracy theory. Second, this sequence acknowledges complicity and assigns responsibility through words like *we* and *us*. The speakers' collective use of first-person pronouns when referring to collusion in the conflict stands in stark contrast to the habitual *theys* and *thems* that litter most reports about Congo. Third, when this sequence transgresses the third wall of cinema as Carney says "you," his articulation of this word makes clear that he is not referring to a proverbial or imaginary "you" but speaking directly to the viewer. By appealing directly to the viewer in this way, the film reveals its underlying objective, which is to catalyze action.

There are important parallels between the paradigm of action Friends of the Congo advocates through this film and the paradigms of action more militant Congolese activists propose, all of which trace back to the historical framing of the conflict. Where Congolese activists call on the roster of facts that lead from Léopold to the present, they do so as the foundation of strategies that address Congo's colonial inheritance, including the less tangible heirlooms such as mental colonization. In an equivalent move, Friends of the Congo calls on the same roster of facts to diagnose the American inheritance, which they argue is evident in the willful ignorance, silence, and complacency that collectively describe the American response—governmental, political, and individual—to the Congo crisis. This diagnosis is made in *Crisis in the Congo* in a sequence early in the film[39]:

There's a pattern to genocide, you can see it coming; I mean—it's like a hurricane. (*Gregory H. Stanton, U.S. State Department 1992–1999, founder and president, Genocide Watch*)

Are we going to have to wait for twenty more years before somebody does something to stop this Holocaust? (*Yaa-Lengi Ngemi, author of* Genocide in the Congo)

There's a global consensus that exists that says that it's OK for nearly six million Black people to die in the heart of Africa and for *us* to be *silent*. (*Maurice Carney, founder, Friends of the Congo*)

So I kept asking our intelligence people: Is there any truth to this? What's happening out there? (*Stanton*)

I don't think policy makers could claim that they didn't know. (*Anneke van Woudenberg, senior researcher for Human Rights Watch*)

There's something wrong. There's something wrong with *us* in terms of the way we think about Africa. (*Howard French,* New York Times *journalist and assistant professor at Columbia Graduate School of Journalism*)

This sequence confirms an important premise of the film: although there are atrocities taking place in Congo, it is in the United States where something is wrong, and that "something" manifests in willful ignorance and silence.

In addition to the overt information conveyed through the film, the cinematic language of *Crisis in the Congo* also challenges the habit of silent ignorance through visual metaphor. Throughout the original version of the film (about which I write), the images that accompany the discussion of the atrocities taking place consistently occupy only a narrow strip of the screen (be it bottom, middle, or top) while the rest of the screen remains black.[40] Whether it is images of emaciated children left to die, bloodied and beaten women and girls lying in makeshift hospital beds, fly-infested scattered corpses, or remnants of mass graves full of anonymous bones, they are limited to a partial screen, as if to represent a picture seen through eyes half shut. On one hand, minimizing these horrific images shows respect for those who are suffering by refusing to gratify voyeuristic fascinations with atrocity. At the same time, this gesture creates within the viewer the subtle psychological effect of restriction

and omission. Ultimately the effect of trying to see beyond the barriers imped-
ing the image makes the viewer try, quite literally, to open her eyes. This visual
metaphor is thus a tactic to trigger a hunger for more information and to call
critical viewers to action.

Accompanying this visual metaphor is an overt call to action. Early on, the
film establishes that "now facing a critical juncture in history, the Congolese
people need *us* to change the way *we're* involved so that they can have the
space to start rebuilding their country."[41] Consistent with its focus on
American (in)actions, *Crisis in the Congo* encourages a change to the Western
paradigm and suggests that space for Congolese autonomy, in conjunction
with strategic legislative change on the part of the West, is ultimately the
necessary formula to bring an end to the crisis. There is a notable difference
between this line of thinking and the idea that simply eliminating conflict
minerals from the picture is sufficient.

The focus on comprehensive action in the West is reinforced toward the end
of the film when Maurice Carney reminds the viewer that "keeping in mind that
the ultimate solution is going to come from the Congolese people themselves,
our role on the outside is to make sure that we create the space for them to solve
and address the challenges that they face."[42] Then, rather than listing the challenges Congolese face, the now-familiar cast of experts lists many of the reasons
Americans should care to change their own behavior, suggesting that, whether as
an environmentally concerned global citizen, or as a child advocate, or as anyone
who has a mother, sister, wife, or daughter, or as the owner of a cell phone, automobile, or pacemaker, or simply as a human being, every citizen ought to be concerned and speak out about what is taking place in Congo. Concomitant with the
litany of reasons to care, the visual metaphor of half-closed eyes that previously
accompanied images of atrocity yields to full screen shots of babies' corpses covered in flies, of young girls looking unflinchingly into the camera from their beds
in the rape clinic. In short, having exposed the complicity of the United States in
the Congo crisis, the wide-eyed visual language underscores the spoken text and
confirms that no one is exempt from action or excused for ignorance.

Ultimately, *Crisis in the Congo* offers concrete suggestions via websites (its
own and Friends of the Congo's) for how motivated viewers can channel their efforts toward catalyzing legislative change in the United States. In addition, they
expose the concrete details—historic and present—of the illegal exploits by the
United States in Congo, which Friends of the Congo ties to the ongoing complacency of the general public. In reading both the film and the accompanying digital
materials critically, this project reveals a very important principle, namely that

when the focus of a campaign includes acknowledging complicity, the resulting tactics are increasingly reflexive. Reflexivity is among the most indicative qualities that distinguish the approaches to activism underlying all projects of social justice or sociopolitical change. It is through reflexive inquiry that individuals and organizations recognize that their own fundamental needs are as entangled in activist work as those of any target population they aim to serve.

It is also through reflexive inquiry that activists must eventually acknowledge the benefits of their work to themselves. I said before that activism is not for credit, but when activists refuse to recognize the material benefits they reap from their work, the natural desire—not need—for recognition often turns activism into a for-credit activity. This is in part because there is a kind of moral capital in doing good. But it is also because many of the activities associated with activism intersect with fundamental human needs even as the language of service deems articulating their satisfaction unspeakable. This is where study of the Needs Matrix benefits activists' reflections on their own needs as well as on the structure of their projects. Recognition, or credit (of the variety that results from aggressive self-promotion), is neither a need nor a satisfier; it is nowhere to be found on the Needs Matrix because it is not an ingredient that fosters protagonism of the collective. Yet, in different ways activist work can and often does fulfill *all* of the fundamental human needs outlined by Max-Neef for at its best, activism is an act of service, a manifestation and embodiment of the values set in motion by economies that prioritize people over things.

If anything, recognizing the personal benefits of activist work increases the impact of that work because it liberates activists from the illusions of benevolence and reveals the personal stakes of intervening in a given situation. This is not the abstract stuff of meditation; the discipline it requires is simply the courage to acknowledge how the work we do is neither more important than nor morally superior to the work of others. I include myself in this. Activist work has certainly brought significant benefits to me. In addition to bringing so many precious people into my life, it has afforded me experience and credibility (not to mention the book you are reading), all of which are real currencies in my profession.

In and of itself, there is nothing wrong with an activism that yields personal benefits to the activist, provided there is sufficient transparency to prevent the perversion of virtue into value. Indeed, if in taking inventory of the personal benefits of activist work we identify the needs and satisfier that motivate our choices, the difference between actions undertaken to fulfill the need for "freedom," "participation," or "identity" and those undertaken for credit, or to justify the spread of morally infused (but ethically suspect) values, becomes painfully clear. In recognizing, for example, that there is a currency to credibility, trading on that currency becomes a conscious act with material consequences for all parties involved, because everyone has something more concrete than imperially infused concepts of morality or heroism at stake. This is not to say that reflexivity guarantees successful development or implantation of a project; for that, there are far too many variables of engaging in activist work. But any project that does not include reflexivity at the foundational level and as an ongoing practice has little chance of doing meaningful good in addressing issues in which human lives are affected.

The force of the preceding reflections might come as a surprise in the context of a book about music, film, and creativity, but the anatomies—and costs—of activism are surprisingly visible in cultural endeavors in and about the east of Congo. This is evident in the many examples throughout this book of the politics of production, the unexpected impacts (positive and negative), and the unintended repercussions of songs, albums, and films. But there is another meta-arena in which the dynamics of culture production are playing out, and that is in arts festivals. Currently there is a particular surge in festival culture in North Kivu. In 2006, Yole!Africa's Salaam Kivu International Film Festival (SKIFF) was the only international arts festival in Goma; in 2007, the group *Union des jeunes artistes dessinateurs et peintres* known as UJADEP (Union of young artists in drawing and painting) launched its Jaki Leo festival of drawing and painting. Since then the number has increased rapidly: in 2012–13 the Amani Festival was launched in Goma by Foyer Culturelle de Goma/ Maison des Jeunes; in 2013 Master Peace took place in Bukavu, organized by the Dutch organization Master Peace; and in 2014 the Peace One Day festival series started in Goma, organized by London-based Peace One Day.

Like the smaller cultural pieces of which they are made, festivals have their own distinct politics of production. In the case of Goma and the Kivus more broadly, these politics center more than ever around peace, which, as the festival titles indicate (*salaam* and *amani* mean peace in Arabic and Kiswahili, respectively), is the topic of urgent concern prompting so many large-scale events. There are many parallels between the claim that music can change the world and the claim that a festival can contribute to peace. The feel-good factor is certainly at work behind the notion that devoting anywhere from one to ten days to music, dance, films, paintings, or any other art form can make material progress in a conflict as deeply rooted as that in the east of Congo. But the feel-good factor sells. Indeed, the budgets for some of these festivals are significant: the $274,000 of the Amani Festival stands alongside a $10 million contribution to Peace One Day from the Howard G. Buffett Foundation to support Peace One Day in Goma for three years (2014–2016). But behind the glamour and the thrill of doing global good, there lurk important questions, not the least of which are, What is the relationship between art and peace? And what is the role of festivals therein?

In 2014 the three highest-profile festivals were Peace One Day (September 21), the Amani Festival (February 14–16), and SKIFF (July 4–13). Each has a distinct concept of the place of art in questions of peace. According to their websites, Peace One Day aims "to shine a global spotlight on the Great Lakes Region of Africa," the Amani Festival aims to "unite . . . innocent victims of the crises [who] want to be the builders of peace," and SKIFF aim to "bring together artists and activists from around the world who share a common vision of positive social transformation through critical creativity."[43] These are distinctly different objectives, which, quite naturally lead to equally contrasting activities. For the purpose of shining a global spotlight on the Great Lakes Region, Peace One Day's primary tactic is to galvanize celebrity support (to date, British actor Jude Law is the Peace One Day Ambassador to Congo) and consistent high-profile media coverage. To unite those who have suffered the daily repercussions of the ongoing conflict, the Amani Festival focuses on creating a forum for celebration infused with a call for peace, or as the organizers describe it, "an incredible party and a fantastic call for peace in the great lakes region."[44] To foster critical creativity, SKIFF organizes a series of workshops and cultural exchanges between local community organizations and partner organizations and artists around the world.

All of these projects have an impressive roster of achievements. As of 2013, Peace One Day had more than 420 million people in two hundred countries who were aware of their work in Afghanistan (their target country before coming to Congo), and that represents a 68 percent increase from 2012. Since 2007, 4.5 million children have been immunized against polio and ten thousand women and children immunized against other deadly diseases in Afghanistan as a result of the ceasefires negotiated for Peace Day. In organizing this scale of activities, Peace One Day has amassed a powerful group of sponsors that includes Coca Cola, Google, Skype, the Execution Charitable Trust, and of course the Howard G. Buffett Foundation.

For its part, the Amani Festival gathered twenty-five thousand people from Great Lakes Countries and Europe for its activities, which also brought an impressive amount of media coverage, including articles in the *Guardian*, TV5Monde, the *EastAfrican*, and *le Potentiel*. The Amani Festival also made great strides toward cultivating a culture of corporate sponsorship for arts events in Goma, as evidenced by their impressive list of sponsors, which includes among others the telecommunications giant Vodacom; one of Congo's biggest beer breweries, Brasimba; Brussels Airlines; and a host of humanitarian and UN agencies such as the UNHCR, UNICEF, and WWF.

In its own right, SKIFF congregated an audience of fifteen thousand from twelve African countries, from Europe, and from the United States for its public performances, offered ten workshops for 247 youth participants that resulted in production of three short documentaries, five new dance choreographies, four new songs, a blog, and a fashion line. SKIFF was also the focus of significant international media attention, including articles in the *New York Times, Al Jazeera*, Africa is a Country, and the *EastAfrican*. In terms of its global support, SKIFF's sponsors and partners include such educational institutions as the University of North Carolina at Chapel Hill, Harvard University, Howard University, and Seattle University; nonprofit funding organizations such as the DOEN Foundation; embassy support from, among others, the American Cultural Center; and small-scale support from other grassroots organizations including Cultures of Resistance, Friends of the Congo, Africa in the Picture, and DRC Apeparel. (For images from various SKIFF festivals, see the companion website.) ▶

In the most general terms, the range and results of activities undertaken by these three cultural entities can be read as working vertically (Peace One Day), horizontally (SKIFF), and diagonally (Amani Festival) to engage culture in the project of peace. Each approach makes an important contribution in seeking to resolve a conflict as complex as Congo's. A vertical approach has the power to put urgent questions on the proverbial table of people and institutions with power the world over. As a result it attracts the attention of a staggering number of ordinary folks whose lives inevitably intersect with the decisions of people and institutions with power. Though often less glamorous, a horizontal approach addresses the dailyness of building and supporting the communities, families, and individuals who collectively shape their own sociopolitical realities. In a horizontal effort, it is more often the host of details than the host of followers that is staggering because in such an approach to activism every interaction matters, no matter how small. What I am calling a diagonal approach tries to achieve a balance between the tactics of vertical and horizontal activism. This approach brings with it the potential financial benefits of larger corporate support and an elevated profile, as well as the capital of greater local credibility; the challenge, of course, is to navigate the great potential for corruption of one (communities or corporate partnerships) in favor of the other so as not to dilute both past the point of efficacy.

In a cultural scene as small as Goma's, it is inevitable that projects eventually intersect with one another. Indeed, there is tremendous cooperation and collaboration between the various festivals and organizing bodies that coexist in the city. But there are also, inevitably, collisions. In these collisions there is much to learn, for they are both the result and the catalyst of the smaller stories that do not make the spotlight, but that do shape the lives of the people affected by the war or the peace in the region. Such stories are often about details that pale in comparison to millions of vaccinated children in war zones but that represent nonetheless the building blocks of sustainable peace.

There is one such story that took place between Yole!Africa and Peace One Day during SKIFF 2014, shedding light on what happens when vertical and horizontal structures collide. Out of an impulse of mutual support, Yole!Africa and Peace One Day entered into an explorative partnership for both organizations' 2014 festivals and activities. This partnership included, among other things, a high-profile screening and community discussion of Peace One Day's signature film *The Day After Peace*, by the organization's founder, Jeremy Gilley; a workshop for aspiring filmmakers about documentary filmmaking, taught by Gilley; and access, through the NYAVU Network,[45] to a number of film and video technicians Peace One Day might call on to document their various activities in the Great Lakes Region. In return for facilitating closer connection with local communities, Peace One Day offered Yole!Africa name and logo promotion on its publicity materials for Congo-related events, which, in light of Peace One Day's impressive list of sponsors, is potentially valuable for an organization with a comparatively small global profile.

In certain ways, this partnership was successful. Indeed it was in the success of the postscreening discussion of *The Day After Peace* that the antagonism between vertical and horizontal activism became clear. One question that arose consistently during the community debate was *where*, in Peace One Day's strategies in Congo, the needs of the local communities were being addressed and, more importantly, *how* Peace One Day was ascertaining information about local needs. The more critical members of the audience were not satisfied with Peace One Day's unilateral support of the UN, arguing instead that civil society actors, and specifically those who were willing to be brutally honest with humanitarian and charitable organizations, would be better targets of Peace One Day's support in Goma's already saturated environment of international NGOs. Musicians in the audience also expressed frustration at the extravagant compensation foreign artists receive for performing (often in English) to local audiences, while *if* local musicians, who can actually speak meaningfully about peace, are even invited to perform, they are not equally respected from a financial point of view, if they are compensated at all. From their side, Peace One Day was advocating for the benefits of elevating the profile of the conflict on the global radar through high-powered cultural events such as the scheduled concert with American-Senegalese hip hop sensation Akon. Peace One Day was adamant about recognizing and congratulating local artists and suggested that by also bringing foreign stars, the overall cultural scene would benefit significantly. By the end of the debate there was a lively, though civil, clash between top-down and bottom-up approaches to sociopolitical change.

Despite the significant energy and resources Peace One Day had already put into building relationships with local organizations such as schools, churches, hospitals, and government officials, the postscreening debate at Yole!Africa was the first encounter they had with criticism from the local community. Absence of direct criticism is typical in Goma when organizations or individuals interact with Western groups. It is important to note, however, that reticence to challenge foreigners is often motivated by the desire to benefit from the power and money foreign projects represent, more than it is motivated by genuine support for the projects themselves. Outside of formal negotiations, representatives of local organizations often express criticism, frustration, or outright disdain for foreign projects while simultaneously justifying the need to partner with them despite gross ideological differences. This is in part another bequest of the legacy of mental colonization and in equal part the inevitable result of an oversaturation of international NGOs. As a result of Yole!Africa's effort to fight mental colonization, debates at the center have become a forum in which people express their questions, and sometimes their criticisms, to representatives of international organizations in an effort to reveal to them how their projects are actually perceived by locals. Encountering critical pushback from within the larger community, which is generally so accommodating, is often a surprise for NGO officials; yet for those who are willing to hear them, many of the local criticisms have tremendous potential value for improving projects.

On many levels, the results of the community debate with Peace One Day are still to be seen. The impact of local criticism on Peace One Day as an organization will become clear only in their future choices over the coming years in Goma. What is certain is that the discussion had a strong impact on members of the community. In a subsequent electronic letter to Jeremy Gilley, the rising Congolese journalist Gaius Kowene articulated the dynamics at work with elegance. As director of communications for Yole!Africa, Kowene was mediator and translator of the community discussion of *The Day After Peace*. Impressed with his obvious competence and familiarity with local criticisms of the organization, Peace One Day approached Kowene the following day, offering him the position of strategic advisor for the organization's programs in Congo. The offer was generous and reflected genuine desire on the part of Peace One Day to partner with and support a promising local young man, which registers on some levels as a symbol of the real desire to do the same for the entire community. Kowene's response is indicative of how such desires are not always viewed by the local individuals and communities in question as partnership. This letter is included in the text with the permission of Gaius Kowene.

POD startegic advisor follow up

2 messages

Gaïus Kowene
To: Jeremy.Gilley, Petna Ndaliko Katondolo

Wed, Jul 16, 2014 at 7:36 AM

Dear Jeremy,

First of all, I would like to thank you for your generous offer to hire me as your strategic advisor at Peace One Day. It is always heartwarming to notice that my work is appreciated and acknowledged both in my community and also amongst expats such as yourself.

Although this seems to be a great opportunity to advance my career unfortunately I cannot accept it. It is important for me to clarify that my decision is not personal but ideological. Let me say clearly that I have nothing against you—I respect your passion and your enthusiasm for peace. At the same time I know from experience that not all good intentions help. In the spirit of mutual exchange perhaps it would be useful for you to understand a bit of where I am coming from. I have two primary concerns that prevent me from accepting your offer.

My first concern has to do with the policies and practices of humanitarian organizations working in Congo. The majority of conscious Congolese—including myself—think that there is a serious hypocritical stance from the West on the question of war and peace.

We were delighted to have you share your experience and your film with our students during SKIFF. As I was mandated to mediate the Q & A after the screening, I could not take part. Had I been able to participate, I would have had a myriad of questions for you and your colleagues at Peace One Day. For example:

- What do you think is the biggest obstacle to peace here in the Congo?

- What is your explanation on why next to nothing has been achieved in the Kivus in the past two decades despite the biggest UN mission in the world and the presence of nearly all existing NGOs?

- Are you worried that this «humanitarian complex» is creating an artificial economy which deepens the dependence of local people and economies on these organizations instead of building strong national institutions, supporting autonomy, and gradually seeing the NGOs and the UN withdraw?

- Do you see how NGOs and the UN only focus on healing the consequences of the problems we Congolese face instead of addressing their roots?

I could go on at length with equally relevant questions, questions we examine and discuss at Yole!Africa regularly. Aside from the many failings of the UN security council to bring peace to the Kivus (as well as elsewhere) after decades of interventions, perhaps my deepest frustration is the glaring fact that mainstream media outlets ignore the realities we face on the ground.

FIGURE 3.4 Letter from Gaius Kowene.

The absence of media attention to the failings of the UN (for example) continues to be a serious obstacle to peace. This is the kind of rhetoric we would like to hear from western organizations claiming to bring peace in the Congo.

My second concern is about the various ways in which humanitarian organizations often unintentionally undermine local autonomy. This tendency can be difficult to recognize so let me give you an example.

The very fact of you offering me this job when I am still at the beginning of building my career, though flattering, puts me in the unsustainable position of advancing in status without building up enough of my own experience. While a high profile job is ultimately what I am working towards, I realize that I need to achieve that through my own efforts and by building the skills that will allow me to advance step by step. Otherwise the risk to me is that when you depart in three years my career will suffer seriously. I say this because I have seen it happen time and time again.

If you are really interested in incorporating local perspectives and needs into your work in Congo, I would advise you to select someone who is experienced and well-established for the role of strategic advisor to Peace One Day. One response you are likely to get from anyone who knows the area is discomfort with the practice of paying international stars substantial amounts of money instead of investing the money in local talents and artists who are much more credible in raising awareness in our country's peace process.

Based on my own experience I encourage you to consider approaching Yole!Africa for advice. As a well-established organization, Yole!Africa understands the local perspective very well and has a strong reputation for integrity. In other words, this is an organization that will tell you the truth even if it is uncomfortable rather than telling you what you, as a foreigner, want to hear. I believe this will make your project stronger.

Sincerely,

Gaius Kowene

--

FIGURE 3.4 Continued

In this letter, Kowene identifies many of the tensions that inevitably arise when the stakes are as high as they are in the east of Congo. Although triggered by an interaction with Peace One Day, the points Kowene makes apply not to any specific humanitarian or charitable organization alone, but to all of the agents— local and global—engaging in Congo advocacy and activism. The concerns he raises are common; they are the fodder for the endless debates that take place out of earshot of foreign "partners." This is not to say that expats are not familiar with local complaints; many are. Indeed, many of the expats who have been working in Goma for an extended period of time share the frustrations of locals when they recognize the systemic failures of humanitarian and charity work. The problem is that changing the system is no small task. Many of the points Kowene outlines are the sticking points of systemic change. That they arise in relation to development or structural aid is no surprise. Less obvious, perhaps, is their relevance to an arts festival.

To fully probe the relationship between art, festivals, and peace, it is useful to expand on a few of Kowene's points, including his questions about the United Nations. Congo has a long history with the UN that dates back to July 1960, when Patrice Lumumba first appealed to the UN to intervene in Congo. Blocked by the government in his attempt to address secessionist wars in Katanga, Lumumba requested UN backing, which was an act Fanon considers a defining "mistake" in Congo's efforts to attain independence.[46] Fanon's analysis warrants quoting at length as it identifies patterns that local communities still criticize in the continued UN intervention in Congo today:

> The UN has never been capable of validly settling a single one of the problems raised before the conscience of man by colonialism, and every time it has intervened, it was in order to come concretely to the rescue of the colonialist power of the oppressing country. . . . It is not true to say that the UN fails because the cases are difficult. In reality the UN is the legal card used by the imperialist interests when the card of brute force has failed. The partitions, the controlled joint commissions, the trustee-ship arrangements are international legal means of torturing, of crushing the will to independence of people, of cultivating anarchy, banditry, and wretchedness. For after all, before the arrival of the UN, there were no massacres in the Congo. After the hallucinating rumors deliberately propagated in connection with the departure of the Belgians, only some ten dead were to be counted. But since the arrival of the UN we have grown used to learning every morning that the Congolese were mutually massacring one another by the hundreds . . . civilian functionaries of the UN had in fact set up a new government on the third day of Lumumba's investiture. The head of the UN made contact with Lumumba's enemies and with them made decisions by which the State of the Congo was committed. . . . The aim sought and achieved is the following: to manifest the absence of authority, to prove the bankruptcy of the State. In other words, to motivate the sequestering of the Congo.[47]

These are strong accusations. Certainly UN spokespersons have a different view of the story. But regardless of the objective truth of this analysis, the fact that many Congolese populations still perceive the UN in this way forces any project that collaborates with the UN to be aware, at the very least, of what such collaboration implies to the local community.[48]

When Kowene articulates the need for critical media attention on the failings of the UN, he speaks for many other Congolese who are deeply critical of the UN's activity in the region. This is based on firsthand experiences ranging from frustration over the parallel infrastructures the UN has built that undermine the Congolese state and its economy, to physical abuses perpetrated by UN peace-keeping troops including rape and other forms of sexual violence. Thus for the conscious Congolese of whom Kowene speaks, the logical role of a media spotlight in the Great Lakes Region would include very critical media attention to the United Nations presence. At the same time, local communities understand the geopolitical pressures that make exposing the UN a dangerous prospect. From this perspective, failure to expose the UN is understandable; however, outright celebration of and noncritical support for the UN's missions to Congo is not perceived as a failure to work meaningfully toward peace, but as an overt undermining of the eventual possibility of achieving it. This is the perspective that leads disillusioned locals to quip that one day of peace is an invitation for 364 days of war.

Another complex issue Kowene raises in his letter is the question of an artificial economy. There is, in this question, the obvious concern about the dependency international NGOs create on the resources with which they temporarily saturate a conflict region. But there is also the question of economies of peace. Advocating for peace is more than ever a lucrative activity. And advocating for peace through culture or art is, from a Western perspective, increasingly attractive—or, to quote my students, sexy. But sex appeal is a dangerous mask for ineffective projects. And sex appeal quickly loses its glamour when the stakes for the local communities are made clear. A brief anecdote suffices to make this point. As part of the exploratory partnership between Peace One Day and Yole!Africa, there was discussion about Yole!Africa organizing dancers to participate in Dance One Day, which is a simultaneous dance manifestation organized annually by Peace One Day. By proposing Yole!Africa for this role, Peace One Day no doubt aimed to respect the power and experience of a local organization and, in inviting a kind of collaboration that gave Yole!Africa artistic autonomy, was honoring an important principle of cooperative activism. The idea was that Yole!Africa would coordinate the dancers of Goma and choreograph a citywide dance installation in the spirit of a flash mob. Both organizations agreed this would be a powerful artistic event. The problem was that, without realizing the implications, Peace One Day informed Yole!Africa that they did not have any funds to put toward the myriad expenses associated with transporting and fueling generators around the city, or compensating artists for their performances.

What to Peace One Day represented an exciting opportunity to share Goma's vibrant dance scene with the world was, for Yole!Africa, a serious problem. The issue was not only that artists resent being asked to perform for free; it is certainly not their preference, but when given ownership over a project at times they agree to forgo compensation (though to them sacrificing their material needs is not perceived as a step toward peace). The problem was that Peace One Day had announced, in a public press conference, the $10 million it received to support its work in Congo. No amount of organizational transparency would convince jaded young people in the NGO capital of the world that Peace One Day was not paying Yole!Africa as a partner. The financial habits of international NGOs are familiar to Gomatriciens, who understand that the presence of a logo on publicity materials (not to be confused with the presence of logos on suffering human bodies) represents an exchange of money or other material goods. Thus, aside from the financial burden for Yole!Africa of fueling and transporting equipment and displacing staff, if the logo of Peace One Day were associated with a Yole!Africa event for which the center did not compensate artists, the only credible explanation from the community would be that Yole!Africa kept whatever money Peace One Day contributed to the project. And when the benchmark is $10 million, Yole!Africa's cut would be sizable in the popular imagination. Thus for Yole!Africa to participate in this collaboration would be to lose, in one fell swoop, the currency of community credibility that it had been painstakingly establishing since 2002 and that, with the center's inconsistent funding, is its greatest capital.

It is understandable that, swept up in the enthusiasm of organizing a synchronized global dance experience, Peace One Day would not connect a press conference from months back with the payment of dancers. But this is precisely why the feel-good factor of art and culture is so dangerous: it overshadows details (and common sense) with grandiose visions of inspiration and global interconnection without allowing mundane material realities, such as the need for artists to eat, the cost of production equipment, or institutional politics, to enter the picture. The consequences of subscribing to the admittedly contagious rhetoric of global connectedness through shared artistic expression are immense when that rhetoric is not grounded in practicality. Indeed, if, in their enthusiasm to partner with local organizations, international NGOs undermine the credibility of community institutions, they leave no structures in their wake to serve the local population when they train their spotlights on new frontiers. And, whatever other strides toward peace might result from such interventions, fragmenting the community and undermining local sources of trust and pride is a form of violence bearing many of the signature characteristics of the ongoing war. These are the concrete casualties of the economies of peace that, for all their earnest efforts to catalyze meaningful change, are fundamentally based on material rather than human truths. (To make this point creatively, dancers at Yole!Africa voluntarily organized a flashmob, which they titled "Peace Every Day" and which depicts the logistical as well as creative aspects of dance in Goma.) ▶

The final idea I want to take up from Kowene's letter is that of autonomy, which he references repeatedly in his text. Clearly, as he means it, autonomy applies to working toward an economy that is independent from international NGOs and features strong community organizations. He is also overt in his advocacy of individual autonomy, and the necessity for foreigners to respect individual effort as a real source of value and self-worth that allows people to participate in their communities and careers on the basis of earned competence rather than the handouts of foreigners. In articulating this, he exposes the complex relationship between autonomy and participation. Though they overlap at times, autonomy and participation are fundamentally different. Returning to the Needs Matrix, "participation" is a need potentially satisfied by "receptiveness," "dedication," and "sense of humor"; "autonomy," by contrast, is a satisfier of the needs for "protection" and "freedom." Yet, in some newer trends of activism, they are often evoked interchangeably.

Max-Neef's inclusion of "participation" in his list of fundamental human needs positions it as universal. The need for participation in some way, however small, is highly visible in the support millions of compassionate people give to organizations working to alleviate suffering around the world. It is this same need for participation that drives the virtual trend of what Petna has come to call Facebook activism: click here to join the movement for _____, like us to bring an end to _____, # to support _____ . Sometimes there are serious movements behind the bombarding appeals for clicks and likes. But just as often, posting, clicking, and liking is a glorified assertion of good-personness in which the stakes of posting provocative photos or scathing denunciations are, for the poster, extraordinarily low. Indeed, there is a new variety of virtual activism that is nothing more than the inevitable collision of the culture of vanity with the inheritance of moral authority. Yet for all its flaws, this variety of activism does, for many people, satisfy the need for participation.

Unfortunately, it is often this conception of participation that is imported into conflict regions on the backs of charitable and humanitarian agendas. Participation becomes an *activity* for the target population rather than a *need* for the people with the power to serve. By contrast, in defending autonomy Kowene is also arguing for a different kind of participation. He is arguing for organizations like Peace One Day to satisfy *their* need for participation with receptiveness, dedication, and a sense of humor so that he and his community can satisfy, through autonomy, their needs for protection and freedom.

This is the anatomy of what Kowene refers to as "mutual exchange." This is also a formula that fulfills Max-Neef's prescription for economies to allow access to the conditions that permit people to satisfy their own fundamental needs. To my reading, this is the most meaningful role an arts festival could possibly play in the struggle for peace. The activities and achievements that might result from a festival built on this principle would, of course, vary with the organization's definition of peace; those that conceive of peace as the saving of lives would most certainly develop different strategies from those that conceive of peace as a state of mind. Of course the spectrum is much broader than that, both for definitions of peace and for the role of art and culture therein. For its part Yole!Africa conceives of peace as "not just a word, but a way of life" as evidenced by the center's holiday card from 2013, reproduced in Figure 3.5.[49] In a place as complex as Goma, advocating peace as a way of life suggests that, whether building, consolidating, negotiating, or struggling for peace, peace is an active practice that plays out as powerfully in the details of daily encounters between ordinary people as it does in the resolutions of geopolitical powers.

Although Kowene's decision is admirable in some respects, there is also a certain irony in the fact that he declined Peace One Day's invitation to assume a position that might allow him to influence their work on the basis of the very critiques he

FIGURE 3.5 Yole!Africa 2013 Holiday Card. Photo courtesy of Yole!Africa.

articulates. From the point of view of foreign organizations, it stands to reason that including voices like his would help improve their projects, and that in denying them he is complicit in perpetuating the status quo. Yet from his point of view, Kowene recognizes that accepting the position without having first fully established himself professionally in his own right would allow him to tackle critical issues in name only and would ultimately corrupt the authority of his voice as a credible expression of dissent. From one angle, the deal would have been fair: Peace One Day would gain credibility and Kowene would gain financial stability and exposure to powerful contacts in the media industry. From another angle, in the event that he were not able to change enough of Peace One Day's policies to appease all the frustrations of the local community (which inevitably he would not), Kowene would sacrifice his future as a bright and potentially powerful leader in exchange for three years of pay. The question is not whether Kowene would be able to secure another paying job when his contract with Peace One Day finished; he most certainly would. The question is what would be lost for the community if the voice of one of its most promising young people were associated with dilution of community autonomy.

Although not without precedent, Kowene's decision to decline this offer does not reflect the norm. Indeed, faced with such an opportunity for money and power (however limited), a majority of people would likely have accepted Peace One Day's offer. Goma is chock full of NGOs with local front people whose presence sures funders that the organization's partnerships are collaborative and whose expressions of gratitude for lucrative employment are interpreted as confirmation that the organization is in fact meeting local needs. In an economy of NGOs, these are the extant jobs that allow people to feed their families, so the politics of survival do not accommodate both ideology and practical needs. But as Arundhati Roy points out, the rhetoric of NGOs creates the illusion that both can coexist, a tactic she warns is in danger of destroying resistance movements: "The NGO-ization of politics threatens to turn resistance into a well-mannered, reasonable, salaried, 9-to-5 job. With a few perks thrown in . . . Real political resistance offers no such short cuts . . . Real resistance has real consequences. And no salary."[50] This dilemma is another symptom of the clash between vertical and horizontal structures, whose respective priorities (power or community) prescribe opposing tactics to fulfilling human needs.

In the context of Congo, this dynamic brings to mind the famous parable of a popular Congolese musician who was invited to a party in the capital city, Kinshasa. As the party was at one of the city's finest hotels, he dressed in his most elegant *boubou*, cut from handmade *kikwembe*, which he completed with high-end accessories and handmade Italian shoes. When he arrived, he produced his personalized invitation to the private security guards at the door, who looked him up and down and refused him entry, citing the organizers' adherence to a dress code that requires Western clothing. After insisting in vain that the security guards should honor his invitation and that he too was dressed appropriately for an event of such caliber, he got back in his car and went home. When, a short time later, he returned in a Versace suit, Dolce & Gabbana shirt, and Martin François Jerbaud shoes, the same guards did not recognize him and hurried to open the magnificent double doors of the hotel without requesting to see his invitation. At the height of the festivities, when food and drink were served, he was seated in the middle of the room, where he began gently pouring champagne down the front of his suit, then lovingly smearing food all over his shirt and tie. When, in horrified concern, the hosts hurried to his table to ask what was wrong, he responded, "Wrong? Why would anything be wrong? You invited us here to eat and drink and that is what I am doing—I'm giving my clothes to eat and drink because you did not invite me, you invited them."

I started this chapter by suggesting that the politics of production reveal the extent to which the underlying orientation of an organization or individual is calibrated to an economy of people or an economy of things. Let me end by suggesting that there is a similar roadmap visible in the politics of producing peace or catalyzing sociopolitical change, and that, to the extent any one of us is willing to acknowledge our own stake in taking or not taking action *with* Congo, there are real possibilities of supporting radical paradigms of activism that symbiotically serve both the people in the east of Congo and the wider world. Despite all odds, the east of Congo has a quiet army of individuals and organizations working beneath the radar that will continue to exist and continue to fight for the needs of their local communities so long as there are human beings with needs. The question is not whether such organizations will carry on when the rest of the world is not paying attention (or money or time); the question is whether, how, and why the rest of the world does or does not support such efforts. And it is an urgent question. For, now, more than ever, there is new resonance to Fanon's reminder that "the fate of us all is at stake in the Congo."[51]

NOTES

1. Arundhati Roy, "The NGO-ization of Resistance," *Massalijn*, Sep. 4, 2014, accessed Oct. 10, 2015, http://massalijn.nl/new/the-ngo-ization-of-resistance/.

2. www.solidarites.org. Accessed Oct. 10, 2015.

3. Robert Stam, "Eurocentrism, Afrocentrism, and Polycentrism: Theories of Third Cinema," *Quarterly Review of Film and Video* 13 (1991), 229.

4. Born in 1970 in Kiwaja, Mack el Sambo studied mechanical engineering when he first came to Goma as a student. As a youth who had always been active in music through

his church, he integrated into Goma's musical scene as solo guitarist for the Congolese rumba band London Musica, where he began his career as bandleader. After releasing his first album, *Sikujuwaka,* in 1996, he became a regional sensation and was able to become a professional musician. Strongly influenced by the music and message of Bob Marley, Mack el Sambo developed Congolese reggae, to much critical acclaim. He released two more albums, *Pacification* (1998) and *Plus jamais par les armes* (2003), before the war dried up the economy and he was forced to start releasing singles. His popularity and the potency of his music have positioned him as one of the most respected local musicians in Goma, which has the dual effect of making him an appealing target for politicians and NGOs seeking musical promotion while also positioning him as a role model of ideological fidelity for less-established musicians navigating the pressures and corruptions of the musical scene in North Kivu. To date, Mack el Sambo has been commissioned by the current minister of the plan, Celestin Vunabandi, whose 2006 and 2011 campaigns he endorsed, and by Provincial Governor Julian Paluku, for whom he wrote a popular song in 2011; Mack el Sambo has also been commissioned by many international NGOs.

5. TD Jack (filmmaker), in discussion with the author, June 2014 in Goma, DRC.

6. Bin G (rapper), in discussion with the author, July 2014 in Goma, DRC.

7. Roy, *NGO-ization.*

8. Bin G (rapper), in discussion with the author, July 2014 in Goma, DRC.

9. Fal G (rapper), in discussion with the author, July 2014 in Goma, DRC.

10. Mack el Sambo (musician), in discussion with the author, June 2014 in Goma, DRC.

11. Emma Katya (rapper), in discussion with the author, October 2010, in Goma, DRC.

12. Holmén, *Snakes in Paradise.*

13. This term, which combines "global" and "local," refers to the deep interconnections between the immediately local issues of exploitation and the global economic forces involved in the conflict. It is a popular word among activist artists in Goma.

14. Videos viewable at https://www.youtube.com/channel/UCufvkji7Wvo_4CHE5v47Dfg.

15. This dynamic is thoroughly outlined in Manji and O'Coill, "The Missionary Position."

16. Fanon, *The Wretched of the Earth*, 176.

17. Solanas and Getino, "Towards a Third Cinema."

18. Stuart Hall, "Cultural Identity and Diaspora," in *Identity: Community, Culture, Difference*, ed. Jonathan Rutherford (London: Lawrence & Wishart, 1990), 222–37.

19. *Episode III: Enjoy Poverty*, directed by Renzo Martens (Autlook Filmsales, 2009), DVD. 0:09:02–0:09:46.

20. Ibid., 0:43:08.

21. Ibid., 0:49:24.

22. Ibid., 0:42:14.

23. Ibid., 1:15:40.

24. Ibid., 0:10:16.

25. Ibid., 0:45:23.

26. Ibid., 1:08:40.

27. Ibid., 1:10:14.

28. Said, *Culture and Imperialism*, xix.

29. Ibid., xvii.

30. Manji and O'Coill, "The Missionary Position," 573.

31. *Crisis in the Congo: Uncovering the Truth* (Friends of Congo Films, 2011), DVD, 0:02:27.

32. Ibid., 0:01:02.

33. Ibid., 0:07:08.

34. Ibid., 0:14:33.

35. Ibid., 0:15:35.

36. Ibid., 0:16:01.

37. Ibid., 0:16:39.

38. Ibid., 0:18:13.

39. Ibid., 0:01:34–0:02:49.

40. The version of *Crisis in the Congo* I write about in this book is the one released originally in 2011. There was subsequently another release that is currently widely available online and is much more graphic—and troublesome—in its depictions of violence (this version includes, among other overt violence, a scene in which a man is thrown off a bridge and shot by soldiers, as well as many additional images of women and children, dead and alive, victims of rape and sexual violence). This latter version does not conform to the aesthetic principles of the original that I discuss in this analysis.

41. Ibid., 0:02:38.

42. Ibid., 0:20:52.

43. The websites are www.peaceoneday.org, www.amanifestival.com, and www.salaamkivu.org.

44. www.amanifestival.com.

45. NYAVU, which literally means "net" in Kiswahili, is the name of a network founded at Yole!Africa in 2008 that includes like-minded urban arts and education organizations in a number of Great Lakes and East African countries (including Congo, Rwanda, Burundi, Uganda, Kenya, Zimbabwe).

46. Franz Fanon, *Racism and Culture: Toward the African Revolution* (New York: Grove Press, 1964), 194.

47. Ibid., 194.

48. Since Fanon launched this critique the UN missions to Congo have changed. The two missions associated with the current conflict are MONUC and MONUSCO. On July 1, 2010, MONUSCO (UN Organization Stabilization Mission in the Democratic Republic of the Congo) took over from the earlier UN peacekeeping operation MONUC (UN Organization Mission in Democratic Republic of the Congo). It was done in accordance with Security Council Resolution 1925 of May 28, 2010, to reflect the new phase reached in the country. The new mission has been authorized to use all necessary means to carry out its mandate relating, among other things, to protection of civilians, humanitarian personnel, and human rights defenders under imminent threat of physical violence and to support the government of the DRC in its stabilization and peace consolidation efforts. http://www.un.org/en/peacekeeping/missions/monusco/.

49. In 2013 this became Yole!Africa's new motto.

50. Roy, *NGO-ization*.

51. Fanon, *Toward the African Revolution*, 197.

Three repetitions should make us pause: the armed militia figure (sentry), the sexually transgressed girl or woman, and the partially redeemed female victim figure. Each opens issues of social roles and subject positions and their repetitions over time. It is important to keep tracking how each becomes symbolic within humanitarian phantasmagoria and within the new Congolese national imaginary still in formation.
NANCY ROSE HUNT, "An Acoustic Register," *p. 244*

4

JAZZ MAMAS

ON TRUTH AND MYTH

Once upon a time Africa was the Dark Continent and Congo was the Heart of that Darkness. The veracity of this story was secondary to its power. It was true because it was told by those with the authority—and technology—to tell. For centuries this story was the foundation of economic, political, and charitable action. It justified projects aiming to civilize, educate, and (re)create Africans in the image of the West, and it rationalized their inevitable failure. And so it was that, with time, the story became true. Over those centuries Africa became a place of war, poverty, and disease, a place of bottomless need. Out of this failure and need grew new stories, many of which tip their hat to the righteous outrage expressed in anticolonial writings or adopt a façade of solidarity with the oppressed; such stories have been honed against the tide of political correctness, but their rhetorical inheritance remains inextricably bound to darkness. Of course, the story told by Africans who inhabit(ed) Africa is different. It is not about darkness or savagery, but about the minute details that cumulatively make home. It might be poignant, boring, profound, nonsensical, but most importantly it is not singular, not a single story, not even a cohesive narrative, but a collection of small, and sometimes contradictory, truths. The problem is that the power of these stories is secondary to their veracity because those with the authority and technology to tell do not often listen themselves.[1]

I am not the first to point out that Africa has been hobbled by a tendentious single story. Generations of activists, artists and scholars from around the world have been amassing potent evidence of this dynamic for more than a century. There are rigorous historical interventions that outline the strategic underdevelopment of Africa by Europe as a means of contesting the inevitability of Africa's current single story of war, disease, and poverty.[2] There are elegant critiques of the scopic regime of Africa, which reduces the continent to an iconic inventory of negative or exotic images, which, ingrained as they are in the psyche of the West, trigger pity, charity, or adventure in brave and compassionate pioneers.[3] There are equally insightful analyses of the insidious practice of celebrating, with exaggeration, the ostensibly inherent connection between Africans and nature, which both naturalizes the brutality of war and illness and eliminates the possibility for Africans to engage as agents with modern forms of technology.[4]

There are also now-popular testimonies, like that of writer Chimamanda Adichie (whose 2009 TED talk has more than nine million views), who warns that "the single story creates stereotypes and the problem with stereotypes is not that they are untrue, but that they are incomplete—they make one story become the *only* story." In her case, the single story of Africa affected her personally when Americans approached her from a "default position . . . of patronizing, well-meaning pity . . . [in which] there was no possibility of Africans being similar to [them] in any way, no possibility of feelings more complex than pity, no possibility of a connection as human equals."[5] Her (and countless others') experiences substantiate analyses of the dynamic between Africa and the West as one in which, far from being a place peopled by human beings, for the West, Africa is nothing more than the backdrop against which to grapple with the "founding metaphor" of light versus darkness that undergirds Western self-conception.[6] Indeed, the single story of Africa continues to substantiate projects (political, economic, cultural, medical, humanitarian, charitable) that "allow the Africans to be consistently present but irrelevant to the project of making Africa safer for Africans."[7]

Within the single story of Africa, Congo occupies a very specific role that has shifted disturbingly little in the Western imagination since the country's branding as the heart of darkness. This is, in part, because Congo has all the accoutrements of exotic Africa: wild and indomitable landscapes; mysterious creatures (okapi, bonobos, and so on); immense forests, jungles, and lakes; active volcanoes; towering mountain vistas; and, of course, diverse tribes. Congo also has the stuff of myths: the sacred springs of the Nile River, relics of the earliest civilizations, (rumors of) the Garden of Eden. Then there are the coveted ingredients of industry and adventure: gold, diamonds, oil, coltan, ivory, rubber, tin, cobalt, copper, uranium, and more than two thousand other valuable mineral resources. This is a potent combination. For centuries it has enticed intrepid explorers, covetous leaders, and extravagant accounts of humanitarianism. For centuries, Congo has been forged into a mythical place of unparalleled savagery and unparalleled wealth in need of unparalleled heroes to bring light to its (unparalleled) darkness. This has generated some of the richest and most skillful iterations of Africa's single story, and has created the most fertile ground for stories of brave and compassionate Western interventions to become Truth. Though the details have changed with time, Congo remains the site of countless charitable and humanitarian projects, each working in its own way to address some social (or political, economic, medical) ill; though the language has changed, Congo remains the source of countless stories of Western heroism. What is, and always has been, missing is the Congolese side of the story.

Nowhere is this trend more evident than in the current response to the epidemic of rape and sexual violence that is plaguing the east of Congo. Much of the increase in popular Western awareness of the current Congo conflict traces back to 2007, when American filmmaker Lisa Jackson made her acclaimed documentary *The Greatest Silence*. This film introduced the epidemic of rape and sexual violence to Western audiences who were (and continue to be) astonishingly unaware of the magnitude of the war that was (and still is) happening during their lifetime. As the film gained traction through festival screenings, awards, HBO play, and articles in the *New York Times* and other notable publications, it catalyzed a movement of Westerners who felt compelled to intervene on behalf of the hundreds of thousands of Congolese women who were (and still are) being systemically brutalized. A number of American celebrities, notably Ben Affleck, Eve Ensler, and Angelina Jolie, turned their attention to the east of Congo, and in their wake a new crop of NGOs, including Affleck's Eastern Congo Initiative (ECI) and Ensler's City of Joy, sprang up and added to the army of NGOs already working in the region.

At the same time, journalists such as the *New York Times*'s Nicholas Kristof were turning attention to the war in the east of Congo. True to his style, Kristof sought to rouse the West from complacency about what he repeatedly calls the most "barbaric" conflict.[8] His tactic is to generate riveting accounts in print, in photographs, online, and in blogs that have a façade of compassion for the victims of this devastating war, but that also revitalize the rhetorical inheritance of darkness in Congo through descriptions of "lush and threatening hills West of Lake Kivu" or "savagery that is almost incomprehensible."[9]

In line with the growing demand to humanize Africans, his articles include detailed descriptions of the suffering of locals—particularly women—but their humanity is circumscribed by designations of victimhood (like nine-year-old Chance, whose "eyes are luminous with fear"), which ultimately positions them as nothing more than a backdrop for the stories of intrepid and compassionate Americans who give up lives of privilege and comfort to come to the aid of their global sisters.[10] For example, in "The World Capital of Killing" (Feb. 7, 2010), readers met Jeanne, a young Congolese woman who was kidnapped, repeatedly, to serve as a sex slave for militia armies who subjected her to gruesome violations that left her permanently incontinent even after years of surgeries performed by the Congolese gynecologist Dr. Denis Mukwege; or in "From 'Oprah' to Building a Sisterhood in Congo" (Feb. 4, 2010) readers the world over learned of Congolese nurse Generose's devastating experience of rape, amputation, and loss, but also of American photographer Lisa Shannon's selfless courage as she gave up everything (thriving business, loving fiancé, comfortable house) to fight for women like Generose. Though untenable from an analytical perspective, this rhetoric is effective in triggering emotional responses by readers who, spurred by the urgency of the situation and feelings of alliance with inspiring heroines, are compelled to take action.

Cumulatively, the work of NGOs and journalists has started to erode the global ignorance of the atrocities taking place in the east of Congo and to initiate action on the ground, but as admirable as such initiatives are, any activist agenda that grows out of a single story has side effects that wreak their own kind of devastation. At present, the single story of Congo is that it is a place of utter savagery, full of depraved militias and powerless victims and that the problem, rather than being one of clashing geopolitical forces that have systematically pillaged Congo of its resources for more than a century, is said to be that "the atrocities continue because nobody care[s]."[11] In this cosmology the only people endowed with the power to "care" are, of course, the "kind, White foreigner[s]" who continue to come to the rescue of "incomprehensible people [Africans] fighting senseless wars, dying of poverty and AIDS, unable to speak for themselves and waiting to be saved."[12] But in reality, caring is, of course, not the issue. "Caring" is the justification for forcing compassion on people as a barometer of the generosity and selflessness of the giver. Caring is also a decoy that diverts attention from the causes of conflict—in Congo or anywhere—to the band-aids that benevolent foreigners rush to put on mortal wounds in the region.

There is an anatomy to this perversion of compassion that involves, among other things, the dehistoricizing of a conflict. Where (in the Western imagination) lack of caring is the problem, fostering compassion is an obvious prescription; but where (in reality) Western hegemony is a fundamental cause of global suffering, solutions lie in complex analyses that are at once self-revealing and uncomfortable for many Western audiences, who, often through no intentional actions of their own, are implicated. Thus drowning out historical truths in a sea of artificial compassion rather than working to rehistoricize and contextualize the conflict has become a staple of charitable action in Congo.

For example, Kristof appeals to readers "to show the same kind of compassion toward Congo that [they] showed toward Haiti."[13] The conflict in Congo, however, is the result not of an earthquake, but of a long history of geopolitical forces actively fighting for the country's natural resources. Comparing the (post)conflict suffering in Congo to the post-earthquake suffering in Haiti effectively eliminates, in one fell swoop, any traces of Western responsibility or accountability and positions the war as a natural disaster rather than a humanmade crisis. And thus the floodgates are flung open for all well-intentioned Westerners to intervene without engaging in critical scrutiny or historical study. Raoul Peck's 2013 documentary *Assistance Mortelle (Fatal Assistance)* makes a powerful case against the many social ills brought to Haiti with the rush of humanitarian and charitable interventions in the aftermath of the earthquake: well-intentioned organizations and individuals introduced a new level of corruption, increased social fragmentation, and undermined local social and political structures all in the name of helping.[14] And that was in a circumstance where all parties agreed on a natural disaster as the (immediate) cause of the problem.

Of course, journalists and documentarians covering the Congo conflict have to offer some historical explanation in order to contextualize the facts. A popular solution is to point back to the Rwanda Genocide of 1994, when fanatic Hutus (among others) fled into the east of Congo. This was a pivotal moment that did trigger the current outbreak of fighting, but the degree of malevolence and the sheer magnitude of destruction in this endless series of wars that have been raging for twenty years now are the result of a much deeper problem that has been festering for more than a century. Popular prescriptions such as "putting pressure on neighboring Rwanda for its possible role in war crimes in [Congo]," "putting pressure on the Congolese president, Joseph Kabila, to arrest Gen. Jean Bosco Ntaganda," or initiating a "U.S.-brokered effort to monitor the minerals trade from Congo so that warlords can no longer buy guns by exporting gold, tin, or coltan," are necessary remedies to certain aspects of the problem, but they fail to historicize the conflict in a way that exposes or addresses its deeper causes. At the core of Congo's history is a pattern of Western interest in Congolese natural resources that, since the era of King Léopold II, has resulted in some of the world's deadliest massacres. The consistency of this pattern suggests that meaningful solutions must also include not just U.S.-brokered efforts to monitor *others*, but overt accountability—historic and ongoing—from Western nations toward their *own* actions.

In previous chapters I have addressed the pattern of dehistoricizing long-term narratives of Congo, but this trend is also apparent in the treatment of immediately recent history, which, were it recognized, would reveal a surprising track record of local action and agency. It is precisely by dehistoricizing the recent examples of local agency that foreign activists, journalists, and international NGOs are in the gravest danger of repeating the very practices that fundamentally contributed to Congo's current crisis by destroying functional existing structures in their zeal to create new ones in their own image.

Unfortunately, if rape and sexual violence most recently landed Congo on the global radar of international do-goodism, rape and sexual violence are also a prime example of the global will to suppress stories of local agency (unless they feature an American hero). When Lisa Jackson made *The Greatest Silence* she was right to point out the uncanny silence surrounding the staggering statistics of rape in Congo, but there is an equal, if not greater, silence surrounding the agency and perseverance of the Congolese who are taking action on a local level. Certainly there are comparatively high-profile figures like Dr. Mukwege, who are getting much international attention, in his case for his gynecological care of survivors of rape, but there are many other well-established local organizations, individuals, and networks in the east of Congo whose medical, educational, and cultural interventions go unnoticed in the West.

And even when Dr. Mukwege gets his due, his agency is often framed in a context of helplessness that positions him as a lone soldier against an impossible tide of violence. Whereas Shannon, founder of Run for Congo, is compared to "an angel and to Jesus Christ"[15] for her efforts to "rescue [Congolese women] from misery,"[16] Kristof's portrait of Dr. Mukwege ends with his defeated statement, "I don't even know what I'm doing here [since] there is no medical solution."[17] Notably, Dr. Mukwege has doctored tens of thousands of women while Shannon's project, though commendable, has had significantly less impact. Yet, in popular coverage of the conflict, in the kind of coverage that attracts flocks of compassionate and idealistic college students to invite Kristof as an inspirational speaker who will initiate them into the ranks of positive global activists, Shannon is framed as a heroine for relentlessly helping one Congolese woman at a time while Dr. Mukwege is positioned at the brink of defeat in his futile effort to do the very same thing. No matter how one looks at it, there is a certain irony in the praise Kristof heaps on the work Shannon undertakes in Congo, which is her "obsession," and the profound defeat he assigns Dr. Mukwege for the work he undertakes in Congo, which is his home.[18]

That Dr. Mukwege and others are not uniformly positioned as empowered agents in international press coverage of the conflict is, on one hand, purely symptomatic of the varying motivations of journalists and filmmakers in telling their respective stories.[19] On the other hand, it is consistent with dominant modes of documenting history that have limited stories of African agency since Africa's encounter with the West. In the abstract, global ignorance of local agency is harmless. But when global actors decide to intervene in what they perceive as local problems, their ignorance of existing local mechanisms is devastating. I am not the first to make this point; it is a cornerstone of the growing volume of criticism against international humanitarian and charitable aid. But for all the lip service they receive, it remains extremely difficult to put theories of "listening to the locals" into practice. That is due, in part, to the long-standing precedent of compassionate foreign audiences turning emotion- (or religiously or politically) driven responses to news reports into plans of action without going through the painstaking and tedious process of gathering sufficient information. But it is also due to what Anthony Smith aptly calls the geopolitics of information. According to Smith:

> The threat to independence in the late twentieth century from the new electronics could be greater than was colonialism itself. We are beginning to learn that de-colonization and the growth of supra-nationalism were not the termination of imperial relationships but merely the extending of a geo-political web, which has been spinning since the Renaissance. The new media have the power to penetrate more deeply into a "receiving" culture than any previous manifestation of Western technology. The results could be immense havoc, an intensification of the social contradictions within developing societies today.[20]

Western technologies have indeed extended, and more disturbingly disguised, imperial power relationships in Congo with dire results. In addition to the overt havoc of conflict and the less publicized havoc wrought by many foreign interventions, Western technologies and new media have increased the power of the single story by creating illusions of multiplicity of voice and democratization of information. Nowhere is this more evident in Congo than in the coverage of rape and violence against women. Indeed, despite the rapidly growing volumes of news reports, documentaries, radio broadcasts, plays, etc., few with global traction are created by locals, if any. For all the urgency about sexual violence, the most penetrating manifestation of Western technologies is the resounding silence when it comes to stories of Congolese agency. This is not an issue of skill, access to technology, or language, but an issue of power—for with power comes, among many other things, the ability to collapse reality into a single story.

But there is no single story of women in the east of Congo. There are, instead, infinite examples of complex human responses to dire circumstances. In many cases these responses reveal astounding perseverance and agency by the very people—Congolese women and men—cast as helpless victims or gruesome perpetrators in the single story of rape and sexual violence that circulates in the West. There is consensus among the more militant Congolese activists that these examples need to be shared to make the point that there are already effective local solutions being implemented and that foreign interventions aiming for sustained positive impact in local communities must take into account the experience and expertise within those communities. Documenting, preserving, and narrating the many stories of local agency and humanity has thus become the focus of such activists who believe that introducing Congolese sides of the story slowly erodes the hegemony of the current single story and thereby begins to shift the imbalance of power.

In this larger dynamic of sexual violence, silence, and assertions of local agency, I see a number of what historian Nancy Rose Hunt refers to as "repetitions."[21] These are historic recurrences of similar dynamics and experiences, but also historic and ongoing recurrences of interpretation. In Congo, what receives most critical attention are the repetitions of silence, which lead to analyses and rhetorics of failure; but there are other repetitions, specifically repetitions of agency, that, when given equivalent critical scrutiny, lead to analyses and rhetorics of possibility. This chapter presents two such examples from Yole!Africa, Twaomba Amani and Jazz Mama, both of which I read as repetitions that are at once "strategic repetitions" in that they cite and then innovate on the agency of Congolese women past, and also embodied variations of this agency that expose "what is novel and different in today's present."[22]

I have structured each case study in this chapter as a "story" in order to underscore my allegiance to the effort of diversifying the single story of rape and sexual violence in Congo. I have had the privilege during my years in Congo of witnessing and in some cases participating in a broad spectrum of community-led responses to and preventive measures against sexual violence. I am calling on those experiences in the very form of this chapter, which, by foregrounding multivocal stories, is its own activist gesture. In terms of content and analysis, this chapter has the dual objective of preserving potent examples of Congolese activism and of applying to them my own observations from my experiences as a researcher and scholar. In the case of Twaomba Amani, this includes investigating the origins and witnessing the afterlife of the project; in the case of Jazz Mama, my knowledge of the project comes from my direct participation as translator of the film and coordinator of the movement, activities that deepened the trust between the local community and myself profoundly. I have reserved these stories for last in this book because they are among the most precious I have gathered in my research in Congo and because they require the extensive historical, contextual, and analytical material of the previous chapters to resonate most fully with readers outside of Congo. In sum, this is a chapter determined to amplify the efforts of Congolese activists by weaving of empirical examples, a critical rubric that begins to substantiate the rhetoric of possibility when analyzing—and proposing—global interventions in the epidemic of sexual violence in the east of Congo.

THE FIRST STORY: TWAOMBA AMANI

In early June 2004, in Beni, North Kivu, a woman was raped, her genitals mutilated, and then eventually she was killed. The frequency of sexual violence in the region having escalated by 2004, her rape and even her death were, statistically speaking, not uncommon. Like many others, her story did not make the news, though it was likely added to the growing tally of brutality against women in the east of Congo. In all, apart from her grieving family, her violation would have gone unnoticed, had it not triggered an unexpected response.

Outraged at the fate of their sister, hundreds of women from Beni gathered together in protest, marching through the city on a path that wound its way from the poorest quarters, past local police stations, to various military bases, and ending finally outside the barred gates of the UN headquarters. Many of the women carried their bed mattresses on their heads or brandished branches in the air; some tore off their clothes. Fueled by years of suffering and pent-up anger, they accused the men—particularly those in official positions—of everything from failing to fulfill their task of protecting the community to blatantly abusing their power, even of taking advantage of the culture of impunity to perpetrate rape themselves. In words and in actions, they challenged the men to come and have sex with them, to fuck them, in public instead of hiding in the shadows—if they dare.

It took tremendous courage to make these statements and gestures in a region where as many as 130 rapes are reported every day and countless others go undocumented. Well before Doctors Without Borders confirmed for the West the staggering magnitude of the rape epidemic in Congo, the women who marched knew full well that no one was immune to such attacks; the horrific reports of gang rapes perpetrated by as many as fifteen men against one women during which guns, spears, or sharp sticks were forced into the vaginas of victims as young as eight months and as old as eighty-eight years, were, for them, not statistics but their own experiences and those of their mothers, sisters, and daughters.[23] The aftermath of rape, including the escalated transmission of HIV/AIDS, unwanted pregnancies, fistulas, trauma, stigma, and shame, were, by 2004, part of their daily realities as the caretakers of the community. When they denounced the culture of impunity it was because they knew, first-hand, that the perpetrators of rape face few consequences or none; they knew, first-hand, what later shocked the world when reports finally confirmed that, in addition to the brutal rapes perpetrated by rebel militias, UN peacekeeping troops and officials were bribing starving women and children in IDP camps to have sex with them for eggs, milk, or one U.S. dollar. That UN soldiers and commanders are presently being investigated for at least 150 rapes and gang rapes, some with children as young as twelve years old, is at once both a triumph and little consolation for the women who risked their lives to make this point years before the world was willing to listen.[24] In short, the women marching in Beni already knew what the international community later flew experts in to discover: in the fight for mineral-rich land, rape—whether the strategic rape of militias or the gratuitous rape of UN troops—is the most effective and least expensive weapon for destroying communities.

Expert testimony has confirmed this point. Addressing strategic use of rape as a weapon of war, former Canadian Ambassador Stephen Lewis (who was also the UN's envoy for AIDS in Africa) argues, with many others, that mass rape in the Congo conflict "has taken a new twist as commanders have used it as a strategy of war."[25] Lewis cites two reasons, the first being the efficacy of rape from a military point of view in a conflict in which terrorizing people off their land is preferable to engaging in a firefight, and the second being that "mass rape attracts less international scrutiny than piles of bodies do, because the issue is indelicate and the victims are usually too ashamed to speak up."[26] Lewis's statement does a number of things when read from the perspective of the women of Beni. Clearly it validates their position by confirming the strategic—and devastating—deployment of rape in this conflict. But it also underscores the profound significance of the women's choice to speak up in protest, even though at the time it did not attract any international attention. Indeed, in a place where rape is so prevalent, it was an extremely courageous choice for the women of Beni to gather in overt protest and to insist that sexual violation and murder are not—and can never be—routine collateral damage, to demand an end to the prevailing culture of silence, impunity, and social paralysis.

From this vantage point, the protest in Beni takes on an important symbolism. It is at once a commemorative memorial of a particular victim as well as an embodiment of collective agency. Clearly it differs from public memorials, which imply state or other official power, but as a community memorial, an embodied and temporary monument, it is nevertheless a powerful mode of preserving memory. Read theoretically, this protest blurs James E. Young's distinction between celebratory honoring of heroes (monuments) and solemn recognition of tragedy and death (memorials), for it is at once both.[27] Compared to neighboring Rwanda, with its plethora of physical, cinematic, literary, and virtual memorials that have sprung up since the 1994 Genocide, the east of Congo has a surprising absence of commemorative sites, despite the fact that genocide and extreme violence had already been occurring for a decade by 2004.[28] In this void of public remembrance, acts of commemoration like the march through Beni are potent not only for their potential psychological benefits, but because of the crucial role they play in influencing how and what the world recognizes, values, and remembers, in determining which stories are told and who has the power to tell them.

Notably, despite the saturation of international journalists in the Kivus, many of whom were notified of the protest in advance, no foreign media group chose to cover the march. The absence of official records of such events is the norm that sustains the single story of rape in Congo, but the absence of a record does not mean the absence of activity. Indeed, whether or not the West was paying attention, a vast network of local organizations understood and responded to this protest in important ways that reveal a thriving culture of activism in the region with deeply established networks and practices.

Most prominent in supporting the women of Beni was the Congolese association Synergie des Femmes pour les Victimes des Violences Sexuelles (Synergie). Founded by Justine Masika Bihamba in 2000, Synergie is a coalition of thirty-five local organizations (most of which are run by women) that work collectively to enforce locally valued aspects of UN Security Council Resolution 1325, which recognizes the essential role of women in brokering peace and encourages their active participation in securing gender-specific needs.[29] Synergie focuses on issues of rape and impunity and insists on the implication of women in peace and reconciliation efforts through three categories of programs: psychosocial, medical, and research. Within the realm of the psychosocial, Synergie has more than seventy-five counselors who provide training, therapy, and mediation to individuals, families, and communities affected by rape and violence. Their medical support is integrated with local hospitals, including Heal Africa and DOCS (Doctors on Call for Service). Synergie's research agenda focuses on subjects such as women's rights and preventive and judicial actions, helping to write and pass laws that enable survivors of rape to prosecute their perpetrators in criminal court, and bringing public attention to legal possibilities for victims and their families.

As part of its commitment to supporting the autonomy of local women, Synergie had a significant presence at the protest in Beni. Thus, when no one from the international press came to film the march, urged by the protesting women, a counselor from Synergie decided to film it herself. This footage, which was far from professional, was then passed like a baton from Synergie to Yole!Africa, with the request that Petna edit it into a short film. Synergie's plan was to feature the film in their next campaign, which had three primary objectives: first, to educate people about rape and sexual violence; second, to offer resources to women who had experienced rape or violence; and last, to gather enough support to push a new law through the legislature that would, for the first time, recognize rape as a criminal offense in Congo.

These were the goals, and from the perspective of Synergie, including a film was essential. But, as a local organization itself, Synergie was very specific that it be a local film by a local filmmaker working with complete autonomy over content and form. From the outset of this project, Synergie was aware that, despite its impressive record in the domains of medical, psychological, and legal matters, it was not equipped to intervene in the realm of art, which has its own integrity as a vehicle of social change. Thus the production of the film is an example of local collaboration that sheds light on dynamics of nonhierarchical interorganizational partnership at the local level. In partnering with—rather than commissioning— Yole!Africa, Synergie relinquished control over aspects of the project and welcomed Yole!Africa's strategic contributions. The result was an expanded project that, in addition to the film, included a song, a music video, and later a full musical album. As the project grew, the title of the film, *Twaomba Amani*, which means "we demand peace," became, in turn, the title of the song, the album and, eventually of the project as a whole.

Twaomba Amani had a significant impact in North Kivu: it sparked new and enduring collaborations between various cultural actors and was directly associated with legal reform. Those are the impacts of the project that are most easily articulated, but in telling the story of Twaomba Amani I am equally concerned with the visible and the invisible. The march through Beni was visible, however fleetingly; the resultant film is visible in a more permanent sense; the legislative and statistical impacts of the campaign are visible to those who look; but there are other impacts, best described as internally transformative, that are invisible. Such internal transformations play an important role in social change as they shift people's opinions one at a time. This is one way in which art has the power to catalyze change. Yet it is often overlooked because it is hard to see, much less quantify. My aim in tracing, in some detail, the creation (supported by Yole!Africa) and dissemination (supported by Yole!Africa and Synergie) of the Twaomba Amani song, music video, and film is to bring some of these internally transformative interactions to the foreground.

This part of the story starts with the song. Yole!Africa had a number of reasons for producing a song about sexual violence. First, on a practical level, music, unlike film, was easy to distribute and reached a much larger population; well before 2004, even in remote areas nearly every household had acquired some means of playing music, whereas television sets were still quite rare. Thus, as a central component of an educational campaign, the potential impact of a song was greater than that of a film. Second, the song "Twaomba Amani" was produced during the period when Congo was effectively divided into two countries (politically, economically, and linguistically) and music was among the few commodities allowed to transcend borders.[30] Much of the music in question was, of course, government propaganda, religious evangelism, or popular dance music. Yet music was omnipresent and unanimously popular (even the guerrilla radio and television channels operated by various rebel groups played music from all over the country), and as such, music provided ideal audience and distribution channels for Yole!Africa to infiltrate with a socially conscious message.

There was further motivation for creating a song in the desire to share Congolese perspectives on the ongoing war with a regional audience. Although neighboring countries in the Great Lakes Region had a vague awareness that there was a war in Congo, in 2004 they too were conditioned by the single story of Congo, which explained the war as an ethnic scuffle that reflected nothing more than the incompetence of Congolese to run a functional state. But if Congo was vaguely associated with war, it was concretely revered for its music. And it was because of the approbation and appetite of surrounding countries for Congo's music that song was such a potent vehicle through which to tell Congo's story from an inside perspective.

However, despite the enthusiasm for and potential power of a song, there was still a problem: *how* to produce a song advocating peace when it was well known that the musicians themselves did not get along with one another and that their fan groups were split along the very ethnic lines associated with the war. In this climate, a song appealing for peace by any musician with a high enough profile to reach a wide audience risked either being seen as further entrenching ethnic divisions or being dismissed as nothing more than empty lip service or even hypocrisy. Although it was effective for politicians to commission popular musicians in Congo to write songs of praise, this practice had created rifts in local audiences that undermined the power of music as a force of social cohesion. Thus the potential of music to shape public opinion was extremely high, while the possibility of applying that potential to negotiating peace was extremely low.

Out of this dilemma Yole!Africa made an experiment. Despite their artistic rivalry and stylistic differences, the organization invited Goma's most popular musicians—Agans Premier, Tilason, Natalie Kabuo, Cecil Walo, Shaba Demandé, Jolie Malonga, Brado Chant, Junior Kashala, Robert King, Witimira Faida, Mack el Sambo, and Jean-Luc Lwango, all of whom are depicted in the right frame of Figure 4.1—and asked them to write a song collaboratively. The idea was that the song should be as much about the process of creation as about the final product, and that if successful it would serve not only through its musical content but also through its very creation as a microcosmic example of the power of music to transform contentious relationships.

Clearly, there were some significant obstacles to overcome in this scenario. There was the obvious challenge of navigating rival adversarial personalities and clashing egos. There was also the musical complication that the performers' styles ranged from Congolese rumba to R&B, to reggae, to raga mafi. Difficulties resulted from bringing together performers from different generations; problems of language preferences and performance practices also arose. Then there were logistical issues, for by 2004 there was no longer a professional recording studio in Goma (by then most of the Rwandese in Goma, including "Jean-Jacques," the recording engineer referred to in Chapter One, were forced into the forest, where they were killed by Kagame's and Kabila's forces). Finally, on top of this were the daily challenges of insecurity: the power cuts, the fuel shortages limiting the usefulness of the generator, the early curfews, and the general ethos of tension, mistrust, and fear.

If anything, these daily reminders of war motivated the musicians to at least consider participating in a project lobbying for peace, and even if they did sit glaring at one another across the room, they all came to Yole!Africa for a preliminary meeting. Rather than getting straight to the point and talking about the song, the meeting began with extended informal chatting that went on long enough that a Yole!Africa staff member was sent to fetch a bottle of water and eleven glasses. This detail is important because it is an example of the kinds of local mechanisms that are in place to navigate social issues but that do not translate to the formalized activities required in project reports for international NGOs. Although "drinking water together" would be a ridiculous item to include in an official summary of activities for a foreign project designed to "facilitate community reconciliation," it was the most effective way to convey a point to the participants. Everyone in the room understood that the gesture of sharing something from a common source, even lukewarm water from a plastic bottle, is symbolic of putting arguments behind and that in agreeing to drink they were agreeing to approach the project with an open mind and willingness to see whether the symbolism of reconciliation might lead to more meaningful forgiveness.

After the lengthy and indirect process of negotiating a tentative truce through traditional channels, the seemingly weightier task of explaining the actual song project was completed in moments. The artists were told that the idea was to produce a song, "Twaomba Amani," then they were given artistic freedom—musically, lyrically, structurally, and instrumentally—to apply their talents and their voices to amplify the call for peace. Without oversight by Yole!Africa, the musicians discussed their ideas about peace, war, and local needs, and then began to craft their respective verses. Given the autonomy to address sexual violence—and war more broadly—from their own points of view, the artists wrote lyrics about human rights abuses, environmental concerns, frustration about corruption in the government, and the negative influence of international NGOs; the lyrics also include critiques of failed regional peace summits, economic analyses that connect the conflict to the legacy of Western colonialism and consumerism, concern about education in Congo, and of course outrage over the epidemic of rape and sexual violence. Nearly a decade later, many of the musicians still recall how fruitful this freedom was for collaboration; within less than an hour, each musician had drafted her or his verse and the group was engaged in an organic process of collaborative revision, which proved to be another important step toward genuine cooperation within the group. Indeed, at the end of the first meeting the song was drafted and rehearsals were set to begin the following day.

For two weeks, the group met daily to polish the song. By all accounts, skepticism about the legitimacy of gestures of cooperation or reconciliation lingered in early rehearsals, but over time sessions became lively as artists stepped outside their comfort zone to learn each other's musical styles and performance practices. There were opportunities for mutual learning and ribbing as older musicians suggested complex rhythms and harmonies and younger musicians retaliated by insisting the group replace outdated dance steps with the latest complex choreographies to accompany their performance. In retrospect, the artists note that the pivotal moment of collaboration was their conscious effort to harness the potential obstacles of the project into strengths in the final song. They dedicated significant effort to cohering their varied musical styles into a relatable sound, they positioned the diversity of languages and generations to expand the potential audience, and they underscored the practical challenges of engaging in cultural work in a war zone as an urgent reminder of the need for the song at the time.

The rehearsals culminated in a three-day recording session (and a few more days at the mixing board) that resulted in a fifteen-minute song in five languages blending four musical styles. Yet much to everyone's surprise, when it was released on the radio "Twaomba Amani" became a popular hit. Even after the initial novelty of cooperation among rivals wore off and the sonic aesthetic had become familiar, "Twaomba Amani" remained popular throughout the region. Part of the appeal was the approach the musicians took to advocating peace, which included a variety of issues rather than the limited foci of political or religious songs. Indeed, "Twaomba Amani" situates rape and sexual violence at the center of a matrix of issues related to the ongoing war in the east of Congo.

The song begins with all the musicians singing a refrain together:

Inji yetu Congo	Our country Congo
tuna omba Amani	we want peace
Congo ya mababu	Congo of our ancestors
tuna teseka sana	we are suffering greatly
inji yetu wote	all of us
tuungane pamoja	let us unite
Congo inji yetu	Congo our country
mutu ache sasa	it's time for others to leave us alone
wa baba na wa mama	our fathers and our mothers
wa kaka na wa dada	our brothers and our sisters

Then, to set the context, Agans Premier sings the first verse, which introduces the scope and magnitude of the suffering caused by prolonged war:

Habari za vita	When it comes to war
usikie lakini usione	it is better to hear about it than to live it
mambo mambo tuna ona	things we are witnessing
mu mashariki ya Congo	in the east of Congo
ni kama ndoto	are like a nightmare
mutupe pole	give us compassion
mauwaji wa kinyama kupita genocide	savage killing is more than genocide
kula nyama ya mutu	eating human flesh
kuzika watu wazima	burying people alive
inji na porwa	the country is being looted
mazingira ina bomolewa	the destruction of the wildlife
wa mama zetu wa bakwa mu macho yetu	our mothers are being raped in front of us
kubaka mpaka na mutoto wa trois ans	they are also raping three-year-old children

tuna lipishwa ki sasia nini	what have we done to earn your vengeance?
muma balabala utaona watoto mayatima	our streets are full of orphans
awana makao nguo ao chakula	they have no place to stay, no clothes, no food

Following this, in verse 2, Tilason introduces the theme of natural resources as the cause of war:

Inji yetu ya bonde na milima	in this beautiful country
tuna kufa bure	we are dying for no reason
Congo yetu ya pesa na zahabu	our Congo full of gold and riches
tuna onelewa eeee—	the people are dismissed eeee—
kwanini wa geni wanawashawishi	foreigners are lying to you
kwa jili ya faida zao	because of their own interests

Then, addressing Congolese politicians, he continues:

kwanini wa geni wanawashawishi	foreigners are lying to you
kwa jili ya faida zao	because of their own interests
na nyini muna kubali	and you accept their lies when you know
kutesa ndugu zenu	that your own people are suffering
wa ongozi wetu wote wa Congo	all our Congolese leaders
mutu mike kazi	get to work
muwache kuleta vita	and stop bringing war
yenye itashimamisha kazi	and respect the peace treaties
ya mukataba wenu	which you have made
yenye mulipatanaka	and agreed upon
kutu mikia inji	to work for the country
watu hawalime tena shamba	people are not farming anymore
kwanini?	why?
kwajuya vita mayisha ina kuwanguvu	because of war life has become very difficult
juu yenu	all this because of you
kweli vita ina bomowa	truly war only destroys
haina hata fayida moja	and there is not any interest
kwa wana inji wote wa Congo	for the people of Congo
na wanyama wote	even the wild animals

ina kimbia mbali na parke yetu	are running far away from our national parks
tuna kosa leo masingira	the wildlife is being polluted
kwa sababu yenu	because of you
kwanini?	why?
hatukujuwaka neno vita	we never knew war
genocider bana Congo	or genocide in Congo

In verse 5, Shaba Demandé introduces another important theme, namely human rights and the series of violated peace accords signed by politicians. Referencing the failed peace accords and the growing dissatisfaction of Congolese with national politicians was (and still is) an important cue to local listeners that the artists were willing to take a bold stance and challenge politicians directly. This stance, which was still fairly rare in the early post-Mobutu era, signaled the commitment of the artists to the lyrics they sang, which was an important factor in galvanizing the local community around the song.

ayé ayé Congo Kinshasa	ayé ayé Congo Kinshasa
la paix bapesi biso	the peace accord the politicians signed
esali cadeau te	is not a gift
mais c'est un droit fundemantal	it is a fundamental right
du peuples Congolais	for all the people of Congo

Demandé's allusion to Lumumba's famous speech, in which he insisted Congo's liberation from Belgium was not a gift but the right of those who fought for freedom, confirms the comparative radicalism of the song and the stance of the group. This phrase is an important framing device for verse 7, in which Brado Chant overtly introduces the theme of rape, which was previously alluded to primarily through metaphor and proverb:

wana inji wa Congo	people of Congo
tusidanganywe kuleta vita	no one should lie to you and create
mbali mbali	unnecessary war
isio namaana	that is meaningless
uporaji wamali	just to loot the wealth
violence kwa wamama wetu	to violate our mothers
yo yo	yo yo
violence kwa wadada	to violate our sisters
ma uwaji mbali mbali	all kinds of killing

Finally, in the penultimate verse (11), Mack el Sambo integrates the outrage about rape and sexual violence with other definitive local complaints, suggesting a symbolic parallel between violation of women and violation of the (feminized) land:

hamu sikie haya	are you not ashamed
kufanya mabaya?	to do all these evil things?
usikuna muchana mubaka wasichana	day and night you rape women
mazingira muharibu	you pollute nature and the environment
mume tugeukia jaribu	you are becoming a true problem
hatu pendi iyi hali	enough of this situation anymore.

By local standards in 2006, this song was considered radical in the way it overtly challenged and criticized politicians, pointed to the economic motivations for the war, articulated rape and sexual violence as a symptom of war, and set the entire critique in a larger context of the struggle for community cohesion. It is noteworthy that, given autonomy over their lyrics, the artists did not choose to write sensational accounts of the specific violence or stigma women face but rather to articulate their solidarity by addressing the magnitude of the greater conflict and the array of geopolitical forces connected to it. In short, the song is neither prescriptive nor is it a conduit of a single story. Instead, it rehistoricized the current problems in ways that spoke directly to regional local audiences.

In response to the popularity of "Twaomba Amani," Yole!Africa decided to make a music video to accompany the song. The video, directed by Petna with cameraman Modogo Mutembwi, was shot in Ndosho (17 kilometers outside of Goma), which was the base of SOS Children, an international NGO dedicated to demobilizing child soldiers. The motivation for shooting the video in Ndosho was to expose young people in that area to positive local role models. But what began as a gesture of social inclusion ultimately contributed to the aesthetic of the video, for the youth were so excited to see popular musical stars in person that they kept encroaching until they were on the periphery of the shot. Eventually Petna and Mutembwi changed their strategy and incorporated the young people into the scene, dancing and singing with the stars to the chorus of the song (they also included footage at the end of the video from the initial "practice" session in Ndosho).

In and of itself, the act of participating in music making was uplifting to the young people, but the real impact of the project became clear when Yole!Africa premiered the finished video in Ndosho. After watching and cheering the video enthusiastically with friends and strangers, one boy, who was among the singing dancing crowd, stood and expressed that it was the first time in his life he had seen himself—literally *seen* himself—contributing to something that made people happy. Prior to seeing himself in the video, he said, his sense of power was rooted in the fear he saw on people's faces as he pointed automatic rifles at them and looted their homes. He struggled to express himself but concluded that, in seeing his body and hearing his voice do something that brought joy to the entire audience, he realized for the first time that his power was not inherently located in his ability to inflict violence. His reaction brings to mind Teshome Gabriel's observation that "once a film enters the spectator's own autobiography, [it] awakens a reconstituted identity."[31] This is not to suggest that seeing this video single-handedly reconstituted this boy's identity, but rather to illustrate, through example, the internal shift that it wrought on his self-perception.

Yole!Africa's ethic is that such personal transformations are private. Nowhere in the video is there reference to the biographies of any of the participants, no personal accounts of the horrors of life as a child soldier or as a victim of rape that yield identifying details. To be sure, many of the participants have harrowing stories, but those stories were not the selling point for the project. Instead of marketing this music video as a project of "rehabilitation for child soldiers" (which, incidentally, is extremely lucrative when looking for foreign donor support), this video offers visual metaphors that speak to the conditions in the region. The aesthetic of this video is different from later works produced by Yole!Africa in that it includes extensive documentary footage of overt violence, some of which conforms to more stereotypical depictions of Congo. At the same time, the video has the hallmark characteristic of visual metaphor. Specifically, as depicted in the center frame of Figure 4.1, throughout the video there are images of a dilapidated truck being pushed through a field by the musicians, sometimes accompanied by children. One of the most prominent musicians in the project, reggae star Mack el Sambo, recalls not understanding why, when music videos generally aimed to show the luxurious side of life, Petna insisted they toil in the hot sun to push around a defunct automobile. Over time Mack el Sambo understood that the truck was symbolic of the definitive intersection of resources, ruin, and technology in the east of Congo. Commenting on this, he says, "What we are pushing here is our country, which is considered wrecked,

FIGURE 4.1 Twaomba Amani Music Video Sequence.

already destroyed. So it is with our own efforts that we must push, that we will restore it to a habitable place."[32]

Speaking more broadly on the visual metaphor, Petna articulates his reflection:

What did the post-Mobutu generation inherit? Ruins. So I ask myself, what can we do with those ruins? Since the ruins are part of the history of my generation, should we think of ourselves as ruins too? Does a ruin become a state of mind? Or do ruins become the symbol that represents our bodies? And if it is our body that is a ruin, that has been through everything— that has been through the cutting of hands by King Leopold, that has been mutilated by people who have been violating the body throughout our history—did they also mutilate our minds? If the ruin is [only] our body, then we can reconstruct it, because we still have our mind . . . but if the ruin has affected and mutilated us completely, how can we liberate our spirit and our soul and our minds? . . . When you put someone in a physical ruin, they realize that they themselves are not the ruin, because they realize the condition of ruin as it applies to the space. But if you avoid physical ruins, people start to think that they themselves *are* the ruin . . . but once you realize that you are *in* this ruin, but you are *not* the ruin, you have a chance to get out of it.[33]

Thus ruin (in the form of a decrepit automobile) became the visual metaphor for a philosophy that sees Congo's social conditions as specifically historic. In this context, the act of rehistoricizing the present generation's narrative through abstract metaphor becomes for some audiences a gesture of militantism, but for others it represents nothing more than the whims of a director who chose, for some inexplicable reason, to focus on an unattractive car that does not even run. ⏵

Despite the inconsistency of people's responses to the video, it did become reasonably popular primarily because Synergie adopted it, with the song and the short film, as part of their larger sensitization campaign about women's rights. Over the years, Synergie has developed effective strategies for reaching mass local audiences in hundreds of communities; representatives speak in schools and churches, facilitate discussions with village chiefs and traditional leaders, and even go door-to-door educating people about a cluster of issues surrounding women's rights. In addition, they have regular airtime designated to messages against sexual violence on local radio stations, they distribute educational pamphlets written in Kiswahili and French, and they edit a publication, released three times a year, that circulates widely. The idea behind the Twaomba Amani project was to add to Synergie's arsenal of activities a mobile cinema unit, which they launched in late 2004 with more than three hundred screenings and public discussions of "Twaomba Amani." To this end, Synergie and Yole!Africa trained a team of six people, four of whom traveled with the mobile unit and two of whom stayed in Goma coordinating logistics.

The international NGO Search for Common Ground, which had long been interested in organizing a mobile cinema project in the east of Congo, cosponsored the projections of "Twaomba Amani." Like the other collaborations in this project, the partnership with Search for Common Ground was distinct; the NGO was integrated only *after* the artistic and educational material was completed (and publicized) and served exclusively as logistical and reporting support with no directorial role in the project. According to representatives from Search for Common Ground, Synergie, and Yole!Africa, this collaborative style worked well at the time, though its success brought the viability of cultural interventions to the attention of other international NGOs, which has subsequently posed challenges for both Synergie and Yole!Africa.

What many of the subsequent organizations have not taken into account is that there already are—and have been for decades—thriving local networks and strategies in place to create, support, and sustain cultural and educational interventions. At the core of these local strategies is a fundamental respect for the humanity of the "target communities," who, despite differences (and sometimes quite grave differences), are for their compatriots human equals, not projects or statistics. In the Twaomba Amani project this was evident in the extreme care Synergie and Yole!Africa took in the extensive preliminary research conducted in each and every village or city before organizing a screening. Logistically this was a nightmare; it meant the team had to travel, multiple times, to remote locations under difficult, often dangerous, circumstances. But it also amplified the impact of the project because it allowed the team to shape every screening and debate so as to meet the most urgent needs of each microcommunity.

The information gathered during preliminary visits included important logistical data about screening conditions. With community leaders the team selected a venue, determined whether modifications would be needed (for example, in areas with an early curfew daytime screenings were necessary, which meant blocking windows), calculated how much fuel would be required to operate the necessary equipment in areas with no electricity, etc. During preliminary meetings the team also gathered more sensitive information about local practices to identify specific issues such as education, stigma, and traditional customs that intersect with rape and sexual violence. Notably, the research for this project was conducted much like the negotiations with the musicians, with a cultural relevance that was often incongruous with formal reporting requirements.

Sometimes members of the Synergie/Yole!Africa team would sit for hours with traditional leaders, drinking local beer while listening to seemingly irrelevant stories and trying to decipher their significance. At times these exercises were simply a test of the respect the team was willing to show for traditions that were not their own; at other times this was a way of conveying critical social information through metaphor or proverb, and often such exercises were a polite way of testing what is best translated as the "b.s. meter" of the Synergie/Yole!Africa team. But whether abstract, concrete, or intentionally misleading, this information eventually became the organizing principle around which every individual screening was structured.

Once negotiations were complete and a date was set for a screening, armies of local organizers took it upon themselves to publicize the event, which speaks to the thriving and established mechanisms for local activism. To prepare for screenings, people took to the streets, winding on foot through crowded markets, churches, and public squares with megaphones in hand; they rode down rugged roads in the backs of beat-up pickup trucks astride enormous speakers blaring screening details; they painted and hung banners in all corners of cities and villages; they saturated the airwaves of local radios; sent mass text messages (in urban areas) explaining the essentials in 130 characters or less. All of these activities happened hundreds of times, in villages as remote as Mubi, and in vibrant urban centers in North and South Kivu. (Incidentally, none of it required the six-figure budgets and cumbersome bureaucracies that commonly accompany foreign efforts; nor were there financial incentives enticing people to participate.)

Eventually, armed with digital copies of the song, the music video, the film, and a cumbersome assortment of screens, speakers, cables, projectors, generators, fuel, tools, and assorted troubleshooting equipment, the team would arrive in a given location. Although each screening was unique, there was a common arc to most Twaomba Amani events: they generally began with popular music from the hosting community playing on loudspeakers as people congregated. The music, often provided by a church, added a communal and often celebratory air to the gathering. After an ample crowd had assembled and exchanged greetings, a local leader would introduce the team, who would make brief preliminary remarks explaining the project as a whole, and then prefacing, and finally playing the song and music video.

Imagine, if you will, a tightly packed room with fabric damping the light from the glassless windows, leaving the air thick and fragrant. More often than not, specks of dust hung in the triangle of light from the projector that cast silhouettes of people as they sat shoulder to shoulder, some on the floor, others packed onto benches, the elders on chairs. Their bodies surrounded a small table holding the projector, a laptop, a power strip, and a knot of worn cables that meandered between people's feet to the speakers in the back of the room, through the window to the generator sitting outside under an overhang, or to spotlights on portable stands. The screen at the front of the room was made from a set of white bed sheets stretched and stapled over a thin veneer of wood, mounted on detachable wooden legs. The sputter and hum of the generator muted the bustle of activity outside the windows as chickens and goats ambled past; combined with the near darkness and the piquant air, the cumulative sensation was one of anticipation, until, after a brief delay, the laptop's hard drive spun to life and the music video began.

After watching the video, there was room for discussion, which ranged from curiosity and often confusion about the more abstract aspects (like the recurring image of the dilapidated car) to appreciation of the compelling relevance of the song's lyrics from a local perspective. Many audiences felt validated by the content of the song and how it spoke for Congolese, and others were simply baffled by the accompanying images, but despite differing receptions the song and video gave audiences a concrete local lens through which to hone in on the specific issue of rape as one in a larger social, economic, and political context about which they too had something to say. When discussion of the video came to a natural pause, the team introduced the film, which was considered the main event.

After another brief delay for the laptop's hard drive to spin back to life, the film began. "Twaomba Amani" (the film) starts with a sound, a percussive pulse, its timbre somewhere between a muted xylophone and an electronic raindrop, that hits once, then again, and then accelerates into a fleetingly audible rhythm.⏵ Overlaid on this audio texture are black-and-white images of women with their backs to the camera as they march down the streets of Beni (Fig. 4.2 left), some striding, some jumping and turning, some waving branches in the air in gestures that could equally convey celebration or protest. Close observation reveals that the opening scene is slightly in slow motion, which, combined with the audio rhythm, enhances its intensity and suggests an element of suspense or latent tension. Images of the march continue behind opening credits and then gently begin to flicker, and, accompanied by a distant rumble that could just as easily evoke thunder or machine gun fire, the screen fades to black.

FIGURE 4.2 Twaomba Amani March Sequence.

But the pulse continues, and soon the image returns. This time the women are facing the camera, bodies running, hands waving fabric in the air, the ambiguity of celebration or protest still intact. The swift movement of their bodies brings the shot quickly from medium-long, where it started, to close-up, but it is more as if the women have zoomed in on the camera than the reverse. As they continue to zoom in, one particularly energetic woman (Fig. 4.2 center) pulls past the others with a swimming gesture, jumping, speaking, and gesturing forcefully until she has brought her face into extreme close-up. At the height of her advance, when only her teeth are visible, she speaks passionately, but inaudibly, into the camera and the main title appears, as if taking the words out of her mouth: "Twaomba Amani: an appeal for peace and living together in the Democratic Republic of the Congo."[34] The camera stays trained on her face as she passes by, and when she marches out of view, the original pulse becomes audible again, enhanced this time by mechanical grinding and ambiguous rustling sounds as the image fades back to black.

The next image is a close-up of a middle-aged woman's face speaking directly into the camera amid a chaos of background noise: "We have to talk. They are saying that we are in democracy, but we don't have the right to say anything. We are underestimated. Enough is enough."[35]

As she speaks, she articulates her words—and sentiments—with her arms, swinging them vigorously. In her hand she carries a branch of leaves, simultaneously evocative of a switch with which to beat an assailant or a symbol of peace. When she finishes talking, the camera pans through the crowd to another woman shouting: "They wanted to have sex with us, that's why they have killed our sister. Let them come and fuck all of us then. Let them come and fuck. We are so despised."[36] After these words the audio pulse is again enhanced by what sounds like a distant clap of electronic thunder, and the image flickers to black.

The following sequence includes close-ups of women speaking into the camera alternating with wider shots of their progression through the city, all offering a glimpse of the nature of the protest: individual women remove their *bikwembe*[37] and lie down in the street, writhing on the ground as the crowd surges by, until, after dragging themselves for some meters on the ground, they rise, retie their bikwembe, and continue. Through all of this, the women's words are inaudible over the crescendo of the pulsing audioscape until, in a final close-up, a powerful matron explains: "We are demonstrating because rape has become worse. We are so angry today. We found a woman raped, her sex swelling, she is undressed."[38] A series of women continue to articulate the community's anger at the increase of sexual violence in their region (Fig. 4.2 right) until their voices and all other diegetic sound is, again, replaced by an amplified version of the pulsing audioscape.

In the final segment of the opening sequence, the camera, as if unbalanced by the sound sphere, seems to roll on the ground with the women. When it rights itself, it gives the disoriented feeling of someone searching through the crowd. Eventually it pauses on a single bed with a simple wooden frame, set up in the middle of the street. This bed, peopled by women and children, is the emblem of the protest. As newcomers sit down, and others stand to reinsert themselves in the flow of the march, the drone rattles louder, and the image becomes seeped in red. Dust flecks of old 35 mm film dance across the angry red background accompanied by a final crash of thunder above the drone.

Audiences in artificially darkened rooms across the region were riveted by the opening of "Twaomba Amani." Clearly the content is captivating. But there is also something important to be said for the cinematic language through which the story is told. Take, for instance, the choice to render the images in black and white. This was due, in part, to the poor color quality of the original images since they were not professionally shot, but more importantly, according to the director, rendering the images black and white reflects an effort to ensure that this moment "remains historical." In his words:

> I [Petna] was looking for a way I could make these images memorable. This action should not be a flash moment, but on the contrary, it should be a flashback, a piece of our history that we never forget. And for me, all the biggest moments in my life—like Lumumba's speeches—are in black and white. If I put [these images] in color people would see them as a day, an event, and that's it, but if I put them in black and white it becomes a memorable moment that everybody will want to keep, it becomes part of our history.[39]

The sense of history is further enhanced by the flecks and scratches of old 35 mm film, which cumulatively have the effect of preserving, memorializing, and historicizing the rally as a protest defined by the intention of its participants in which generations past and future might see themselves reflected.

Another significant aspect of the cinematic language in the opening sequence is the unfailing return (flicker, fade, or cut) to black after every glimpse of the rally. Like the use of black and white, this aesthetic choice has a dual explanation, the first half of which is that only short segments of consecutive footage were viable. However, this technical challenge contributed to a very intentional aesthetic of erasure and renewal that brings attention to film as the specific medium of commemoration. Instead of inviting the viewer to lose herself in the scene, these interruptions are a repeated reminder that it is only through the camera that she gains access to this knowledge at all. Underlying this aesthetic is an interesting duality: on one hand, the insistent returns to black screen allude to the larger history of erasure and silence that surrounds stories of agency or empowerment in Congo. The very technical difficulties that contribute to this aesthetic result from lack of access to and training in the use of film equipment (to say nothing of international disinterest), which has literally erased the stories of women and men fighting against violence and oppression in the east of Congo. On the other hand, the constant renewal of the images underscores the determination, resilience, and progress depicted in a march and a film that challenge Congo's single story.

Perhaps ideas like these crossed the mind of more-critical viewers after watching the images of the rally, but more often the slight pause after the opening sequence provided a moment of sensory reflection before the start of the second half of the film, which is in full color. As the scene fades in from black, the camera is already panning over a murky stream cascading between vibrant green banks. The camera leaves the stream and begins to advance slowly through the lush grass. Objectively, the scene is picturesque and idyllic; however, the camera trembles slightly, which, in conjunction with the cautious hyperrealistic sounds of someone trying to advance silently, creates an ominous tension. The image then cuts to a woman wrapped modestly in worn but colorful fabrics washing dishes in the stream. Just when the babbling diegetic sounds of splashing, scrubbing and far-distant crying of roosters and children begin to calm the previous suspicions, the image cuts back to the grass, the sound returns to a stalking silence, and there is no doubting the ominous. The image then undergoes a series of cuts and zooms that establish the proximity of predator and prey, until a man comes into view, clad in jeans and a collared shirt. He emerges from the grass, looks cautiously to the left and right, then trots confidently toward the woman, grabs her from behind, and puts his hand across her mouth to silence her erupting scream, all before she can even drop the cookpot she is washing.

Her reflex to struggle erupts with force, and for a moment she frees herself of his hold, pushing past him and running for cover (Fig. 4.3 left), only to be overtaken and thrown to the ground, where she continues to struggle, kicking, clawing, screaming; yet he pins her down and overpowers her. Throughout this struggle the trembling of the camera increases, speaking her terror in its own language until it has shaken itself free of image and color and the viewer is left with nothing more

FIGURE 4.3 Twaomba Amani Attack Sequence.

than a writhing negative of violence. As the image dissolves, a deep drone crescendos, like the perpetual reverberations of a resonant drum struck too hard. The struggle continues through a kaleidoscope of colliding negatives moving in opposition to their own colors that float on the surface, pinned down under the heavy vibration of rhythmless sound. The center frame of Figure 4.3 shows the height of abstraction, with multiple shots of her legs struggling against his imposing body.

Just as the oppression becomes unbearable, the woman heaves for breath and releases a bellowing scream, her mouth momentarily distinguishable through the abstraction (this moment is visible in Fig. 4.3 right frame). The sound of the scream disintegrates as it sustains, splintering into competing echoes, timbres, and tempos, until in her agony one can hear the screams of hundreds of women. She continues to wail as his negative overpowers hers and they multiply ferociously, her kicking legs doubling then quadrupling exponentially—but in vain—against his mounting force. Though the layers of image are in slow motion, cutting and shifting at different times, their cumulative effect produces a feeling that this act is happening both too slowly and too fast at the same time, that it will last only fleeting seconds, but yet never end.

When the struggle does finally subside, it does so by receding into an even more gruesome reality. Her screams eventually fade the image to black—though whether the blackout is of death or unconsciousness remains unclear. When the image returns, it fades foggily through a white screen dancing with the same gritty texture associated with history in the first half of the film. This time, the combination of texture and color emphasize history and reality in equal measure as the images transition, hazy and obscure at first, from blackout into an indigo-infused scene of documentary footage accompanied by an ambient drone: soldiers standing detached and unconcerned among a collection of bodies strewn on the ground, the neglected corpse of a woman, a close-up of the vacant eyes and open mouth of another anonymous dead woman's face, live hands beating the face of a dead body, disgracing it one last time as it lies in a heap of unclaimed dead. Each image fades in turn to a textured indigo emptiness.

Eventually the documentary footage gives way to the familiar image of women marching through Beni waving their branches and bodies in slow motion through the indigo haze that ultimately consumes them. The final image is of the women marching toward the camera again, until, when the same particularly energetic woman pulls past the others and zooms her face into extreme close-up, the image freezes on her open mouth. Yet this time, instead of taking words out of her mouth and inscribing them in text, the intensity of her force is articulated by a final clap of thunder, or perhaps gunfire, that fades the screen to a deep red. The sound continues to reverberate, but the red eventually turns to black as the song of the closing credits begins and the viewer is left to grapple with rap lyrics denouncing the conflation of circumstances and (in)actions that led to the social and political climate of Congo (lyrics and translation to this song are on the companion website ⏵).

The only thing to do after watching this film is pause. The content is too real to provoke applause; who, and what, would one be clapping for anyway? The most common response to screenings was, at first, collective silence. But as comments inevitably began to trickle into discussion, it became clear that it was not a silence of trauma. Despite the obvious discomfort of witnessing a rape scene, the unconventional depiction of violence in "Twaomba Amani," the particular aesthetic woven out of sound, movement, color, texture, and narrative, effectively invited viewers to lose themselves in another's experience without losing hold of their own dignity or sense of self in the process.

Instead of assaulting the viewer with graphic depictions of realistic violence, the film makes its point on a different level, exposing insight into the nature of sexual violence while protecting the humanity of those who have experienced it. It is one thing to speak of mutilation by showing literal disfigurement of people, and another thing entirely to speak of mutilation by dismembering images of assault or through the violence of rending negative from color and superimposing multiple iterations of aggression one upon another until the images appear to be fighting among themselves. For audiences for whom sexual violence is often all too real, setting sight and hearing at odds in such a way that sound and image contradict provides a sensory experience that is at once tolerable while still expressive of the brutality of rape. This approach does not lessen the viewer's appreciation of the impacts of rape by rendering the image "nonrealistic." On the contrary, by not assaulting the viewer with overly dogmatic images of violence, there is space for the viewer to feel empathy, through which the reality of the pain and mutilation of the victim become enhanced. Or, to borrow from Frank Ukadike, "it is the mental anguish illuminated with artistic devices . . . that enables the viewer to share the experience of the tortured victim."[40]

Even where the film does include real images of mutilation, their impact comes as much from the artistic aesthetic as the actual content. For one thing, the melding of documentary and fictional footage blurs the distinction between fiction and reality, shifting focus away from questions of truth versus the imaginary and toward the simple awareness that through all of these images, the common thread is the human experience. After the opening sequence of the film has conditioned the viewer to experience the potency of documentary footage, the indigo-blue haze through which the pile of corpses becomes visible buffers the viewer from a direct assault and redirects the impulse toward blatant voyeurism or the urge to turn away into a deeper psychological experience. Because the heavy blue color, which, in other circumstances would be calming, is inseparable from the carnage it shrouds, it implies a deep and seething sense of injustice, metaphorically subverting the power of a soothing force to foreground the painful denial of the daily dignities of peace. In theoretical terms, this example conforms to Ukadike's suggestion that "the fictional and the documentary coexist to illuminate and expand the borders of reality . . . they not only contribute to the resuscitation of popular memory, but also construct an active audience as witnesses of that history."[41]

Of course, no one articulated it like this in postscreening discussions. But in many communities people felt empowered to share their own stories, which in important ways amounts to much the same thing. Quite a few women expressed that seeing this film, sharing the emotional agony of being overpowered and the righteous outrage of protesting, gave them a very different perspective on experiences they themselves had had. Others shared that the film helped them understand the nuances of rape—that it is not just the horrific instances of violation that are tallied as evidence of war, but *any* forced sexual encounter. In one instance, a woman, visibly moved by the film, stood up to tell the packed room that, if the violence she saw in the film was called "rape," then she had been raped many times, but before seeing the film she had not understood that rape was the word for what she had experienced, or that she had the right to the same services provided for women who had been raped by soldiers or militia men. Observations such as these often led to more complicated conversations, specifically in villages that still observed certain traditional practices such as having the fathers-in-law of a newlywed groom test the virginity of the bride or "giving" a widowed woman to her brother-in-law after her husband's death.

If women often shared personal experiences, men tended to demonstrate a more emotional response to the film, expressing shock as they attempted to incorporate the visceral details of violation that had previously been abstract to them. Confounded by the obvious innocence of the woman in the rape scene, one man repeated again and again his dismay that he had blamed his wife for being raped and driven her out of the house instead of avenging, or better yet protecting, her. Stories like this were not uncommon as men slowly began to question the traditional beliefs that women are responsible and should be ostracized if they are raped. In many cases, these reflections led to dialogues about measures to help ensure the safety of vulnerable women. As much of the sexual violence being committed at the time was by soldiers passing through remote areas, one popular suggestion among men was to organize task forces to accompany women to the isolated areas where they washed dishes, children, and clothes, or to join them on their long walks to and from distant markets and planting fields.

But recognizing the brutality of sex forced aggressively on a defenseless woman going about her daily chores did not necessarily lead to comparable recognition of the violation implicit in certain traditional practices. It is one thing to acknowledge the horror of sexual assault, but another thing for communities to question deeply ingrained customs that force women into unwanted sexual relationships. Traces of Yole!Africa's ideology are evident in the fact that Twaomba Amani was not about telling people what to do or how to live but about inspiring people to start asking questions. In communities most deeply committed to traditional practices, sometimes the best possible outcome of a screening was the mere willingness to look at tradition from another angle, if only for a moment, perhaps to ask a question. From this standpoint, it matters as much that communities ask, "We have always lived like this; how can we change our tradition?" as that they answer immediately.

On many scales this outcome is too small to register. It certainly does not come with much by way of concrete results, and would be nearly impossible to justify through analyses comparing resources to outcome. From the perspective of most international NGOs operating in the east of Congo, projects like this simply did not (and still do not) make sense, and understandably not; what organization wants to spend thousands of hours and whatever dollar equivalent just to get people to ask a question they cannot answer? But from a local perspective that recognizes, with equal urgency, the profound value of tradition and the need to honor women's rights, this shift, however slight, is significant. From the vantage point of Synergie and Yole!Africa, the goal was not immediate behavioral change, but a chipping away at the many steps that necessarily precede it, beginning with a shift in understanding that led, over time, to organic community-driven shifts in practice.

It is in the willingness for the magnitude of this project to be at once so great and so small that it calls to mind the doctrines of Third Cinema. Clearly, task forces of men accompanying women on their daily chores do little to alter the larger epidemic of rape in the east of Congo; indeed, this idea poses its own dangers as men are themselves targeted in systematic deployment of rape as a weapon of war and men are more likely to be killed, while women are more likely to be kidnapped. Equally insignificant is the subtle psychological shift evident in people's willingness to question previously accepted practices when compared to the staggering statistics of ongoing—indeed escalating—violence. These actions, however small, are nevertheless, an "extra-cinematic" response to Twaomba Amani that underscores the importance of alternative aesthetics. Teshome Gabriel argues, and rightly so, that

the aesthetics of Third Cinema . . . are as much in the after-effect of the film as in the creative process itself. This is what makes the work memorable, by virtue of its everyday relevance . . . within the context of Third Cinema, aesthetics do not have an independent existence, nor do they simply rest in the work *per se*. Rather, they are a function of critical spectatorship.[42]

Like all effective screenings in the tradition of Third Cinema, the postscreening discussions of "Twaomba Amani" yielded widely varying results. Some moved in the direction of legislative action, others focused on reintegrating raped women into communities instead of stigmatizing them, and still others prioritized further education on the subject. In many instances, the best-case scenario was simply to introduce the concept of sexual violence against women. Just as there was no script, however delicate, and no series of bullet points, however flexible, that could adequately address the multiple aspects of gendered violation in various traditions encountered during the project, there was no set of intended results against which the success or failure of a given screening was measured. Clearly some screenings went better than others, but the distinguishing characteristics were intangibles such as the amount and quality of energy in the discussion, the safeness of the space for dialogue, the "vibe" (to quote the team), which is not easy to quantify. Search for Common Ground did keep detailed records of the number of screenings and the number of participants per screening, as well as data gathered from a brief survey participants took at the end of the event. But as a locally driven project, Twaomba Amani was not subject to the cumbersome reports required by funders whose demands for concrete statistics raise ethical nightmares for organizations that believe divulging numbers of victims or perpetrators of rape "rehabilitated" through a given project obscures the project's greater impacts.

But the lack of reporting does not reflect a lack of concrete results. Beyond the psychological shifts for many individuals and communities and the project's contribution toward unseating Congo's single story of rape, Twaomba Amani was also central to Synergie's larger effort to formalize a legal definition of rape and an associated law that recognizes rape as a crime. Synergie understood that, in order to reform the culture of impunity and raise the stakes—and punishment—for perpetrating rape, there had to be a legal definition of rape as a punishable crime, and understood that changes to Congo's legal code had to come from Congolese. Accordingly, concurrent with the launch of the Twaomba Amani campaign in 2004, *Synergie* submitted a formal petition to President Joseph Kabila. With proof of effective sensitization efforts, notably Twaomba Amani, and growing regional support for state action, Synergie continued to pressure the president until, on July 22, 2006, he officially signed Law 006, *La loi sur la répression de la violence sexuelle faite aux femmes* (repression of violence against women act), into being. With the law came celebration, but also the recognition that a law is meaningless unless it is known and enforced, two tasks that became the focus of Synergie's next project, which continues in various iterations to this day.

My point in telling the story of Twaomba Amani is to introduce it into the collection of stories that represent rape and sexual violence in the east of Congo. If nothing else, it is an indication that there is more to the spectrum of Congolese agency than savagery and victimhood. The efficacy of this project, and the impact it made on so many social and political levels, makes it hard to understand why, three years later, after Twaomba Amani had reached hundreds of communities and after Synergie had succeeded in pushing Law 006 through parliament, the film (*The Greatest Silence*) that introduced the issue of rape to the Western world made no mention of these powerful local mechanisms that were already making concrete advances in addressing the issue. True, Twaomba Amani's primary measurable outcome was establishing the legal channels through which rape could become punishable, which by necessity shifted the focus of the project to rape as an individual act rather than a systematic weapon of war. But that was an extremely important step in the process of addressing mass strategic rape. And it seems worth mentioning that an army of "gentle angry women" was already making real change.[43]

THE SECOND STORY: JAZZ MAMA

By 2008 the single story of rape in Congo had taken root in the American imagination. Late that year, Petna took his first trip to the United States, where he was invited to screen his films and give presentations at a number of prestigious universities, colleges, and cultural centers across the country. Despite the fact that the films he programmed were not directly about rape, during the postscreening discussions members of the audience almost always asked some version of the question, "Why do you Congolese men rape your women?" According to Petna, this question shocked and offended him for many reasons. First, it diverts attention from the strategic use of rape as a weapon of war and implies instead the kind of uncontrolled savage male sexuality conjured in the single story of Congo that is rooted in darkness; second, it collapses the range of motivations for Congolese men, who in his experience profoundly respect women and often join armed groups with the primary aim of protecting the women they love. Hindered by his agony over the question, he was never able to offer his audiences an answer that satisfied him.

By 2008 the single story of rape in Congo had also taken root in the European imagination. Later that year Petna was approached by the director of SESAM, a national educational and cultural project of the French Embassy in Congo, to document the Congolese adaptation of Koffi Kwahulé's one-woman play *Jaz*, about a rape scene in Paris, which was to be staged in Kinshasa in 2009. According to Petna, what bothered him was the suggestion that a rape scene in Paris had anything to do with the kind of systematic rape taking place in Congo. The problem was not in drawing parallels between the trauma that survivors of either experience suffer, but rather in the conflation of motivations on the part of the respective perpetrators, some of whom are motivated by sexual desire however corrupted and others of whom are motivated by strategic (also corrupt) political and economic forces.

In response to these experiences, in 2010 Petna made *Jazz Mama*, a film that expanded into a movement about the dignity of Congolese women despite the many obstacles they face. *Jazz Mama* is a thirty-minute documentary shot in Kinshasa that tells a web of stories of women in Congo. It introduces Mama Brigitte, who sells fabric at the market to feed her family since the state no longer pays her husband, who is a civil servant. As the film follows her through work in the market and home life with her five children, it creates a portrait of the hundreds of thousands of anonymous Congolese women whose remarkable strength is overlooked in the more sensational stories of victimhood. Mama Brigitte, the woman on the right in Figure 4.4 left frame, is intelligent and energetic, and most notably she embodies a kind of contagiousagency that inspires her customers and fellow vendors alike. Perhaps this agency is most evident when, looking directly into the camera, Mama Brigitte says:

> Selling fabric is not as lucrative as it was, but I have to do it to feed my children. Some people want to discourage me, to make me feel guilty, diminish my dignity, punish me for being stronger than they are by dismissing me as a "seller of nothing." But I am not nothing. I make sure my children get an education, I feed my husband, whose salary the state no longer pays. *I am not a nobody.*[44]

The film also introduces Ornella Mamba (the actress who featured in *Jaz* when it was staged in Kinshasa), who ties the narrative together as she navigates different

FIGURE 4.4 *Jazz Mama* Women of Congo Sequence.

parts of the city, indirectly introducing viewers to the crowded public buses of Kinshasa, the outdoor urban bars and cafés, the gridlocked traffic on the multilane boulevards, the public squares and government buildings, the lingering dilapidated high-rises that intersperse thriving urban centers, the tight quarters of makeshift retail shops. Through Mamba's encounters, the film also introduces a host of characters that inhabit Congo's capital city: two *shegue* (street boys), visible in the center frame of Figure 4.4, who accost her for money and then, after trying to justify their attempt to take her mobile phone by telling her they have not eaten in days, respond to her rather personal questions with snapshots of their life stories in which they reflect poignantly on what their mothers would think of their behavior; the film also includes the acclaimed Congolese musician Simaro Lutumba, who reflects on the role of women in traditional society and reminds viewers that the ornate *bikwembe*[45] that traditionally adorn women's bodies have a long history associated with the dignity of and respect accorded to women in Congolese cultures.

These are (some of) the concrete ingredients of *Jazz Mama*. But the film is also infused with potent visual metaphors. Among the most prominent is the presence of traditional Congolese fabric. On one level, *Jazz Mama* tells the history and meanings of various kikwembe patterns through Mama Brigitte's description of fabrics worn by married women to shame rivals for their husbands' affection, and through Lutumba's description of the intricate patterns of knotting kikwembe that signal gendered social statuses of marriage or motherhood (for example). Examples of kikwembe are visible in the right frame of Figure 4.4. Having established the centrality of fabric to the cultural conception of women in Congo, the film makes of kikwembe a metaphor. Throughout the film there are scenes of Ornella Mamba in an outdoor setting adorned from head to toe in kikwembe, holding a flowered piece of fabric that she tears apart (see Fig. 4.5). In most instances, her gesture is accompanied by the amplified sound of the fabric rupturing. This combination of image and sound leaves no doubt that the

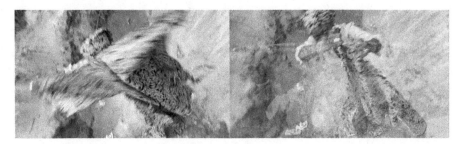

FIGURE 4.5 *Jazz Mama* Tearing Sequence.

rending of cloth is symbolic of the destruction of the bodies, dignity, and history of women in Congo.

But despite its potency, this visual metaphor is not traumatizing. The need to address the brutality of sexual violence without further wounding communities who experience rape first-hand is one of the most powerful motivating factors behind *Jazz Mama*. In the director's statement, and in countless postscreening discussions, Petna poses the question, "Must a bloody story be written in blood for people to understand?" For anyone who has experienced rape or ushered a loved one through the experience, the force of films that aim to catalyze action often triggers tremendous pain by forcing survivors to relive horrific experiences. This is certainly common in depictions of rape in Congo, which rely on shocking and horrifying images to rouse viewers out of complacency, or as Hunt so eloquently puts it, in which the "signature of horror serv[es] as humanitarian fuel."[46] But, in the case of Congo (as elsewhere), this has two interrelated effects: for people who have not experienced sexual violence it positions those who have as de facto victims in need of help, and for people who have experienced sexual violence it reanimates trauma, often forcing them to focus on the suffering in their past rather than on taking action. By insisting on the visual metaphor of kikwembe, *Jazz Mama* works, subtly, to rehistoricize Congo's story of sexual violence and in so doing underscores how dignity and respect for tradition are at stake in the way women's stories are narrated.

A second visual metaphor that runs through the film is industry. Throughout *Jazz Mama* there are shots of women's hands busily engaged in activities that range from braiding hair, sewing, caring for children, and cooking to soldering motherboards, programming computers, repairing electronics, and writing. In short, women's hands are occupied with many of the small tasks that collectively drive progress. In this way, women are cast as the force that creates, sustains, and repairs the structures of everyday life. Like the hundreds of thousands of women represented by Mama Brigitte's infectious agency, these women are anonymous, but their anonymity should not be confused with passivity or helplessness. If nothing else, *Jazz Mama*'s repeated evocation of female industry shows, beyond the shadow of a doubt, the many ways in which women are already engaged in addressing the needs of their communities.

A third, and particularly pointed, visual metaphor is introduced through an original poem that was written for the film by the acclaimed Congolese author Bibish Mumbu. The poem is delivered in short sections by Mamba, whose face is often in extreme close-up as she recites stanzas looking directly into the camera and wearing the same flowered kikwembe as a headdress that, in other scenes, she tears apart. The poem itself is a reflection on the disturbing inversions of sound and silence that increasingly characterize life in Congo. Early in the film Mamba delivers the beginning of the poem first in extreme close-up against a black background and then later projected from the digital screen of Kinshasa's largest billboard:

En un mot, le refus du silence	In short, I reject silence
Car il tue la marge	because the absence of silence
entre le personnel	kills the space between an individual
et le reste.	and the others.
Chaque existence devient alors	Each existence becomes
une place publique	a public place
où chacun a son mot à dire.	where everyone has a say.

As she continues, the camera zooms further and further out, showing the urban chaos that is Kinshasa as her voice fights to compete with the city's daily cacophony:

vie publique	Public life,
confiance publique	Public confidence,
place publique	Public place ...
Par peur du silence, cette bête qui tue	For fear of silence, that beast that kills.[47]

Later in the film, the poem continues with a black-and-white extreme close-up of Mamba, her face occasionally obscured by a drift of fog or smoke competing with her teeth for whiteness, against the black background.

On peut dire—et croire	One could say—and believe
que je suis contrast avec cette ville de bruit	that I am a contrast with this city of noise
mais on n'est qu'on	But in fact we are one . .[48]

When she finishes, silence lingers with the image, and then slowly, as color seeps into the following shot of Kinshasa's famous traffic, the noise of daily lifereturns. The penultimate iteration of the poem, visible in Figure 4.6 (left frame), is accompanied by a close-up of half of Mamba's face on the right side of the screen against a backdrop of traditional fabric.

Ma culture est celle du bruit.	My culture is that of noise.
Le silence me gène.	Silence disturbs me.
Il me pèse.	It weighs on me.
Comme s'il cachait quelque chose	Like it hides something

comme un porteur de mauvaise nouvelle	like a bearer of bad news
C'est pour ça que les coupures d'électricité	that is why (electrical) black outs
sont calamité	are disastrous
parce qu'elles me plongent dans le silence.	because they plunge me into silence
Or, quand tu regardes les gens vivre,	when you observe how people live
tu te rends compte de ce refus du silence.	you recognize their rejection of silence.[49]

The final iteration of the poem concludes the film as Mamba, perched high above the city of Kinshasa wearing a kikwembe headdress (see Fig. 4.6 right frame), looks directly into the camera.

Place publique,	public place
vie publique,	public life
confidences publiques,	public confidence
compréhension publique,	public understanding
justifications publiques,	public justification
téléphone publique,	public telephone
conversations publiques,	public conversations
injustices publiques,	public injustice
faim publique,	public hunger
appel public,	public call
réponse publique,	public response
questionnement public,	public questioning
déshumanisation publique,	public dehumanization
regard public,	public scrutiny
femme publique . . .	public woman
Culture publique du silence!	public culture of silence!

FIGURE 4.6 *Jazz Mama* Poem Sequence.

At the core of this poetic reflection on sound and silence is a strong critique of the inversion of the most potent conduits of positive change. Silence, which in other circumstances might be a blessed opportunity for reflection or contemplation, has become a premonition of crisis, while sound, instead of denouncing crises, has become a distraction and a buffer. Thus both sound and silence are rendered impotent to prevent destruction, and omnipotent to maintain a status quo of chaos. This critique is as applicable to Congolese popular culture as it is to Western activism. Indeed, what Lisa Jackson terms the *greatest* silence might well be called the *wrong* silence—for the most characteristic silences in Congo's story of violation are evident in the gaping absence of Congolese stories documented and publicized by Congolese people. And the silencing of Congolese stories in international media coverage, which has become its own cacophony, inevitably leads to the wrong noise. In Congo, the balance between speaking out *for* Congolese and listening *to* Congolese has been dangerously skewed in the urgency to intervene in the current crisis. The practice of listening has become secondary to the need to speak out, but without first hearing—deeply—the nuances buried in local stories, the act of speaking often adds to the cacophony that diverts relevant action.

Whether or not local audiences would articulate their interpretation of *Jazz Mama* in these words, the impact of the film was overt. When it premiered in Kinshasa, it was referred to as revolutionary for the way it portrayed Congolese women. In a particularly poignant postscreening discussion, Pauline Katupa (who is the wife a highly respected Congolese political journalist who also serves as coordinator of media research in DRC for European countries) told Petna, "*je te dis merci de la part de toutes les femmes du monde pour ce film, qui parles de la femme Africaine avec dignité. Ç'est rare qu'on c'est retrouve en présence d'une honnêteté pareil*" (I thank you on behalf of all the women in the world for this film that speaks of African women with dignity. It's rare to find such honesty). There are many reasons for *Jazz Mama*'s popularity in Congo. There is the sheer novelty of a film about sexual violence in Congo by a Congolese filmmaker, for *Jazz Mama* was the first. There is also the communal sense of ownership of a project that, for the first time (according to Congolese audiences), provided an equitable portrait in which people from all walks of life could see themselves. Of course, not everyone liked everything in the film, but the issues of contention were about Kinshasa (the traffic, the street children) and Congo (the corruption, the war) as flawed places, not about the representation of people's lives as exaggerated, partial, or outright false. Another element that increased the popularity of the film was the presence of Ornella Mamba and Bibish Mumbu, two powerful female Congolese artists who, when *Jazz Mama* was filmed, were rising to international fame. Thus the broad spectrum of women portrayed in, contributing to, and behind the scenes of the film was representative of the equally broad spectrum of Congolese women engaging with the world.

The consistent enthusiasm the film received coupled with the repeated requests by Congolese women to share their voices with the world through the film prompted an international tour, which, over time, cohered into the Jazz Mama Movement, which I helped coordinate. The more than thirty-five screenings of *Jazz Mama* in the United States and the more than twenty in Europe had a decidedly different flavor from screenings of the film in Congo, where the sights, sounds, and languages are familiar enough to allow audiences to focus on the artistic details of the film. American and European screenings also differed in that audiences often needed to be briefed about the political context before watching the film in order to understand some of the content that was obvious to Congolese viewers. But there were also other very revealing differences.

One of the more striking differences between Congolese and Western screenings of *Jazz Mama* was the respective audiences' response to the film's two most overt political critiques, which offer a clear diagnosis of the epidemic of rape and sexual violence. The first of these is delivered through a filmic recreation with the camera of the popular headshaking gesture that accompanies the words of a middle-aged woman who, halfway through the film, says, "they intentionally attack women because we are the source of life . . . attacking women is a way of destroying the whole society."[50] The second overt critique is delivered toward the end of the film by a local man in a bus who is sitting in front of the window (center right) in Figure 4.7:

> You know, rape has become a weapon to destabilize our people. Especially in the east, gang rape is creating terror. As a result, women are fleeing their villages, abandoning their lands to the control of their attackers who exploit the minerals and other riches of our country. You see? Like this they are raping the land as well! In the east we are witnessing total destruction— they are using illegal guns to kill people and rape to dehumanize us. It's a strategy of extermination! They are using rape to disguise systematic looting. This is pure sabotage, they are sabotaging our country![51]

Without fail, Congolese audiences are animated in their response to these scenes, often clapping, shouting, and voicing agreement, even adding detail to the explanations. Equally consistent is the silence with which American and European audiences consume these scenes. In postscreening discussions, many Western audience members recall being disoriented by unfamiliar visual and sonic cues and consequently missing the force of the words in these scenes. And this makes

FIGURE 4.7 *Jazz Mama* On the Bus.

sense. In the first instance the brief visual metaphor of head shaking dissolves into a delightful scene of children running blissfully (and naked) through an urban rainstorm, which, for unaccustomed audiences, frequently draws attention away from the woman's words. In the second instance, the bus is loud and crowded with many distractions: a young mother nervously comforting her newborn, the bouncing and jostling of the passengers as the decrepit vehicle navigates Kinshasa's rugged streets, the competing sound of the engine, the speaker's voice and the voices of other passengers on mobile phones.

It is easy to understand that the overwhelming quantity of sensory input distracts viewers from the gravity of the speakers' words, but ironically it is precisely such conditions that the most important information is communicated in Congo. Public buses are where locals go to get inside information about major political and economic issues, and it is through body language more than words that many opinions are conveyed. When postscreening discussions in Europe and America (inevitably) hone in on the importance of frequenting gritty public spaces like buses in order to stay abreast of public opinion, questions often arise about the disconnect between foreign activists and NGO workers who cruise through cities in private air-conditioned SUVs accompanied by personal translators. In sum, even though both Congolese and Western audiences tend to react strongly to these scenes, their divergent points of focus—the content versus the conditions of denunciation— yield different (though not necessarily contradictory) lingering insights.

Another important distinction that arose when screening *Jazz Mama* in Europe and America was the unexpected impact the film had on viewers according to their preconceived expectations of films featuring Congolese women. "Jazz

Mama" is advertised as "a film and a movement inspired by the uncompromising strength and dignity of Congolese women despite the obstacles and violence they face."[52] Smaller print at the bottom of posters tells prospective viewers that

> Jazz Mama aims to bring awareness to gender based violence in Congo without reducing the women to victims whose lives are circumscribed by rape, but instead to recognize that, while sexual violence is indeed a devastating problem, these women are often not only survivors but the pillars of the community.[53]

This text alerts viewers to the fact that the film addresses issues of sexual violence, but the predisposition of many Western viewers toward stories from Congo led them to expect a more didactic film about rape. This became clear when, consistently, such expectations were not met.

One scene in particular triggered many passionate conversations in the United States and Europe about unmet expectations. The scene takes place close to the end of the film, when Mama Brigitte's daughter, Rachelle, announces to her mother that she has something to tell her that she has been afraid to say. The scene is set in the idyllic front yard of the family's home, with chickens and chicks happily pecking scraps of rice out of the sand. Rachelle is shyly nervous, though not obviously fearful, as she sits down next to her mother after much anticipation. There is nothing ominous about this scene (depicted in Fig. 4.8), yet after the fact many viewers share that they were braced for Rachelle to deliver a heartbreaking confession to her mother that she was brutally raped and has been suffering trauma, pregnancy, and perhaps disease in privacy and isolation. Instead, when Rachelle finally screws up her courage, she says,

> *Quand je voir comment ma maman se comporte avec moi, et tout ce qu'elle fait pour nous, j'ai toujours envie de lui dire quelque chose mais je sais pas par respect ou par honte, je manque de le lui dire. Maman, c'est ta fille Rachelle, je voulais juste te dire que je t'aime beaucoup.* (When I see how my mother behaves toward me, and everything she does for us, I've always wanted to tell her something but, I don't know if it's out of respect of fear, I never tell her. [facing her mother] Mama, this is your daughter Rachelle, I just wanted to tell you that I love you very much.)[54]

The shock of such a heartfelt expression of normalcy—and love—in a place shackled by references to the heart of darkness is, for many Western viewers, among the most impactful moments of the film that challenges the single story of rape in Congo in deeply personal ways. In one particularly poignant postscreening discussion, an American woman expressed, with great emotion, disappointment

FIGURE 4.8 *Jazz Mama* Mama Brigitte and Rachelle.

in herself when she realized that her expectation of Congolese women was, by default, calibrated to stories of rape and violence. Prior to watching *Jazz Mama*, she said, her understanding of Congolese women was an amalgamation of unimaginable horror that cohered around collective suffering without any individual agency; the phrase "Congolese woman," in her mind, had a sole implication that left no space for easily relatable daily human interactions of her global peers, like Rachelle, who is working diligently toward a medical degree and yearning to confess love and admiration for her mother. For this viewer, Rachelle's confession was striking not only because of its obvious tenderness but also because of what it taught the viewer about the limitations of her own biases.

The goal of the Jazz Mama Movement was (and still is) to catalyze precisely this kind of shift in thinking in Western audiences. At the same time, the movement is equally focused on shifting paradigms of action on the ground in Congo, which, for Yole!Africa, meant introducing activities that encourage the participation of women and girls. From the center's launch in 2002, Yole!Africa predominantly served male students. By 2009, the overall ratio of male to female participants in workshops and trainings was approximately 4:1, which does not reflect local gender demographics in the least. The intense focus the Jazz Mama Movement put on the historic and ongoing strength and dignity of Congolese women forced Yole!Africa to grapple, in earnest, with the reasons the gender balance at the center was so skewed. The majority of women who were participating were enrolled in English language courses and computer literacy courses, and a few in journalism classes, but not in artistic workshops or trainings.

Research revealed that one major problem was that Yole!Africa's activities in the domains of music and dance were perceived by parents as belonging to the hip hop genre, which was not a genre in which they wanted their daughters to participate for fear of stigma that could ultimately diminish their daughters' marriageability. Filmmaking activities by contrast were often perceived as too technical or not feminine enough for young women (though there were some female participants in ALT2TV). Another complication was (and still is) the additional burden on women to support household function before engaging in extracurricular activities, especially activities that are not associated with earning money. There were, at the time, no female role models in the east of Congo who had successful or lucrative careers in art, which served as proof to parents that it was not a viable career choice for their daughters.

However, despite the concerns of parents, there were a number of young women hungry to participate in artistic activities. In response to both the families and the young women, Yole!Africa started the Kivu Choir in October 2010, which was the first concrete project of the Jazz Mama Movement on the ground in Congo. The rationale behind starting a choir was that few families if any would object to their daughters singing choral repertoire. At the same time, the center did not want to create a choir limited to "traditional" genres that could be perceived as isolated from the other activities. So Yole!Africa organized a collaborative pair of workshops, one for aspiring documentary filmmakers and one for the choir. In the choral workshop, which I had the privilege of teaching in its first iteration, the choir (which consisted of sixteen women and men between the ages of sixteen and sixty-eight) learned not only preexisting songs but also the principles of film scoring and had the opportunity to contribute to composing the final piece, which was performed, live, accompanying the projection of the short documentary created in the filmmaking workshop. The left and center frames of Figure 4.9 show the choir in rehearsal in 2010; the right frame shows the Kivu Choir immediately following a performance in 2011 accompanying a different film projection. A careful look behind the performers reveals the white wooden screen against which the film was projected.

The performance, which was public, was received with great enthusiasm by the local community, for whom such an installation was a surprise. Many of the young women's parents were present and later expressed appreciation for the performance itself and for the impact that participating in the choir had on their daughters. (One mother confessed she had told her daughter she could only participate in the choir if she finished her household chores before practice *and* raised her GPA, both of which her daughter did, much to her mother's delight.) In this way the parents began to perceive artistic activity (at least of the choral variety) as motivational for

FIGURE 4.9 Kivu Choir. Photos courtesy of Yole!Africa.

their daughters and also as a boon to the families, who received many compliments on the performances of the choir. But the impact for participants was different from that on community audience members or parents. What was, from the public perspective, a project of giving voice to images in the most literal sense also created a certain dynamic that worked on a much more private level for participants. As one in the ongoing rotation of conductors of the Kivu Choir, I have been privy to many of the subtler interactions that take place behind the scenes.

Like all of Yole!Africa's projects, the Kivu Choir integrates people from vastly different social, ethnic, religious, age, and economic groups. As such, rehearsals facilitate a kind of all-inclusive social space that is comparatively rare. Since the beginning the choir has included a group of "church mamas" (respected elderly widows associated with various churches) as well as young women from differ-ent backgrounds, including, inevitably, women who have experienced sexual violence. The choir's intergenerational makeup provides important opportuni-ties for members of the group to reconstruct, if temporarily, traditional means of knowledge transmission that have been fragmented both by the prolonged conflict and by the prolonged intervention by international NGOs in issues that would generally be resolved by community structures. Of course, cultivating such relationships takes time. When the choir first started, small groups of people clung to their familiar cliques, until, after they were divided by voice type and in-vited to participate in intensive sectional rehearsals, the initial barriers softened and new alliances eventually started to form.

It was through these unexpected alliances that the power of the choir, or per-haps the power of collective music making, first became evident in the group. A pointed example was when, after participating in a nonrelated Yole!Africa event about gender-based violence in Congo, a pregnant young woman, who had always been particularly shy, approached one of the widowed church mamas and tenta-tively posed the question, "How can I learn how to love this baby I am carrying if I am so angry about being raped?" The widow immediately took her aside and had a private conversation with her. I do not know the content of their exchange; nor is it any of my (or anyone else's) business. What I witnessed was that, from that moment on, this young woman began to engage directly with the church mamas during rehearsals, often arriving early or staying late to discuss with and learn from them. The point of this anecdote is not what the older woman said to the younger one, or even that music was the context in which their exchange took place, but rather that it is a powerful form of activism to engage in activi-ties that support existing cultural structures rather than further dismembering an already traumatized community into silos of victimhood. Indeed, if cumula-tively the international NGOs and charitable groups targeting rape victims or widows in the east of Congo as recipients of "help" combined their resources and put local women in charge, it is highly likely that organic interaction between the two groups would be infinitely more effective for all than isolated activities that stigmatize everyone involved.

Another important lesson that came from my work with the Kivu Choir is about stigma. I had long accepted the vehemence with which Yole!Africa refuses funding that requires the organization to divulge statistics about the personal lives of participants in reports. In theory I understood the center's argument that organizing activities for "rape victims" or "child soldiers" might momentarily provide people with support, but in drawing attention to their most traumatic experiences as the currency that qualifies them to participate, such activities ultimately do more harm than good. In theory I even encouraged the organization to turn down grants (often grants I had painstakingly written) when funding institutions added a "workshop for HIV/AIDS positive youth" or the production of a short film "profiling the life of a rape survivor" to the projects Yole!Africa proposed. But I had to experience the power of stigma directly before I fully grasped how devastating it is and how easily it poisons otherwise positive initiatives.

The incident that made this clear to me was when a group of six young women from the Italian-based international Catholic NGO Don Bosco joined the Kivu Choir. The regional director of Don Bosco's project in Goma at the time suggested that singing in a community choir might be a positive experience for the young women as it would allow them to participate in the locally respected Salaam Kivu International Film Festival. As acting director of the choir, I readily accepted the young women into the group, without pausing, until later, to reflect that reintegrating women into the very community from which they come is a suspicious activity for Europeans to be undertaking in Congo.

The subtle negative effects of this otherwise wonderful initiative to address the needs of rape survivors was painfully clear to me when, the following day, the women were brought to rehearsal in one of Don Bosco's SUVs, which broadcast their most intimate experiences to the entire community by virtue of getting out of the car. The women's arrival prompted a series of quiet but snide remarks delivered by the musicians and dancers who were engaged in rehearsals and other activities when the car, plastered with logos for Don Bosco, pulled up in front of Yole!Africa. The young people, who are fluent in deciphering extensive information from NGO logos, openly pondered what shenanigans the *muzungus* (foreigners or white people) were subjecting the "raped women" to this time.

Of course, teenagers in all cultures make snide remarks. In this case their comments on comparative cultural priorities were in fact rather insightful ("Why" they asked, "do Westerners pay thousands of dollars for airfare and accommodations to come teach us yoga for three months when we have better ways of dealing with our problems? Why can't they just give that money to our local organizations instead of teaching us things we're not interested in?"), but seeing the women's posture diminish and their eyes drop to the ground as they passed their peers on the short walk from the compound gate to the rehearsal space for me brought into strong relief the deep stigma participants suffer when they are branded by ostensibly healing projects that are in fact fundamentally based on their status as victims.

Fighting this and other varieties of stigma was the impetus behind the creation of another of the local projects, Femmes de Yole (women of Yole!Africa), which grew out of the Jazz Mama Movement in Congo. Over time, the women who first came to Yole!Africa through the Kivu Choir began to integrate—with the blessing of their parents—into other artistic activities, including music, dance, and filmmaking. Although still disproportionate, the ratio of male to female participants in workshops (including music production, filmmaking, and dance as well as English language, computer literacy, and journalism) shifted to 3:2 by 2012. The young women participating often excelled in their domains and earned the respect of their male peers with ease. However, they still grappled with gender-specific obstacles that challenged them. In an effort to address some of these obstacles, a group of sixteen young women came together to form Femmes de Yole; these women are between the ages of eighteen and thirty-six and study various disciplines at Yole!Africa (among them, cinema directing, acting, music, dance, and journalism).

Femmes de Yole began simply as a support group for women in navigating gender-specific challenges. As the young women got to know one another better, they realized they were not alone in many of the psychosocial barriers they experience; they realized others too were battling the same questions of self-doubt, low self-esteem, and lack of familial support for their interest in art. This discovery prompted them to investigate the roots of a problem they began to realize was nearly ubiquitous for young women in their age group. What they discovered was that it is very common for young women in Congo to face extremely challenging—and often contradictory—realities.

On the one hand, women in Congo are, traditionally speaking, the most respected members of a given community. Historically many of Congo's traditional cultures were matrilineal, and some were also matriarchal. In learning about this history, members of Femmes de Yole uncovered stories about Congolese heroines whose history is omitted from their school curricula. They discovered Kimpa Vita, the twenty-year-old woman who led a social movement against the Atlantic slave trade and the disintegration of the Kongo Kingdom in 1704 (and who was burned at the stake in 1706); they discovered Nyiabingi, a histori-cal woman who opposed colonial forces in the east of Congo (killed by British forces, who severed her head and buried it in a different village from where her body was interred, for fear she might come back to life) and whose spirit is said to reincarnate regularly in women to support resistance movements and protect communities throughout the region. Indeed, they (re)discovered the profound respect embedded in the term *mama* and learned about the period from the 1960s through the mid-1990s when adding the word *jazz* to describe a mama was the highest indication of power, respect, and esteem. In short, they discovered Congo's history was similar to that of many other colonized nations in which patriarchy was imposed on matricentric communities because the latter, with no central authority to overthrow or corrupt, were the hardest to dominate and colonize. Figure 4.10 shows a mural featuring an artistic rendering of Nyiabingi that resulted from a Jazz Mama workshop at Yole!Africa in 2012.

This prompted the Femmes de Yole to investigate the roots of patriarchy in Congo. They learned that patriarchy was introduced to many communities with the arrival of European missionaries in the fifteenth century and imposed with growing force through the colonial period. Under King Léopold II and with offi-cial Belgian rule, patriarchy was institutionalized into the structure of the state. The patriarchal culture imposed by Belgium was later adopted, restructured, and formalized by Mobutu in the infamous *code de la famille*, which dictates absolute

FIGURE 4.10 Nyiabingi Mural. Photo courtesy of Yole!Africa.

male authority. Patriarchy thus became part of the legacy of mental coloniza-tion that led men to strive for a kind of mimicry of the superiority asserted by colonizers, while also retaining remnants of the traditional respect for women they inevitably inherited from their families. The result is that Congo remains in a kind of schizophrenic limbo in which women are both deeply revered and materially restricted.

The Jazz Mama Movement's emphasis on the dignity of and respect accorded to Congolese women introduced this history to the Femmes de Yole, who had pre-viously been mired by the gendered restrictions they experienced without under-standing how these restrictions came to be. Understanding the source as well as the experience of Congo's specific gender-bias inspired Femmes de Yole not only to identify the limitations young women in the east of Congo face, but to develop concrete strategies to empower future generations. At the time of writing, they have created a formal mentoring program for young girls interested in art and journalism, and are negotiating with elementary, middle, and high school admin-istrators to formulate and implement a gender-specific after-school program of cultural education.

The impact of this project on younger generations in Goma is yet to be de-termined, but its impact on the existing Femmes de Yole demonstrates that the revolution of gender dynamics is often a matter of minute details. A poignant example is the story of Doris Lokwatere, who begged her parents for years for permission to participate in ALT2TV workshops at Yole!Africa. Concerned by the ratio of male to female participants, her parents were hesitant, but eventually she wore down their resistance. With many stipulations about curfews (among other things), at eighteen Doris enrolled in a beginner's workshop, where she was the only female participant. Initially she needed tremendous effort to assert herself, but she quickly became the pivotal student in the group. As her confidence grew, the effect was not limited to filmmaking, but began to influence her studies at school as well. Noticing the shift, her parents gave her more responsibilities and more freedom. Eventually she was allowed to participate in evening screenings at Yole!Africa, provided she confirmed to them that she had secured transportation home with the Yole!Africa vanpool. After witnessing, for months, Doris return to her house protected by her male classmates (all of whom insisted that, regardless of geographic inconvenience, Doris be dropped home first), her parents eventu-ally abandoned their habit of waiting up for her at night. Shortly thereafter, Doris arrived at Yole!Africa glowing with pride and produced the key her parents had given her with much ceremony the preceding night. It was the first time, in her family of eight siblings, that a female child was given a key to the family home. For both Doris and her family, this simple act was pivotal; it marked a distinct shift in their evaluations of her competence and confirmed that her gender was not an inherently inhibiting obstacle of her ambition.

Doris's story is both revolutionary and banal. Its happy conclusion, though important for one family, is not unique; it is the story of young women the world over struggling to assert themselves against systems of domination. In this story, the revolution is in the details, in the small interactions between one young women and her family, between one young woman and her male peers. Everyone in this story was changed by these interactions: Doris gained confidence, her parents and brothers opened their minds (which, in combination with her success, has since influenced other parents), and her classmates recognized and changed some of their own gender biases.

But Doris Lokwatere receiving a key from her family is a story that will never make the news. It is a story of revolution too mundane to translate to global media interest. Yet against the backdrop of the single story of Congo, the banality of her story is precisely what makes it remarkable and worth telling. It is the kind of story that helps shift the default expectation of young women and men in Congo from de facto victims or perpetrators of war to ordinary people whose challenges and triumphs are as mundane and sublime as anyone else's. It is the kind of story that reminds the world that, even if Congo is the site of a deadly conflict, it is a nation peopled by human beings. It is, perhaps, the best answer Petna could have given to Western audiences to shift their perspective of Congo, and with it their ways of helping.

THE MORAL

There are many morals one can draw from the stories in this chapter, but let me focus on two: that Congo is simultaneously the site of dire conflict and also the stage of powerful community organizations, and that women and women's bodies are at the heart of both. Feminist scholar Susan Roche says, "If . . . '[o]ur stories are active—if they constitute us,' then it matters to our change missions which stories we tell, which ones we seek, and which ones we hold close to us."[55] There are many change missions at work in Congo, and consequently many stories. Most prominent are iterations of the historic single story that casts Congo as a perpetual heart of darkness. In gendered terms, this translates to the common statement that Congo is "the rape capital of the world," or "the worst place in the world to be a woman" (two phrases commonly bandied about on the basis of per capita statistics of rape in Congo). That is one story, and its point is to convey urgency and magnitude. Stories like Twaomba Amani and Jazz Mama, on the other hand, work to unseat the hegemony of Congo's single story by adding to accounts of history and records of Truth, the daily activities undertaken by a broader spectrum of individuals and organizations. These stories coexist with stories of urgency and magnitude, but seeking, holding close, and (re)telling small stories of local agency (rather than reducing Congo to a place of unparalleled horror) is more likely to shift change missions or activist agendas toward strategies that better serve local needs because they position local communities as peopled by able human beings rather than disempowered embodiments of statistics.

Precisely because rape is now the focus of such urgent global attention in Congo, it is high time that the stories of local agency, of which Twaomba Amani and Jazz Mama are but two examples, also become part of the global dialogue when it turns to questions of intervention. It is also high time to balance labels of magnitude ("the rape capital of the world") with concrete snapshots of what local populations are doing about their situations, so that in addition to seeing in the horrific suffering of survivors of rape an imperative to take action on their behalves, foreign donors (of money *or* time) begin to recognize that meaningful interventions come from supporting the local structures that already exist. And this comes back to the importance of history—of rehistoricizing not only the global actions of geopolitical forces but also the local actions of community organizations. Herein lies the importance of storytelling as a mode of cultural activism. Literary theorist Trinh Minh-Ha says:

> Aware that oppression can be located both in the story told and in the telling of the story, an art critical of social reality neither relies on mere consensus nor does it ask permission from ideology. Thus, the issue facing liberation movements is not that of liquidating art in its not-quite-correct, ungovernable dimension, but that of confronting the limits of centralized conscious knowledge, hence of demystifying while politicizing the artistic experience.[56]

But the project of making of Congo's story a web that becomes three-dimensional, for all its complexity, is not an esoteric phenomenon restricted to the hallowed spheres of academe; it is a real and gritty project self-consciously being undertaken by a growing army of militant activists who are aware that the price of a single story is the lives of their nation's people. In the director's statement for *Jazz Mama*, Petna grapples publicly with this:

> Daily life in the heart of Africa, in this region named and renamed—DRCongo, Zaire, maybe the Belgian Congo or Congo Free State . . . is it fiction? science-fiction? documentary? As a teller of stories how can I situate myself in this

complexity where rumors have become the primary source of information, where the border between the truth and lies does not exist, where pastors sell miracles on street corners, where noise has replaced prayers, where the force of the people and the pulse of culture never subside despite having its history torn asunder...? What is the meaning of "documentary" in a place where daily life is already a melodrama and a fiction? In my attempt to seize daily life, narrative arises from truth, fictions emerge through documentation and I find myself telling the beautiful disorder of reality.[57]

If, in listening to what Petna calls the beautiful disorder of reality, the power, dignity, and agency of Congo's women becomes audible, then the project of storytelling offers an essential amendment to the single story of darkness that circulates in the West. If volunteers and program coordinators from Europe and America begin to understand the historic role of women in Congolese societies, indeed if instead of calibrating their vision to victimhood they learn to recognize the many jazz mamas in local communities, perhaps they will hesitate before proposing predetermined activities and instead sit with these women and listen in order to learn whether—or not—there might be some role their compassion can play in helping to restore the women of Congo to what is historically their rightful place. Indeed, what global strategies of aid might arise if images of victimhood were balanced with images of powerful active women like her?

FIGURE 4.11 Anonymous Woman in Crowd at SKIFF 2015. Photo Courtesy of Yole!Africa.

Chimamanda Adichie says:

Stories matter. Many stories matter. Stories have been used to dispose and to malign. But stories can also be used to empower and to humanize. Stories can break the dignity of a people, but stories can also repair that broken dignity. When we reject the single story, when we realize that there is never a single story about any place, we regain a kind of paradise.[58]

Regaining paradise in the east of Congo is perhaps an overly ambitious task for stories, but repairing broken dignity is not; nor is shifting paradigms of action too great a step to expect individuals and organizations to take when confronted with stories that prove, beyond the shadow of a doubt, that in addition to being a backdrop of the volatile history of greed, Congo is also a place of vibrancy, innovation, and determination peopled by everyday heroines.

NOTES

1. Nancy Rose Hunt, "An Acoustic Register, Tenacious Images, and Congolese Scenes of Rape and Repetition," *Cultural Anthropology* 23, no. 2 (2008), 244.

2. Walter Rodney, *How Europe Underdeveloped Africa* (Washington, DC: Howard University Press, 1982).

3. See, among others, Chinua Achebe, "An Image of Africa," in *Hopes and Impediments: Selected Essays 1965–1987* (London: Heinemann, 1988); Milton Allimadi, *The Hearts of Darkness: How White Writers Created the Racist Image of Africa* (New York: Black Star Books, 2002); Stefan Andreasson, "Orientalism and African Development Studies: The 'Reductive Repetition' Motif in Theories of African Underdevelopment," *Third World Quarterly* 26, no. 6 (2005), 971–86; Elleke Boehmer, ed., *Empire Writing: An Anthology of Colonial Literature 1870–1918* (Oxford: Oxford University Press, 1998); David Campbell and Mascus Power, "The Scopic Regime of 'Africa'," in *Observant States: Geopolitics and Visual Culture*, eds. Fraser McDonald et al. (London: I. B. Tauris, 2010); Jacques Derrida, *Writing and Difference* (London: Routledge, 1978).

4. See, among others, Kay Anderson, "Culture and Nature at the Adelaide Zoo: At the Frontiers of 'Human' Geography," *Transactions of the Institute of British Geographers* 20, no. 3 (1995), 275–94; Annie Coombes, *Reinventing Africa: Museums, Material Culture and Popular Imagination in Late Victorian and Edwardian England* (New Haven, CT: Yale University Press, 1997); Robert J. Gordon, '"Captured on Film': Bushmen and the Claptrap of Performative Primitives," in *Images and Empires: Visuality in Colonial and Postcolonial Africa*, eds. Paul S. Landau and Deborah D. Kaspin (Berkeley: University of California Press, 2002); Lucy Jarosz, "Constructing the Dark Continent: Metaphor as Geographic Representation of Africa," *Geografiska Annaler Series B, Human Geography* 74, no. 2 (1992), 105–15.

5. Chimamanda Adichie, "The Danger of a Single Story," *TED video*, July 2009, posted October 2009, accessed October 10, 2015, http://www.ted.com/talks/chimamanda_adichie_the_danger_of_a_single_story?language=en.

6. Derrida, *Writing and Difference*, 27.

7. Kathryn Mathers, "Mr. Kristof, I Presume?" *Transition* 107 (2012), 14–31.

8. Examples include Nicholas D. Kristof, "Orphaned, Raped, and Ignored," *New York Times*, Jan. 30, 2010, accessed Oct. 10, 2015, http://www.nytimes.com/2010/01/31/opinion/31kristof.html?_r=0; and Nicholas Kristof, "Death by Gadget," *New York Times*, June 26, 2010, accessed October 10, 2015,. http://www.nytimes.com/2010/06/27/opinion/27kristof.html.

9. Kristof, "Orphaned, Raped, and Ignored," 11.

10. Kristof, "Death by Gadget," 11.

11. Nicholas Kristof, "From 'Oprah' to Building a Sisterhood in Congo," *New York Times*, Feb. 3, 2010, accessed Oct. 10, 2015, http://www.nytimes.com/2010/02/04/opinion/04kristof.html.

12. Adichie, "Danger of a Single Story."

13. Kristof, "Orphaned, Raped, and Ignored," 11.

14. *Assistance Mortelle*, directed by Raoul Peck (Velvet film, 2013), DVD.

15. Kristof, "From 'Oprah' to Building a Sisterhood in Congo," 11.

16. Nicholas Kristof, "D.I.Y. Foreign-Aid Revolution," *New York Times*, Oct. 20, 2010, accessed Oct. 10, 2015, http://www.nytimes.com/2010/10/24/magazine/24volunteerism-t.html?pagewanted=all&_r=0.

17. Nicholas Kristof, "The World Capital of Killing," *New York Times*, Feb. 6, 2010, accessed Oct. 10, 2015, http://www.nytimes.com/2010/02/07/opinion/07kristof.html.

18. Kristof, "From 'Oprah' to Building a Sisterhood in Congo," 11.

19. As the November 2016 elections in Congo approach, Dr. Mukwege, who has been nominated to run for president and received substsantial American support, has begun to receive very positive press coverage. There is some debate in Congo, however, about whether this coverage is motivated by the ongoing desire of the United States to influence political actors in Congo.

20. Anthony Smith, *The Geo-Politics of Information: How Western Culture Dominates the World* (New York: Oxford University Press, 1980), 176.

21. Hunt, "An Acoustic Register," 237.

22. Ibid., 243–44.

23. François Grignon, "Rape as a Weapon of War in Congo," *Spiegel Online International*, June 11, 2009, accessed Oct. 10, 2015, http://www.spiegel.de/international/world/opinion-rape-as-a-weapon-of-war-in-congo-a-629885.html.

24. UN officials are also under investigation for operating pornographic video rings in their bunkers, and for selling and circulating videos of forced sex with starving women and children from IDP camps. http://www.timesonline.co.uk/tol/news/world/article512959.ece, http://articles.latimes.com/2005/feb/12/world/fg-unsex12.

25. Stephen Lewis, "Women Targeted or Affected by Armed Conflict: What Role for Military Peacekeepers?" Remarks delivered by Stephen Lewis, co-director of AIDS-Free World, at the annual convention of Wilton Park on Women Targeted or Affected by Armed Conflict, Sussex, UK, May 27, 2008.

26. Ibid.

27. James E. Young, *The Texture of Memory: Holocaust Memorials and Meaning* (New Haven, CT: Yale University Press, 1993), 3.

28. Ngwarsungu Chiwengo, "When Wounds and Corpses Fail to Speak: Narratives of Violence and Rape in Congo (DRC)," *Comparative Studies of South Asia, Africa and the Middle East* 28, no. 1 (2008), 10.

29. UN Security Council Resolution 1325 was unanimously approved in October 2000. This resolution aims to "adopt a gender perspective that includes the special needs of women and girls during repatriation and resettlement, rehabilitation, reintegration and post-conflict reconstruction" and "includes measures that support local women's peace initiatives and indigenous processes for conflict resolution, and that involve women in all the implementation mechanisms of the peace agreements, as well as measures to ensure the human rights of women and girls, particularly as they relate to the constitution, the electoral system, the police and the judiciary." United Nations Security Council, Resolution 1325, "Women, Peace, and Security," Oct. 31, 2000, accessed Oct. 10, 2015, http://www.un.org/womenwatch/osagi/wps//.

30. I discuss this historical moment in greater detail in Chapter One.

31. Gabriel, "Third Cinema as Guardian," 59.

32. From an interview conducted by the author with Mack el Sambo on July 8, 2014, in Goma, DRC. Original reads: ". . . ce que nous sommes en train de pousser la c'est notre pays, qui est considéré comme déjà en lambo, comme déjà détruit. Alors c'est avec nos efforts que nous allons pousser, nous allons le révéler qu'il soit encore vivable, qu'il soit encore remable, qu'il soit encore frequentable."

33. Petna Ndaliko Katandolo (artistic director and founder of Yole!Africa), in discussion with the author, December 2010, in Kampala, Uganda.

34. "Twaomba Amani," 0:00:31.

35. Ibid., 0:00:41.

36. Ibid., 0:00:51.

37. Bikwembe (plural of kikwembe) are the traditional fabrics women wrap around their waists.

38. "Twaomba Amani," 0:02:00.

39. Petna Ndaliko Katondolo, in discussion with the author, November 2010, in Goma, Congo.

40. Frank Ukadike, "African Cinematic Reality: The Documentary Tradition as an Emerging Trend," *Research in African Literatures* 26, no. 3 (1995), 92.

41. Ukadike, "African Cinematic Reality," 92.

42. Gabriel, "Third Cinema as Guardian," 60.

43. Susan Roche, "Gentle, Angry Women Creating Change," *Journal of Women and Social Work* 24, no. 4 (2009), 345–47.

44. *Jazz Mama*, directed by Petna Ndaliko Katondolo (Alkebu Productions, 2010), DVD, 0:22:05.

45. See note 36.

46. Hunt, "An Acoustic Register," 244.

47. *Jazz Mama*, 0:03:36.

48. Ibid., 0:11:49.

49. Ibid., 0:17:04.

50. Ibid., 0:23:47.

51. Ibid., 0:26:07.

52. Petna Ndaliko Katandolo, "The Film: Jazz Mama, a Film by Petna Ndaliko," *Respect*, accessed Oct. 10, 2015, www.jazzmama.org/the-film/.

53. Ibid.

54. *Jazz Mama*, 0:27:31.

55. Roche, "Gentle, Angry Women Creating Change," 346.

56. Trin Minh-Ha, *When the Moon Waxes Red: Representation, Gender and Cultural Politics*. New York: Routledge, 1991, 6.

57. Ndaliko Katandolo, "The Film: Jazz Mama, a Film by Petna Ndaliko."

58. Adichie, "Danger of a Single Story."

Hatukupanda kwa bega ya wazee wetu kuangalia vidole
yao ya miguu.
(We did not climb on the shoulders of our elders to look
at their toes).
SWAHILI PROVERB

EPILOGUE

IN JULY 2014, the *New York Times* published an article, "Arts Sanctuary in a War-torn City: In Congo Salaam Kivu Festival Brings Performers to Goma," that featured Yole!Africa on the front page of the arts section with full-color photographs and celebratory prose. In uncanny synchronicity, within days of this article's publication Petna was quite nearly killed by an extremely agitated and heavily armed lieutenant of the army who was intent on preventing him from filming a contemporary dance sequence for the creative documentary film he was making to recount Congo's history through dance. These events were entirely unrelated, yet I cannot but read in their confluence a microcosmic narrative that mirrors my own throughout this book.

For the *New York Times*, a respected arbiter of opinion in the West, this article was an exercise in control of perceptions, in this case perceptions of beauty and perceptions of wreckage. For the military, which has long been struggling with the power to assert its own self-image into international debates on Congo's governance, inflicting physical violence was an effort to control dangerous *mis*perceptions. The pen and the sword, the camera and the machine gun in their ever-evolving opposition. On one hand, the details matter: the *New York Times* was laudatory, describing SKIFF as a "quixotic arts festival amid . . . ruins," a space where, to quote Petna, "art can transcend where dialogue has been blocked"[1]; the military, on the other hand, were mistrustful, threatening Petna's life because of their volatile anger about the gross perversions of Congo that circulate the globe and the brutal foreign policies that result from how the nation's story is often told. On another level the details are irrelevant, and more important is the fact of simultaneity and contradiction, a fact substantiating my larger point in this book: storytelling, art, and creative expression are real currencies in conflict regions, currencies with the power to dismember and to re-member, to erase and to immortalize. On that front I rest my case.

But this is also a book about cultural activism. Thus I must point out, one final time, that not all storytelling, art, or creative expression taking place in a conflict region is necessary noise. As the examples in these chapters illustrate, in the east of Congo art is being made (and sponsored) by a wide variety of people for a wide variety of reasons. From a distance it is alarmingly easy to accept—even promote—the necessity of any creative expression in a war zone, to celebrate beauty against the backdrop of wreckage. But on closer inspection, there are critical dynamics that require rigorous investigation lest the illusion of artistic empowerment obscure lethal manipulations and manifestations of power. To that end, I have set out a number of principles throughout this book that collectively serve as a barometer I use in my own effort to hear through the cacophony of global activism and identify necessary noise. I have argued, among other things, for the critical importance of plural narratives and the value of diverging truths; and for the inalienability of the link between artistic autonomy and sociopolitical change. I have argued that revolution is in the details; that activism is not for credit; that peace is not for sale; that listening means being open to the things we might prefer not to hear. Let me conclude by articulating a final principle: I do not believe in the notion of "giving voice." If my work in the east of Congo has taught me anything it is that people—from the most meek to the most powerful—already have voices. And they know how to use them. In my final analysis then, the potential power of activism (cultura, political, or otherwise) is in *amplifying* voice, not in giving it.

The issue of "voice" reverberates on many levels in debates about global activism. Depending on how it is wielded, voice can be a justification for charitable imperialism or a vehicle for necessary noise. To idealists intent on making the world a better place, I have often issued a caution: any project proclaiming to give voice to oppressed people in Congo, other parts of Africa, or anywhere else on the planet implies two things. First, it establishes a false hierarchy in which one party is imbued (in his or her imagination, of course) with the power to bequeath on his or her fellow human beings one of the most fundamental aspects of human existence. And second, it suggests the omnipotence on the part of the benefactor to know whose voice is worthy of cultivating. To me this is not activism; it is egotism of the variety that fuels charitable imperialism in its worst forms. The alternative, for which I have been advocating so vehemently in this book, is about cultivating a new way of listening that penetrates beyond the sensationalism and urgency of global distance to the contrapuntal and mundane texture of daily life. Indeed, the aim of this book is to fill in one of the gaping craters in the global imagination of the east of Congo, which I have chosen to do by curating an array of details that render the human lives in this "conflict zone" more vivid. I took this approach because I am convinced that citing names and describing interactions between ordinary individuals and rendering lived physical spaces seeable provides the necessary context that promotes radical listening. And, from what I have witnessed at Yole!Africa, I am equally convinced that radical listening is a mandatory prerequisite to effective activism on both local and global scales.

To make this point, I want to offer one final story that zooms out in concentric circles through time and space, connecting minutiae to revolution via a chorus of local voices. In response to the dramatic week in July 2014 when Yole!Africa made international news and then almost lost its founder, students from the center came together for a barazza to process this schizophrenic series of events. The conversation began with informal reminiscing about Yole!Africa, its past, and its founder, Petna, until one young woman reminded all of us of a pivotal moment when Yole!Africa was on the brink of shutting down in its early years. This story took place in 2006, during a particularly unstable political moment when Joseph Kabila was attempting to integrate former rebel leaders into the transitional government, with precarious results in the east of Congo. Yole!Africa was still relatively new in Goma at the time, and there was tremendous skepticism about the value or viability of an arts organization in such a political climate. After failing to raise the necessary funds to pay the center's rent and encountering other significant obstacles, Petna was on the verge of closing Yole!Africa. While he was contemplating this course of action, he had to fulfill a commitment he had made to organize a film screening in the wing of a local hospital that treats survivors of rape. He selected a provocative fiction film from Senegal, which, during the post-screening discussion, prompted a woman to stand up and furiously denounce the film's protagonist, threatening, in all earnestness, to avenge his victim by her own hand. When Petna later inquired why the other patients in the room responded with such utter shock to her outburst, the doctor told him that despite various therapies, prior to the film screening this woman had not uttered a single word for the more than three years, since she was raped and nearly burnt to death in her home, where her family were all killed.

Petna tells this story frequently, describing it as a pivotal moment in his own understanding of and commitment to artistic activism. Witnessing this anonymous woman shift her own self-perception from a patient/victim to an active spectator with the power to give—even something as intangible as an opinion—clarified to him the opposing impulse (and impact) of approaching another human being on the basis of perceptions of what she *needs* or perceptions of what she has to *give*. Further, this moment confirmed, experientially, to Petna the theories that the educator and philosopher Paolo Freire put forth in his *Pedagogy of the Oppressed*, namely that creativity and art, as both practices and products, have the power to liberate people from the real and imagined constructs that restrict imagination and constrain self-perceptions and thus limit agency. Collectively these two realization were what compelled Petna to soldier on, at all costs, in the fight to sustain Yole!Africa.

There is an undeniable elegance to this story. Having dedicated years of my life to researching, supporting, and benefiting from Yole!Africa, it is poignant to recall, through story, the voice of a woman I have never met, who inspired Petna to stay the course of revolution. Indeed, her voice inspires an entire generation who have heard this story and who understand that the material resources and intellectual skills they access through study at Yole!Africa are a physical echo of her voice. From this perspective she, as much as Petna and the early pioneers of Yole!Africa, is the ancestor on whose proverbial shoulders they stand as they chart their course for the future. And recognizing this means recognizing their inheritance—and their power—in a lineage of activism that grows out of the protagonism of the people.

This was the gist of the conversation during the barazza in July 2014. As I sat listening to the debate, I found myself registering its meaning on multiple levels. I was struck that a story about the voice of an anonymous woman could have such a rousing effect on a new generation of young people a decade after her utterance. I could not help but catalog, again, the many categories that position her—a Congolese woman, raped, abandoned, impoverished, victimized, traumatized—as an ideal candidate for the countless projects aiming to give voice. She is the poster-child target of such projects, and yet clearly she has a voice—a voice that was powerful enough to inspire Petna, who in turn sustained Yole!Africa, which has become a powerful platform on which radical transformation is taking place at the local level in North Kivu.

Thinking about her voice in this context tells me something about necessary noise. It draws attention to the echoes and reverberations that, like the repetitions Nancy Rose Hunt identifies, map hidden iterations—and possibilities—of local agency. It recalibrates necessity not as a metric of statistics or urgency but as a metric of analysis, which introduces proximity and perspective as qualifications that rival pedigrees of accreditation. From this perspective, necessity is measured in relation not to wreckage but to possibility. This is a radical shift. It is also a sobering reminder of the profound difficulty of hearing necessary noise across the many global divides that filter local voices in the east of Congo through a web of networks, channels, systems, protocols, hierarchies, measures, analyses, and organizational criteria. The truth is that much of the most necessary noise is drowned out in the steady hum of bureaucracy, which labels victims and target populations as chasms of need without recognizing what they, too, might give; without stopping to imagine what radical creativity might be born of the utterance of one mutilated and abandoned woman.

As a scholar, this pattern troubles me deeply. Indeed it poses a dangerous paradox: there is at once no reliable prescription to remedy the shortcomings of charitable aid and at the same time no recipe that guarantees the audibility of the most truly necessary noise. This puts a burden of responsibility on those who would intervene that is substantially heavier than the reflexes cultivated by the desire to appease a vague sense of guilt or perform good-personness are prepared to handle in the digital age. As a scholar, I am torn. I feel compelled to identify a formula that would allow the successes of organizations like Yole!Africa to be replicated in other geographic locations, or a formula to ease the burden of the young (and not so young) people around the world yearning to make it a better place. And at the same time, I recognize the impossibility of any such formulas. Instead, I have come to value stories as capable of modeling precedent and catalyzing critical thought. Like the youth at Yole!Africa, I see myself standing on the proverbial shoulders of intellectuals and activists before me who have demonstrated the value of putting scholarship to the service of society. In this, like Petna I take a cue from Freire's suggestion that "discovery cannot be purely intellectual but must involve action; nor can it be limited to mere activism, but must include serious reflection: only then will it be a praxis."[2]

I propose the form and content of the handful of stories in this book as a gesture toward a new praxis in socially engaged scholarship. These stories, from the east of Congo, put studies of human catastrophe in dialogue with studies of human creativity to make the point that we cannot effectively learn about one without the other. My hope is that this approach to activism and to scholarship is contagious, and that globally, those of us who feel compelled to intervene in the world's crises will choose to start by filling in the remaining craters in our imaginations and then by tracing—and at times amplifying—the echoes and reverberations of local voices as they cohere into a distinctly necessary kind of noise.

Such noise traverses time and space. It might emanate from a brutalized body and reverberate in the songs and films of hundreds of young people that circulate the globe. But its significance is not the fact that it made its way into our ears; its significance is the fact that it animates the imaginations and the critical capacities of people everywhere. The discipline that comes with listening to this kind of noise is the discipline of remembering what takes place in our absence, of remembering that activism is not a measure of our heroism but of our ability to imagine the daily experiences and responses of individuals and communities navigating dire circumstances with creativity, and continuing to do so whether or not we are paying attention. As I bring this book to a close and zoom out—beyond the compound walls of Yole!Africa with its vibrant murals and bustling roster of activities, beyond the city of Goma with its legacy of violence and artistic radicalism, beyond the national boundaries of Congo with its struggle for economic autonomy, beyond the outline of the African continent and its legacy of cultural domination and resistance—as I zoom out into a world segregated by global orders of "North" and "South," "First" and "Third," "Developed" or "Developing," I invite you to keep the voices in this book ringing in your ears. I invite you to remember the host of ordinary people you have met through these stories of Goma and to know that, whether or not you or I continue to listen, they will continue to make beautiful, dissonant, extraordinary, and most decidedly *necessary* noise.

NOTES

1. Somini Sengupta, "Arts Sanctuary in a War-Torn City," *New York Times*, July 11, 2014, accessed Oct. 10, 2015, http://www.nytimes.com/2014/07/12/arts/in-congo-salaam-kivu-festival-brings-performers-to-goma.html?_r=0.

2. Paulo Freire, *Pedagogy of the Oppressed*, trans. Myra Bergman Ramos (New York: Continuum, 2000), 65.

Filmography

50 ans et au-delà (50 Years and Beyond). Directed by Petna Ndaliko Katondolo. Alkebu Film Productions, 2010. DVD.

An African Journey. Featuring Jonathan Dimbleby. BBC, 2010.

Afro@Digital. Directed by Balufu Bakupa-Kanyinda. Dipanda Yo! RD Congo and Akangbé Productions, 2003. DVD.

"Aigle de fer (Iron Eagle)." *Alternative to TV*, 2011. Accessed Oct. 10, 2015. http://www.youtube.com/watch?v=p1CR8l5aZoI.

Anna from Benin. Directed by Monique Phoba. Women Make Movies, 2000.

L'art de la guerre. Written and performed by Lexxus Legal. Directed by Ronnie Kabuika. 2009.

Article 15 bis. Directed by Balufu Bakupa-Kanyinda. Dipanda Yo!, and Akangbé Productions, 2000.

Assistance Mortelle. Directed by Raoul Peck Velvet film, 2013. DVD.

Balangwa Nzembo. Directed by Balufu Bakupa-Kanyinda. Dipanda Yo!, and Akangbé Productions, 1999.

A Bewitched Life. Directed by Monique Phoba. Karaba Productions, Lagunimages and Néon Rouge Productions, 2004. DVD.

Boma-Tervuren: le Voyage (de juin à septembre 1897). Directed by Francis Dujardin. Cobra Films, 1999. DVD.

"Congo: Knowing the Enemy." Directed by Susan Schulman, and Elliot Smith. *The Guardian*, Dec. 9, 2009. Accessed Oct. 10, 2015. http://www.guardian.co.uk/world/video/2009/dec/08/congo-fdlr-rwanda.

Congo's Tin Soldiers—Democratic Republic of the Congo. Featuring Jonathan Miller. Journeyman Pictures, 2006.

Crisis in the Congo: Uncovering the Truth. Friends of Congo Films, 2011. DVD.

Les Damiers. Directed by Balufu Bakupa-Kanyinda. Dipanda Yo!, RD Congo Central Productions, and CENACI Gabon, 1996.

The Day After Peace. Directed by Jeremy Gilley. BBC, Passion Pictures, and Peace One Day, 2009.

Dix milles ans de cinema. Directed by Balufu Bakupa-Kanyinda. Scolopendra Productions, 1991.

Entre la coupe et l'éléction. Directed by Monique Phoba, and Guy Kabeya Muya. Lagunimages e Kabola Films, 2007.

Episode III: Enjoy Poverty. Directed by Renzo Martens. Produced by Peter Krüger, and Renzo Martens. Autlook Filmsales, 2008. DVD.

"Gimme Shelter." Directed by Ben Affleck. Working Title Films and Williamsworks, 2010. Accessed Oct. 10, 2015. https://youtu.be/i1PkzjxIX5A.

The Greatest Silence: Rape in the Congo. Directed by Lisa Jackson. Jackson Films, 2007.

Les habits neufs du gouverneur. Directed by Mweze Ngangura. Mweze Ngangura, 2004.

"How Long?" Written and performed by Katya Emma and Ndungi Githuku. Feb. 6, 2012. Accessed Oct. 10, 2015. http://www.youtube.com/watch?v=5Rn4edmLchM&feature=player_embedded.

Jazz Mama. Directed by Petna Ndaliko Katondolo. Alkebu Productions, 2010. DVD.

"Le jour d'après/Siku ya Badaaye." Written and performed by Baloji, May 5, 2010. Accessed October 10, 2015. http://www.youtube.com/watch?v=-h4kPKcAotU&feature=channel.

Juju Factory. Directed by Balufu Bakupa-Kanyinda. Dipanda Yo!, RD Congo Central, and Akangbé Productions, 2007.

Jupiter's Dance. Directed by R. Barret and F. de La Tullaye. Belle Kinois Films (copyright Idéal Audience International), 2007.

Lamokowang. Directed by Petna Ndaliko Katondolo. Alkebu Productions, 2004. DVD.

"Leadership à l'université de Goma (Leadership at the University of Goma)." *Alternative to TV*, 2011. Accessed Oct. 10, 2015. http://www.youtube.com/watch?v=SBqdNNF7IYA&feature=related.

"Makayabo à Goma (Makayabo in Goma)." *Alternative to TV*, 2011. Accessed Oct. 10, 2015. http://www.youtube.com/watch?v=2eyELBYy-Ko&feature=related.

Mandabi. Directed by Sembene Ousmane. Filmi Domireve, and Comptoir Français du Film Production, 1968, 2005. DVD.

Matamata and Pilipili. Directed by Tristan Bourland. First Run/Icarus Films, 1997. DVD.

La Mort du Prophet. Directed by Raoul Peck. California Newsreel, 2008. DVD.

"Ndoto Yangu." Alternative to TV. Alkebu Productions, 2007. Accessed Oct. 10, 2015. http://metropolistv.nl/en/correspondents/petna-goma/balume-15-years-old-and-already-a-producer.

"Pandisha Bandera." Directed by Petna Ndaliko Katondolo. Alkebu Productions, 2006. DVD.

Pièces d'identité. Directed by Mweze Ngangura. Mweze Ngangura, 1998.

"Plage du peuple, Goma (People's Beach, Goma)." *Alternative to TV*, 2011. Accessed Oct. 10, 2015. http://www.youtube.com/watch?v=Yjwu2iAmFeU&feature=related.

"Raise Hope for Congo." Directed by Ryan Gosling. 2011.

Rape as a Weapon of War in DR Congo. Michael J. Kavanagh and Taylor Krauss for World Focus, 2009.

"Renzo Martens in Discussion with J. J. Charlesworth, Part I." Posted July 22, 2010. Accessed Oct. 10, 2015. https://youtu.be/j8ueB-tMlIo.

"Renzo Martens in Discussion with J. J. Charlesworth, Part II." Posted July 22, 2010. Accessed Oct. 10, 2015. https://youtu.be/SoU3IgRVMnk.

Rouch in Reverse. Directed by Manthia Diawara. California Newsreel, 1995.

Rumba: deux rives au même tempo. Directed by Olivier Lichen. Home Sweet Home, 2009.

"Saisir l'avenir." Performed by Salaam Kivu Allstars. Alkebu Productions, 2010. Accessed Oct. 10, 2015. http://www.youtube.com/watch?v=SgqZPcXyyFw&context=C3f1292fADO EgsToPDskLRIgnDtojNQQKLTvTlwnzo.

Silent Elections. Directed by Sarah Vanagt. Balthasar, 2009. DVD.

State of Mind: Healing Trauma. Directed by Djo Tunda wa Munga. Suka! Productions, 2010.

"True Story." Directed by Petna Ndaliko Katondolo. Alkebu Film Productions, 2008.

Tuko Tayari. Yole!Africa, Alternative to TV, 2006. Yole!Africa archive.

"Twaomba Amani." Directed by Petna Ndaliko Katondolo. Alkebu Productions, 2005.

La vie est belle. Directed by Mweze Ngangura. Lamy Films, 1986.

Viva Riva! Directed by Djo Tunda wa Munga. Suka! Productions, 2010.

Who's Afraid of Ngugi? Directed by Manthia Diawara, and Balufu Bakupa-Kanyinda. K'a-Yéléma Productions, 2006.

Bibliography

Achebe, Chinua. "An Image of Africa." In *Hopes and Impediments: Selected Essays 1965–1987*. London: Heinemann, 1988.

Adichie, Chimamanda. "The Danger of a Single Story." *TED video*, July 2009. Posted October 2009. Accessed Oct. 10, 2015. http://www.ted.com/talks/chimamanda_adichie_the_danger_ of_a_single_story?language=en.

Allen, Karen. "Bleak Future for Congo's Child Soldiers." *BBC News*, Apr. 25, 2011. Accessed Oct. 10, 2015. http://news.bbc.co.uk/2/hi/africa/5213996.stm.

Allen, Tim, and Jean Seaton, eds. *The Media of Conflict: War Reporting and Representations of Ethnic Violence*. London: Zed Books, 1999.

Allimadi, Milton. *The Hearts of Darkness: How Writers Created the Racist Image of Africa*. New York: Black Star Books, 2002.

Anderson, Kay. "Culture and Nature at the Adelaide Zoo: At the Frontiers of 'Human' Geography." *Transactions of the Institute of British Geographers* 20, no. 3 (1995), 275–94.

Andreasson, Stefan. "Orientalism and African Development Studies: The 'Reductive Repetition' Motif in Theories of African Underdevelopment." *Third World Quarterly* 26, no. 6 (2005), 971–86.

Askew, Kelly. *Performing the Nation: Swahili Music and Cultural Politics in Tanzania*. Chicago: University of Chicago Press, 2002.

Askew, Kelly. "As Plato Duly Warned: Music, Politics, and Social Change in East Africa." *Anthropological Quarterly* 76, no. 4 (2003), 609–37.

Askew, Kelly. "Jack-of-all-Arts or Ustadhi? The Poetics of Cultural Production in Tanzania." In *In Search of a Nation: Histories of Authority and Dissidence in Tanzania*, edited by Gregory H. Maddox and James L. Giblin, 304–27. Oxford: James Currey, 2005.

Aumont, Jacques. *The Image*. London: BFI, 1997.

Baaz, Maria Eriksson, and Maria Stern. "Whores, Men, and Other Misfits: Undoing 'Feminization' in the Armed Forces in the DRC." *African Affairs* 110, no. 441 (2011), 563–85.

Bakari, Imruh, and Mbye Cham, eds. *African Experiences of Cinema*. London: British Film Institute, 1996.

Balfour, Ian, and Eduardo Cadava. "The Claims of Human Rights: An Introduction." *And Justice for All? The Claims of Human Rights* 103, nos. 2–3 (2004), 277–96.

Barnett, Michael, and Thomas Weiss, eds. *Humanitarianism in Question: Power, Politics, Ethics*. Ithaca, NY: Cornell University Press, 2008.

Barret, Helena. "In the Stills Gallery: Renzo Martens 'Enjoy Poverty.'" *In Theory*, Dec. 11, 2010. Accessed Oct. 10, 2015. http://helenabarrett1987.wordpress.com/2010/12/11/in-the-stills-gallery-renzo-martens-enjoy-poverty/.

Baxi, Upendra. *The Future of Human Rights*. New Delhi: Oxford University Press, 2006.

Berger, James. *After the End: Representations of Post-Apocalypse*. Minneapolis: University of Minnesota Press, 1999.

Bhabha, Homi. "Foreword." In *The Wretched of the Earth*, by Franz Fanon, vii–xlii. New York: Grove Press, 2004.

Bhinda, Nils, Jonathan Leape, Matthew Martin, and Stephany Griffith-Jones. *Private Capital Flows to Africa: Perceptions and Reality*. Amsterdam: Forum on Debt and Development, 1999.

Binet, Jacques, Victor Bachy, Ferid Boughedir, and Alain Ricard. *Cinemas noirs d'Afrique*. Paris: L'Harmattan, 1983.

Bisschoff, Lizelle, and Stefanie Van de Peer, eds. *Art and Trauma in Africa: Representations of Reconciliation in Music, Visual Arts, Literature and Film*. New York: I. B. Tauris, 2013.

Blom, Eric, ed. *Grove's Dictionary of Music and Musicians*. New York: St. Martin's Press, 1954.

Boehmer, Elleke, ed. *Empire Writing: An Anthology of Colonial Literature 1870–1918*. Oxford: Oxford University Press, 1998.

Bone, James. "UN Peace Keepers Banned from Sex with Congolese." *The Times*, Feb. 11, 2005. Accessed Oct. 10, 2015. http://www.timesonline.co.uk/tol/news/world/article512959.ece. http://www.thetimes.co.uk/tto/news/world/article1979692.ece

Bouveignes, Olivier de. "La Musique Indigène au Congo Belge." *African Music Society* 1, vol. 3 (1950), 19–27.

Brown, Jayna. "Buzz and Rumble: Global Pop Music and Utopian Impulse." *Social Text* 28, no. 1 (2010), 125–46.

Burton, Julianne, ed. *The Social Documentary of Latin America*. Pittsburgh: University of Pittsburgh Press, 1990.

Campbell, David, and Mascus Power. "The Scopic Regime of 'Africa'." In *Observant States: Geopolitics and Visual Culture*, edited by Fraser McDonald, Rachel Hughes, and Klaus Dodds, 167–98. London: I. B. Tauris, 2010.

Canclini, Néstor Garcia. "The State of War and the State of Hybridization." In *Without Guarantees: In Honor of Stuart Hall*, edited by Paul Gilroy, Lawrence Grossberg, and Angela McRobbie, 38–52. New York: Verso, 2000.

Carrington, John F. "Tone and Melody in a Congolese Popular Song." *African Music* 4, no. 1 (1966/1967), 38–39.

Carrington, John F. "The Musical Dimension of Perception in the Upper Congo, Zaire." *African Music* 5, vol. 1 (1971), 46–51.

Caruth, Cathy. *Trauma: Explorations in Memory*. Baltimore: Johns Hopkins University Press, 1995.

Caruth, Cathy. *Unclaimed Experience: Trauma, Narrative, and History*. Baltimore: Johns Hopkins University Press, 1996.

Césaire, Aimé. *Cahier d'un retour au pays natal*. Paris: Présence Africaine, 1971.

Charry, Eric, ed. *Hip Hop Africa: New African Music in a Globalizing World*. Bloomington: Indiana University Press, 2012.

Chatellier, Sarah. "We Have Suffered in Silence Too Long ... Women's Narratives and Peacebuilding in the Democratic Republic of Congo." M.A. thesis, Utrecht University, 2009.

Chernoff, John Miller. *African Rhythm, African Sensibility: Aesthetics and Social Action in African Musical Idioms*. Chicago: University of Chicago Press, 1979.

Chiwengo, Ngwarsungu. "When Wounds and Corpses Fail to Speak: Narratives of Violence and Rape in Congo (DRC)." *Comparative Studies of South Asia, Africa and the Middle East* 28, no.1 (2008), 78–92.

Clark, John F., ed. *The African Stakes of the Congo War*. New York: Palgrave Macmillan, 2002.

Clarke, John. "Unfinished Business? Struggles over the Social in Social Welfare." In *Without Guarantees: In Honor of Stuart Hall*, edited by Paul Gilroy, Lawrence Grossberg and Angela McRobbie, 83–93. New York: Verso, 2000.

Clifford, James. *The Predicament of Culture: Twentieth-Century Ethnography, Literature and Art*. Cambridge, MA: Harvard University Press, 1988.

Collective. "Une Plaie Encore Ouverte: La Problématique des Violences Sexuelles au Nord Kivu." In *Regards Croises: Revue Trimestrielle No. 011*, 6–14. Goma: Pole Institute, April 2004.

Collins, Patricia Hill. *Black Feminist Thought: Knowledge, Consciousness, and the Politics of Empowerment*. New York: Routledge, 2000.

Convents, Guido. *Images et démocratie: Les Congolais face au cinéma et à l'audiovisuel. Une histoire politico-culturelle du Congo des Belges jusqu'à la république démocratique du Congo (1896–2006)*. Brussels: Aden Diffusion, 2006.

Coombes, Annie E. *Reinventing Africa: Museums, Material Culture and Popular Imagination in Late Victorian and Edwardian England*. New Haven, CT: Yale University Press, 1997.

Crockett, Clayton. "Technology and the Time-Image: Deleuze and Postmodern Subjectivity." *South African Journal of Philosophy* 24, vol. 3 (2005), 176–88.

Dahlhaus. "Counterpoint: 12. The Term Counterpoint after 1600." In *The New Grove Dictionary of Music and Musicians*, Vol. 1084, edited by Stanley Sadie. New York: Macmillan, 2001.

Dawes, James. *That the World May Know: Bearing Witness to Atrocity*. Cambridge: Harvard University Press, 2007.

De B'béri, Boulou Ebanda. *Mapping Alternative Expressions of Blackness in Cinema: A Horizontal Labyrinth of Transgeographical Practices of Identity*. Bayreuth, Germany: Thielmann & Breitinger, 2006.

Deibert, Michael. *The Democratic Republic of Congo: Between Hope and Despair*. London: Zed Books, 2013.

Deleuze, Gilles. *Kant's Critical Philosophy*. Translated by Hugh Tomlinson and Barbara Habberjam. Minneapolis: University of Minnesota Press, 1984.

Deleuze, Gilles. *Cinema 1: The Movement-Image*. Translated by Hugh Tomlinson and Barbara Habberjam. London: Athlone Press, 1986.

Deleuze, Gilles. *Cinema 2: The Time-Image*. Translated by Hugh Tomlinson and Robert Galeta. London: Athlone Press, 1989.

De Waal, Alexander, ed. *Who Fights? Who Cares? War and Humanitarian Action in Africa*. Trenton, NJ: Africa World Press, 2000.

De Witte, Ludo. *The Assassination of Lumumba*. New York: Verso, 2002.

Diawara, Manthia. *African Cinema: Politics and Culture*. Bloomington: Indiana University Press, 1992.

Diawara, Manthia. *In Search of Africa*. Cambridge, MA: Harvard University Press, 1998.

Diawara, Manthia. *We Won't Budge: An Exile in the World*. New York: Basic Civitas Books, 2003.

Evans, Tony. "International Human Rights Law as Power/Knowledge." *Human Rights Quarterly* 27, no. 3 (2005), 1046–68.

Fabian, Johannes, and Tshibumba Kanda Matulu. *Remembering the Present: Painting and Popular History in Zaire*. Berkeley: University of California Press, 1996.

Fanon, Frantz. *White Skin Black Mask*. New York: Grove Press, 1952.

Fanon, Frantz. *The Wretched of the Earth*. New York: Grove Press, 1961.

Fanon, Frantz. *Racism and Culture: Towards the African Revolution*. New York: Grove Press, 1964.

Fanon, Frantz. *Toward the African Revolution: Political Essays*. New York: Grove Press, 1967.

Ferguson, James. *Global Shadows: Africa in the Neoliberal World Order*. Durham, NC: Duke University Press, 2006.

Fletcher, Yaël Simpson. "'History Will One Day Have Its Say': New Perspectives on Colonial and Postcolonial Congo." *Radical History Review* 84 (2002), 195–207.

Freire, Paulo. *Pedagogy of the Oppressed*. Translated by Myra Bergman Ramos. New York: Continuum, 2000.

Gabriel, Teshome. *Third Cinema in the Third World: The Aesthetics of Liberation*. Ann Arbor, MI: UMI Research Press, 1982.

Gabriel, Teshome. "Third Cinema as Guardian of Popular Memory: Towards a Third Aesthetics." In *Questions of Third Cinema*, edited by Jim Pines and Paul Willemen, 53–64. London: British Film Institute, 1989.

Gabriel, Teshome. "Introduction: Third Cinema: Exploration of Nomadic Aesthetics & Narrative Communities." *Teshome Gabriel: Articles & Other Works*, Feb. 14, 2012. Accessed Oct. 10, 2015. http://teshomegabriel.net/introduction.

Givanni, June, ed. *Symbolic Narratives/African Cinema: Audiences, Theory and the Moving Image*. London: British Film Institute, 2001.

Gordon, Robert J. "'Captured on Film': Bushmen and the Claptrap of Performative Primitives." In *Images and Empires: Visuality in Colonial and Postcolonial Africa*, edited by Paul S. Landau and Deborah D. Kaspin, 212–32. Berkeley: University of California Press, 2002.

Grignon, François. "Rape as a Weapon of War in Congo." *Spiegel Online International*, June 11, 2009. Accessed Oct. 10, 2015. http://www.spiegel.de/international/world/opinion-rape-as-a-weapon-of-war-in-congo-a-629885.html.

Gugler, Josef. *African Film: Re-Imagining a Continent*. Bloomington: Indiana University Press, 2003.

Hafez, Hai. *The Myth of Media Globalization*. Cambridge: Polity Press, 2007.

Hall, Stuart. "Cultural Identity and Diaspora." In *Identity: Community, Culture, Difference*, edited by Jonathan Rutherford, 222–37. London: Lawrence & Wishart, 1990.

Hall, Stuart. "Cultural Identity and Cinematic Representation." In *Black British Cultural Studies: A Reader*, edited by Houston A. Baker Jr., Manthia Diawara, and Ruth H. Lindeborg, 210–22. Chicago: University of Chicago Press, 1996.

Hall, Stuart. "New Ethnicities." In *Identities: Race, Class, Gender and Nationality*, edited by Linda Alcoff and Eduardo Mendieta, 90–95. Oxford: Blackwell, 2003.

Haskin, Jeanne M. *The Tragic State of the Congo: From Decolonization to Dictatorship*. New York: Algora, 2005.

Harrow, Kenneth. *Postcolonial African Cinema: From Political Engagement to Post Modernism*. Bloomington: Indiana University Press, 2007.

Herman, Edward S., and Noam Chomsky. *Manufacturing Consent: The Political Economy of the Mass Media*. London: Vintage, 1994.

Hochschild, Adam. *King Leopold's Ghost*. New York: Mariner Books, 1999.

Holmén, Hans. *Snakes in Paradise: NGOs and the Aid Industry in Africa*. Sterling, VA: Kumarian Press, 2010.

Hunt, Nancy Rose. "An Acoustic Register, Tenacious Images, and Congolese Scenes of Rape and Repetition." *Cultural Anthropology* 23, no. 2 (2008), 220–53.

International Crisis Group. "Beyond Victimhood: Women's Peacebuilding in Sudan, Congo, and Uganda." Africa Report No. 112. *International Crisis Group*, June 28, 2006. Accessed Oct. 10, 2015. http://www.crisisgroup.org/en/regions/africa/horn-of-africa/112-beyond-victimhood-womens-peacebuilding-in-sudan-congo-and-uganda.aspx.

International Crisis Group. *Congo: Consolidating the Peace*. Africa Report No. 128. Kinshasa, DRC: ICG, July 5, 2007.

International Crisis Group. "Congo: Bringing Peace to North Kivu." Africa Report No. 133. *International Crisis Group*, Oct. 31, 2007. Accessed Oct. 10, 2015. http://www.crisisgroup.org/~/media/Files/africa/central-africa/dr-congo/Congo%20Bringing%20Peace%20to%20North%20Kivu.pdf.

International Crisis Group. "Congo: Four Priorities for Sustainable Peace in Ituri." Africa Report No. 140. *International Crisis Group*, May 13, 2008. Accessed Oct. 10, 2015. http://www.crisisgroup.org/en/regions/africa/central-africa/dr-congo/140-congo-four-priorities-for-sustainable-peace-in-ituri.aspx.

International Crisis Group. "Congo: Five Priorities for a Peacebuilding Strategy." Africa Report No. 150. *International Crisis Group*, May 11, 2009. Accessed Oct. 15, 2015. http://www.crisisgroup.org/en/regions/africa/central-africa/dr-congo/150-congo-five-priorities-for-a-peacebuilding-strategy.aspx.

International Crisis Group. "Conflict in Congo." *International Crisis Group*, June 15, 2010. Accessed Oct. 10, 2015. http://reliefweb.int/sites/reliefweb.int/files/resources/644802B7530B82DBC125774300076FFB-Full_Report.pdf.

International Crisis Group. "Congo: A Stalled Democratic Agenda." Africa Briefing No. 73. *International Crisis Group*, Apr. 8, 2010. Accessed Oct. 10, 2015. http://www.crisisgroup.org/en/regions/africa/central-africa/dr-congo/b073-congo-a-stalled-democratic-agenda.aspx.

Irele, Abiola, and Biodun Jeyifo. *The Oxford Encyclopedia of African Thought*. Vol. 2. Oxford: Oxford University Press, 2010.

Jaji, Tsitsi Ella. *Africa in Stereo: Modernism, Music, and Pan-African Solidarity*. New York: Oxford University Press, 2014.

Jarosz, Lucy. "Constructing the Dark Continent: Metaphor as Geographic Representation of Africa." *Geografiska Annaler Series B, Human Geography* 74, no. 2 (1992), 105–15.

Journeyman Pictures. "Congo's Forgotten War." Apr. 7, 2008. Accessed Oct. 10, 2015. http://www.youtube.com/watch?v=peHo2zuQ29Q&feature=bf_play&list=WL77BE4C1E6E5EA4A3&index=1. 1 May, 2011.

Kajese, Kingston. "An Agenda of Future Tasks for International and Indigenous NGOs: Views from the South." *World Development* 15, no. 1 (1987), 79–85.

Kennedy, David. *The Dark Side of Virtue: Reassessing International Humanitarianism*. Princeton: Princeton University Press, 2005.

Kingsolver, Barbara. *The Poisonwood Bible*. New York: HarperCollins, 1998.

Kristof, Nicholas. "The Weapon of Rape." *New York Times*, June 15, 2008.

Kristof, Nicholas. "Orphaned, Raped, and Ignored." *New York Times*, Jan. 30, 2010. Accessed Oct. 10, 2015. http://www.nytimes.com/2010/01/31/opinion/31kristof.html?_r=0.

Kristof, Nicholas. "From 'Oprah' to Building a Sisterhood in Congo." *New York Times*, Feb. 3, 2010. Accessed Oct. 10, 2015. http://www.nytimes.com/2010/02/04/opinion/04kristof.html.

Kristof, Nicholas. "Death by Gadget." *New York Times*, June 26, 2010, accessed Oct. 10, 2015. http://www.nytimes.com/2010/06/27/opinion/27kristof.html?_r=0.

Kristof, Nicholas "The World Capital of Killing." New York Times, Feb. 6, 2010. Accessed Oct. 10, 2015. http://www.nytimes.com/2010/02/07/opinion/07kristof.html.

Kristof, Nicholas. "D.I.Y. Foreign-Aid Revolution." *New York Times*, Oct. 20, 2010. Accessed Oct. 10, 2015. http://www.nytimes.com/2010/10/24/magazine/24volunteerism-t.html?pagewanted=all&_r=0.

Kubik, Gerhard. "Neo-Traditional Popular Music in Eastern Africa Since 1945." *Popular Music, Vol. 1, Folk or Popular? Distinctions, Influences, Continuities* (1981), 83–104.

Lala, Raoul Yema de. *Franco le Grand Maître*. Kinshasa: Centre de Recherche sur les Mentalites "Eugomonia," 2011.

Lammers, Ellen. *Refugees, Gender, and Human Security: A Theoretical Introduction and Annotated Biography*. Holland: International Books, 1999.

Lewis, Stephen. "Women Targeted or Affected by Armed Conflict: What Role for Military Peacekeepers?" Presentation at the annual convention of Wilton Park on Women Targeted or Affected by Armed Conflict: What Role for Military Peacekeepers? Sussex, UK, May 27–29, 2008.

Lierde, Jean van, ed. *Lumumba Speaks: The Speeches and Writings of Patrice Lumumba, 1958–1961*. Translated by Helen R. Lane. New York: Little, Brown, 1972.

Locher, G. W., P. L. Duchartres, T. Galestin, J. M. Jadot, and Luis Valcarcel. "Preservation and Development of Indigenous Arts." In *UNESCO Occasional Papers in Education*. No. 8. Paris: Educational Clearing House, 1949.

Maira, Sunaina, and Elisabeth Soep, eds. *Youthscapes: The Popular, the National, the Global*. Philadelphia: University of Pennsylvania Press, 2005.

Mamdani, Mahmood. *Citizen and Subject: Contemporary African and the Legacy of Late Colonialism*. Princeton: Princeton University Press, 1996.

Mamdani, Mahmood. *Saviors and Survivors: Darfur, Politics, and the War on Terror*. New York: Pantheon Books, 2009.

Manji, Firoze, and Carl O'Coill. "The Missionary Position: NGOs and Development in Africa." *International Affairs* 78, no. 3 (2002), 567–83.

Maren, Michael. *The Road to Hell: The Ravaging Effects of Foreign Aid and International Charity*. New York: Free Press, 1997.

Martin, Angela, ed. *African Films: The Context of Production*. London: British Film Institute, 1982.

Mathers, Kathryn. "Mr. Kristof, I Presume?" *Transition* 107 (2012), 14–31.

Max-Neef, Manfred. "Development and Human Needs." In *Real-life Economics: Understanding Wealth Creation*, edited by Paul Ekins and Manfred Max-Neef, 197–213. London: Routledge, 1992.

Mbembe, Achille. "Variations on the Beautiful in the Congolese World of Sounds." *Politique africaine* 100, no. 4 (2005), 69–91.

Mbiti, John. *African Religions and Philosophy*. Portsmouth, NH: Heinemann, 1990.

McCalpin, Jermaine. "Historicity of a Crisis: The Origins of the Congo War." In *The African Stakes of the Congo War*, edited by John Clark, 33–50. New York: Palgrave Macmillan, 2002.

McLaren, Peter, and Peter Leonard, eds. *Paulo Freire: A Critical Encounter.* London: Routledge, 1993.

Memmi, Albert. *The Colonizer and the Colonized.* New York: Orion Press, 1965.

Memmi, Albert. *Decolonization and the Decolonized.* Minneapolis: University of Minnesota Press, 2006.

Merriam, Alan P. "African Music Re-examined in the Light of New Materials from the Belgian Congo and Ruanda Urundi." *African Society Newsletter* 1, no. 6 (1953), 57–64.

Michael, Sarah. *Undermining Development: The Absence of Power Among Local NGOs in Africa.* Oxford: James Currey, 2004.

Minh-Ha, Trin. *When the Moon Waxes Red: Representation, Gender and Cultural Politics.* New York: Routledge, 1991.

Minns, John. "The Post Cold-War Predicament." *Third World Quarterly* 22, no. 6 (2001), 1025–43.

Monson, Ingrid. *Freedom Sounds: Civil Rights Call out to Jazz and Africa.* Oxford: Oxford University Press, 2005.

Moore, David. "Neoliberal Globalization and the Triple Crisis of 'Modernization' in Africa: Zimbabwe, the Democratic Republic of the Congo, and South Africa." *Third World Quarterly*, 22, no. 6 (2001), 909–29.

Mudimbe, Valentin-Yves. *The Invention of Africa: Gnosis, Philosophy, and the Order of Knowledge.* Bloomington: Indiana University Press, 1988.

Mudimbe, Valentin-Yves. *The Idea of Africa.* Bloomington, IN: Indiana University Press, 1994.

Mukuna, Kazadi wa. "The Evolution of Urban Music in Democratic Republic of Congo during the 2nd and 3rd Decades (1975–1995) of the Second Republic—Zaïre." *African Music* 7, no. 4 (1999), 73–87.

Murdock, Heather. "Rape Victims in Congo Call for Justice." *VoaNews English*, Apr. 12, 2011. Accessed Oct. 15, 2015. http://www.voanews.com/english/news/africa/Rape-Victims-in-Congo-Call-for-Justice-119779379.html.

Mutua, Makau, ed. *Human Rights NGOs in East Africa: Political and Normative Tensions.* Philadelphia: University of Pennsylvania Press, 2009.

Naficy, Hamid, and Teshome H. Gabriel, eds. *Otherness and the Media: The Ethnography of the Imagined and the Imaged.* Chur, Switzerland: Harwood Academic, 1993.

Ndaliko Katondolo, Petna. "Lamokowang Press Release." *Alkebu Productions.* Accessed Oct. 10, 2015. http://alkebu.org/index.php/film-productions/lamokowang/.

Ndaliko Katondolo, Petna. "The Film: Jazz Mama, a Film by Petna Ndaliko." *Respect.* Accessed Oct. 10, 2015. www.jazzmama.org/the-film/.

Ndegwa, Stephen N. *Two Faces of Civil Society.* West Hartford, CT: Kumarian Press, 1996.

Nichols, Bill. *Representing Reality.* Bloomington: Indiana University Press, 1991.

Nielsen, Nikolaj. "'Enjoy Poverty.'" *Foreign Policy Association*, May 11, 2009. Accessed Oct. 10, 2015. http://foreignpolicyblogs.com/2009/05/11/enjoy-poverty/.

Nkashama, Ngandu P. "Ivress et Vertige: Les nouvelles danses des jeunes au Zaïre." *L'Afrique littéraire et artistique* 51 (1979), 94–102.

Nkashama, Ngandu P. "La chanson de la rupture dans la musique zairoise moderne." In *Papier blanc, encre noire: Cent ans de culture francophone en Afrique central (Zaire, Rwanda et Burundi)*, edited by Marc Quaghebeur, and Emile can Balberghe, 477–89. Brussels: Labor, 1992.

Nketia, Joseph H. *Funeral Dirges of the Akan People.* Exeter: Achimota, 1955.

Nketia, Kwabena. *The Music of Africa.* New York: Norton, 1974.

Nolen, Stephanie. "'Not Women Anymore . . .' The Congo's Rape Survivors Face Pain, Shame and AIDS." *Ms.* 15, no. 1 (2005), 56.

Nzongola-Ntalaja, Georges. *Revolution and Counter-Revolution in Africa: Essays in Contemporary Politics*. London: Zed, 1988.

Nzongola-Ntalaja, Georges. *The Congo: From Leopold to Kabila: A People's History*. London: Zed, 2002.

Nzongola-Ntalaja, Georges. *From Zaire to the Democratic Republic of the Congo*. Uppsala, Sweden: Nordiska Afrikainstitutet, 2004.

O'Connell, John M., and Salwa El-Shawan Castelo-Branco, eds. *Music and Conflict*. Urbana: University of Illinois Press, 2010.

Olaniyan, Tejumola. "The Paddle That Speaks English: Africa, NGOs, and the Archaeology of an Unease." *Research in African Literatures* 42, no. 2 (2011), 46–59.

Olema, Debhonvapi. "La satire amusée des inégalités socio-économiques dans la chanson populaire urbaine du Zaïre: Une étude de l'oeuvre de Franco (François Luambo) des années 70 et 80." Ph.D. diss., Université de Montréal, 1998.

Olema, Debhonvapi. "Societé zairoise dans le miroir de la chanson populaire." *Canadian Journal of African Studies* 18, no. 1 (1984), 122–30.

Onwudiwe, Ebere, and Minabere Ibelema, eds. *Afro-Optimism: Perspectives on Africa's Advances*. Westport, CT: Praeger, 2003.

Penny, Joe. "'Enjoy Poverty': Interview with Renzo Martens." *Africa Is a Country*, July 16, 2010. Accessed Oct. 10, 2015. http://africasacountry.com/2010/07/16/poverty-for-sale/.

Petty, Sheila. "Black African Feminist Filmmaking?" *Visual Anthropology Review* 6, no. 1 (1990), 60–64.

Pfaff, Françoise, ed. *Focus on African Films*. Bloomington: Indiana University Press, 2004.

Pfaff, Françoise. "Africa from Within: The Films of Gaston Kabore and Idrissa Ouedraogo as Anthropological Sources." *Society for Visual Anthropology Review* 6, no. 1 (1990), 50–59.

Pike, John. "Congo Civil War." *Global Security*, Apr. 25, 2011. Accessed Oct. 10, 2015. http://www.globalsecurity.org/military/world/war/congo.htm.

Pinkney, Robert. *NGOs, Africa and the Global Order*. Basingstoke: Palgrave Macmillan, 2009.

Ploch, Lauren. Congressional Research Service. *Africa Command: U.S. Strategic Interests and the Role of the U.S. Military in Africa*. July 22, 2011. Accessed Oct. 10, 2015. https://www.fas.org/sgp/crs/natsec/RL34003.pdf.

Quarry, Wendy, and Ricardo Ramirez. *Communication for Another Development: Listening Before Telling*. London: Zed Books, 2009.

"RDC Elections: Adam Bombole candidat à la présidentielle sous la casquette d'indépendant." *Radio Okapi: MONESCU, Fondation Hirondelle*, Sep. 12, 2011. Accessed Oct. 10, 2015. http://www.radiookapi.net/actualite/2011/09/12/rdc-elections-adam-bombole-candidat-a-la-presidentielle-sous-la-casquette-dindependant.

Rieff, David. *A Bed for the Night: Humanitarianism in Crisis*. New York: Simon and Schuster, 2002.

Roberts, Allen F. *A Dance of Assassins: Performing Early Colonial Hegemony in the Congo*. Bloomington: Indiana University Press, 2013.

Roche, Susan. "Gentle, Angry Women Creating Change." *Journal of Women and Social Work* 24, no. 4 (2009), 345–47.

Rodney, Walter. *How Europe Underdeveloped Africa*. Washington, DC: Howard University Press, 1982.

Roelandt, Els. "Episode 3: Analysis of a Film Process in Three Conversations." *A Prior* 16 (2008). Accessed Oct. 10, 2015. http://aprior.schoolofarts.be/pdfs/ap16_martens_roelandt.pdf.

Roy, Arundhati. "The NGO-ization of Resistance." *Massalijn*, Sep. 4, 2014. Accessed Oct. 10, 2015. http://massalijn.nl/new/the-ngo-ization-of-resistance/.

Sadie, Stanley, ed. *The New Grove Dictionary of Music and Musicians*. Vol. 1084. New York: Macmillan, 2001.

Said, Edward. *Culture and Imperialism*. New York: Vintage, 1994.

Sartres, Jean-Paul. "Introduction." In *Lumumba Speaks: The Speeches and Writings of Patrice Lumumba, 1958–1961*, edited by Jean Van Lierde, translated by Helen R. Lane, 3–52. Boston: Little, Brown, 1972.

San JuanJr., E. pifanio. *Beyond Postcolonial Theory*. New York: St. Martin's, 1999.

Sen, Amartya. *Development as Freedom*. New York: Knopf, 1999.

Sengupta, Somini. "Arts Sanctuary in a War-Torn City." *New York Times*, July 11, 2014. Accessed Oct. 10, 2015. http://www.nytimes.com/2014/07/12/arts/in-congo-salaam-kivu-festival-brings-performers-to-goma.html?_r=0.

Shelemay, Kay. *A Song of Longing, an Ethiopian Journey*. Chicago: University of Illinois Press, 1991.

Shelemay, Kay. "Crossing Boundaries in Music and Musical Scholarship: A Perspective from Ethnomusicology." *Musical Quarterly* 80, no. 1 (1996), 13–30.

Shelemay, Kay. "'What's up, Doc?' A View of 'Reel' Musicologists." *Musical Quarterly* 81, no. 2 (1997), 204–9.

Shivji, Issa G. *Silences in NGO Discourse: The Role and Future of NGOs in Africa*. Oxford: Fahamu, 2007.

Shohat, Ella, and Robert Stam. *Unthinking Eurocentrism: Multiculturalism and the Media*. New York: Routledge, 1994.

Shohat, Ella, and Robert Stam. *Multiculturalism, Postcoloniality and Transnational Media*. New Brunswick, NJ: Rutgers University Press, 2003.

Shohat, Ella, and Robert Stam. "The Cinema after Babel: Language, Difference, Power." In *Taboo Memories, Diasporic Voices*, by Ella Shohat, 106–37. Durham, NC: Duke University Press, 2006.

Simone, AbdouMaliq. *For the City Yet to Come: Changing African Life in Four Cities*. Durham, NC: Duke University Press, 2004.

Simone, Phillipe. "Boma-Tervuren, le Voyage de Francis Dujardin." *Cinergie Webzine*, Mar. 1, 2002. Accessed Oct. 10, 2015. http://www.cinergie.be/critique.php?action=display&id=223.

Sivanandan, Ambalavaner. "Imperialism and Disorganic Development in the Silicon Age." *Race & Class* 21, no. 2 (1979), 111–26.

Slobin, Mark. *Global Soundtracks: World of Film Music*. Middletown, CT: Wesleyan University Press, 2008.

Smith, Anthony. *The Geo-Politics of Information: How Western Culture Dominates the World*. New York: Oxford University Press, 1980.

Soja, Edward. *Postmodern Geographies: The Reassertion of Space in Critical Social Theory*. London: Verso, 1989.

Solanas, Fernando, and Octavio Getino. "Towards a Third Cinema." *Tricontinental* 13 (1969): 1–54.

"Soundtrack." *The Oxford English Dictionary*, 1949. Accessed Oct. 10, 2015. http://www.oed.com/view/Entry/185124?rskey=8kWRX5&result=1&isAdvanced=false#eid21825362.

Stam, Robert. "Eurocentrism, Afrocentrism, and Polycentrism: Theories of Third Cinema." *Quarterly Review of Film and Video* 13 (1991), 217–37.

Stam, Robert, and Louise Spence. "Colonialism, Racism, and Representation." *Screen* 24, no. 2 (1983), 2–20.

Steinberg, Donald. "Beyond Words and Resolutions: An Agenda for UNSCR 1325 Women and War: Power and Protection." *International Crisis Group*, June 30, 2010. Accessed October 10, 2015. http://www.crisisgroup.org/en/publication-type/commentary/steinberg-beyond-words-and-resolutions-an-agenda-for-unscr-1325.aspx.

Stoler, Ann Laura, ed. *Imperial Debris: On Ruins and Ruination*. Durham: Duke University Press, 2013.

Tadjo, Véronique. *The Shadow of Imana: Travels in the Heart of Rwanda*. Translated by Véronique Wakerley. Portsmouth, NH: Heinemann, 2002.

Tarkovsky, Andrei. *Sculpting in Time: Reflections on the Cinema*. Austin: University of Texas Press, 2003.

Tchebwa, Manda. *La terre de la chanson: La musique zairoise hier et aujourd'hui*. Brussels: Duculot, 1996.

Tegera, Aloys, Christiane Kayser, and Onesphore Sematumba. "Devoir de mémoire et responsabilité collective pour l'avenir." *Regards Croises*, Revue Trimestrielle 13 (2004).

Thiong'o, Ngugi wa. *Decolonizing the Mind: The Politics of Language in African Literature*. Portsmouth, NH: Heinemann, 1986.

Thiong'o, Ngugi wa. *Something Torn and New: An African Renaissance*. New York: Basic Civitas Books, 2009.

Thiong'o, Ngugi wa. *Dreams in a Time of War: A Childhood Memoir*. New York: Anchor Books, 2010.

Thiong'o, Ngugi wa. *Globaletics: Theory and the Politics of Knowing*. New York: Columbia University Press, 2012.

Trefon, Theodore. *Congo Masquerade: The Political Culture of Aid Inefficiency and Reform Failure*. London: Zed Books, 2011.

Tsambu Bulu, Léon. "Musique et violence à Kinshasa." In *Ordre et désordre à Kinshasa: Réponses populaires à la faillite de l'état*, edited by Theodore Trefon, 193–212. Paris: L'Harmattan, 2004.

Tshongo, Onyumbe. "Le thème de l'argent dans la musique zaïroise moderne de 1960 à 1981." *Zaire-Afrique: économie, culture, vie sociale* 23, no. 172 (1983), 97–111.

Turino, Tom. *Music as Social Life: The Politics of Participation*. Chicago: University of Chicago Press, 2008.

Ukadike, Frank. *Black African Cinema*. Berkeley: University of California Press, 1994.

Ukadike, Frank. "African Cinematic Reality: The Documentary Tradition as an Emerging Trend." *Research in African Literatures* 26, no. 3 (1995), 88–96.

United Nations. MONUSCO. "Why the DRC Matters?" Jan. 18, 2012. Accessed Oct. 10, 2015. http://www.un.org/ar/peacekeeping/missions/monuc/documents/drc.pdf.

United Nations. Office for the Coordination of Humanitarian Affairs. "DRC: Mass Rapes Escalate in Fizi, South Kivu." Feb. 28, 2011. Accessed Oct. 10, 2015. http://www.irinnews.org/report.aspx?reportid=92062.

United Nations Organization Stabilization Mission in the DRC. Jan. 18, 2012. Accessed Oct. 10, 2015. http://www.un.org/en/peacekeeping/missions/monusco/.

United Nations Security Council. Resolution 1325, "Women, Peace, and Security." Oct. 31, 2000. Accessed Oct. 10, 2015. http://www.un.org/womenwatch/osagi/wps/.

United Nations Security Council. Resolution 1925, "Withdrawal of Forces." May 28, 2010. Accessed Oct. 10, 2015. http://www.un.org/press/en/2010/sc9939.doc.htm.

Vlassenroot, Koen, and Timothy Raeymaekers. *Conflict and Social Transformation in Eastern DR Congo*. Ghent, Belgium: Academia Press, 2004.

Wamba Dia Wamba, Ernest. "Some Remarks on Culture, Development, and Revolution in Africa." *Journal of Historical Sociology* 4, no. 3 (1991), 219–35.

Wenzel, Jennifer. "Remembering the Past's Future: Anti-Imperialist Nostalgia and Some Versions of the Third World." *Cultural Critique* 62 (2006), 1–32.

Wheeler, Jesse Samba. "Rumba Lingala as Colonial Resistance." *Visual Narrative: The Visualization of the Subaltern in World Music: On Musical Contestation Strategies (Part 1)* 10 (2005), 1–53. Accessed Oct. 10, 2015. http://www.imageandnarrative.be/inarchive/world-musica/worldmusica.htm.

White, Bob W. "Modernity's Trickster: 'Dipping' and 'Throwing' in Congolese Popular Dance Music." *Research in African Literatures*, 30, no. 4 (1999): 156–75.

White, Bob W. "Congolese Rumba and Other Cosmopolitanisms." *Cahiers d'Etudes Africaines* 43, no. 168 (2002), 663–86.

White, Bob W. "L'Incroyable Machine d'Authenticité: l'Animation Politic et l'Usage Public de la Culture dans le Zaïre de Mobutu." *Anthropologie et Sociétés* 30, no. 2 (2006), 43–63.

White, Bob W. *Rumba Rules: The Politics of Dance Music in Mobutu's Zaire*. Durham: Duke University Press, 2008.

Whitlock, Gillian. "Remediating Gorilla Girl: Rape Warfare and the Limits of Humanitarian Storytelling." *Biography* 33, no. 3 (2010), 471–97.

Wilson, Amos N. *The Falsification of Afrikan Consciousness: Eurocentric History, Psychiatry, and the Politics of White Supremacy*. New York: African World Infosystems, 1993.

Yoleafrica. "Hiphop Artist from DRC Wins Award." *Yolé!Africa*, Apr. 19, 2010. Accessed Oct. 10, 2015. http://yoleafrica.org/2010/04/19/hiphop-artist-from-drc-wins-award/.

Young, James E. *The Texture of Memory: Holocaust Memorials and Meaning*. New Haven, CT: Yale University Press, 1993.

Young Smith, Barron. "An End in Sight for Congo?" *New Republic*, Apr. 25, 2011. Accessed Oct. 10, 2015. http://www.tnr.com/blog/the-plank/end-sight-congo.

Zacks, Stephen A. "The Theoretical Construction of African Cinema." *Research in African Literatures* 26, no. 3 (1995), 6–17.

Index